WELCOME TO IDG BOOKS ONLINE!

Thank you very much for selecting *Building Successful Internet Businesses,* a unique blend of paper and online publishing. We hope you'll not only enjoy the contents of the book that you now hold in your hands but also take advantage of the wealth of information related to this title that we'll be publishing on our Web site in the months to come.

In the back of this book we've enclosed a CD-ROM containing an assortment of tools and software to help you get started with your Internet business. You can find this book's Web site by pointing your browser at the IDG Books Online area of our Web site:

www.idgbooks.com/idgbooksonline/

The online medium is an evolving one, and one that we believe will allow us to deliver the highest quality information to you in the fastest way possible. In order to help us improve our future products, we encourage you to send your suggestions and comments to online@www.idgbooks.com.

We hope that you'll enjoy and benefit from this and future titles that we will be publishing. We look forward to hearing from you and we'll strive to make each and every title in our line a quality, information-rich reading experience both online and in print.

David Ushijima
Vice President and Publisher
IDG Books Online

BUILDING SUCCESSFUL INTERNET BUSINESSES

BUILDING SUCCESSFUL INTERNET BUSINESSES

The Essential Sourcebook for Creating Businesses on the Net

by David Elderbrock and Nitin Borwankar
with contributions by Leslie Lesnick

IDG BOOKS WORLDWIDE, INC.
AN INTERNATIONAL DATA GROUP COMPANY

Foster City, CA ■ Chicago, IL ■ Indianapolis, IN ■ Southlake, TX

Building Successful Internet Businesses
Published by
IDG Books Worldwide, Inc.
An International Data Group Company
919 E. Hillsdale Blvd., Suite 400
Foster City, CA 94404

Library of Congress Catalog Card No.: 96-077601
ISBN: 0-7645-7001-3
Printed in the United States of America
10 9 8 7 6 5 4 3 2 1
1B/RT/QY/ZW/FC

Distributed in the United States by IDG Books Worldwide, Inc.
Distributed by Macmillan Canada for Canada; by Contemporanea de Ediciones for Venezuela; by Distribuidora Cuspide for Argentina; by CITEC for Brazil; by Ediciones ZETA S.C.R. Ltda. for Peru; by Editorial Limusa SA for Mexico; by Transworld Publishers Limited in the United Kingdom and Europe; by Academic Bookshop for Egypt; by Levant Distributors S.A.R.L. for Lebanon; by Al Jassim for Saudi Arabia; by Simron Pty. Ltd. for South Africa; by Pustak Mahal for India; by The Computer Bookshop for India; by Toppan Company Ltd. for Japan; by Addison Wesley Publishing Company for Korea; by Longman Singapore Publishers Ltd. for Singapore, Malaysia, Thailand, and Indonesia; by Unalis Corporation for Taiwan; by WS Computer Publishing Company, Inc. for the Philippines; by WoodsLane Pty. Ltd. for Australia; by WoodsLane Enterprises Ltd. for New Zealand. Authorized Sales Agent: Anthony Rudkin Associates for the Middle East and North Africa.

For general information on IDG Books Worldwide's books in the U.S., contact our Consumer Customer Service department at 800-762-2974. For reseller information, including discounts and premium sales, contact our Reseller Customer Service department at 800-434-3422.

For information on where to purchase IDG Books Worldwide's books outside the U.S., contact our International Sales department at 415-655-3078 or fax 415-655-3281.

For information on foreign language translations, contact our Foreign & Subsidiary Rights department at 415-655-3018 or fax 415-655-3281.

For sales inquiries and special prices for bulk quantities, contact our Sales department at 415-655-3200 or write to the address above.

For information on using IDG Books Worldwide's books in the classroom or for ordering examination copies, contact our Educational Sales department at 800-434-2086 or fax 817-251-8174.
For authorization to photocopy items for corporate, personal, or educational use, contact the Copyright Clearance Center, 222 Rosewood Drive, Danvers, MA 01923, or fax 508-750-4470.

ABOUT IDG BOOKS WORLDWIDE

Welcome to the world of IDG Books Worldwide.

IDG Books Worldwide, Inc., is a subsidiary of International Data Group, the world's largest publisher of computer-related information and the leading global provider of information services on information technology. IDG was founded more than 25 years ago and now employs more than 8,500 people worldwide. IDG publishes more than 270 computer publications in over 75 countries (see listing below). More than 90 million people read one or more IDG publications each month.

Launched in 1990, IDG Books Worldwide is today the #1 publisher of best-selling computer books in the United States. We are proud to have received eight awards from the Computer Press Association in recognition of editorial excellence and three from *Computer Currents*' First Annual Readers' Choice Awards. Our best-selling *...For Dummies®* series has more than 25 million copies in print with translations in 30 languages. IDG Books Worldwide, through a joint venture with IDG's Hi-Tech Beijing, became the first U.S. publisher to publish a computer book in the People's Republic of China. In record time, IDG Books Worldwide has become the first choice for millions of readers around the world who want to learn how to better manage their businesses.

Our mission is simple: Every one of our books is designed to bring extra value and skill-building instructions to the reader. Our books are written by experts who understand and care about our readers. The knowledge base of our editorial staff comes from years of experience in publishing, education, and journalism — experience which we use to produce books for the '90s. In short, we care about books, so we attract the best people. We devote special attention to details such as audience, interior design, use of icons, and illustrations. And because we use an efficient process of authoring, editing, and desktop publishing our books electronically, we can spend more time ensuring superior content and spend less time on the technicalities of making books.

You can count on our commitment to deliver high-quality books at competitive prices on topics you want to read about. At IDG Books Worldwide, we continue in the IDG tradition of delivering quality for more than 25 years. You'll find no better book on a subject than one from IDG Books Worldwide.

John Kilcullen
President and CEO
IDG Books Worldwide, Inc.

IDG Books Worldwide, Inc., is a subsidiary of International Data Group, the world's largest publisher of computer-related information and the leading global provider of information services on information technology. International Data Group publishes over 276 computer publications in over 75 countries. Ninety million people read one or more International Data Group publications each month. International Data Group's publications include: **ARGENTINA:** Annuario de Informatica, Computerworld Argentina, PC World Argentina; **AUSTRALIA:** Australian Macworld, Client/Server Journal, Computer Living, Computerworld, Computerworld 100, Digital News, IT Casebook, Network World, On-line World Australia, PC World, Publishing Essentials, Reseller, WebMaster; **AUSTRIA:** Computerwelt Osterreich, Networks Austria, PC Tip; **BELARUS:** PC World Belarus; **BELGIUM:** Data News; **BRAZIL:** Annuário de Informática, Computerworld Brazil, Connections, Super Game Power, Macworld, PC Player, PC World Brazil, Publish Brazil, Reseller News; **BULGARIA:** Computerworld Bulgaria, Networkworld/Bulgaria, PC & MacWorld Bulgaria; **CANADA:** CIO Canada, Client/Server World, ComputerWorld Canada, InfoCanada, Network World Canada; **CHILE:** Computerworld Chile, PC World Chile; **COLOMBIA:** Computerworld Colombia, PC World Colombia; **COSTA RICA:** PC World Centro America; **THE CZECH AND SLOVAK REPUBLICS:** Computerworld Czechoslovakia, Elektronika Czechoslovakia, Macworld Czech Republic, PC World Czechoslovakia; **DENMARK:** Communications World, Computerworld Danmark, Macworld Danmark, PC Privat Danmark, PC World Danmark, PC World Danmark Supplements, TECH World; **DOMINICAN REPUBLIC:** PC World Republica Dominicana; **ECUADOR:** PC World Ecuador; **EGYPT:** Computerworld Middle East, PC World Middle East; **EL SALVALDOR:** PC World Centro America; **FINLAND:** MikroPC, Tietoverkko, Tietoviikko; **FRANCE:** Distributique, Golden, Hebdo-Distributique, Info PC, Le Guide du Monde Informatique, Le Monde Informatique, Reseaux & Telecoms; **GERMANY:** Computer Partner, Computerwoche, Computerwoche Extra, Computerwoche Focus, I/M Information Management, Macwelt, PC Welt; **GREECE:** GamePro, Multimedia World; **GUATEMALA:** PC World Centro America; **HONDURAS:** PC World Centro America; **HONG KONG:** Computerworld Hong Kong, PCWorld Hong Kong, Publish in Asia; **HUNGARY:** ABCD CD-ROM, Computerworld Szamitastechnika, PC & Mac World Hungary, PC-X Magazine; **ICELAND:** Tolvuheimur/PC World Island; **INDIA:** Information Systems Computerworld, PC World India, Publish in Asia; **INDONESIA:** InfoKomputer PC World, Komputek Computerworld, Publish in Asia; **IRELAND:** ComputerScope, PC Live!; **ISRAEL:** People & Computers; **ITALY:** Computerworld Italia, Computerworld Italia Special Editions, Macworld Italia, Networking Italia, PC Shopping, PC World Italia, PC World/Walt Disney; **JAPAN:** DTP World, HP Open World Japan, Macworld Japan, Nikkei Personal Computing, Open World Japan, OS/2 World Japan, SunWorld Japan, Windows World Japan; **KENYA:** East African Computer News; **KOREA:** Hi-Tech Information/Computerworld, Macworld Korea, PC World Korea; **MACEDONIA:** PC World Macedonia; **MALAYSIA:** Computerworld Malaysia, PC World Malaysia, Publish in Asia; **MEXICO:** Computerworld Mexico, Macworld, PC World Mexico; **MYANMAR:** PC World Myanmar; **NETHERLANDS:** Computer! Totaal, LAN Magazine, LanWorld Buyers Guide, Macworld, Net Magazine, Totaal! Beurskrant; **NEW ZEALAND:** Absolute Beginner's Guide, Computer Buyer, Computer Industry Directory, Computerworld New Zealand, MTB, Network World, PC World New Zealand; **NICARAGUA:** PC World Centro America; **NIGERIA:** PC World Nigeria; **NORWAY:** Computerworld Norge, Computerworld Privat (Datamagasinet), CW Rapport Norge, IDG's KURSGUIDE, Macworld Norge, Multimediaworld, PC World Ekspress, PC World Nettverk, PC World Norge, PC World's Produktguide, Windows World Spesial; **PAKISTAN:** Computerworld Pakistan, PC World Pakistan; Panama: PC World Panama; **P. R. OF CHINA:** China Computer Users, China Computerworld, China Infoworld, China Telecom World Weekly, Computer & Communication, Electronic Design China, Electronics Today, Electronics Weekly, Game Camp, Game Soft, Network World China, PC World China, Popular Computer Weekly, Software Weekly, Software World, Telecom World; **PERU:** Computerworld Peru, PC World Profesional Peru, PC World Peru; **PHILIPPINES:** Computerworld Philippines, PC World Philippines, Publish in Asia; **POLAND:** Computerworld Poland, Computerworld Special Report, Macworld, Networld, PC World Komputer; **PORTUGAL:** Cerebro/PC World, Computerworld/Correio Informático, Dealer World Portugal, MacIn/PCIn, Multimedia World Portugal; **PUERTO RICO:** PC World Puerto Rico; **ROMANIA:** Computerworld Romania, PC World Romania, Telecom Romania; **RUSSIA:** Computerworld Russia, Mir PK, Sety; **SINGAPORE:** Computerworld Singapore, PC World Singapore, Publish in Asia; **SLOVENIA:** MONITOR; **SOUTH AFRICA:** Computing S.A., InfoWorld S.A., Network World S.A., Software World; **SPAIN:** Computerworld España, COMUNICACIONES WORLD, Dealer World, Macworld España, PC World España; **SWEDEN:** CAP&Design, Computer Sweden, Corporate Computing, MacWorld, Maxi Data, MikroDatorn, Nätverk & Kommunikation, PC/Aktiv, PC World, Windows World; **SWITZERLAND:** Computerworld Schweiz, Macworld Schweiz, PCtip; **TAIWAN:** Computerworld Taiwan, Macworld Taiwan, PC World Taiwan, Publish Taiwan, Windows World; **THAILAND:** Thai Computerworld, Publish in Asia; **TURKEY:** Computerworld Turkiye, MACWORLD Turkiye, PC WORLD Turkiye; **UKRAINE:** Computerworld Kiev, Computers & Software, Multimedia World Ukraine, PC World Ukraine; **UNITED KINGDOM:** Acorn User, Amiga Action, Amiga Computing, Appletalk, Computing, GamePro, Macworld, Network News, Parents and Computers, PC Advisor, PC Home, PSX Pro UK, The WEB; **UNITED STATES:** Cable in the Classroom, CD Review, CIO Magazine, Computerworld, Computerworld Client/Server Journal, Digital Video Magazine, DOS World, Federal Computer Week, GamePro, InfoWorld, I-Way, JavaWorld, Macworld, Multimedia World, Netscape World Online, Network World, PC Entertainment, PC World, Publish, SunWorld Online, SWATPro Magazine, Video Event, WebMaster; **URUGUAY:** PC World Uruguay; **VENEZUELA:** Computerworld Venezuela, PC World Venezuela; and **VIETNAM:** PC World Vietnam.

7/16/96

To Eric and Evan, who will grow up along with the Internet.
—David

To my parents, Anant and Prabha Borwankar, whose insistence on a strong education has stood me in lifelong stead.
—Nitin

PREFACE

In the last three years, amid a great deal of hype and hoopla, the business community has flocked to the Internet. What the upshot of the Internet communication revolution will be—or if it even *is* a revolution—is still anybody's guess. A fair number of businesses have yet to feel the ripple effect of this revolutionary activity. Some never will, and will not be the worse for it. Others will join the fray and wish they hadn't. Like any significant change, this one will not benefit everyone equally.

Whatever the outcome, it is fair to say that in the final analysis, business as a whole will never be the same. The Internet is transforming the way businesses operate internally, the way they relate to one another, the way they deal with their customers, the way they collect information, and the way they market and distribute their products and services.

What is going on here?

The first wave of the business community's love affair with the Internet focused primarily on designing Web sites for marketing purposes. At first blush, the Internet appeared to be the perfect advertising venue—inexpensive development, enticing graphical capabilities, and a captive audience variously estimated to be between 10 and 30 million strong. Imagine a world in which your target audience was already "plugged in" to you and all you had to do was put up your message on a page for all to view. Free advertising was the carrot that attracted many of the early adopters.

As many pioneering companies discovered, though, building a Web site may be easy, but there is no guarantee anyone will notice it. In addition, maintaining a Web site requires a good deal of ongoing effort. Marketing brochures are usually changed every year or so, if that. The culture of the Internet dictates weekly, if not daily, changes. Most businesses are not set up for this kind of publishing effort.

Without a clear business case for developing an Internet presence, without a clear plan for promoting and managing a site, and without a long-term vision of how the site should be built and enhanced, many businesses that went online early are now being forced to reassess their strategy. Many of the early Web sites already have been abandoned, or *stabilized* as they say, left like billboards littering the information backroads, the victims of failed enthusiasm or an excessive fear of losing that vital competitive edge.

On the one hand, then, experience with nonproductive Web sites is producing a backlash of disillusionment. On the other hand, a deeper realization is emerging that the Internet can be used in other ways to improve a company's productivity. In this picture, what is important is less the medium that the Internet offers for communication than the channels it offers for conducting business. The Internet offers a powerful new means of aggregating, distributing, and exchanging goods and services.

To tap the power of this new vision, new business models are needed, as well as a deeper understanding of the technologies that underlie that vision, and new ways to educate the users to the advantages of these models. The recent shift toward more functional uses of the Internet—a shift exemplified in part by the recent excitement over *intranets*—and what it entails for businesses is the subject of this book.

What this book is about

This book details what it takes to devise and develop Internet business applications. Unlike a number of Internet books, this one does not attempt to convince you that building a Web site is painless, fun, and profitable. The processes we discuss may drive you and your company to re-examine its existing practices and to envision new ones. You will have to combine an understanding of technological capabilities with a sharpened business acumen. Not necessarily easy, but rewarding when it succeeds.

The book is organized around the major types of business applications being built today on the Internet. Within each section, we offer two valuable ways of understanding the business trends and opportunities available. First we describe in detail some of the hottest, most successful businesses on the Internet, focusing not only on what they built, but how and why they built it that way. We then provide an in-depth discussion of the crucial issues related to building your own application as well as the tools you may want to use to do it.

The book is divided into four main parts. The first three parts discuss the most important types of Internet business applications. Within each part, the initial chapters present the case studies. The last chapter in each part looks at what you will need to build your own application.

Part I is devoted to communication systems.

Part II discusses publishing applications.

Part III focuses on electronic commerce and transactions.

Part IV provides a detailed and specific look at what it takes to plan and implement your own Internet business. We placed this section at the end of the book because we believe you will be better equipped to understand and appreciate the details if you have first surveyed the whole terrain. Of course, if you are eager to get started learning about Internet software and tools, you are welcome to jump right to this final section and return to read the rest at a later date.

The CD-ROM

In addition to more than a dozen in-depth case studies and expert advice, this book also comes with a CD-ROM that contains a number of the development tools describe in Chapter 13, "The Essential Applications." For instructions on installing the software on the CD-ROM, see the Appendix, "Using the Companion CD-ROM and Web site."

Who this book is for

This book is written for anyone who is setting up or thinking about setting up an Internet business. Maybe you are an entrepreneur with a great idea about how to seize an Internet business opportunity while it is still hot. More likely, though, you are part of an existing company that wants to explore the Internet as a medium for expanding, supplementing, and enriching the business.

If you are just building a standard Web site, this book is calculated to give you a wider perspective of the possibilities so that you can build a site that won't be headed for obsolescence. If you are in the more probable position of having to assemble and direct the team that will be defining your company's Internet strategy, this book gives you the ground-level understanding you need to make informed decisions and get started.

This book is for those individuals—project managers, product designers, as well as business and technical developers—who are responsible for envisioning, creating, justifying, maintaining, and enhancing a company's business presence on the Internet.

If you are a manager or executive, this book will give you the high-level understanding of the technological tools and cultural issues you need to formulate a plan for your business.

If you are a developer or producer, this book will help you gain an understanding of the underlying business rationales that should inform a successful development project.

What this book doesn't do

This book is not a cookbook for do-it-yourself Web projects. In fact, it is not a Web book at all, although a great deal of emphasis is placed on the World Wide Web as an interface for Internet applications. There are any number of excellent how-to books that can help you build a Web site. Those books do not, however, help you think through the business issues involved in such a project; nor do they provide glimpses "backstage" at some of the Net's most successful sites. To our knowledge, this is the first book to prepare concrete case studies to illustrate the principles of successful business applications.

Likewise, there are many good books that provide a how-to perspective about using the Internet for business. Most of those focus exclusively on making money on the Internet. They tend to gloss over the nuts and bolts of building a profitable Internet application. We will also examine the most successful ways of using the Internet to generate revenues, but our wider perspective is on the mix of business planning and technology you will need to extend your company's resources and productivity via the Internet.

You can think of this book as a series of aerial snapshots of the commercial cyber-landscape. It is your essential guidebook to planning, designing, and building an Internet business.

Beyond this book

One of the themes of *Building Successful Internet Businesses* is the fact that the Internet has forced traditional industries to rethink how they do business. In fact, this book not only reports this phenomenon; it is also an example of it.

Writing a book on the state of the Internet, which is always changing and growing, is a challenge. We believe that the structure of the Internet as we have described it and the essential principles we have espoused will stand the test of time (at least as it is measured in Internet terms).

We recognize, however, that new information, new technological breakthroughs, and new industry coups appear every day, augmenting and in some cases overturning yesterday's wisdom. For that reason, and also because we have plenty of information that did not make it into the book, this book has a Web site of its own, where new case studies will be posted, information about and demonstrations of new and updated tools and applications will be provided, and other fun stuff will be added. You can get to the book's Web site by pointing your browser at **www.idgbooks.com/idgbooksonline/**.

Feedback

Most of all, we hope you find this book a valuable resource, and we encourage your comments and suggestions on ways we can improve future editions of the book as well as the Web site. To tell us what you think, send e-mail to **online@www.idgbooks.com**.

ACKNOWLEDGMENTS

David Elderbrock

A number of smart and dedicated folks have helped to make this book possible. First and foremost is publisher, David Ushijima, who deserves the credit for bringing us all together and forcing us to stop talking and start writing. Our editor, Corbin Collins, who should be in line for an honorary degree in psychology, managed to remain calm and keep us moving forward throughout the process as well as offered an abundance of good editorial advice. Stuti Garg, our technical editor, and Katharine Dvorak, our copy editor, helped to ensure that the book was intelligible to read.

I would also like to thank my coauthor, Nitin, for lending his experience and technical expertise to this project. A special debt of gratitude is owed to Leslie Lesnick, who brought some superb journalism to bear on a good number of the case studies. Thanks, too, to all of the Internet executives and managers who took time away from hectic schedules to be interviewed for the case studies in this book.

My deepest affections and thanks I reserve for three very special people: for Tamar, whose support, as always, has made all things possible, and for Eric and Evan, who were quite persistent in reminding me that losing to them on the basketball court was far more fun than pounding on a keyboard.

Nitin Borwankar

Many thanks to my wife, Garima, and one-year-old daughter, Vanita, for the crazy schedules and demands I made on their time. This book would not have been possible without my wife's patient encouragement.

I would like to thank my coauthor, David Elderbrock, for putting up with my erratic delivery schedule, the people at IDG Books—especially Corbin Collins and David Ushijima—for being very flexible as the book metamorphosed in vision and content. Without their persistence this book would not have seen the light of day.

Contents at a Glance

Contents

PART ONE

Online Communication Services

From e-mail and newsgroups to chat, from Internet phone and video conference to virtual world environments, the Internet has proven fertile ground for the development of communication technologies. In Part One, we look at some of the successful businesses and business applications that are being built up around such communication models, and we examine some of the tools used to conduct Internet-based communication.

In Chapter One, "The New Internet Models," we provide a general survey of the business models emerging as a result of the convergence of technology, marketing, and business goals on the Internet.

Chapter Two, "Mail and Discussion Forums," focuses on examples of asynchronous communication, while Chapter Three, "Real-time Chat Services," focuses on case studies of businesses using synchronous communication.

The last chapter in this section, Chapter Four, "Applications for Messaging and Chat," examines the major issues and technologies involved in the construction of communication-based business applications on the Internet.

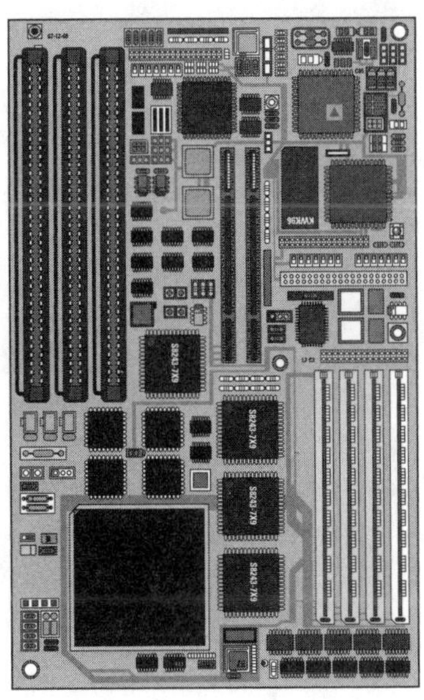

CHAPTER ONE

THE NEW INTERNET MODELS

It is difficult to recall that just three years ago the Internet was still almost exclusively the province of the academic community. All of the Internet services were character-based, only a small number of dedicated UNIX jockeys really understood how the technologies worked, and the principal people sending e-mail were research scientists.

All that changed with the introduction of the World Wide Web and, more crucially, Mosaic, the first graphical browser. Slowly at first, but with an increasing sense of urgency (some might say delirium), businesses began to pay attention to the Internet and wonder if they weren't missing out on something revolutionary. Government played its part in the promotion by spinning notions of the Internet as the realization of an "information superhighway" that connects citizens in a perfect democracy.

Now the landscape of the Internet continues to expand and change at a dizzying pace, so much so that Internet books are out of date by the time they hit bookstores. People have begun to speak of "an Internet year," meaning a compacted amount of time, something like dog years, to convey the sense of rapid change.

A Starting Point

How, in the midst of such a frenetic, hype-filled environment, does one make intelligent, informed, business decisions about venturing into the new world of Internet presence?

Our goal in this book is to guide you though the labyrinth of smoke and mirrors, separate hype from reality, and call attention to what is most promising, in order for you to make reasonable, informed decisions about how to catch the cyberwave without taking a bath.

As a starting point, we first explore how the Internet has impacted the business world. We then examine the new models for conducting business that are emerging as a result of this impact. In subsequent chapters, we will introduce the major types of Internet businesses and examine the practices of some of the highly successful businesses that have taken the plunge into the online world. We will also guide you through your initial steps as you put together a plan for your own business. Along the way we will focus on two elements: detailed case studies of already successful businesses, and nuts and bolts information to help you put together your own plan for the next killer Internet site.

A Marriage of Opposites

In order to tap into the Internet's opportunities, you need to understand its underlying structure and what it is about the Internet the business world has found so appealing.

When the Internet was first conceived by ARPAnet in the 1960s, it was intended as a medium in which to transfer and share vital information and communications. For most of its existence, the Internet was considered to be an inhospitable world of cryptic UNIX commands like *grep* and *chmod* and protocol acronyms like TCP/IP, NNTP, SMTP, and FTP. As the Internet expanded, however, an increasing number of non-computer experts began to discover the value of e-mail as well as information delivery services such as gopher.

At the same time academic institutions were honing their Internet skills, businesses were gradually acclimating themselves to the notion that desktop computers linked together in local area networks could make it possible for employees to not only share data and resources, but also to communicate with one another without having to call another meeting. In this environment they encountered some of the same functions, with different technologies and different applications, that the universities were using on the Internet.

In addition, company road warriors and telecommuters wielding laptops, cellular phones, and Personal Digital Assistants (PDAs) began to appear on the scene. They needed the ability to dial into the company LAN to access their databases, check their e-mail, and fax important documents.

All of this contributed to the wave of enthusiasm that converged around the introduction of Mosaic, the first graphical Web browser to appear for Windows and Macintosh computers.

The main appeal of this new "network of networks" was the extension of the LAN combined with an economic trend that favored "downsized" companies to provide more services with a smaller staff. And the World Wide Web offered an inviting, seemingly effortless way to get customers to come and check out the latest information about a business' products or services.

The Ideal Internet Presence

In the fall of 1994, the *New York Times* ran an article about the increasing commercial use of the Internet. The article featured a local florist who started to use the Internet to take flower orders. There was a big photo of the man in his shop, looking pleased that the Internet had brought him more business in the last month than FTD. And he didn't even own a computer. He paid another company approximately $30 a month to give him a page of advertising and then fax him any requests he received online.

This was not the first news article about Internet commerce to appear, nor by any means the last. It did, however, set forth the appeal of the Internet to businesses in a way that was highly alluring. Imagine that for essentially no money down and without any appreciable learning curve, anyone with something to sell could stake a claim on the Internet, put up a home page, and tap into the Internet mother lode. Sounds appealing, no?

It is worth noting that the flower shop story has many analogs in the tales of some of the most legendary Internet successes. Is there anyone who does not yet know the overnight-millionaire story of the group of undergrads from Illinois hired by a savvy CEO who together took the name *Netscape* public and made their fortunes? Or the one about two Stanford graduate students who started to make Web hotlists in their spare time and who have now amassed a minor industry under the unlikely name of "Yahoo!"?

Bursting the Bubble: Internet Fallacies

It does not take a genius to realize that to pay $30 a month to put up a page of ad copy on the Internet and reach a potential market of over ten million users is a bargain when compared to the ad prices for print and broadcast media. But what happens when you build a home page and nobody visits it? And even if they do show up, how do you ensure that your marketing will have any impact?

This no-hassle advertising approach works as long as you are a novelty item on the Net. Unfortunately, the half-life of novelty items on the Internet is shrinking every day. When only a handful of florists advertise online, the chance that any one of them will be found is pretty good. Now there are hundreds—possibly thousands—of florists on the Net (anyone care to count?), which is certainly more than you would ever find in your local yellow pages. In such circumstances the return on the investment diminishes rapidly.

The Internet has the potential to be a significant vehicle for corporate advertising, but advertisers are beginning to learn that traditional advertising models do not necessarily work on the Internet—a place where most users are either looking for entertainment or information, or just browsing. It takes a special kind of advertising to capture these folks. We will examine some of the most creative and effective approaches to advertising in later chapters.

In the future, specialized Internet advertising will become increasingly the norm as competition for market attention continues to escalate and consumer tolerance for strict advertising declines. This is not to say that you shouldn't consider profit motives in setting up your Internet strategy. Just be aware that selling on the Internet is still anything but guaranteed income.

There is nothing really wrong with the florist's approach to business on the Internet, which at least has the virtue of being low risk, and it apparently worked, at least for a time. The problem is with some of the assumptions hovering just beneath the surface of the story. Let these notions take hold of your thinking, and you are likely to find yourself at first beguiled and then disenchanted by the opportunities the Internet affords. Before we go any further, it is worth uncovering and exposing the most dangerous of these fallacies.

Fallacy 1: Everybody needs a home page today

There are plenty of good reasons for wanting or needing an Internet presence. Most of the reasons center around developing a new channel for your business. But this assumes that both the people involved in your business and any potential clients or customers have Internet access. This may not be a valid assumption for you—yet. Let good business instincts guide your decision. It may look like your competition is getting the jump on you, but if they don't have a good reason for their Internet presence, it is more likely to stagnate than to grow. Meanwhile, plan your own timing and strategy.

Fallacy 2: I don't need to know or use the Internet to tap customers

There is no denying that it takes time to really understand the Internet, and it is always possible to delegate the responsibility for knowing how the Internet operates to others. But think of the Internet as a foreign country (some might say it's more like another planet). Would you send a sales team to a foreign country if they couldn't speak the language and didn't know the first thing about how to conduct themselves in that country? We hope not.

Similarly, it will help you immensely in planning your Internet strategy if you have explored this foreign territory yourself and learned something of its conventions as well as its limitations. You will better understand the needs and frustrations of Internet users, making you less likely to mass e-mail thousands of unsuspecting readers or fill your Web site with oversized graphics. Plus, Internet users like to feel that the person on the other end is "one of them" and someone to be trusted.

Fallacy 3: To advertise on the Internet, I can reuse my existing collateral materials

Okay, you *can* do this. In fact, reusing existing marketing copy on the Internet is standard practice at the moment. Lots of companies do it because it is a quick way to get up and running. But if you were planning a TV spot, would you shoot a film of the CEO reading your company backgrounder? Would you scroll the text of it across the screen?

Different media have different strengths and weaknesses. Trying to convert content from one to the other usually leads to mediocre results. How good will that 5MB EPS graphic look as a dithered 40KB GIF? How readable will that nice three-page brochure be on one long, scrolling Web page?

Realistically, of course, you probably don't want to start reinventing content from scratch. But don't let the format of existing content dictate your project design. Instead, start by identifying what the medium offers you, and let that drive how you present the content you either have available or that you have the time and budget to create. In the long run, this will help you expand your Internet presence more effectively.

Fallacy 4: The Internet is a teeming market just waiting to be tapped

This attitude seems to be fairly pervasive, perhaps because the Internet is not yet (thank goodness) saturated with advertising. It looks like virgin real estate. (Just look at all those unsuspecting cyber-nabobs waiting to be sold widgets!)

This view has several problems. In the first place, demographic studies suggest that most users are either students or business people who use the Internet for purposes other than shopping. It is not yet a consumer market.

Second, many users still hesitate to buy online. Much of this has to do with uneasiness about the security of money transactions online. This is likely to change over time, as reliable standards are developed to handle these transactions and as users become acclimated to buying online. After all, we have become used to ordering via catalogs, dictating our credit card numbers over the phone, and using bank automated teller machines.

A large appeal of the Net, though, is the ease with which you can go on to something else. But in such an environment, how does one capture and hold the attention of a potential customer long enough to make a sale? At the moment, the Internet appears to be a better tool for the online equivalent of window shopping and for doing product comparisons than for making actual purchases. It is even an open question whether traditional advertising techniques will work in the more active, task-oriented atmosphere of the Internet.

The real problem with this notion of *tapping* the audience—a concept inherited from television culture, we suspect—is that it separates the world into *tappers* and *tappees*. But the Internet, in part because it has interactive capabilities, operates much more like an extended community environment. Certainly the Internet has the potential to offer your business a marketplace and a channel to customers. But you will have to build those channels and become a part of them yourself if you want the marketplace to flourish and repay you for your efforts.

Fallacy 5: Having a business presence on the Internet means advertising

This is not so much a fallacy as simple short-sightedness. At the moment it is true that most of what passes for commercial Internet development is advertising. As the previous sections suggest, however, this may not be the best use of the Internet as a business tool.

Advertising has been the easiest way for businesses to establish an Internet presence, but especially with the explosion of commercial Web sites, the jury is still out on whether Internet advertising is cost-effective. If you are only paying $30 a month and spending three hours of your time to advertise on the Web, it probably doesn't much matter. On the other hand, if you are paying $30,000, you are going to want to see some pretty concrete returns on your investment. Even at the low end, once the novelty of the project wears off, you are likely to abandon the project rather than augment it if the response is not strong.

Web Sites With Vision

For most companies, the idea of establishing an Internet presence still looks primarily like a marketing exercise. A home page feels like a digital company brochure, and in fact, many Web sites have been constructed largely from reworked marketing material.

It is our contention that although advertising and self-promotion will always be a component of what happens on the Internet, this is not what the Internet is best suited for, as many companies are discovering. The Internet is really only good for marketing in specialized circumstances.

This does not mean that the value of the Internet to business is all empty hype. The Internet is first and foremost a channel for circulating information. The trick for businesses is to find ways to use that channel effectively, and in the process make their place on the Internet an essential node through which traffic is channeled.

FedEx

The Federal Express Web site (**www.fedex.com**) represents for many people the quintessential demonstration of doing something useful on the Internet. The site has a clean, appealing interface design, with a cool black background, simple colors, and a sleek navigation button bar. It provides basic service information about FedEx delivery options, reprints the requisite FedEx press releases, and even enables you to download software for preparing your packing slips.

The main attraction of the site, though, is the fact that you can track packages you have sent or expect to receive by simply typing in the tracking code number. It is an extremely simple function, and in fact it is this simplicity that is so satisfying. Tracking a package this way is significantly easier than it would be to try to get a customer service representative on the phone to track the package for you.

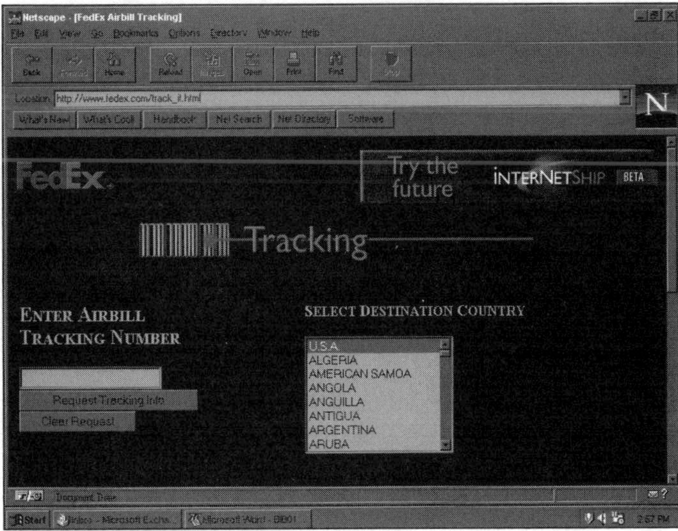

Figure 1-1
Tracking your package through cyberspace.

Of course there is a great deal of sophisticated technology at work behind the scenes to make it possible for this feature to work. But that is not what matters to the user, nor for that matter to FedEx. Once the system is set up, it more or less runs itself. Users are willing to do the tracking work themselves in exchange for quick service. FedEx wins by saving costs and by satisfying customers. It is a perfect illustration of the "ATM effect" which the banking industry so successfully introduced several years ago (and that most of us now depend on).

IRS

Have you ever tried to find an IRS tax form to do your last-minute taxes, or tried to get last-minute answers to questions? If you have, you know what a nightmare it can be. Your local library has the forms, but they just ran out. The IRS phone lines are snarled for hours.

Now the IRS has a Web site (**www.irs.ustreas.gov**) that makes it easy to get IRS publications, official tax forms, and even some free advice. Like the FedEx site, the interface of the IRS site is colorful and appealing, with a "mom-and-pop" look clearly designed to try to make the harried tax-preparing citizen feel at home. After all, filing taxes is not one of life's more pleasant tasks. The real success of the IRS site is not the sheer quantity of information it makes available so much as the atmosphere it creates around that information.

Figure 1-2
The IRS delivers attitude on the Web.

What the designers of the IRS site have done is attempt to convey a sense of community with their content. You could argue about whether the sense of community is sincere or artificial, but at least the agency attempted to make an onerous task more bearable, both by making lots of information readily available, and by lightening the typically bureaucratic atmosphere.

The IRS Web site is located at **www.irs.ustreas.gov**.

Hot Hot Hot

The last site we examine here is a small business venture called Hot Hot Hot (**www.hot.presence.com**). It is the Web site of a retail operation in southern California that specializes in chili sauces. Around its sales pitch, the company has woven an inviting and informative set of features that convey a sense that the site is really providing a service while at the same time fostering community among lovers of the hot stuff. It is a story worth telling in some detail, as it offers several lessons for small businesses wanting to undertake successful Internet projects.

Figure 1-3
Some like it hot.

As the hot sauce business is a niche business, certainly without the kind of competition florists face, the company might easily have chosen to take out a home page with one of the many services in California that offer presence on the Internet. Hot Hot Hot started out with a simple site, but chose a strategy that would establish its Web site as the cyberplace to go for anything pertaining to hot sauces.

On its Web site, Hot Hot Hot has a database of its products with brief descriptions and a hotness rating. The company has made this data accessible in various ways: by name, ingredients, or heat. Once you find the sauce you want, you can buy it, either online or by calling a toll-free number.

If the product database is the core of the Web site, though, it is the additional features that give the site its life and attract first-time and returning customers. Many of these features have been added over time, as the owners familiarized themselves with the demands of managing the site on an ongoing basis.

For the site, the company produces a weekly newsletter, selecting a product to feature and offering it at a discount. It enhances the site by providing information and anecdotes related to the chief ingredients—primarily chili peppers. It solicits feedback from visitors to the site and posts on a weekly basis the best stories they receive.

Having set out to build an Internet site to buy their products, the owners of Hot Hot Hot have ended up constructing a forum for exchanging "hot" information. In the process they demonstrate both their knowledge of and enthusiasm for their products; their users provide testimonials and amusing anecdotes to spice up the content offerings. As a result, their Web site feels more like a club for hot sauce aficionados than a virtual condiment market.

The Hot Hot Hot Web site is located at **www.hot.presence.com**.

Some Rules of the Road

Some general lessons can be distilled from the experience of online businesses. We offer these in no particular order, but each one contains a key concept that you would do well to note.

Regard information as a value-added service

It's the Information Age, right? And everybody wants it to be free. One of the chief differences between the Internet and other information services—even the commercial online services—is that information has lost some of its value as a commodity. In other words, nobody has figured out how to *sell* information on the Net, a place not only where users are used to free access, but also where a glut of information sloshes around, much of it of questionable quality.

In time, no doubt, quality information will command a price. However, until such time as people can easily tell high-quality from low, providing information will be most valuable to its owners as a service they can provide users. A business that provides information about its products or services demonstrates an interest in educating, not just milking, customers. Providing information to customers also helps to position the business as an expert in its field.

Include your customers and users in the production of content

The flip side of the fact that information is given away on the Net is that users can be solicited to contribute information as well. Publishing such information can be a good way to generate fresh content and encourage return visitors to your site. This is yet another gesture that conveys the sense that a business is fostering a community of users.

Build in real functionality

There are several reasons for doing this. The Internet encourages interactivity, so visitors to your site are always looking for something to do. The first reason you should add functionality to your site is to encourage the curious and keep them from catching the next wave out. Useful functionality will also keep visitors coming back. There is a limit to the number of times you can read an HTML Web page, but the potential for function-based information is endless. Similarly, the final reason for designing a functional site is that it becomes much easier to add to and manage the content base.

The launch is only the beginning. We have already mentioned this one, but it bears repeating. As Web site managers discover, there is much to do after the site is alive in order to keep it healthy and fit and at the head of the class. The good news from several sources is that, if properly planned for, the work can be fun. It is not "extra" work, but rather an integral part of the business. You should also look for spin-off benefits from your Internet presence to the non-Internet aspects of your business, such as reusing content produced on or for the Web site in other aspects of the business.

COUNT ON NEW JOBS TO DO ONCE THE SITE IS UP

The Internet Models

With the preceding examples in mind, we can begin to distill some of the basic models that businesses are using to develop their sites. Many of the basic concepts behind these models are familiar, based on existing media and business operations, and provide an adequate starting point. Later, when we turn to the actual case studies, we will be able to hone the models more exactly.

The Internet as broadcast medium

In some ways the real-time broadcast model exemplified by radio and television gives a better feel for what maintaining an Internet presence is like. It is no accident that people are beginning to experiment with the World Wide Web as a performance space. For example, interactive, cyber "soap operas," such as the Spot, Ferndale, and Brentwood, have already appeared on the Web. Another trend that is pushing the Net towards a broadcast model is the implementation of *streaming* audio and video, which lets you view content as it arrives, replacing the notion of downloading content and then viewing it.

But broadcasting, like publishing, imagines that all content emanates from a central authority. This is not to say that broadcasting does not happen on the Internet, but the full thrill of the Internet lies partly in the sense that there is no authority, and no intermediary editing, censoring, or filtering done to the content.

A more technical way to say this is that whereas the broadcast model is a "one-to-many" communication model, the Internet is at its best as a "many-to-many" communication medium.

The other drawback of the broadcast model is that broadcasting is by nature ephemeral. If you miss a show and are too busy to program the VCR, you miss it. The Internet is much more naturally a content-on-demand environment. This, too, is likely to change, as we see more event-oriented content, such as cybercast concerts, on the Internet. But the fact remains that content is much more archivable, even as—ironically—the half-life of its interest decreases.

The Internet as party-line phone/CB/ham radio network

Remember the popular fascination with Citizen Band radios in the '70s? Did you have a "handle?" Much of what was sexy about CB radios has re-emerged on the Internet—we are surprised, in fact, that none of the many Internet phone services has thought to call itself "CyberCB." The virtue of this particular model is that it highlights the degree to which the Internet is a many-to-many environment. It also helps to convey some of the "power to the people" sensibility that still echoes across the T-1 cables, even as the big players are rushing to gobble up any semblance of this frontier feeling.

The biggest problem with this model is that unless you happen to sell CB radios, there is not much room in the CB model for doing business. There is, however, a place for a third party to host the kinds of conversations that take place over these airwaves, such as TalkCity (**www.talkcity.com**). And it is important to recognize this phenomenon as part of the challenge and beauty of the Internet as a communication medium.

The Internet as publishing medium

As a publisher, your role would be to collect and edit content for your Internet project that would then be delivered to users on a periodic basis. This model gives a good feel for the input-output flow, but it is misleading in several ways.

The first problem is with the idea of *periodic*. The Internet is 24/7/365, as they say, so even though no one can reasonably update content continually, the compulsion is there to do so as often as possible.

Real-time updating, on the other hand, strains the editorial role you would probably like to have with the content. Similarly, the whole concept of revision is thrown out with the bath water. *Morphing* content might better describe what happens in the Internet environment. One result is the dreaded "Under Construction" syndrome, in which your site is being continually worked on.

Another drawback of the publishing model is its implicit notions of authorship and intellectual property. In the publishing model, the publisher or author typically owns the content. On the Internet, such is not always the case. And even if it were, it would be difficult to enforce. It is perhaps more accurate to imagine that the publisher—that is, you—own the space in which content and content consumers join up.

The Internet as forum/marketplace

Finally a model to warm the heart of any businessperson. The notion of the Internet as a forum or marketplace emphasizes the extent to which the Internet is really more about being a place than a channel. They don't call it cyber*space* for nothing. (This is also where the frontier metaphor comes in.)

But a marketplace conjures up images of vendors hawking their wares and vying for the attention of roving hordes of consumers. In point of fact, the Internet is—at its best, anyway—much more interactive than that. It is more than tens of thousands of digital billboards littering the virtual highways of the infobahn. In the Internet marketplace, it becomes more difficult to distinguish the vendors from the consumers, just as it becomes more difficult to tell the authorities from the charlatans.

New Business Models

In the remainder of Part I as well as in Parts II and III, we will examine how these various models have emerged on the Internet in three identifiable business types: communication sites, publishing sites, and transaction sites.

Communication Sites

These sites have focused their energies on ways to allow people to communicate easily and effectively, either in real-time chat environments or in newsgroups or bulletin board structures.

Publishing Sites

Given that the Web was originally envisioned as an information delivery system, it is no surprise that the collection, organization, and presentation of publishing content has become big business on the Internet.

Transaction Sites

These sites are less interested in exchanging communications or information than in transacting business. The obvious examples are Internet malls that enable shoppers to make purchases online. As we will discover, however, there are many other transactions that can take place in cyberspace.

A Sneak Preview

In each of the sections in this book, we will examine in detail several prime examples of each of the three types of sites identified above. We will show you the model around which they built the site, how they built it, and how they generate revenue. In reading the case studies, several business principles begin to appear again and again. Here is a sneak preview of some of the things you will discover:

Business Principles

1. Businesses, even traditionally product-oriented ones, have assumed an information-service component as part of their ability to attract and retain customers. This service has blurred the boundaries between information and advertising, particularly where "educating the consumer" is part of attracting customers to a business.

2. The notion of customer service in general has moved increasingly in the direction of enabling (or forcing, depending on your point of view) customers to have direct access to the information they need to help them get things done, whether this means technical support information or a means of making a purchase. This do-it-yourself-whenever-it-is-convenient model is one principal attraction of the Internet.

One variation of this model is the tendency of Internet businesses to involve customers in the development stages of their business operations. The most obvious example of this is the proliferation of beta test software to be found on the Internet. This, too, changes the relationship of the customer with the business, making the customer feel closer to the source and encouraging a sense of community—we're all in this together and your participation matters—which is the hallmark of the Internet.

3. The Internet offers a two-way channel for the flow of information, of which smart Internet-based companies will take advantage. We call this the aggregation-packaging-distribution model. The Internet can be used not only to disseminate information in a broadcast fashion, but also to collect it. Indeed, building content through the contributions of users is an important aspect of developing an Internet business.

Different companies locate their strengths at different places along this continuum. Some excel at aggregating information for consumers. Others take information and package it effectively, either by organizing it, or filtering it, or evaluating it in order to reduce the information overload we all suffer from these days. Still other companies provide distribution services and add their value to the process in that way.

Necessary Adaptations

Although conceptually some similarities exist between local area networks and the Internet, the fact is most businesses have had to ramp up to deal with this new way of doing business. This ramp up typically includes:

- New hardware and software purchases
- Adapting or converting existing data to new environments
- Identifying new ways of gathering/storing/retrieving data
- Revamping business models to work in this environment
- Training and/or re-deploying employees
- Developing applications to deliver the data

- Deciding how much of a project to outsource and how much to control in-house

This book alone does not provide the answers to all of the questions you may have if you embark on building your own Internet business. But along with the case studies, we provide a framework for understanding what will be involved in setting up your own Internet business and point you to additional, more specialized, resources that you may want to consult.

Some Assumptions

Let's look at some of the principles this book will illustrate and expand on throughout Part I and in later case studies.

The Internet is a volatile, rapidly changing place

Depending on whether you are a "glass-half-full" or "half-empty" type, this principle may sound encouraging or disheartening. The fact that the Internet is an easily changeable information delivery mechanism is one of its chief virtues. This distinguishes it from print and CD-ROM publishing on the one hand, and one-directional broadcast media, such as TV and radio on the other, where media content is never changed because it ceases to exist as soon as it is broadcast. By the same token, the ease with which content can be updated on the Internet again gives rise to the dreaded "Under Construction" syndrome, which can seriously de-value an otherwise useful Web site.

This principle suggests a few other words of advice. For starters, don't bite off more than you can chew. Internet technology is evolving on what seems like a daily basis. Competition to outdo one another is intense among Internet technology companies. Standards keep changing in an attempt to keep up with or dictate customer demand. In such a climate it would be foolhardy to stake everything on one technology.

Don't be afraid to take some chances—those who hesitate are lost, too, you know—but bear in mind that, for better or worse, your project will not be a one-time development effort. Don't do anything you will later regret having to undo. If you can afford to experiment, by all means do—this is how the Internet advances. If you are worried about loss of time or money, however, invest only a small amount at first. Build something small that you can be proud of. You will have plenty of time to expand your project as your confidence increases and response warrants it.

This leads to the second word of advice on this topic: be prepared to change what you have. On the Internet, the medium is a large part of the message, to paraphrase Marshall McLuhan. Part of keeping your Web site current is keeping it up to date with the evolving technical standards. As long as the medium keeps changing, you will have to update your message if you want to communicate it effectively.

Even if the Internet technology wasn't changing, the climate of the Internet is such that you have to update, renew, and expand frequently. (Lest you think the Internet is the primary cause of short attention spans, recall that the average television image stays on screen a little over one second.) Time is so fleeting on the Net that an "Internet year" has come to signify a very short period of time.

In this environment, content that is not updated rapidly loses value and legitimacy. How can you trust information that has not been reviewed for two months? Is anyone even monitoring the site? One answer to this need for constant updating is the familiar "What's New?" section on many Web sites. Fresh, updated content, or at least the anticipation of new content, brings people back for more.

The key lesson here is that you need to enter into any Internet project knowing that it is a long-term relationship that will require continual work on your part. And that if it is to remain a happy marriage, you must keep in mind that this relationship will likely involve changes not only to your Internet presence, but to your business as well.

Joining the Internet will change the way you do business and the people you need to do so

Remember, we are talking about a commercial revolution here. You cannot join a revolution and expect to remain untouched by it. Your business practices, even the structure of your business, are likely to undergo changes as a result of going online. Maybe not today, maybe not tomorrow, but soon—and for the rest of the life of your business.

How *much* your business practices will be changed obviously depends on how deeply you involve the business in the project. Perhaps it will simply mean designating a person to check and respond to e-mail on a regular basis. Or someone to produce a weekly newsletter to be posted on your Web site. And someone else to figure out how to give employees access to the Internet, and... well you get the picture.

The main point is to plan for change up front by including it in your estimates of how much your business can reasonably accomplish.

The best Internet implementations leverage existing corporate assets and take into account the strengths of the online medium

In a nutshell, our advice to anyone planning their Internet strategy is this: take into account what your audience wants, what you have to offer, and what the medium permits within your budget.

For now, suffice it to say that the online world is good for viewing, browsing, searching, participating, experimenting ("try this...") and simulating ("imagine this..."). It is not so good at presenting large blocks of textual information (like a book, for instance), or in directing users in a particular way (towards a sale, for instance). (I would like to see a research project that set up some "slide presentations" and then tracked how far into the presentation the average viewer went before giving up. My guess, trying to be generous, would be about three screens). In a word, it is hard to constrain users to a linear path in a hypertextual world.

See Chapter 3, "Real-time Chat Services" for more information about how to best take advantage of the strengths of the Internet.

You should also consider ways your Internet project can help to counteract some of the less-than-desirable characteristics of cyberspace. For instance, as everyone who has ever read a "History of the Internet" knows, the network architecture was designed to encourage decentralization and redundancy. That way it would be harder for an enemy to figure out where to drop its bombs. That's great if you're a government, more interested in self-perpetuation than in efficiency. It's not so great if you are searching for a certain fact you are given only thirty minutes to find and you are returned a list of 247 places where you could look to find it. In this kind of environment, information filtering and quality control are high-value activities.

The Internet is a medium for increasing business productivity and communications, not just a vehicle to augment sales

In the first wave of enthusiasm over the commercial possibilities of the Internet everyone leapt at the idea of the Internet as a marketing vehicle. Now, that excitement is beginning to be tempered by reality. While marketers try to figure out how to make advertising work in this new environment, others are realizing that businesses might use the Internet to make themselves more productive doing what they already do, thus derive revenue indirectly.

The Internet holds vast potential as a channel for corporate communications. This can mean communication between the company and existing as well as potential customers. Many companies are moving their customer service and technical support online and finding that not only are customers happier, but work flow is easier to manage.

Similarly, some companies are using the Internet as a means of conducting business-to-business operations, from building alliances to sharing information and resources. Other companies are turning to the Internet as a solution to their internal communications and work flow needs.

Even the recent rumors, announcements, and commentary regarding the $500 network computer—which would use the Internet as a massive client/server network with applications residing on remote hosts with inexpensive computers accessing them on a per-need basis—adds weight to the argument that the trend is towards making the Internet a place where business is conducted, not just a place where products are bought and sold.

The trend in Internet development is changing from document-based Web sites to multi-functional applications

This principle is as close as the book will come to a theme song. The first wave of commercial development on the Internet has clearly been using Web sites as marketing tools. That wave is cresting as the demand for more sophisticated network functionality combines with the appearance of new programming capabilities (such as Sun Microsystem's Java and Netscape Corporation's plug-in capabilities), as well as with commercial-grade database and development tools.

The result is a shift in Internet development from simple publishing models to something more akin to traditional software application development. We are already seeing an increasing emphasis on Web sites that perform one or more functions. They still contain marketing information, but judiciously contained within a functional application. We will be examining a number of these kinds of Internet projects in the chapters ahead.

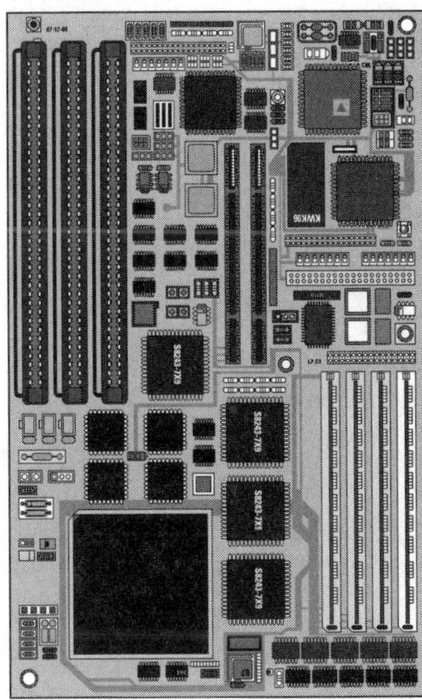

CHAPTER TWO

MAIL AND DISCUSSION FORUMS

Communication services are a venerable part of the Internet. E-mail, Listserv e-mail-based discussion lists, and USENET newsgroups were among the first network communication services to appear on the Net. These services may not be as glamorous as that media darling, the World Wide Web, but even so, every user survey discovers that e-mail is still the function most widely used by the Internet community.

In the following two chapters, we look at several businesses that are trying to seize the opportunity to help people communicate over the Internet. In this chapter, we look at the services that provide store- and forward-type of messaging services, often called *asynchronous* to denote the fact that the communication takes place at different times. In Chapter 3, "Real-time Chat Services," we look at companies that are building synchronous, or real-time, communication environments, known (not always affectionately) as "chat servers." Finally, in Chapter 4, "Applications for Messaging and Chat," the last chapter in Part I, we will consider the direct business implications of communication services and glance at the latest breed of multimedia communication and collaboration technologies.

Communication Models

There are two basic models used to describe the value an Internet business can bring to a communication system. These models apply equally to both asynchronous and synchronous communication services.

Providing Channels of Communication

First, the role of the communication channel service is both to make possible and to simplify the act of communication between external parties. In this model, the company that provides the communication service does not participate in any capacity in the discussions that take place between external parties. The business is merely offering the environment and, in the best cases, optimizing that environment for the kind of communication provided.

Depending on the type of communication provided, the channel service model can take on various metaphoric qualities. If the communication is e-mail-based, as is the case with Pobox.com, a company we discuss later in this chapter, the service looks something like the U.S. Postal Service. If you are maintaining a discussion service, whether based on e-mail, newsgroups, or one of the forum applications discussed in Chapter 4, your role looks more like that of the host of a convention center, a town hall, or possibly a singles bar. Here, too, your purpose is simply to create the space and let conversation or discussion happen.

ASYNCHRONOUS VS. SYNCHRONOUS COMMUNICATION

The distinction between asynchronous and synchronous communication plays a key role in our discussion in Part I, so it would be good to define these terms now.

Asynchronous communication is broken up over time intervals. The participants in the discussion are not necessarily connected online at the same time. Synchronous communication, then, is just the opposite. It is real-time, remote communication conducted by having all participants logged onto the communication service simultaneously.

The difference between these two types of communication is perhaps best characterized in the non-computer world by the difference between trading voice mail with one or more persons (asynchronous) and actually talking to a person via a regular voice or conference call (synchronous). As far as the Internet is concerned, the distinction is between e-mail and various types of discussion—forum (asynchronous) or chat (synchronous).

Expert Content/Moderating

The alternative to the channel service model is to assume the role of a central participant in the communication. In this case, your business will actively define the content for the communication, which, for example, may be done in a question and answer format—much like a standard "letters to the editor" section or advice column. A variation of this model that recently gained in popularity involves sponsoring featured respondents to serve as moderators for a discussion, either ongoing or on a one-time basis.

Another example of this model are the services such as Match.Com, that define what kind of communication will take place, and use technology to limit the content (see the Match.Com Spotlight later in this chapter). For example, Match.Com may facilitate communication leaning toward people meeting and socializing. It does not, however, encourage the buying and selling of products. Nor is it really conducive to seminar-like, online conferences.

To learn more about the "nuts and bolts" of building a communication-based Internet application, turn to Chapter 4, "Applications for Messaging and Chat."

Pobox.com (**www.pobox.com**) is a novel way to manage and find e-mail addresses on the Web. Subscribers to pobox.com can forward all of their e-mail through the system and have it delivered to one final destination, or they can have their e-mail forwarded to more than one address if they wish—no more having to remember to check all of their e-mail accounts. For one set fee, subscribers can choose up to three aliases and have them all forwarded. This service is particularly useful for users who have more than one identity on the Internet, or more than one e-mail account.

Most importantly, the service is useful to anyone who at any time will change e-mail providers. With pobox.com, you don't have to send out a "change of address" message, because to those you communicate with, your address remains the same. You only need to update pobox.com's database.

The system also makes your e-mail address easy to locate for someone who wants to get in touch with you but who has forgotten your address, which, through pobox.com, is searchable by anyone on the Internet through the World Wide Web and through Finger, a standard UNIX command. Pobox.com is managed by IC Group, Inc., an internet service business based in Philadelphia, Pennsylvania.

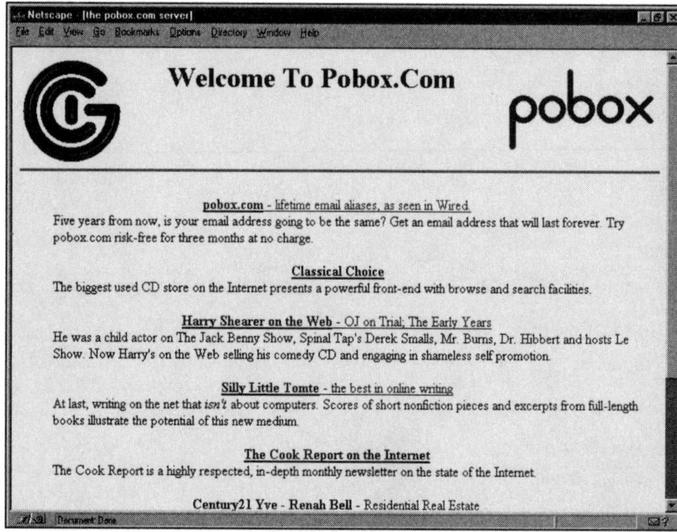

Figure 2-1
Pobox.com was the first e-mail redirection service on the Web.

POBOX.COM AT-A-GLANCE

The Product	E-mail redirection service
URL	www.pobox.com
The Company	IC Group, Inc.
Owners	Reuven Bell and Meng Weng Wong
The Team	Seven employees
The Customers	Individuals and businesses with multiple aliases and e-mail accounts that want one permanent destination e-mail address
Start Date	January, 1995
Lessons Learned	Plan ahead and read everything in your contract when you are looking to form business partners and use the law to your advantage. Always keep the customers in mind, and make sure your hardware is capable of doing more than you ask of it. You never know when you will have a sudden growth spurt.
Software/Hardware	UNIX-based architecture
Subscribers	7,000 with 30-40 new subscribers daily

COMPANY BACKGROUND

Reuven Bell and Meng Weng Wong, two college students and friends from the University of Pennsylvania (who discovered each other online), developed the concept behind pobox.com. They came up with the idea in the summer of 1994. From September of that year to January, 1995, they did some preliminary programming, conceptualization, and investigation of the equipment needed to run such a service. In January, 1995, they officially launched the site.

The layout of money to get up and going was only $2,500 for the initial SPARC station from Sun Microsystems. Everything else was added thanks to favors from friends and other business relationships—for example, they were able to secure free connectivity for the first few months.

After the initial launch, they cautiously let only a few people know that the service was available—friends and a few people on IRC (Internet Relay Chat), so that they could test the system without getting inundated with users. Within three to four weeks, they had 200 users solely by word-of-mouth. Today, the user base stands at 9,000 subscribers.

PRODUCT DESCRIPTION

With pobox.com, you never again have to notify anyone when you change your e-mail address. Subscribers only have to contact pobox.com to change their forwarding address, and then all of their mail is automatically forwarded to them. The address changes are transparent to the recipients of a subscriber's e-mail messages.

By registering three aliases—your full name, current username , and a unique nickname with pobox.com, you increase the odds that someone can locate you through pobox.com. Subscribers with long, cumbersome usernames or machine names will truly benefit from this system.

Businesses that want to present a uniform front-end to the public can create multiple aliases so that all e-mail is forwarded to one address. For example, if a small business owner has an account with America Online, a CompuServe account, and an Internet account with a local ISP provider, she can arrange to have all of the e-mail from the various accounts forwarded to her pobox.Com account. She can also give out her pobox.com account as her primary address, which never changes, if she finds that she is changing accounts frequently. Another example is if a small business owner wants to create the illusion of size, he or she can create multiple aliases at

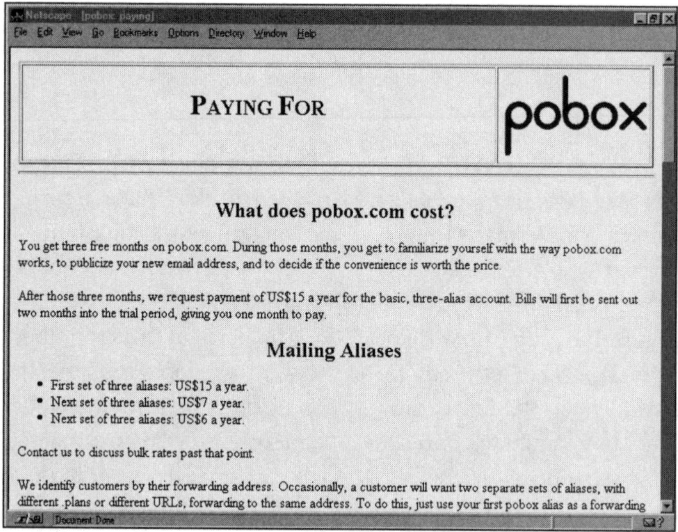

Figure 2-2
Pobox.com charges an affordable flat-rate yearly fee.

pobox.com, all of which will be forwarded to the same e-mail account(s).

Also, if the business owner is primarily a commercial online service user and does not have an Internet e-mail account, pobox.com can make it appear that she does.

PRODUCT FEATURES AND BENEFITS

Pobox.com offers a free three-month, no-risk, trial period, after which the service charges $15 a year. According to Reuven Bell, President of the IC Group, your pobox.com address is good for a lifetime, so you can use the address with confidence on your resume or business card. No entity except pobox.com needs to be notified of address changes for your other accounts.

URL redirection is another feature offered by the service. If your URL changes, Web clients are automatically redirected to your real home page. The entire process is invisible to end users, who don't have to put up with annoying "404 Not Found" messages. For example, if your URL is **http://www.pobox.com/~rbell** you can have it redirected to another address such as **http://www.nyx.net/~rebell.**

Subscribers can register for a pobox.com account with the sign-up form on the site or by sending an e-mail message to new@pobox.com. When you register, you will be asked to list your requested aliases, forwarding address, home page URL (if you have one), and biographical information for your searchable profile. Pobox.com will then send you a return e-mail message within a few seconds, so that you can confirm your choices. Your account is officially activated within 24 hours.

All subscribers are assigned a "magic cookie" when they first subscribe. This magic cookie is your pobox.com password and is necessary for any information or alias name changes. You can change your account at any time either through the Web or through e-mail as long as you use your magic cookie. All changes take place at noon, Greenwich mean time.

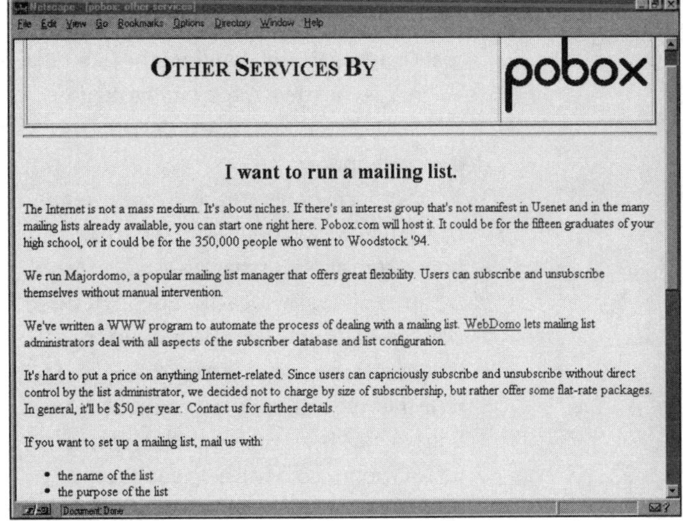

Figure 2-3
Subscribers can also use pobox.com to set up their own mailing lists.

BUSINESS/MARKETING MODEL

Pobox.com's free trial period is used to get potential subscribers to try out the system. If they sign-up for the system, they are billed yearly according to the number of aliases registered. The first set of three aliases is $15/year; the second set of three aliases is an additional $7/year; and the third set of aliases is an additional $6/year. A single URL redirection is free regardless of the number of aliases.

Subscribers may also pay online with a credit card or with the electronic payment system, First Virtual. Pobox.com supports PGP ("Pretty Good Privacy") encryption: encrypt the message with pobox.com's key, sign it with your key, and e-mail the payment to payment@pobox.com. PGP messages are downloaded to a secure computer that is physically isolated from the Internet where they are decrypted. Offline credit billing, checks, and money orders are also payment options.

In order to generate additional revenue by offering value-added Web services, pobox.com also runs mailing lists. You can set up a mailing list for a flat rate of $100 per year. Special scripts have been developed that permit the owner of a list to administer it via the Web, rather than through the traditional e-mail-based commands alone. Also, for $50, pobox.com will help you secure a domain name from InterNIC. They also provide various services for URL and mail forwarding based on a customer's domain. Prices are service-specific. If you are looking for a place to register your PGP public key, pobox.com can do that as well. Pobox.com was the first white pages directory to market and was followed four months later by its first competitor. Currently, there are about eight to ten other services. However, because of press coverage and name recognition, pobox.com is still the largest. Some competitors are investing in serious marketing efforts both online and offline, so Bell and Wong are pursuing corporate financing. Even though they have a substantial user base and a viable business idea, they are facing some resistance from some financiers due to their age and status as college students.

Marketing efforts, for the time being, still consist of word-of-mouth and press pieces (Wong and Bell also ask their subscribers to spread the word), but they plan to start advertising in print computer journals and other more traditional media such as radio.

TECHNOLOGY BACKBONE

Pobox.com runs Majordomo, a popular, flexible mailing list manager that enables users to subscribe and unsubscribe themselves without manual intervention. WebDomo, written in-house, automates the process of administering a mailing list by letting administrators deal with all aspects of the subscriber database and list configuration.

Pobox.com currently runs UNIX on Intel-based computers (it started with a Sun Sparc Station II), and is using leased lines for connectivity: a T1 line and a T3 line, one hop away from the MAE-East backbone.

LESSONS LEARNED AND HELPFUL SUGGESTIONS

- Initial mailing list offering was done at too low a price, so pobox.com is getting a large number of people signing up, putting a strain on their server.
- You can never can have enough memory, especially when you are running mailing lists.
- Network connection points do go down, so they plan to get back-up service from multiple major service providers.
- Bill early and often and have a good invoicing system. Collecting money in an automated and efficient fashion has been the most difficult challenge.
- Offering a free trial period is effective for traffic generation.
- Secure trademarks or service marks on anything that may be proprietary and follow-up on it. Make your business as distinct as possible.
- Realize that the Web is a niche marketplace.
- Plan ahead.
- Internet service is a global marketplace. Make no assumption that all of your users will be American. Work to accomodate foreign markets.
- The importance of automation in all aspects. Human intervention is much more difficult to scale up than is a well-designed computer system.
- Get all the press coverage you can. It's free advertising.
- Keep your technology one to two steps ahead of your needs. You don't want to be caught unaware in a sudden growth spurt.

FUTURE PLANS

Bell and Wong want to get into more services and hire more people. They plan to offer Web site hosting by the end of Summer, 1996, as well as POP accounts (Post Office Protocol—an Internet e-mail account you can dial into to receive your e-mail) and additional security technologies. Pobox.com is also exploring strategic partnerships, and will accept payment using First Virtual technology in the immediate future. They plan to propose low-level modifications into the basic protocols on which e-mail is transmitted in order to make the e-mail redirection service one that is built into the Net, and much more bandwidth efficient.

Eventually, the day-to-day operation will be moved to New York while still keeping a presence in Philadelphia.

Match.Com (**www.match.com**) is the leader in online matchmaking, providing professional, single adults with a new and effective way to find one another. The service offers browsing and matching of participants on more than a dozen criteria. Other features include anonymous e-mail exchange among members, integrated member photos, a helpful online e-zine, and advice columns.

The service combines the advantages of interactive technology—interaction, searchable databases, instantaneous response time, and a multimedia environment—with the existing practical benefits of print classifieds.

COMPANY BACKGROUND

Electric Classifieds, Inc., is headquartered in San Francisco, California. Its mission is to be the leading provider of services and technology that enable classified advertisement publishers to take advantage of the online market. Since its founding in 1993, ECI has singularly focused on building an online classifieds advertising platform that facilitates the connection of buyers and sellers. Match.Com is ECI's first functioning business unit on the Web. In March of 1996, ECI received $7.5 million in its second round of venture and corporate funding.

The running joke is that Match.Com was the first matchmaking business entity launched because the owner, Gary Kremen, wanted to find a date. He thought that if he could put women in a database and sort through them based on his own criteria, he would find the perfect woman for him and thereby solve his romance problems. Even given the success of the site, Kremen still finds he is too busy to date as much as he would like.

The truth is that Kremen became interested in Web technology back in 1993 and had the foresight to see its potential. He thought that classified advertising was a natural for the Web, because it is information-based and would benefit from being fully searchable. As he started to look at the different classified vertical markets, he discovered that the personals are very much the revenue backbone of the alternative and weekly newspapers. He also thought that personals online, if done well, would generate quite a bit of press.

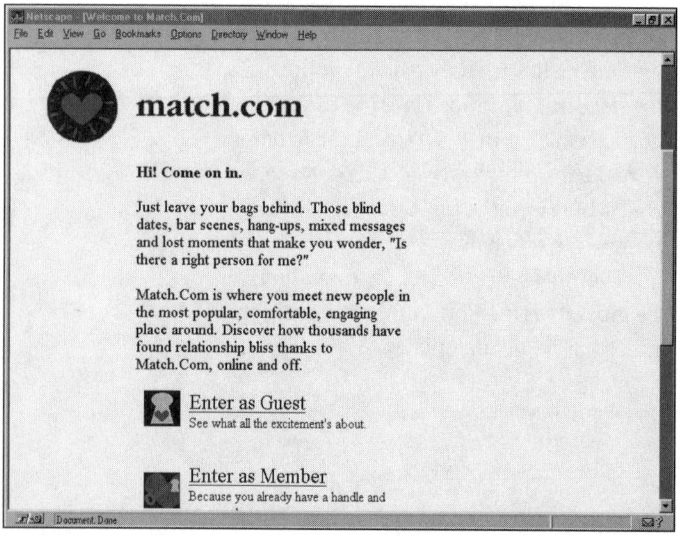

Figure 2-4
Match.Com welcomes users on its opening page.

Match.Com At-a-Glance

The Product	Professional matchmaking service for singles that protects identity and ensures anonymity while they get to know other online members
URL	www.match.com
The Company	Electric Classifieds, Inc.
Owner	Jordan Graham
The Team	30 and growing rapidly
The Customers	Single professionals looking for meaningful relationships with other singles
Start Date	April 12, 1995
Lessons Learned	Understand your target audience and build the site and market to the needs of that specific group.
Software/Hardware	The Geneva system developed by ECI
Volume	More than 10,000 anonymous e-mails are exchanged among members each day. The site has more than 200,000 Web pages.
Subscribers	Over 100,000 members have registered and placed profiles—more than 2,000 men and women register each week.

PRODUCT DESCRIPTION

With the online dating service, users can anonymously narrow down the person or persons they may want to pursue by looking through the computer-matched profiles. If they want, they can exchange anonymous e-mail messages with potential matches and protect their anonymity.

Match.Com is one of the fastest-growing Internet services, increasing business at a rate of approximately one percent per day. At the time of this writing, more than 100,000 members have registered and placed profiles, with more than 2,000 men and women registering each week. More than 10,000 anonymous e-mail messages are exchanged among members each day.

International customers are also very active in Match.Com's online community, accounting for almost 15 percent of the online participation. Australia is a particularly active geographic region.

The Match.Com site was designed to draw in women, who do not use the Internet as often as their male counterparts. Currently, 26 percent of the online membership are women, which may be a better percentage than on the Internet as a whole. Forty percent of female members claim to have met another member in person since joining Match.Com. Some have met at offline events organized by the users themselves in various locations across the country. Dozens of engagements, ten marriages, and at least one baby on the way have resulted directly from Match.Com's online environment.

PRODUCT FEATURES AND BENEFITS

The friendly environment of Match.Com makes placing a profile, browsing other members' profiles (and viewing photos when available), and interacting anonymously with other members easy and entertaining. Anonymity and other security features have proven especially appealing to women, who, from their homes and offices, can get online and meet potential dates.

At Match.Com, all members remain anonymous because no names or actual e-mail addresses are revealed. Members are always in control of the amount of information a potential match receives. The tone is upbeat and friendly and encourages intelligent exchanges among users. The service is inexpensive and well below the cost of personal ads with 900-numbers, video-dating services, or high-priced matchmakers that can charge as much as $5,000-$10,000 for their services.

New members can register and receive a 10-day free trial of the service. After that, a monthly fee of $9.95 buys unlimited access to all of Match.Com's features. In order to protect user anonymity, all users must complete questionnaires and create a secret identity before they can begin searching the database for potential matches. Messages sent to members are sent to their alias addresses then forwarded to their real e-mail boxes by Match.Com.

After becoming a member at Match.Com, you fill out a profile form that asks many basic questions about age, body characteristics, religion, ethnicity, and so on. After the profile is completed, you can perform a two-way match where you can find out which people in the database fit your criteria as well as dis-

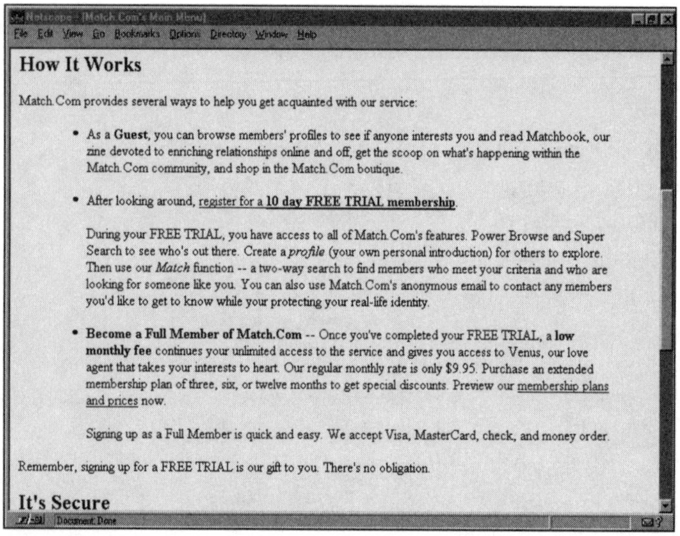
How It Works

Match.Com provides several ways to help you get acquainted with our service:

- As a **Guest**, you can browse members' profiles to see if anyone interests you and read Matchbook, our zine devoted to enriching relationships online and off, get the scoop on what's happening within the Match.Com community, and shop in the Match.Com boutique.
- After looking around, register for a **10 day FREE TRIAL membership**.

  During your FREE TRIAL, you have access to all of Match.Com's features. Power Browse and Super Search to see who's out there. Create a *profile* (your own personal introduction) for others to explore. Then use our *Match* function -- a two-way search to find members who meet your criteria and who are looking for someone like you. You can also use Match.Com's anonymous email to contact any members you'd like to get to know while your protecting your real-life identity.
- **Become a Full Member of Match.Com** -- Once you've completed your FREE TRIAL, a **low monthly fee** continues your unlimited access to the service and gives you access to Venus, our love agent that takes your interests to heart. Our regular monthly rate is only $9.95. Purchase an extended membership plan of three, six, or twelve months to get special discounts. Preview our membership plans and prices now.

  Signing up as a Full Member is quick and easy. We accept Visa, MasterCard, check, and money order.

Remember, signing up for a FREE TRIAL is our gift to you. There's no obligation.

It's Secure

Figure 2-5
Explaining how to use Match.Com.

cover whose criteria you fit. Members can also browse the database by entering various criteria and search for one-way matches.

BUSINESS/MARKETING MODEL

ECI's approach is unique in the Internet arena. By partnering with classified ad publishers and community-oriented service providers, ECI shares its Internet experience and technology for the mutual benefit of all members of the partnership. ECI offers the economics of a service bureau with the added value and competitive differentiation of a custom-developed system. In the future, ECI plans to expand its offerings into many other classified vertical markets.

Presently, Match.Com is also offered as a co-branded service with GNN (a unit of America Online), NetNoir, Lifetime TV, Latino Link, and Parent Soup (part of iVillage). Through these business relationships, Match.Com is able to expand its user base while the other businesses are able to offer a valued-added service to their sites.

Match.Com also has a business relationship with PC Flowers and Gifts, Godiva Chocolatier, and Greet Street Greeting Cards, so that users can send flowers, fine chocolates, or romantic cards to their special someone. On occasion, Match.Com also sponsors contests to boost user interest. For example, the Valentine's Day issue of Matchbook, Match.Com's e-zine, featured an e-mail courting contest with prizes for the top five romantic e-mail messages.

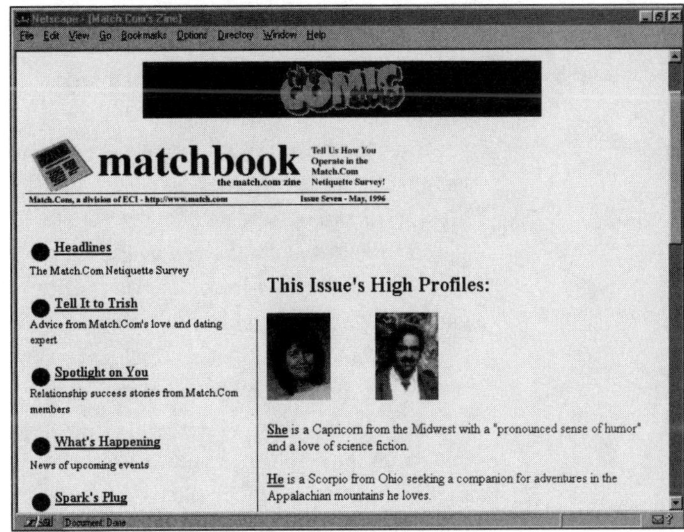

Figure 2-6
Matchbook, Match.Com's online zine.

Matchbook was designed as a resource specifically to help members get the best results from the site. The zine includes tips on how to make effective matches, the love expert "Tell Trish" answers questions, online and offline events are announced, and plenty of success stories are shared, which helps to showcase the success of the online community.

To help members move from online to offline courting, Match.Com sponsors parties in cities across the U.S., including New York, Los Angeles, Chicago, San Francisco, Atlanta, Washington D.C., Seattle, Denver, and Cleveland. Details about other offline events can be found in Match.Com's zine.

So far, Match.Com has not had to censor its profiles. The staff attributes this fact to the environment that was carefully and conscientiously built to be attractive, professional, "clean-cut," and safe. When the site was first launched, not many women were surfing the Web, and in order to create a successful site, the staff knew that it had to do everything it could to attract enough women. Much effort went into creating a friendly, non-threatening environment to attract professional women. As the result of careful planning and a clear understanding of the market they were after, the Web site has attracted exactly that professional membership base, which continues to build on itself. Also, plenty of alternatives exist on the Web for more risqué adventures, so Match.Com rarely has to deal with inappropriate participation.

From a business perspective, the online environment is essentially self-generating in terms of continually adding new content. With the constant addition of new members, users have reason to return on a regular basis without Match.Com having to spend extensive amounts of money coming up with original content.

In order to get the word out about Match.Com, the business put considerable effort in online marketing in terms of linking to other sites. Word-of-mouth and press coverage also helped to spread the word. Recently, the site has invested in ad banner advertising on other sites; however, to get the first beta testers, a traditional offline direct mailing campaign was used to generate traffic.

Match.Com first built a critical mass of users before it began charging for the online service. It carefully built a perception of value before hooking a charge on to it. According to Fran Maier, Director of Marketing at Match.Com, the competition in online matchmaking is currently not very strong on the Web. Match.Com continues to be the largest site with the best functionality, most features, and easiest navigation.

TECHNOLOGY BACKBONE

Match.Com uses the Geneva system developed by Electric Classifieds, Inc., owner of Match.Com. The actual data is stored in an Oracle database, and each Web page is generated by the Geneva system. The Web pages are customized according to the customer's desires and platform capabilities (type of computer, browser, software, and so on).

In addition, each Web page contains a unique signature enabling publishers using the Geneva system to track copied material. If a company suspects that some of its Web pages have been copied, it can use the signature to identify the user that originally downloaded the pages.

The Geneva system does not require that an entire database be stored on a single computer. Information can be distributed over several computers. This architecture enables the Geneva system to handle very large and heavily-used Web sites. Information can be stored in several computers, providing reliability seven days a week, 24 hours a day.

Also, Match.Com offers the intelligent search agent, Venus, which searches the database for you while you are offline. Venus sends messages once a day to your e-mail account when it discovers new matches for you.

LESSONS LEARNED AND HELPFUL SUGGESTIONS

- Success of the online classifieds market requires the formation of partnerships that leverage the unique core competencies of each participant—publishers, technology providers, as well as information and research services.
- It is important to provide a good service that has a real practical benefit to doing it on the Web. You need to offer convenience and functionality that users can't get anywhere else, while at the same time create a sense of community with plenty of interaction.
- The technology should be sound so that the site works properly and reliably.
- Have a clear sense of who you are trying to reach and what is compelling to them. Let that criteria guide your marketing and product development.
- The site must be interactive, immediate, and intimate.
- Users need to be able to easily and quickly do exactly what they want to do.

FUTURE PLANS

Immediate plans include offering more search options, building live chat rooms and bulletin boards, and enhancing the content so that people can interact more effectively. The company also plans to tighten its relationship with the vendors currently online, so that Match.Com members can send gifts anonymously.

In order to continue driving up revenue, plans are being developed to offer more services that users may be willing to purchase on an á la carte basis, and form more strategic business partnerships to increase site traffic. In addition, the staff will be considering new products for new market segments.

Electric Classifieds is also looking to build more online vertical classifieds, but probably not on a branded basis.

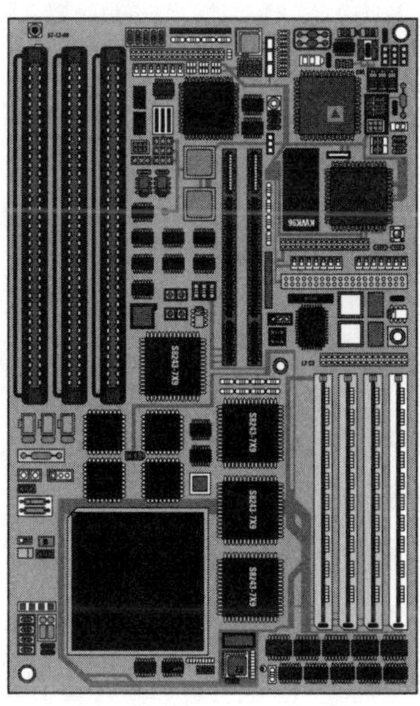

CHAPTER THREE

REAL-TIME CHAT SERVICES

In Chapter 2 we described two Internet businesses that provide asynchronous communication services for its customers. In this chapter we look at real-time, synchronous communication services, commonly referred to as "chat servers."

Later in this chapter we examine two companies, WebChat and Time Warner, that have developed chat software and operate a chat service based on that software.

The Evolution of Internet Chat

The evolution of chat applications on the Internet has occurred in three phases. Initially, text-based chat services were created—Internet Relay Chat and Multi-User Dimensions (MUDs) are the primary examples. Although neither of these entities has caught on to any great extent in the business community, we provide a brief description of them here, as they have served as the backdrop for many subsequent chat environments.

IRC

Internet Relay Chat is an Internet protocol designed for chatting purposes. It is essentially the ham radio of the Internet. Developed in Finland in 1988 by Jarkko Oikarinen, IRC is a multiuser chat system with virtual topical channels where people can meet to talk publicly or in private.

Use of IRC involves setting up a client application that communicates with one of several central IRC servers. Once connected to a server, users can join any of an overwhelmingly large number of channels and chat with folks from all over the world.

MUD/MOO

A MUD, which stands variously for "multi-user dungeon" or "multi-user dimension," is an Internet-based client/server application that allows multiple users to occupy text-based spatial environments for the purpose of communicating or interacting. Users can access a MUD via a standard Telnet connection or by using a specialized MUD client, most of which provide a split-screen interface with one window for entering text and another for viewing the scrolling dialogue.

MUDs were initially developed with the idea of developing networked, role-playing adventure games, hence the *dungeon* part of its name. As in IRC, participants in a MUD can participate in a running dialogue that scrolls across the screen as each person sends his or her input to the discussion. One of the main differences between the two environments is that a MUD creates a text-based spatial environment. Upon entering a MUD, the user is presented with a textual description of a space. Navigation is performed by issuing directional commands, such as "go up," or "go east."

In addition, a MUD allows users to perform virtual actions by issuing commands. If they have the proper authority, users can program new actions, place new objects in rooms, or even construct new rooms.

There are many variations of the MUD family. A MOO, for example, is an object-oriented MUD. Other varieties include, MUSEs (Multi-User Simulated Environments), and MUSHs (Multi-User Shared Hallucinations). Each type has its own programming dialect and its own type of environment.

Web-Based Chat Environments

The second phase in the evolution of chat applications emerged out of the popularity of the World Wide Web. Businesses wanted to offer chat as one component of their Web sites. Users wanted the simplicity of a Web browser interface to use for chatting. As a result, several companies attempted to create Web-based chat environments. In addition, companies have begun to create proprietary versions of an IRC-like environment, but with a GUI (Graphical User Interface) that could either be run as a stand-alone application or as a plug-in to a Web browser that recognizes plug-ins, such as Netscape Navigator or Microsoft Explorer.

Implementing chat via the Web is not as easy at it may seem. Store-and-forward type messaging forums, like those discussed in Chapter 2, lend themselves fairly readily to Web implementations. The Web is designed to support temporary, rather than sustained, connections. Each time a user accesses a Web page, the user's browser opens a connection to the Web server and requests the appropriate file(s). Once the files are delivered, the client is disconnected. The Web is called a "stateless" environment, because once the browser has been disconnected, the server itself retains no information about the state of the previous request.

For examples of Web-based chat environments see Chapter 4, "Applications for Messaging and Chat."

IS THERE A BUSINESS CASE FOR CHAT?

Chat has a bad reputation. It is generally regarded even by those who enjoy it as a frivolous activity where you can squander away long hours online pretending to be someone else in conversation with a group of like-minded people all pretending the same thing. Stories are beginning to show up in the media about people who are addicted to online chat environments. We would not be surprised to learn that there are Chatter's Anonymous (rather an ironic name, under the circumstances) organizations springing up even now.

Little wonder, then, that the business community has expressed some reservations about embracing chat systems as a means of conducting business communications. At the moment, we see three main uses for chat systems in business.

The first, which describes both of the cases in this chapter, involves Internet businesses that set up and maintain chat environment on a membership basis. In this case clearly, chat *is* the business.

The second case involves businesses that have set up chat environments as part of a larger Internet presence, either as a convenience to their customers and an attempt to build community, or as an alternate means of providing customer support (although asynchronous forums of the type described in Chapter 4 are usually a better choice for this function).

The third case involves a new generation of communication tools aimed directly at business communication needs. These tools, which fall under the category of *collaboration* tools, or *groupware,* are all beginning to appear as this book goes to print. Most of the use for these applications will be internal, on corporate intranets. For more information on such issues, see Chapter 4, "Applications for Messaging and Chat," and the Epilogue, "Intranets."

In the Web's stateless environment, it is difficult to achieve the effect of simultaneous connection necessary to conduct online chat. This is not to say that many have not tried, with varying degrees of success. Of the many versions of Web-based chat environments that have been developed, the most successful to date is WebChat. (We present our case study of Web Chat later in this chapter.)

WebChat Communications, Inc. (**wbs.net**) produces, designs, implements, and sells WebChat software, which enables multimedia chat at a Web site with no client download (by "client download," we mean that the user has to take the time to manually download and install the client). Other chat software available on the Web require a client download, which is a major usage barrier for most computer users. WebChat software provides the backbone for WebChat Communications' Web Broadcasting System (WBS)—the largest multimedia interactive chat and event environment on the Web. As of this writing, the site was drawing, on average, approximately 37,000 unique visitors per day and was growing by 20 to 30 percent each month.

Most people on the Web will not download a client because either they don't know how to download it or they don't want to take the time to do so. By eliminating that task for users, and being first to market, WebChat has been able to hit a larger share of the marketplace.

WebChat Communications created the WebChat Broadcasting System for people who want to chat about a variety of different topics. The effort has been so successful that WBS has become the primary business focus of WebChat Communications, much more so than the business of selling its WebChat software package. Essentially, WebChat has proved more successful as a backbone for WBS than as a stand-alone product.

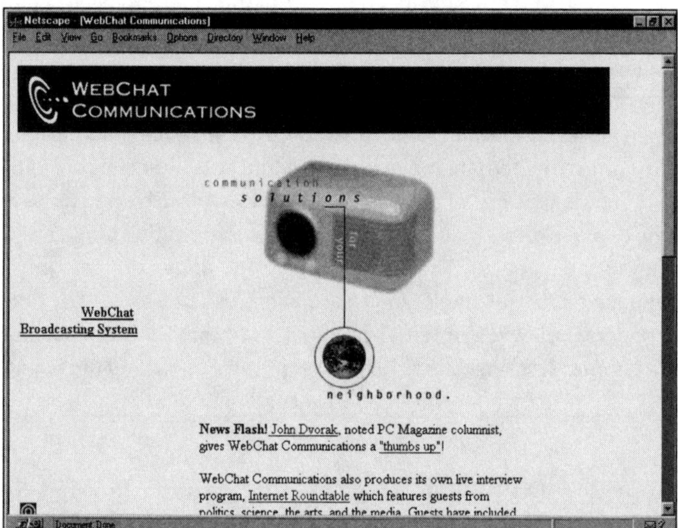

Figure 3-1
WebChat Communications developed the hugely successful Web Broadcasting System.

WebChat At-a-Glance

The Product	WebChat Server Software, The Web Broadcasting System (WBS)
URL	wbs.net
The Company	WebChat Communications, Inc.
Owner	Wendie Bernstein Lash, President; Michael J. Fremont, Chairman & CEO; Robert E. Lash, Executive Vice President
The Team	13 people
The Customers	Computer users, businesses, and companies interested in purchasing WebChat software, consumer Internet users who want to interact with individuals or be entertained by live events, companies that want to advertise on the Web and have access to focused demographics
Start Date	Development began in the summer of 1994. WebChat launched in February of 1995. WBS launched in March of 1995.
Lessons Learned	Focus on what you do best and do not spread yourself too thin.
Software/Hardware	Specially modified and enhanced WebChat software, Progressive Network's RealAudio server and real-time transcription with Cheetah's CAPtivator Online software
Volume	More than 200 channels with more added every day, over 100 scheduled events and over 350 hours of events each week
Subscribers	450,000 registered members with a growth rate of 30–40% per month.

COMPANY BACKGROUND

WebChat was introduced in February of 1995. The WebChat Broadcasting System was launched in March of 1995 and currently boasts over 450,000 registered users with a growth rate of approximately 30 to 40 percent per month. The company is also putting together some strategic relationships that are expected to increase the growth rate to between 50 and 60 percent per month.

WBS was initially created to leverage the sale of the WebChat software product. The initial chat environment launch was done in conjunction with Digital Equipment Corporation and was simply called WebChat. WebChat Communications did all of the development of WebChat in-house, but in the early days, before WebChat had a major server and bandwidth to hold the capacity, Digital housed the chat environment. Even-

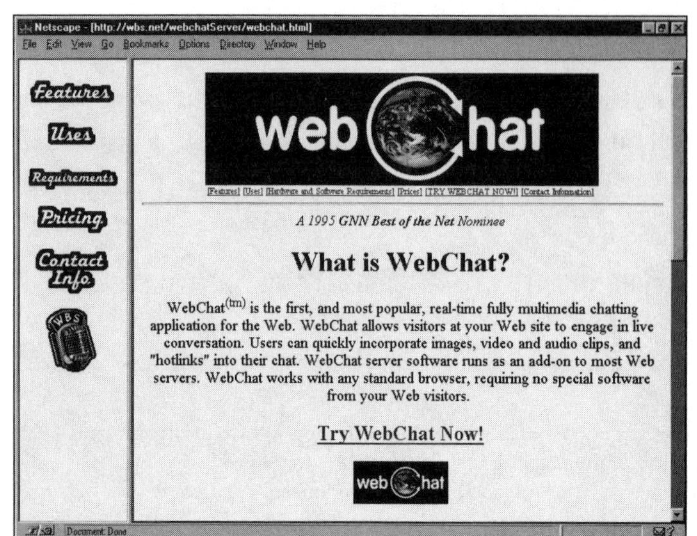

Figure 3-2

WebChat software runs as an add-on to an existing Web server, and chatting requires no special software on the client side, other than a Web browser.

tually, WebChat Communications launched its own independent chat area, which became WBS. For a while, Digital continued its own chat area, but today that area no longer exists.

Because of the success of WBS, the business model shifted from the software product to WBS as the main service and revenue source, but WebChat will continue to be sold to other Web sites and businesses looking to add chat software.

WebChat Communications started out creating a bulletin board system (BBS) in the community. The small team of developers had the idea that they wanted to produce a current events show where users could come and discuss the issues. The company developed a real-time visual chat for Grlact.com's Major BBS, called SuperChat. With SuperChat, users could select an image to identify themselves and type their comments next to the picture. It created a different level of interaction from the straight text talk available on the Internet.

The next stage of evolution at WebChat was the Internet Roundtable, which was done in IRC (Internet Relay Chat) because at the time, it was the only real-time chat component on the Internet. As the Web further took hold in the summer of 1994, they decided to take that idea and combine it with the Web. The developers used the research and development that had been done to create SuperChat, took it to the Web, and created WebChat—the current backbone for WBS. Funding for the WebChat development came mostly from doing Web site designing on the side.

Prior to January, 1996, WebChat Communications was called the Internet Roundtable Society (IRS). The IRS created the Internet Roundtable—a weekly interview show for policy makers, innovators, authors, and artists to communicate with each other and discuss issues that shape today's political and cultural world and interact with the Internet community. The Internet Roundtable required considerable attention and content development, and the small company found it difficult to not only deal with the research and product development for WebChat, but also manage the content development necessary for the Internet Roundtable, deal with the end user customers registered on WBS, and arrange for strategic relationships and partnerships. As a result, the decision was made to no longer do content development in-house, so the Internet Roundtable was dropped as a regular feature. Thus the name change. Currently, WebChat Communications is forging new business relationships with people who can bring in additional programming, such as the Internet Roundtable, to enhance WBS.

PRODUCT DESCRIPTION

WBS's multimedia chat environment is and will remain a free service to the end user. The Web service is a direct competitor to the online services, which charge customers anywhere from $3 to $10 an hour to chat in a text-based environment. Revenue is primarily generated through the sale of on-site advertising. WebChat's strong technology is one of the major reasons WBS is so successful, because anyone that has access to the Web can participate without having to download any special programs.

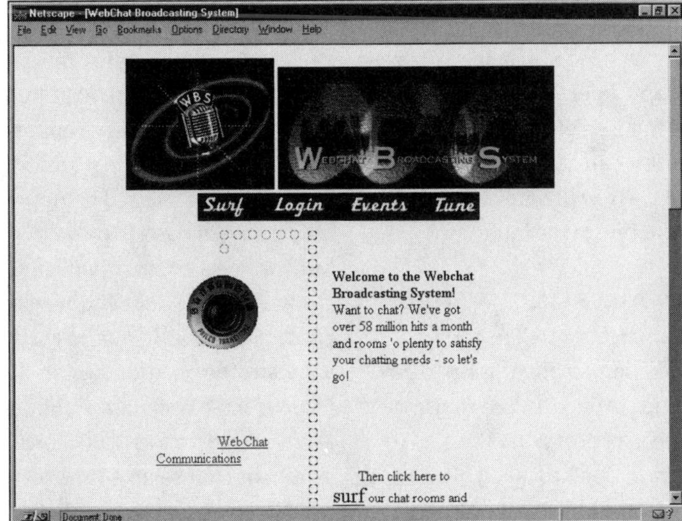

Figure 3-3
With more than 450,000 registered members, the WebChat Broadcasting System is the Web's largest chatting center.

PRODUCT FEATURES AND BENEFITS

At any time, a user can come to WBS and find hundreds, if not thousands, of people chatting about various topics and join in a conversation. There are more than 200 WebChat Broadcasting System stations with many channels about such topics as entertainment, business and finance, travel, current events, home and living, and community support (the most popular area). WBS also hosts Web events for companies, such as product release announcements coupled with live interviews with the key developers.

Users can participate in various chat sessions, with channel names such as soc.singles, Fifty Plus Chat, Fortysomething, Thirtysomething, Twentysomething, Young-Adult Chat, College Chat, Teen Chat, and Johnny Depp's Viper Club around the clock. For more focused discussions with fewer people, users can try an existing private room, create a new private room, or invite people into one of the lounges.

BUSINESS/MARKETING MODEL

WebChat Communications offers the traditional Web-based banner advertising to pay for the cost of supporting the free transmission and the free access of WBS. Although, considerable discussion has taken place online and offline about the viability of ad banner advertising on the Web. Many critics don't expect it to last, because the mechanisms that exist to determine the kind and amount of traffic generated on a Web site are far from conclusive. In addition, only a limited amount of advertising dollars is available. Sites must have a compelling reason and just the right demographics to draw in a healthy revenue stream with advertising dollars. Also, not that much money is being spent on the Web compared to other traditional forms of media, and most of it is being pulled by the major search sites and the high-traffic sites.

Given all of the obstacles, the staff at WebChat Communications still believes that advertising dollars are a viable revenue stream for their chat environment. WBS claims to be in the top 100 Web sites in terms of traffic among all the sites on the Net, and it is growing every day.

WebChat expects to draw in significant advertising dollars due to its huge audience and focused ad delivery. Those two factors combined give WebChat an edge over a site that either has focused demographics but little traffic, or has a large amount of traffic but unfocused demographics.

Revenue is also still coming in from companies interested in purchasing the WebChat software. The price for the package starts at $5,000 for a 100 simultaneous user license, and it grades up to $15,000 for an unlimited simultaneous user one-time license.

A major expense that WebChat Communications sidesteps is content generation. Original content generation is expensive. At WBS the users generate the content.

Business relationships in the making include one with Search Site. WBS can provide a source of community for Search Site, and Search Site can provide more traffic and greater visibility to WBS. For example, when a user is looking for certain type of chat areas, she can find out through Search Site what specific rooms or channels WBS has available in those areas.

WebChat Communications is also looking at relationships with content providers who can enhance and build the site's content and available programming. Currently, WBS operates approximately forty hosts, but it wants to bring in more programming in the following content areas: arts and entertainment, current events, travel and leisure, computers, and the Internet.

Essentially, the majority of the programming scheduled on WBS is generated by the users. For example, if someone wants to find out about sports medicine, she can attend the scheduled program on the topic; however, the majority who visit WBS come because they just want to connect with friends that they've made online.

Wendie Bernstein Lash, President of WebChat, believes that people are drawn to the site because they want to connect with other people and be part of a Web community. They want to be able to do more than just interact with pages of text and information. WBS provides an easy way for them to gain unique access to a worldwide community at no charge.

WebChat Communications has not made any serious marketing efforts other than distribute press releases. The users have come to WebChat mostly through word-of-mouth and listings in search sites. Recently WebChat Communications has purchased ad banners on directory sites. Now that they have a seed round of capital, they plan to do more offline publicity and marketing.

Large companies such as Intel, Borland, and Novell have hired WebChat Communications to produce a public relations chat for them on WBS. Companies such as these are starting to use the Web to interact in real-time with their customers, business partners, and investors. In the past, they have relied on such Internet service providers as America Online, CompuServe, and Prodigy, but they are now gravitating more and more toward the Web. Currently, the only place that can emulate the professional online services to some degree is WBS. Companies can schedule events, have them moderated on WBS, and do their own advertising. For example, a company buys advertising on WBS, receives a limited amount of exposure by announcing an upcoming press conference, and then WBS assists them in holding a virtual press conference.

Web Communications positioned WBS as an excellent forum for businesses to build relationships with customers and business partners. Businesses can have a customer representative available online through a WBS channel to answer questions 24 hours a day. Businesses can also use the chat environment to talk to potential new hires before going through the expense of flying them across the country for a personal meeting. It is also a good place to maintain public relations because it offers a forum to discuss quarterly returns and announce latest product releases.

WebChat Communications' clients use WebChat software for a wide variety of applications. Eastman Kodak holds fireside chats with the Chairman and product talks with the senior technical staff. The British Broadcasting System uses WebChat in conjunction with an interactive children's television show. The *Toronto Sun* holds celebrity events—the first was with hockey star Wayne Gretsky. Price-Costco plans to hold chats with bands and then sell their CDs online. The American Association of Neurosurgeons facilitates dialogues with its membership. The University of Oklahoma holds private fund-raising chats with football stars. And the Fayetteville Technical College uses WebChat for distance learning.

WebChat Communications is in a growth phase and is not currently profitable, like most Internet businesses. Instead, it is looking to continue financing the staggering growth that the company is currently experiencing. Nevertheless, the company expects to be profitable in the not too distant future.

TECHNOLOGY BACKBONE

The core technology behind WBS is WebChat, which was built using Perl and CGI scripting. WBS optionally supports Progressive Network's RealAudio server and plans to add streaming video in the near future.

ChatCam software was developed in-house and supports sequential in-line photos. The program basically provides the ability to take a video feed and grab images from it so that users of WBS can see a sequence of images as well as text. In an attempt to hit the broadest market possible, the company chose to develop this capability instead of using one of the streaming video technologies available—because the majority of the users logging into WBS and the Internet in general are using 14.4K modems.

Future technology plans include adding frames technology and server push (both Netscape technologies) and a similar functionality that will enable users to see video streams and other kinds of flicker presentations.

The environment will be tailored to meet different levels of users, but for now the goal is to hit a level that is easily accessible by most people.

The real push as far as chat is concerned has been toward a communication environment that simulates a real, spatial environment, with provision for people and actions, much as MUDs have attempted to do in a text-only environment. These efforts, sometimes called virtual worlds, or habitats, loom on the horizon as this book is being written. Many of the current efforts surrounding audio and video conferencing, as well as virtual worlds and VRML 2.0, are discussed in Chapter 4.

Time Warner's chat product, The Palace (spotlighted next in this chapter), mixes a rich, graphical environment with traditional text-based communication features. It may be that The Palace is simply an early precursor to other, more elaborate chat worlds. On the other hand, it may be that for the purposes of facilitating conversation, the simpler environment offered by The Palace will turn out to be preferable. Time will tell.

VIRTUAL WORLDS

LESSONS LEARNED AND HELPFUL SUGGESTIONS

- Stay focused on what you do best.
- The world of the Web moves so quickly that you cannot afford to spread yourself too thin and try to be all things to all people.
- Successful business relationships and partnerships are critical to enhancing your business and staying competitive.

FUTURE PLANS

WebChat Communications plans to sell sponsorship of special areas and events on WBS. For example, if there is a cowboy chat area on WBS, Wrangler may decide to purchase all the advertising in that chat area. In other words, Wrangler becomes branded in the cowboy chat area and they would underwrite the cost of the users to chat. The company—in this case, Wrangler—is advertising to a target market and appears to be doing something nice for the users. Although this is a for-profit business, the advertising model resembles the kind of sponsorship found in public broadcasting.

Future plans for WBS also include enhancing the site's content by partnering with content providers. By leveraging the content creation of other companies, WebChat Communications can focus on what it does best—continuing to make WBS a place where hundreds of thousands of individuals come to interact. Eventually, Java enhancements will be added to make chatting quicker and more efficient.

The Palace (**www.thepalace.com**) is a virtual world entertainment architecture that is essentially a collection of multimedia sites where users can go and chat, flirt, gossip, play games, role play, and discover secrets in a 3-D graphic mansion. Each individual palace is owned and operated by an independent proprietor who can be located anywhere in the world. Palace owners have complete control of the look, feel, and activities that take place at their sites.

COMPANY BACKGROUND

The project, a graphical chat environment, was initially started in the cable division of the Full Service Network at Time Warner, but was eventually dropped because it lacked game features. The project then moved to Time Warner Interactive, the CD-ROM division, with plans to release it on CD-ROM. At that point, the concept of letting users develop their own server was not developed, nor was there a UNIX server option, but some discussion was starting about users being able to create their own rooms.

Mark Jeffrey, the current Director of Online Ventures for Time Warner's Palace Group, joined the group from the world of the Internet, added the few additional pieces that the product has today, and suggested making the product purely an online offering.

When Time Warner Interactive faded as a division, The Palace project was without a home and almost became a part of Pathfinder, Time Warner's main Web site. However, Jeffrey convinced Time Warner to let The Palace Group operate on a shoestring budget independently for a year as a project supported by the Time Warner Music Group. Fortunately, The Palace garnered a great deal of press early on, which enabled the project to survive and grow.

The project has now spun out and become its own independent company with shared ownership by Time Warner, Intel, and other venture capitalists.

PRODUCT DESCRIPTION

The Palace approach provides a fully customizable and speedy social environment. The emphasis is on speed, high customization, and real-time shared experiences. Guests in The Palace are welcome to enter a select number of first floor rooms for free—for example, the Venetian spa, game room, and Harry's Bar. Guests can try on costumes, chat with other guests and members, play games, and check out the membership offer.

When guests decide to become members for a one-time nominal fee, they enjoy expanded privileges including access to the private suites upstairs and the all-important authoring capabilities to create their own palace.

The Palace is a fairly free environment with few restrictive rules. Almost anything goes in The Palace. Each Palace is linked to others, forming a distributed network of servers that are always expanding and changing.

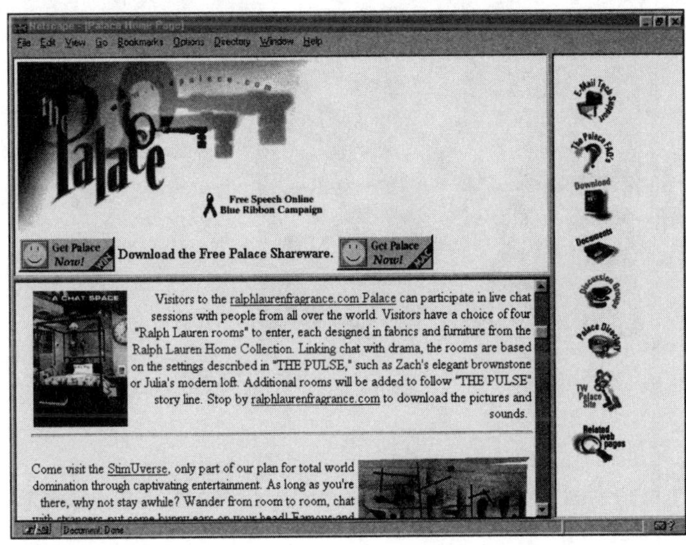

Figure 3-4
The Palace is a completely interactive multimedia environment.

The Palace At-a-Glance

The Product	Multimedia chat environment
URL	www.thepalace.com
The Company	Time Warner, Inc.
Owners	Time Warner, Intel, other venture capitalists
The Customers	Presently the majority are Internet-savvy and very tuned-in to the online world
Start Date	Fall, 1995
Software/Hardware	Windows and Macintosh systems are able to link together on The Palace. The Palace also runs on UNIX machines. Client/server software is necessary and can be downloaded for $20.

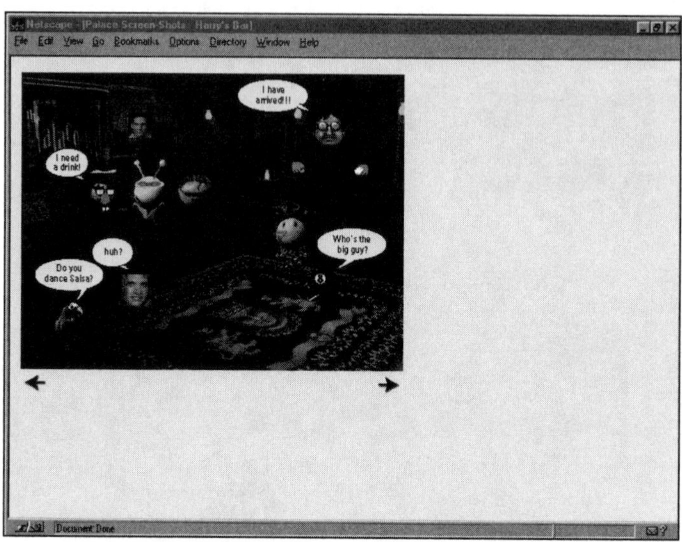

Figure 3-5
Harry's Bar at The Palace.

PRODUCT FEATURES AND BENEFITS

Macintosh and Windows users on the Internet can create their own graphic identities and their own Palace server sites. Palace servers are connected through *hyperdoors,* which act much like the hypertext capabilities of Web pages.

Anyone can create custom Palace environments and maintain his or her own Palace server with a registered version of the software, which is the key Palace feature. Users can completely control, author, and run their own servers as well as add their own functionality.

Also, visitors to Palace sites can modify any environment they find, so that there is a continual ebb and flow of new content and ideas at the site. Visitors can upload new objects into the environment. The Palace server (Pserver) operator can even elect to give visitors privileges to re-author or augment the site while they visit, as the Pserver operator has full control over what is and what is not permissible.

A registered version of The Palace for Macintosh and Windows is available for $20 and includes both the 1.0 client and server software. The Palace 1.0 UNIX server software is available as an unsupported beta application from The Palace Web site.

At the Time Warner Palace server, up to 200 users at a time can explore dozens of rooms in a virtual mansion. Users have com-

Figure 3-6
Hosts of Palace sites can modify and control The Palace environment.

plete control over their appearance in The Palace. What you look like is known as your *face* or *avatar*—it might be a picture of a user's real face or a Bugs Bunny head, for example. In every room, users have places to explore and objects to manipulate. One of the most popular areas is the game room, where users can challenge each other to games of chess, checkers, and backgammon.

The Palace Directory enables others with The Palace software to locate your Palace server. One of the strengths of The Palace server is that other people can find you even if your server is up only sporadically. The Palace Directory is dynamic—as soon as a Palace server comes up anywhere on the Internet, it sends a message to The Palace Directory. The Directory automatically adds The Palace server to the Directory for the duration of that Palace server's time online, enabling servers to come up and go down dynamically.

BUSINESS/MARKETING MODEL

The Palace was designed to combine some of the best advantages of the virtual world: interpersonal communication, the creation of new spaces, and scripting ability, while also being interesting to look at and relatively easy to use. Jeffrey hopes to evolve The Palace to the point where it becomes the standard metaworld environment on the Internet.

Like many other Internet companies, The Palace is giving away quite a bit up front in the hopes of "ubiquity now, revenue later." Giving away the service helps to get a large number of metaworlds up and running by other people, and drives up the demand for the clients. What The Palace sells is not really software but the capability within the client to customize the avatar and functionality. And it turns out that customers are very willing to pay $20 for that ability. (Jeffrey wanted to keep the price within impulse-buy range.)

For $20 users get a registration number, so there are no products to ship, which helps to keep overhead costs to a minimum. Currently, The Palace is set up with a simple 1-800 infrastructure. Once enough clients are sold and enough people are using it, and it becomes the graphical/chat metaworld environment of choice, The Palace will begin to sell the UNIX and NT servers. It also has plans to sell a smaller personal server for PCs and Macs, which it now gives away for free. Other sales plans include add-on products that provide new capabilities built around The Palace's client/server architecture. The Palace may also consider licensing the technology.

Many high-profile clients, such as Ralph Lauren, MTV, VH1, Fox Television, Sony Pictures, HBO, and Capitol Records, have servers up, and the client sales continue to increase. Between word-of-mouth and Jeffrey's connections in the entertainment world, more high-profile sites continue to be added. Also, many people who currently produce Web sites are expanding their business by moving into doing Palace servers. The plan is to capitalize on this activity by making it easy for developers to make money creating palace servers.

TECHNOLOGY BACKBONE

The Palace architecture employs a decentralized server scheme that distributes the processing load across the entire Internet—no centralized server or authority exists. This enables a site built using The Palace archetecture to handle large numbers of users as its popularity grows.

The Palace requires users to download a client before they can participate in a Palace environment. The Palace client is not an add-on to your browser but is a completely independent program. Both the client and server are available for Macintosh and Windows platforms. A UNIX server (for several different platforms) is also available. All you need to run an effective server is a Mac or PC with a TCP/IP connection to the Internet. Both the Mac and Windows Pservers are capable of supporting up to 40 simultaneous users on a single computer. Large numbers of concurrent users (anything over 40) require additional servers. UNIX servers are able to better handle more concurrent users, especially if they are using a high-bandwidth connection such as a T1 or T3 leased line. Both The Palace client and server are TCP/IP compliant, just like Web browser clients and Web servers.

Most of the processing is done at the client. The client downloads any custom graphics for a Palace environment and creates the visual environment for the user. When a Palace client jumps to a Pserver URL, the client presents a virtual environment in which other users and Palace environments that are also on that server are visible. By having the client do most of the processing, the server is free to handle more users.

Authoring tools are included with The Palace server software—making it easy to add your own functionality to your Palace site. A scripting language (called IPTSCRAE) enables users to build their own functionality much like Perl CGI scripting does for Web pages.

The Palace is also interconnected with the Web—URL hyperlinks are embedded in the virtual environment of The Palace. Netscape (or whatever your default browser) is invoked when a URL is selected. Palace URLs can be embedded in an HTML document. Because both are TCP/IP clients, movement between browser and Palace environments is fluid and immediate.

LESSONS LEARNED AND HELPFUL SUGGESTIONS

- Jeffrey believes that The Palace did the right thing in the online world in terms of erring on the side of freedom, rather than keeping everything locked down and tightly controlled in hopes to curb some of the more outrageous behavior.
- Keeping the price down was another significant decision that turned out well in terms of building the business.

FUTURE PLANS

The immediate future plans are to take The Palace to the next level in terms of advertising and marketing, and to get even more high-profile palace servers up and running. Other plans include better integration into existing Internet content and standards, as well as working with the Internet community to leverage large business partnerships.

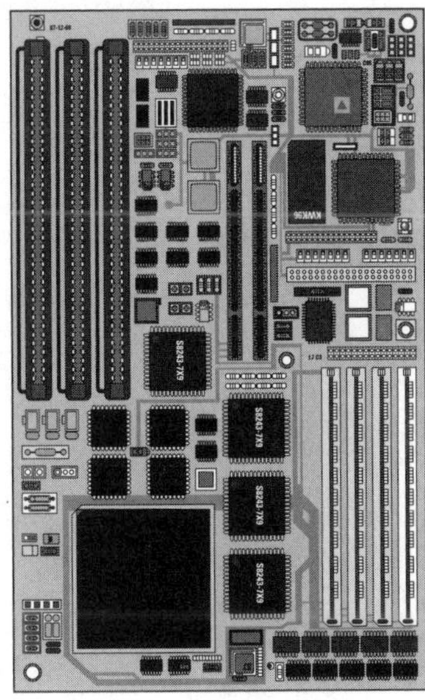

CHAPTER FOUR

APPLICATIONS FOR MESSAGING AND CHAT

If you mention the idea of Internet-based communication to people, many of them immediately assume you are talking about *chat,* which usually means the online equivalent of bar-stool conversation. To most people, chatting has very little bearing on the operation of a business. In fact, the two seem contradictory. Chatting, in this view, is what you do when you don't want to get anything done—as if anything could get done without communicating.

In this chapter, we examine a variety of communication technologies to show that there is a great deal more to communication services on the Internet than chat, and even more potential for chat than most people assume. For each technology discussed, we explain the crucial issues involved in designing a communication service, identify the applications and tools you can use to build your communication service, and provide brief, spotlighted examples of businesses already using these services.

For detailed case studies of businesses that maintain communication-based services, see Chapter 2, "Mail and Discussion Forums," and Chapter 3, "Real-time Chat Services."

In Chapter 2, we examined two businesses that have set up services that allow users to send and receive messages—in one case among themselves, in the other, to the world at large. Chapter 3 looked at two prominent examples of businesses that have developed chat technologies and then set up successful chat environments based on those technologies.

This chapter expands on those cases by providing a conceptual framework for understanding communication services generally.

Factors in Communication Systems

Several criteria, or factors, are available that you can use to classify online communication systems. The three main criteria we will consider are *timing, channel,* and *medium.*

For purposes of clarity, we will refer to real-time communication systems as conversing, or *chat,* services; and store-and-foward systems as *messaging* services.

Timing

The timing of a communication service refers to whether all of the participants are present at the same time or not. A system that enables real-time, remote communication requires all participants to be connected simultaneously. The alternative is to use a system that provides a store-and-forward mechanism of delivering messages, such as the postal service or a voice mail system.

Channel

By communication channel, we mean *how* the participants are connected to one another. Some technologies, of which e-mail is the most prominent example—and more recently "Internet phone systems"—are most often used for one-to-one communication. The real power of Internet communication, though, is in fostering one-to-many (such as a conference presentation or forum), many-to-one (such as "Dear Abby"-type of forum) or even many-to-many (such as chat) communication.

In addition, communication can be a one-way broadcast (or *narrowcast* for that matter) much like TV or radio, or two-way, like ham radio. Our emphasis in this chapter is on one-to-one (two-way), one-to-many, and many-to-many forms of communication, since these take most advantage of the Internet's special qualities.

Medium

The third factor to consider is the medium itself. All of the early communication systems were exclusively text-based. Next came a push to allow these text-based mechanisms to transmit non-textual information, such as pictures, sound files, or other file formats. Recently, the trend has been toward non-text-based communication environments, using audio transmission, video, 3-D worlds, and document-sharing environments.

Business Uses of Communication

In addition to understanding the various communication technology options available to your business, it is important to consider what your business objective is when designing or adopting a communication system.

Listed below are some of the more prominent types of business uses for communication services.

Communication Centers

Communication centers are businesses that are established to implement and maintain a virtual space where communication can occur. A real world analogy would be that of a convention center or singles bar, depending on the type of communication supported. At the moment this is the primary revenue generating means of using communication. All of the other types of communication systems are designed not as profit centers but as support services, or as a means of improving a company's productivity. All four of the communication case studies described in Chapters 2 and 3 fit into this category.

Some examples of the kinds of communication centers being constructed on the Internet include: socializing centers (cafes, bars, and so on), conference centers, and post offices for e-mail. The distinguishing characteristic of this form of communication is that the business itself does not participate in the communication in any capacity. The business simply provides the space for others to communicate.

Customer Service and Outreach

Turn to the Epilogue for a detailed spotlight of Sybase's technical support system.

Perhaps the most useful application of communication services as far as customers are concerned is in the area of customer support. Typically, online customer support communication systems are designed as extensions of, or alternatives to, existing customer support mechanisms such as 800-phone services. Many companies are building their Internet applications with a mixture of information and communication services to serve as a means of easing the burden of often-overloaded phone lines.

Customer-support technologies range from relatively simple e-mail-based communication systems to more elaborate real-time problem-solving environments. The case study of Sybase's technical support system included in the Epilogue of this book is one example of an extensive customer support system that includes communication components as well as tracking mechanisms.

Community Discussion Groups

In the jargon of Internet marketing, *community* has come to be the word of choice to describe the universe of people who are likely to be the customers for a given company's products and/or services. Supporting your company's business community through discussion groups provides the opportunity for people to cultivate the kinds of interests and tastes that make them targets for your business in the first place.

Community building is essentially a form of customer support except that it is directed at supporting the lifestyle that makes your customer a customer in the first place, rather than directly supporting his use of your products. Like customer service, community building is a form of communication that links the company with its constituents. It is also typically positioned as a value-added service that demonstrates a company's commitment to and expertise in the community in question.

Several of the case studies in subsequent sections include community-support communication components. Both Salon (described in Chapter 5) and C|NET (Chapter 6) have discussion forums, as does the Discovery Channel Online (Chapter 5).

Groupware Applications

This last form of business communication is typically used internally for communication among team or department members working toward a mutual goal. The main differences between groupware communication and those described earlier is its goal orientation and the close relationship among the various participants. In spite of these differences, many businesses are simply using generic communication applications for their groupware needs. More sophisticated applications build in mechanisms for tracking the progress toward the desired goal, and typically allow for annotations or comments on the messages of others in ways that would not be as appropriate in a more anonymous communication environment.

Rather than try to discuss every possible combination of communication system imaginable, in the sections that follow we look at the most prominent types of communication technologies, the issues involved in selecting one for a business application, and some examples of tools used to build each type.

Messaging Systems

As mentioned earlier, a messaging system, as we define the term, refers to any communication system that does not require the participants to be connected online simultaneously. Instead, a messaging system uses some version of a store-and-forward method of delivering messages to each participant and allowing them in turn to send, or *post*, new messages or replies to the system. The principal examples of messaging systems are e-mail, newsgroups, mailing lists, and bulletin boards, all of which amount to not much more than a way of managing e-mail-based discussion groups.

Principal Features

All messaging systems have some means of sending, receiving, and replying to messages. In some cases, the receiving of messages is done on-demand—when the user himself seeks out the messages. In other cases, delivery is automatic, usually with some user-controlled options. Whenever a message is sent to the system, it is routed immediately to all participants. In addition to these basic functions, messaging systems typically provide a number of other activities, including organizing messages, archiving messages, and managing participants.

THE WEB IS NOT THE NET

Most of the attention lavished on the Internet by the business community has focused on the World Wide Web. Many people conflate the Internet itself as a means of connecting networks of computers with the Web, but in fact, the Web is merely one information service that runs on the Internet.

This distinction is important to understand when thinking about communication services on the Internet, since the majority of them are based on non-Web technologies. It is only the pervasiveness of the Web and the desire on the part of businesses to offer communication and information services together in one place, that has encouraged the development of Web-to-communication-service gateways to be built.

In this chapter we offer a survey of the various kinds of communication services available on the Internet. Some of them predate the appearance of the Web; others have emerged only recently, as interest in non-text communication systems as grown.

Messaging Applications

The following applications provide a sampling of the commercial Web-based conferencing products available for adding to your Internet application.

DEC'S ALTAVISTA FORUMS Formerly called Workgroup Web Forum, the AltaVista Forums is now part of Digital Equipment Corporation's growing line of Internet software integrated under the AltaVista brand name. Forums is a feature-rich environment for conducting online post-and-reply conferencing and real-time polling, providing common access to shared files, offering the ability to circulate and attach comments to documents, and multi-level password security. The AltaVista Forums is available for Digital UNIX or Windows NT.

For more information about AltaVista products, go to the AltaVista Web site at **www.altavista.software.digital.com**.

O'REILLY WEBBOARD WebBoard is a conferencing system product for 32-bit Windows operating systems distributed by O'Reilly & Associates, Inc., in cooperation with Duke Engineering, the developers of the program. WebBoard includes an intuitive administrator module that allows you to set up and maintain multiple, threaded, subject-based forums. Access levels can be set for each forum, so that either read-only, private, moderated, or public forums can be created. Messages can be searched, or previewed, and automatically quoted in replies.

In addition, WebBoard provides an activity log for system status reports, user listings, and user Profiles that allow you to track who has logged in on a particular day or who your most active members are. The WebBoard interface is also customizable. Menu bar items can be added or deleted, and the HTML used for page displays can be revised.

For more information, or to download an evaluation copy of WebBoard, visit the WebBoard Web site at **webboard.ora.com**.

ALLAIRE FORUMS Allaire Forums, developed by Allaire using its Cold Fusion product (a 30-day demo version of Cold Fusion is available on the CD in the back of this book), is a multi-threaded conferencing system for the Windows NT platform. Administration can be performed via a Web browser, and easy-to-use wizards are included for all setup and configuration functions. Forums can be created with read-only, read/write, and moderated access permissions.

All messages are displayed in a color-coded threaded hierarchy, and can be searched by author, date, keyword, or discussion area. The HTML interface format can be customized by the administrator. Users can also create custom views of the forums. In addition, Allaire Forums enables the use of transparent user identification (via Netscape cookies) and e-mail-back user verification.

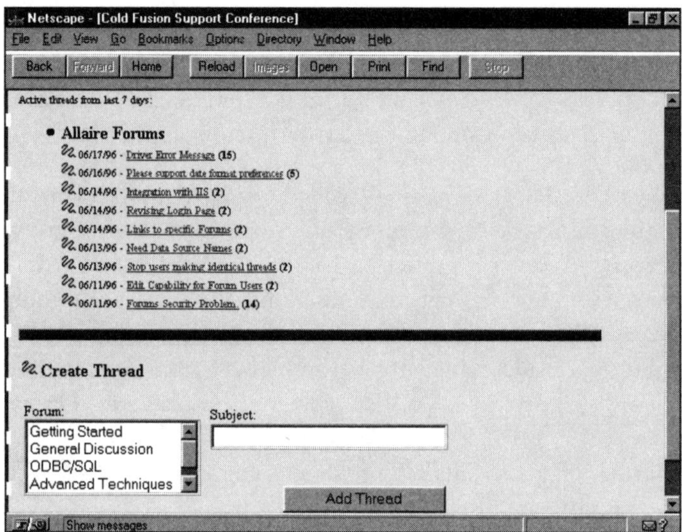

Figure 4-1
Allaire uses its Forums product for its own product and technical support.

For more information, or to download an evaluation copy of Allaire Forums, visit the Allaire Web site at **www.allaire.com**.

WEB CROSSING Web Crossing is a discussion group application from Lundeen & Associates. It is available for several platforms, including Windows NT, Macintosh, DEC Alpha NT, and several varieties of UNIX.

Web Crossing discussions are organized hierarchically in nested folders. Related messages compose a single discussion thread. Users can post and respond to messages as well as create new discussion topics and folders. Web Crossing also includes support for non-indexed keyword searching of messages, and both guest and registered user access is supported.

Web Crossing does not support the multi-layered threading of messages. It uses a simpler, single-level of threading. Any responses to responses in a discussion become a new discussion folder, thus minimizing the layers of messages typically found in standard threaded discussion groups. For this reason, Web Crossing works best in a topic-based discussion environment, such as a classroom for example, where the assumption is that most responses from users will be generated from an initial posted topic.

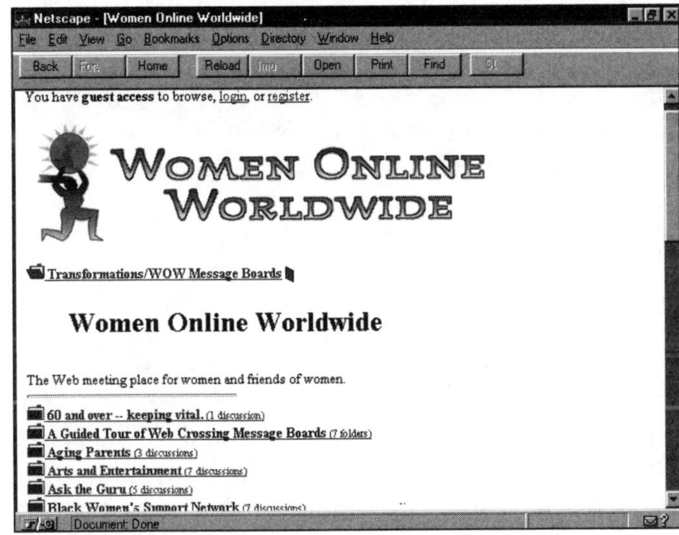

Figure 4-2
A view of the Women Online Worldwide forums illustrating Web Crossing folder structure.

The Web Crossing HTML interface can be customized by changing any of the HTML templates used to display messages and message lists. Discussions can be public, private, or moderated. In the case of a moderated discussion, all messages are first sent to a queue to be checked by a designated discussion moderator, or host, before being posted to the list. Users are granted access permissions ranging from no access, through read only, moderated, participant, and host. In addition, Web Crossing recognizes a sysop-level access for the site administrator.

In addition to supporting standard HTTP authentication methods, Web Crossing has its own, certificate-based authentication. Each time a user logs in, Web Crossing automatically generates a new unique certificate for that session. This certificate automatically expires when the sysop configurable logout interval has been reached. Use of this certificate method is appropriate for guest access to discussions or for automatic user registration.

For more information, including a list of sites running Web Crossing software, or to download an evaluation copy of the Web Crossing server, visit the Lundeen & Associates Web site at **webx.lundeen.com**.

HYPERNEWS HyperNews is a freely available UNIX source code for building discussion forums. Developed by Daniel LaLiberte at the University of Illinois, HyperNews first appeared in 1994, and as of this writing was currently available in version 1.9.

Like other discussion applications, HyperNews creates a hierarchical tree of user messages and responses. It also supports a subscription feature. Users who subscribe to a particular message will be sent an automatic e-mail notification any time a new response is sent to that message or to any of the messages in its sub-branches.

More information about HyperNews and a link to the source code is available from the HyperNews Web site at **union.ncsa.uiuc.edu/HyperNews/ get/hypernews.html**.

Web Site Integration

By far the majority of businesses that implement a communication-based system do so in conjunction with their information-based Web sites. For this reason, it is highly advantageous to integrate the two functions into a single Web-based application. This section describes some existing applications to simplify the integration task.

The applications discussed in the previous section are all CGI programs that connect to Web servers and have all of their functionality built into the CGI itself. The applications described below are also CGI programs, but they provide gateway functions between a Web site and a non-Web messaging communication service such as e-mail, a mailing list, or newsgroup. Web-based chat applications will be discussed in the chat section that follows.

HYPERMAIL HyperMail is a program that converts UNIX e-mail messages into a set of cross-referenced HTML documents. Each file created represents a separate message in the mail archive and contains links to other articles. The entire archive can be browsed in a number of ways by following links.

Each HTML file that is generated for a message includes information about the subject of the article, the name and e-mail address of the sender, the date, and links to the next and previous messages. In addition, URLs can be converted to hypertext links and e-mail addresses can be converted from mail to URLs or links to a CGI mail program.

HyperMail is currently in version 1.2. The program was originally developed by Tom Gruber for Enterprise Integration Technologies (EIT) in Common Lisp. It was later rewritten in C by Kevin Hughes at EIT. It is available for UNIX.

For more information, or to download the software, check out the HyperMail home page at **www.eit.com/software/hypermail/**.

COCOBOARD The CoCoBoard, which stands for Collaborative Cork Board, is a UNIX e-mail to HTML gateway developed by Ben Johnson, Paul Walker, and Joan Masso at NCSA. CoCoBoard allows users to post messages via e-mail that then are posted on an HTML page.

In addition to its basic functionality, CoCoBoard supports two enhanced features. First, the system allows projects to be defined with a designated set of project members. Whenever a message is sent to a particular project, all of the members are notified of the changes.

CoCoBoard is also MIME (Multipurpose Internet Mail Extension) compliant. Users can attach MIME files to their e-mail messages. When translated into an HTML page, a small icon will be placed in the e-mail message with a link to the MIME document.

CoCoBoard requires Perl 4 and the Image Magick tools, both freely available, in order to work. For more information, or to download the CoCoBoard software, visit **jean-luc.ncsa.uiuc.edu/Codes/CoCoBoard/**.

POLYFORM Unlike HyperMail and CoCoBoard, which convert e-mail messages to HTML, PolyForm from O'Reilly & Associates, is a rapid, form-building application. It allows Web site developers to build HTML forms that deliver their data via e-mail messages. PolyForm can be used for anything from collecting registration information and surveys to building full-fledged communication systems.

PolyForm features a GUI-based form-building component with easy-to-use wizards and templates. Forms can be configured to send data to a designated e-mail mailbox or to store the input in a common data format text file for later importing into spreadsheet or database applications. In addition, each form can be set to send an automated e-mail confirmation message to the user. PolyForm also comes with a built-in SMTP mail server for the purpose of sending e-mail messages.

For more information on PolyForm, or to download an evaluation version of the software, visit the PolyForm Web site at **polyform.ora.com**.

Chat Systems

A chat system, as we use the word in this book, refers to any real-time communication environment in which the users are connected online at the same time. In contrast to the messaging services, a chat service is only usable if you and others are logged in together. To converse in a chat system, you must be virtually present in the chat environment. In more recent systems, users have a visual avatar or substitute visual representation of themselves, which further reinforces the sense of "being there" as you converse remotely.

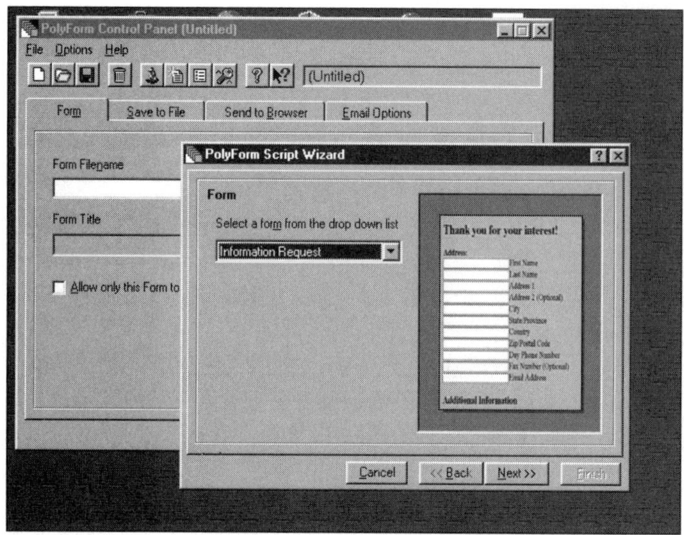

Figure 4-3
O'Reilly's PolyForm wizards provide easy-to-use templates for building e-mail forms.

One of the main differences between chat systems and messaging systems is the kind of communication that takes place. When people send messages, they tend to be complete, that is to say they deal with one or more issues in their entirety. The conversations that take place in a real-time environment tend to be much more granular. This may be partly why chat environments tend to encourage "chatter," but it can also be more appropriate for a meeting situation which involves several small agenda items, each of which may have several issues that need to be treated separately or sequentially.

One of the difficulties in using chat environments to conduct meetings concerns familiarity—most people are still more comfortable talking face to face about business, where they can judge reactions as they speak (although, a great deal of business is conducted over the phone already). Another difficulty with chat has to do with maintaining control of a conversation. Chat conversations tend to be free-wheeling rather than goal-oriented. Many of the more recent applications geared toward business communication have built-in mechanisms for moderating a conversation and maintaining a level of control over the direction a discussion takes. This is a topic we will discuss in more detail later in the chapter.

Principal Features

Standard text-based chat environments are typically organized into "rooms" that designate different topic areas. Individual chat rooms can be configured with different access privileges, in the same way that bulletin board software does. Some chat applications allow participants to submit HTML coded text or other media files, graphics, sound, even video, attached to their message.

Other prominent features of chat software include:

- The ability to list room occupants
- A "balcony" overview of room occupants and/or discussion
- Whisper function to speak privately to someone in a chat room
- A "bozo" filter which allows you to filter out offensive chatters
- Search capabilities
- The ability to assign a moderator to the chat
- A "tour guide" feature that allows a group of chatters to surf the Web together

Chat Technologies

In the following sections, we will look briefly at a number of chat technologies. These include many text-based technologies, such as IRC, MUD/MOO, and Web-based chat; multimedia technologies, including graphical and 3-D worlds, audio, and video conferencing; and collaborative tools for communication and working in a shared document environment.

In this section we provide an overview of some of the prominent text-based chat environments. In later sections, we will examine recent development efforts in building graphical chat environments, most of which use the Internet, but not the Web directly.

IRC/MUD TO WWW GATEWAYS

There are a number of attempts to build gateway applications between IRC and the Web. One of these is wwwirc, a free gateway CGI script written in C by Zhong Yang. There are two different versions of the application: wwwirc and wwwirc-isp. Wwwirc is a single-user gateway, and wwwirc-isp is a multi-user gateway. For more information, check out **www.fiu.edu/~zyang01/wwwirc/**.

Recently, as with IRC, efforts have been made to gateway MOOs to the Web. Called WOOs (what else?), two of the more prominent examples are The Sprawl (**sensemedia.net/sprawl**), developed by SenseMedia, Inc., and WaxWeb (**bug.village.virginia.edu/**).

As this book was being finished, The Sprawl had just completed its v3.0 beta, which implements SenseMedia's latest server design, known as VooDo, for Virtual Object Oriented Domain. VooDo combines support for interactive chat, interactive HTML, interactive VRML, and plug-in modules.

We will return to the VRML and the creation of 3-D communication environments towards the end of this chapter, when we take up the subject of virtual worlds.

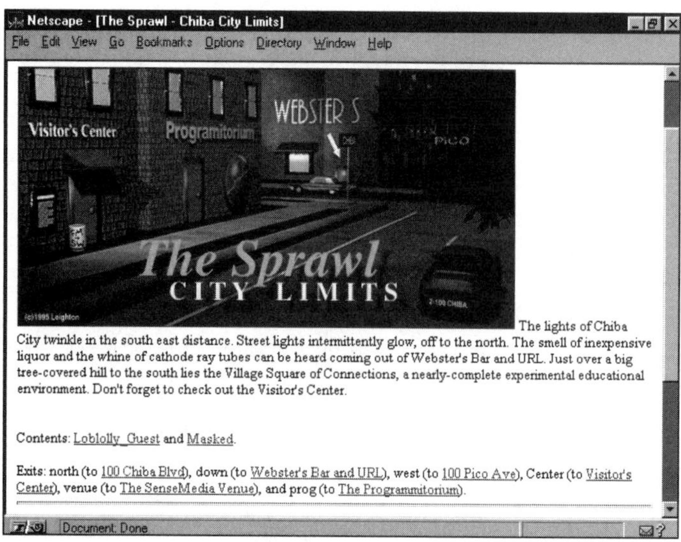

Figure 4-4
The Sprawl, a MOO with a Web interface.

GLOBAL CHAT Global Chat, developed by Prospero Systems Research, Inc., and now distributed by Quarterdeck, Inc., is a graphical IRC client, which can be called from a Web page as a helper application. It is currently the IRC client of choice among many smaller discussion sites.

Global Chat also has a corresponding server component, called Global Stage, which is available in various configurations.

For more information on Global Chat, consult the Quarterdeck Web site at **www.qdeck.com.**

ICHAT ichat, developed by ichat, Inc., is an IRC-compatible client that operates as a plug-in to compatible browsers such as Netscape Navigator and Microsoft Explorer. Users enter a conversation by accessing an ichat-enabled Web page. With the ichat client plug-in installed, the Web page will display an HTML frame in the browser window. Within that frame, ichat displays a real-time chat session among all the visitors on that Web page. Users can communicate with one another simply by typing into the frame.

In addition, ichat has two enhanced features. An add-on options allows ichat sessions to be moderated, so that all messages pass through a host rather than being sent directly to the chat display. ichat also has a tour guide feature that enables site administrators or users to take users connected to the server on a tour of designated Web pages.

ichat is based on a proprietary server technology that also supports IRC protocols. Unlike standard IRC, however, users can in fact connect to the server via a normal Telnet session if they prefer.

For more information about ichat, visit the ichat Web site at **www.ichat.com.**

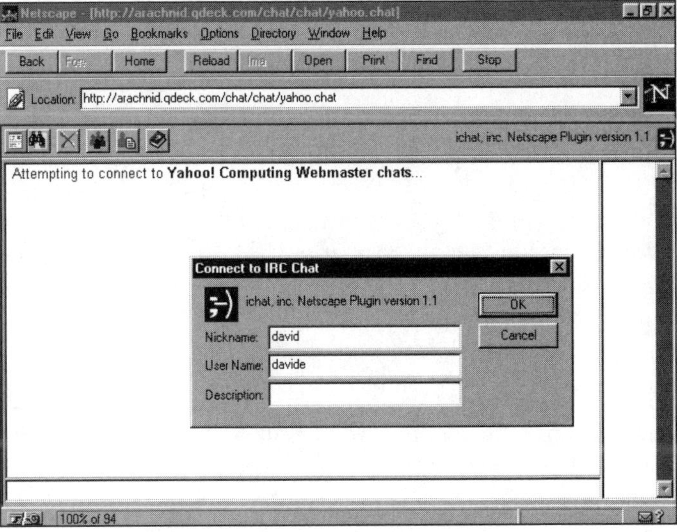

Figure 4-5
The ichat client operates as a plug-in to the Netscape browser.

Web-based Chat Systems

WebChat is the most impressive of several Web-based chat systems. It is discussed at length in Chapter 3, in the context of the WebChat Broadcasting System.

For more information and a detailed spotlight on the WebChat system, see Chapter 3, "Real-time Chat Services."

All of the Web-based chat systems have had to account for the fact that the Web does not retain any state information between requests from a given client. The simple solution to this is to require users to click a submission button whenever they want to send a message to the chat room as well as any time they want to refresh their page with the latest messages. This is a clumsy mechanism at best. Alternatives include performing a server push to the page at designated intervals, but this still requires a complete reloading of the page, which is not particularly elegant either.

Content Services (Classifieds)

Messaging and chat systems are intrinsically content neutral. They merely provide a structure and mechanism for communicating. At the next level, several popular services have emerged that provide content-specific communication services. In case that sounds a bit vague, we are basically referring to online classifieds—services that stipulate what kind of messages you can or should send. These range from job listings and classified sales, to personals.

Granted, these systems have a somewhat limited definition of communication. You will not find lengthy discussions taking place in these environments. Insofar as they do allow for messages to be posted, retrieved, and replied to, however, they may be classified as real communication/exchange environments.

Interestingly, most of the major classified services have built their technology from scratch rather than using existing Internet services or applications. The majority of these services are Web-based, using custom CGI programming connected to database applications for their store-and-forward interface. This greatly complicates the task of building the application, but simplifies components such as archiving and searching the content.

Event Programming and Netcasting

It took a while for the concept of scheduling events on the Internet to take hold, perhaps because the culture of the Internet eschews punctuality. With the advent of audio and video on demand technologies, such as Progressive Networks' RealAudio and Xing Technolgoies' StreamWorks, the notion of the Internet as a broadcast medium began to catch on.

Currently, a new Net phenomenon is brewing. Called *Netcasts* or *Webcasts*, these productions involve live audio or video feeds of special events—sports, music, politics seem to be favorites. Unlike a standard TV or radio broadcast, however, these netcasts frequently mix the ability to interact with the event, either through chat or some other means.

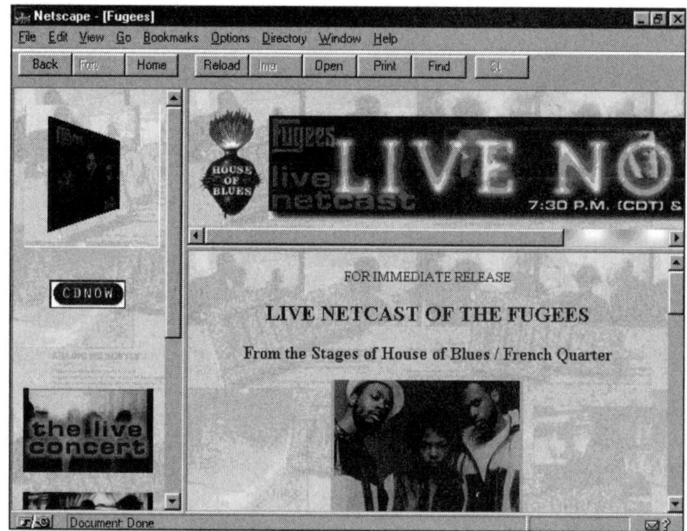

Figure 4-6
Scene from a House of Blues (www.hob.com) Netcast featuring the band, The Fugees.

This discovery of the potential for time-sensitive programming has in turn had its effect on the way forums and chat are used by businesses. Now it is not uncommon for Web sites to announce that a well-known guest will participate in an online discussion or a moderated interview at a given place and time. Such events draw people to the Web site, and it cuts down on the tendency for chat rooms to be underpopulated most of the time. There is nothing worse than a chat room with only one person in it.

Audio/Video Conferencing

One of the areas of Internet development that has recently begun to explode is the audio and video conferencing technologies. There are currently well over half-a-dozen Internet phone products, several of them proclaiming the ability to do low bandwidth video conferencing over the network. These products are still in their infancy, but the intensity of interest in them suggests that they may ultimately supplant text-based communication tools in importance.

In this section, we describe some of the more promising of the many applications in this category. Many of the rest are mentioned at the end of the chapter in the Short List.

Audio Conferencing

Voice on the Net (VON) technologies are a relatively recent and still controversial addition to Internet communication services. A VON is software that enables a point-to-point audio connection to be established over the Internet. The effect is roughly analogous to turning your PC into a phone, enabling you to talk long-distance to anyone for the price of your Internet connection. The catch is that you can only converse with another PC user who has the same application. There are no VON standards and the various products are not currently interoperable.

VOCALTEC INTERNET PHONE One example of VON software is VocalTec's Internet Phone. It has all of the basic functionality of a telephone. You can connect another party either directly, if you know how to reach them, or by accessing a chat room and locating them in the directory. In addition, the VocalTec IPhone has all of the enhanced telephone features, such as call holding, call waiting, and call screening. Callers can even leave voice mail for you if you do not answer the call.

The most recent release of the product also incorporates some basic groupware functionality as well. Users can transfer files between one another, share documents, and edit them in real-time with whiteboard functionality. And a Web linking feature allows you to add a direct voice link to your Web home page.

For more information about VocalTec's Internet Phone software, visit the VocalTec Web page at **www.vocaltec.com**.

Other examples of VON Internet telephony products, which share many of the same features with VocalTec, include:

- Netscape CoolTalk (**www.netscape.com**)
- Quarterdeck WebTalk (**www.qdeck.com**)
- Third Planet Publishing Digiphone (**www.planeteers.com**)
- Voxware Televox (**www.voxware.com**)
- FreeTel Communications (**www.freetel.com**)

Video Conferencing

Full-color motion video conferencing over the Internet remains something of an elusive dream. We will briefly examine two products working to bring the dream to reality.

CU-SEEME Originally developed at Cornell University Medical College (hence the CU part of the name) and now available in an enhanced commercial version from White Pines Software, Cu-SeeMe is TCP/IP video conferencing software for real-time person-to-person or group conferencing. The enhanced version from White Pines, for both PC and Macintosh, includes full-color video, audio, a text chat window, and whiteboard communications.

For more information about CU-SeeMe, check out the White Pines Software Cu-SeeMe Web site at **goliath.wpine.com/cu-seeme.html**.

VDOPHONE VDOnet, developers of VDOlive, a streaming video plug-in for Netscape Navigator, recently released a product called VDOPhone. VDOPhone lets you call another Internet user with the VDOPhone software and transmit two-way color video and audio, or audio only, over dial-up connections. As of this writing, VDOPhone was only available for the Windows 95 operating system.

See the VDOlive Web site at **www.vdolive.com** for more information.

Collaboration Systems (Microsoft NetMeeting)

Trying to distinguish between audio/video conferencing products and collaboration software—also known as groupware—is sometimes difficult. In general, though, conferencing applications allow communication to occur, either person-to-person or multi-person. Collaboration applications typically add to this the ability to work collectively on a task, by sharing access to documents, and so on.

In this section we present Microsoft's latest addition to Internet-based collaboration software. Information on other collaboration applications and groupware can be found in the Epilogue, which discusses Intranet development.

NetMeeting is an Internet-based collaboration application from Microsoft. It enables real-time voice and data communications over the Internet, including shared applications, file transfer, shared whiteboard, and chat. The application-sharing features work with existing Windows-based programs. Each person who shares the application can review and edit the document in real-time. Only one person is required to have the actual application or file resident on his or her computer.

Turn to the Epilogue for further information about Internet-based collaboration applications and groupware.

The whiteboard is a multipage, multiuser drawing program that enables you to sketch, draw, or type into the shared space. You can use a remote pointer and highlighting tool to call attention to items on the whiteboard as you collaborate.

The file transfer features enable you to send a file to all of the participants in a conference by dragging it into the NetMeeting window. The file transfer occurs in the background so you can continue to share programs using the whiteboard, or by chatting.

Microsoft NetMeeting has been bundled with version 3.0 of the Internet Explorer, available to download from the Microsoft Web site. For more information about NetMeeting or Internet Explorer, see Microsoft's Web site at **www.msn.com**.

Virtual Worlds

Virtual worlds, also known as habitats, are graphical online worlds in which the people present are represented by graphical stand-ins called "avatars." Typically, a world environment allows you to select, or possibly create, your avatar which then represents you in the graphical representation of the place you are visiting remotely.

The technology for building viable virtual worlds is still evolving. Just before this book went to press, support for the Moving Worlds, which adds programmable behaviors to the static VRML 1.0 standards, was announced for VRML 2.0. Even as some agreement is reached on the standards, however, many companies continue to develop proprietary technologies which may or may not conform to the standards.

The Palace

The Palace is a standalone graphical client/server chat application developed by Time Warner, Inc. It incorporate a 2-D graphical scene as the background for its environments, and then adds 2-D avatar graphics into the scene to represent participants. Chatting is done in a separate scrolling text box.

The Palace is described in detail in Chapter 3, "Real-time Chat Services." For additional information, visit The Palace Web site at **www.thepalace.com**.

Worlds, Inc.

Worlds, Inc. was one of the earliest companies to explore 3-D chat environments. Their first product, a client-based 3-D application called World Chat, predates the VRML 1.0 standard. To chat using World Chat, you first select an avatar and then enter a 3-D virtual environment. Objects can be hotlinked to Web pages and you can chat, by sending text-based messages, with others who are virtually present in the same space.

Worlds, Inc.'s most recent efforts have been directed toward a new product called AlphaWorld. Like World Chat, AlphaWorld is a 3-D environment, but here the concept is extended to embrace a virtual simulation of a community. In AlphaWorld you become a virtual citizen, assume an online persona, and can acquire and develop your own virtual corner of cyberspace.

Currently AlphaWorld is still in its beta version, which means that you can participate in this experiment in social computing for free. It is quite possible that AlphaWorld will sooner or later be overtaken by Moving Worlds, the latest VRML standards. However, Worlds, Inc. has been closely involved in the discussions of this standard. It is likely that their products will eventually support the new standards. In the meantime, AlphaWorld may be the closest thing to what VRML 2.0 will feel like.

For more information, or to download client software, visit the Worlds, Inc. Web site at **www.worlds.net**.

OnLive! Traveler

OnLive! Technologies recently introduced a beta version of their software called Traveler, which allows multiperson voice communication within a 3-D environment. As with other graphical environments, Traveler allows a user to select an avatar and to navigate through virtual environments, meeting and talking with others.

OnLive! also markets a Community Server which would allow a business to develop and operate its own virtual communication environment. For more information about OnLive! products check out their Web site at **www.onlive.com**.

Successful Internet Chat and Messaging Applications

Here we spotlight some of the better chat and messaging systems to be found on the Internet.

UTNE CAFE (**www.utne.com**) Part of the Utne Web site, Utne Cafe is a feature-rich discussion forum that uses Motet software. Utne makes available a schedule of planned events, as well as excerpts from the archives of previous discussions.

CLUB WIRED (**www.hotwired.com/club/**) Part of HotWired, the online publication for the digitally hip, Club Wired is the moderated event room. All HotWired chats take place on a separate server, talk.com. There is a Java version (still in beta testing at this writing) for those who qualify; others can

Telnet to talk.wired.com. There are several chat rooms available at talk.com and users are able to create new ones as well.

THE WELL ENGAGED (**engaged.well.com**) The WELL is arguably the most active of the Internet online communities. The Engaged Conferences system is the WELL's proprietary Web interface to its PicoSpan conferencing system. It includes many topical areas with lots of activity; however, paid membership is required for entrance.

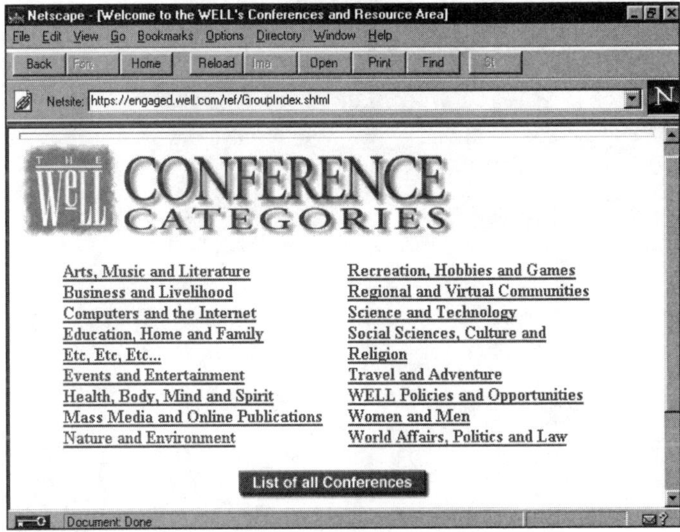

Figure 4-7
The WELL has a large number of heavily-used forums.

THE GLOBE (**www.theglobe.com**) The Globe is the online community system developed by WebGenesis, a Macintosh software development company. It features two chat areas: Globe Chat and Rapture. Globe Chat features four general purpose chat rooms: "Circus," "Day Trip," "Psycho," and "Red Square." Rapture, a more culturally-focused chat area offers "an open forum for the exchange of political, intellectual, cultural, and sometimes just plain weird ideas." Two new chat areas: TV chat and the Singles Bar, have recently been added. The Globe chat environment comes in three interfaces, including a java interface.

GNN VIRTUAL PLACES (**www.vplaces.com**) Formerly developed by Ubique before being purchased by GNN, Virtual Places chat environment recently re-emerged with a spiffy, "outer space" new look. Virtual Places is a client application that allows you to create an avatar for yourself and then join others at any Web site to either engage in conversation or participate in group tours. In addition, GNN sponsors chat locations, where people can congregate and mingle in virtual space.

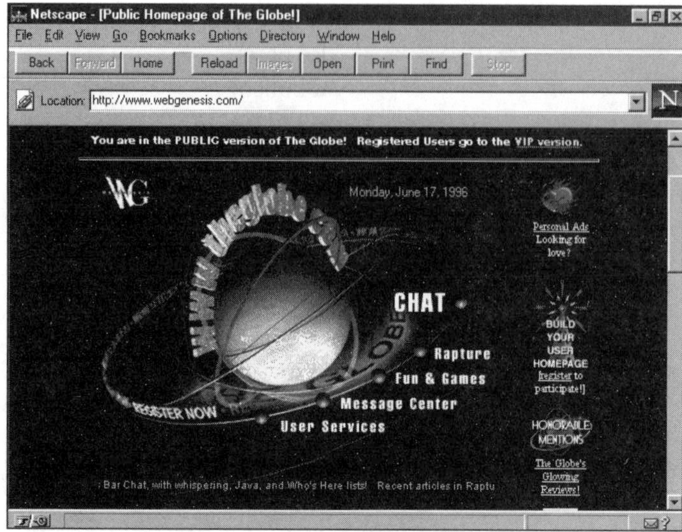

Figure 4-8
The Globe is an online community with several forum areas developed by WebGenesis.

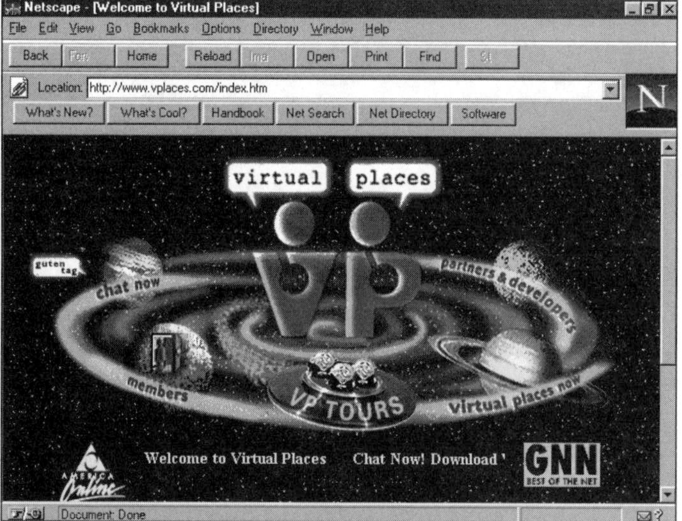

Figure 4-9
Virtual Places has a new owner, GNN, and a new look.

PARENT SOUP (**www.parentsoup.com**) Parent Soup is a Web site devoted to parenting issues, which includes advertising targeting the '90s mom and pop. In addition to a long list of departments and features, Parent Soup includes an extensive topic-based bulletin board system as well as a chat system, which features both an open chat area and feature events. Parent

Soup uses Global Chat software for its chat sessions. The site includes a technical help section for chat-related problems and also posts a statement of "House Rules" that defines acceptable use of the chat and bulletin board services.

The following table encapsulates some data for each of the preceding examples.

Table 4.1 Chat and Messaging Systems

NAME	URL	SUB-TYPE	SIZE	COMMENTS
Utne Cafe	www.utne.com	BBS/forum	M	uses Motet software
Club Wired	www.hotwired.com	chat	L	an active chat scene
The WELL Engaged	engaged.well.com	BBS/forum	XL	the WELL's proprietary application
The Globe	www.theglobe.com	Chat	L	WebGenesis' WebJive
GNN Virtual Places	www.vplaces.com	Chat	L	formerly Ubique
Parent Soup	www.parentsoup.com	Chat	M	parenting with Global Chat

The Short List

What follows is a list of additional examples of sites related to online publishing. This list is intended to be representative rather than comprehensive. For more directories of publishing sites, see the following section, Additional Resources.

Table 4.2 The Short List

NAME	URL	SUB-TYPE	SIZE	COMMENTS
SF Gate	www.sfgate.com	chat	M	San Francisco newspaper chat; uses Motet
SAID	www.said.com	chat	M	new, hip chat interface
OmniChat	www.4-lane.com	chat	L	various chat topics
Pathfinder BBS	pathfinder.com/pathfinder/bbshome.html	BBS/forum	L	various topics
The Chicago Tribune	tribapps.tribune.com	BBS/forum	M	uses Web Crossing
Juno	www.juno.com	e-mail service	n/a	free e-mail service

(continued)

Table 4.2 The Short List (continued)

NAME	URL	SUB-TYPE	SIZE	COMMENTS
Freemark Communications	www.freemark.com	e-mail service	n/a	free e-mail service
NY Times	www.nytimes.com/ comment	BBS/forums	M	various topics
BookWeb	www.bookweb.org	chat	M	scheduled author chats
Women Online Worldwide (WOW)	www.wowwomen.com	chat	M	women's issues
Fun City	www.funcity.com	chat	L	various topics
ESPN Sportzone	espnet.sportszone.com/ editors/talk	chat	L	sports, sports, sports
Peachweb Plantation	plant.peachweb.com/pyr	chat	L	a commercial chat environment
PowWow	www.tribal.com	collaboration	L	free collaboration application
Virtual Vegas—Lizard Lounge	www.virtualvegas.com/ quicker/lizard/lizard.html	chat	M	various technologies
Apple Computer Webcasts	live.apple.com	webcast	L	Apple site for video telecasts
Talk City	www.talkcity.com	chat	L	culture, politics, arts, society
Online Health Forum	healthnet.ivi.com/ common/ html/home.html	chat	M	bulletin board discussions and scheduled chats with physicians
Z-DNet Community Center	www.zdnet.com/home/ filters/talk.html	chat	L	computers, mainly
Youth Central	yc.apple.com	chat	L	kids and teens
Sonic Net	www.sonicnet.com	chat	M	music and musicians
Sony World Networks ChatSpace	www.swnetworks.com	chat/club moo	M	music and musicians

Additional Resources

DAVID R. WOOLLEY'S CONFERENCING ON THE WORLD WIDE WEB **(freenet.msp.mn.us/people/drwool/webconf.html)** An excellent resource for information links and software related to online asynchronous conferencing.

DANIEL LALIBERTE'S WWW COLLABORATION RESOURCE PAGE **(union.ncsa.uiuc.edu/HyperNews/get/www/collaboration.html)** An exhaustive list of conferencing and collaboration tools and information maintained at NCSA by the developer of HyperNews.

JEFF PULVER'S VON RESOURCES **(www.von.com)** The consummate resource page for Voice On the Net technologies. Includes references to both audio and video products as well a lots of information.

THE CONFERENCING METAPHOR, GEOFFREY BOCK AND RONNI T. MARSHAK, COLLABRA **(www.collabra.com/articles/seybold.html)** This article is excerpted from "The Conferencing Metaphor," by Geoffrey Bock and Ronni T. Marshak.

INFOSEEK WEB TIMES **(www.infoseek.com)** Features a calendar of events including "interesting chats, webcasts, and more."

QUARTERDECK'S CHAT SCHEDULE **(arachnid.qdeck.com/chat/schedule.html)** A good listing of chat events, updated daily.

META CHATS **(sunsite.unc.edu/dbarberi/chats.html/)** Sponsored by MetaLabs and Sunsite.

SOL CHAT-O-RAMA **(www.solscape.com/chat/)** More chat links than you could ever wish to follow.

ELECTRONIC COMMUNITIES **(www.communities.com/habitat.html)** Electronic Communities maintains a list of virtual worlds and habitats at their Web site.

Future Directions

Three trends are emerging for the next generation of communication tools on the Internet. In the next months, we may see communication services evolving...

- from text-based to multimedia
- from pages to worlds, using VRML 2.0
- from single-user to shared application groupware

It is only a question of time, money, and bandwidth before such applications proliferate.

More importantly, though, for anyone contemplating Internet business applications, we should start to see some of the dust begin to settle, and standards and stable technologies begin to emerge. Today's toys will become tomorrow's tools.

Probably the first and primary uses of these emerging technologies will be on corporate intranets, where bandwidth issues are somewhat reduced, and where application of the technologies can be more closely controlled.

PART TWO

Online Publishing and Information Delivery

We now turn to businesses centered around information delivery—the online equivalent of the publishing industry. Information publishing via the Internet really came into its own with the advent of the World Wide Web, the Internet's answer to interactive multimedia.

The Web is quite adequate to the needs of most simple publishing applications. As we will see, though, the Web presents a number of challenges and limitations to information publishers who want to take full advantage of the Internet's potential.

The main case studies in this section are divided into two chapters. In Chapter Five, "Digital Publications," we examine the applications that are based most closely on traditional publishing metaphors—the digital version of news magazines.

In Chapter Six, "News Delivery and Directory Services," we discuss information services focused on the collection, organization, and delivery of information.

Chapter Seven, "Joining the Publishing Revolution," discusses the various ways online publications are conducting their business on the Net today.

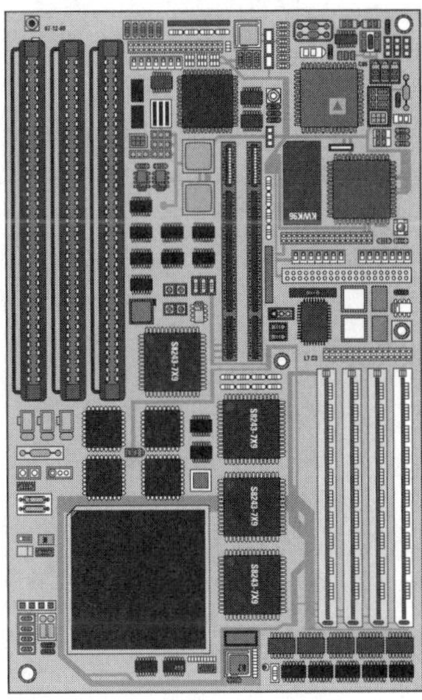

CHAPTER FIVE

DIGITAL PUBLICATIONS

In this chapter we examine case studies involving online publishing, which is currently one of the hottest areas of Internet development. Publishing companies recognize that the Internet is an attractive medium in which to provide readers with new information. Publishers already have the electronic content, and although converting this content is no trivial matter, it is more like extending the current market for their content than it is like creating a whole new enterprise. In addition, magazine publishers are used to thinking in terms of *features*. From the print-based magazine environment to the feature-rich, interactive, online world is a relatively easy conceptual transition.

Information Wants to be Free

To publishing companies, the online model provides a relatively inexpensive means by which to deliver information to customers. It is easy to update—even to change at the last minute before publishing.

The biggest challenge for publishers, however, has been figuring out how to generate revenue from their online content. Customers are reluctant to pay for information, partly because the legacy of the Internet dictates that all information should be freely available. This "information wants to be free..." business is more than just a cyberpunk manifesto.

Look around on the Net and you will find a large amount of digital content that is written, organized, and maintained by private individuals during their free time. Collecting information is a '90s equivalent of collecting model trains or salt and pepper shakers.

By the same token, advertisers have been reluctant to invest large sums of money in online publishing ventures, as long as the whole digital publishing enterprise remains speculative, and until they have provision in their budgets for a form of advertising that barely even existed a year ago.

It is quite likely that this reluctance, especially on the part of advertisers, will diminish as the Internet is more fully assimilated into consumer culture. Most online publishing, like most current publishing, will be driven by ad revenue. On top of that, publishers are likely to offer value-added, "premium" features, which customers will pay extra for. This is essentially the model that online services such as CompuServe and America Online introduced successfully several years ago.

This model will be successful for news-oriented content, where it is possible to predict that a customer will return regularly for the next installment. Content that is more static, such as technical documentation or literary works, for example, is more likely to follow a pay-per-use model. In this case, charges to the customer are based on the quantity of information they request. This requires a mechanism for calculating small, incremental charges, like the Newshare model discussed in Chapter 6.

Finally, it is worth noting that many publications now request (or require) that users register with the service. Some sites have begun to successfully introduce subscription-based services. Even if no charges are associated with this registration, a publication that registers its users can develop a valuable database of user information. What use a company makes of that data varies from publication to publication, but even if it is only used for internal purposes and is not sold to advertisers, it can still provide publications with a wealth of marketing information.

The Publication Model

Most accounts of online publishing focus on the delivery end of the publication model. In fact, a true online publishing venture requires network-based systems (not to mention a staff capable of managing these systems) for all of its operations: aggregation of content, content management, subscription, and ad sales accounting, as well as content delivery.

It is possible, of course, to continue to perform the back-end functions manually, but only as a transitional phase. If online publishing is to become a large-scale operation, it will require the economies that only fully electronic systems can provide.

Many of the early ventures into online publishing started by simply re-producing content from existing print publications. Time Warner's *Pathfinder*, *USA Today*, Conde Nast *Traveler*, even *HotWired* were jump-started with existing content. As these online publications have matured, however, they have increasingly taken on a life of their own, one that takes advantage of the Internet medium and one that speaks to their online audience.

In addition, a number of recent ventures have been launched to produce an exclusively digital magazine, or "digizine" as these are now called. As a result of these newly introduced *streaming* multimedia technologies, we are starting to see publishing ventures that look more like broadcast media—Internet-based audio and video publishing.

THE DIGIZINE SCENE

Getting Down to Cases...

There are really three types of electronic publications.

- Reformatted print publications
- Exclusively electronic publications
- Multimedia/broadcast publications

An increasing number of print publications are now placing their content online, in part as a way of promoting the print publication, but also, at least in some cases, looking forward to a new medium in which to deliver subscription-based information.

Publication sites range from those that have simply "cut and pasted" content from the publication into a Web format to more elaborate sites that combine original content and Web-based functionality with information and/or articles from the print publications.

In addition, an increasing number of publications are designed entirely around the electronic environment.

As for the more broadcast-like applications, those are still experimental. It is evident that the demand for delivering real-time audio and video content exists, and that the technology is progressing. But bandwidth constraints will keep these from becoming viable business opportunities for a while longer. When they do arrive, chances are good that it will be first on Intranet sites, where bandwidth is typically greater as is the ability to control bandwidth usage.

To learn more about the nuts and bolts of building an online publishing system, turn to Chapter 7, "Joining the Publishing Revolution."

SALON (**www.salon1999.com**) is a free, interactive, literary zine on the Web that's gaining quite a following in the online world. Even the print world is enamored with it.

Many online zines have print counterparts, but not SALON. Inspired by the creative potential of the Internet, the SALON founders wanted to create a zine that stimulated discussions about books, authors, politics, entertainment, and ideas. Daily updates and colorful writing in features such as "Newsreel," "Media Circus," "Sneak Peaks," and "Table Talk," keep the site fresh and readers coming back.

SALON's great strength is that it provides strong content from professional journalists and writers and then gives readers a place to go for ongoing discussions. For example, after reading a fresh perspective of a current news event, you can immediately join Table Talk and participate in a discussion about the event with other readers online.

Readers can also enjoy the comics, read the music reviews, keep up with their favorite SALON columnists, and peruse back issues. Many zines are popping up on the Web, but this particular electronic publication has the financial backing, writing talent, technology backbone, and vision to turn itself into a serious commercial venture.

COMPANY BACKGROUND

David Talbot created the concept of SALON when he was working at the *San Francisco Examiner*. Discouraged by what he describes as the "dumbed down media of the '80s" that is focused mostly on glamour and celebrities, Talbot decided to create a publication that stimulated the kinds of discussions he used to have in college about books and issues. He believed there was a market for SALON, given the recent resurgence of book clubs, public readings, and the appearance of weightier, more substantive books on best-seller lists.

SALON At-a-Glance

The Product	Interactive literary zine on the Web
URL	www.salon1999.com
Owners	venture capital investors
Start Date	November, 1995
Software/Hardware	Apple Macintosh 6150s servers, Web Crossing chat software and custom software development

His first thought was to create a modest print magazine with just a few employees featuring books and authors. Then, along came the Internet. Talbot quickly realized that this new medium was a way to economically produce an ambitious magazine with a larger staff that could do more than provide interesting, provocative content—it could provide an environment for conversation about what people were reading.

He also had a potential audience of highly educated people who, he believed, were seriously undernourished by the traditional print media. Talbot, with a clear vision in mind, began searching for a partner that understood the business side of publishing. That person was David Zweig, and together they wrote a successful business plan, selling intelligence as the next growth market in media.

Four people created the prototype and launched the first issue of SALON in November of 1995. At the time of this writing, SALON employs 16 people, and the company is well on is way to hiring more.

SALON's popularity took off faster than they thought.

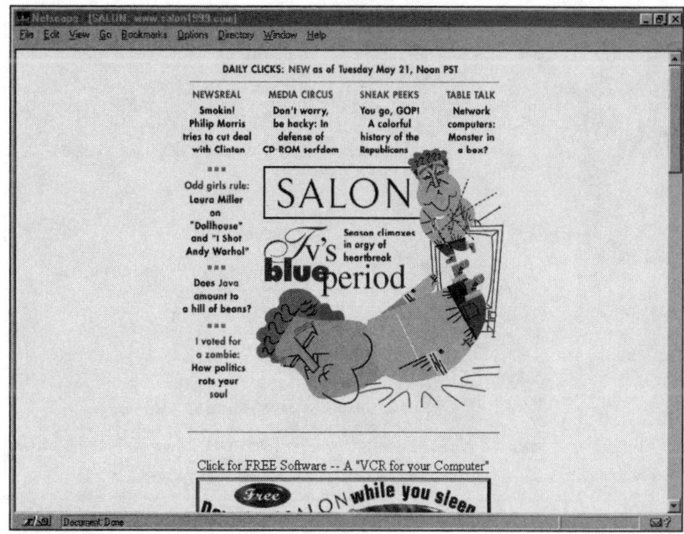

Figure 5-1
SALON's home page.

PRODUCT DESCRIPTION

SALON is attempting to offer a variety of views and perspectives—an eclectic mix. Editorially, the publication is aiming for a centrist view as its anchor, but actively seeks both left-wing and right-wing perspectives. For example, SALON has a deal with City Hall in New York, a very conservative organization; yet in its current issue offers a compelling piece on gay marriages from a more liberal perspective. The overall goal is to provide well-written, solid content.

Among the provocative pieces that have appeared in earlier issues of SALON are:

- Denis Johnson's first-person account of a gathering for Christian bikers
- Jamaica Kincaid's put-down of Tina Brown
- Harvey Keitel's defense of Quentin Tarantino
- Camile Paglia's defense of trash TV shows
- Novelist Mary Gaitskill's probing essay about Vladimir Nabakov
- Oliver Sacks on why Mozart makes him a better neurologist

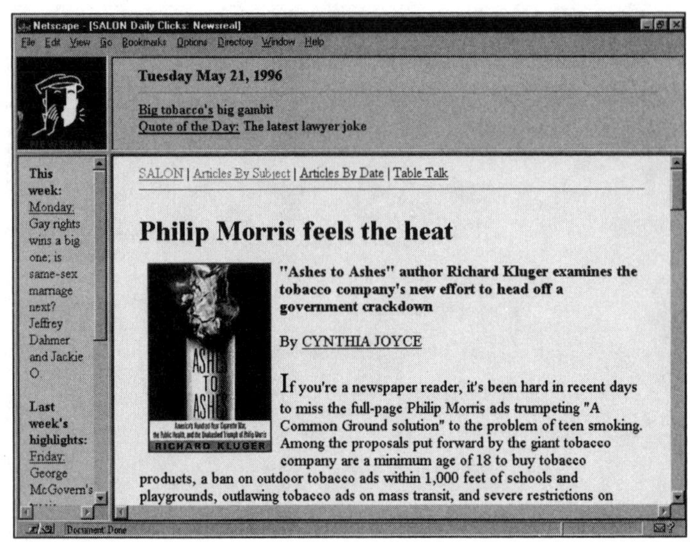

Figure 5-2
The edgy pieces in News Real are designed to stimulate conversation.

PRODUCT FEATURES AND BENEFITS

Currently, SALON offers two daily features geared to stimulate more site traffic: "Media Circuit," a daily review of recent news events, and "News Real" (see Figure 5-2), a commentary piece with an attitude on a daily news item.

Some of SALON's features are visited more frequently than others. The editorial staff gets a sense of what features are popular from reader surveys and tracking where people travel on the site. Questions and answer interviews are popular, as they work well on the screen. Readers can scan the questions and select the responses they want to read. Favorite interviews are typically the ones featuring famous writers, such as John Updike or Amy Tan.

Certain columnists are popular, too, because of their colorful writing, which is effective on the Internet. Cartoonists also do well—Tom Tomorrow has a big following. Also, readers enjoy responding to "Hot Button" essays—they generate considerable conversation in the Table Talk area, which is, of course, the goal behind selecting essay topics. The more stimulating the essay, the more people will participate in discussions, and the more likely that they will return to the site.

Sneak Peaks offers reviews and articles on books, movies, and music. After reading a book review, you can click to go to the Borders Books and Music site and order a copy.

Virtually all the writing in SALON is original. It is produced by SALON's editorial staff and a strong pool of authors and professional journalists who are paid a competitive rate by online standards. The only non-original pieces that SALON publishes are from the Pacific News Service, a labor of love maintained by one woman, Sandy Close, who won one of the MacArthur Fellowships last year for her work with the independent news service. She works largely with teenagers and other young people, many of them from disadvantaged backgrounds. SALON subscribes to that news service and the editors use it fairly frequently to bolster the News Real feature.

SALON has set out to be different from other zines when it comes to technology. It covers technology but not as a primary focus and not from the perspective of the technologist. Rather, the viewpoint is one of social commentary from an informed technological perspective.

BUSINESS AND MARKETING

SALON has three important alliances that came about in very different ways. Zweig and Talbot thought seriously about what sort of strategic partners would help them accomplish their marketing goals. They decided that a relationship with a bookstore chain would be ideal.

After evaluating their options, they approached Borders, Inc., because it was both a responsive and innovative company. Drawing on their connections in the publishing world, they adamantly pursued the company until they got their ideas in front of the right people. They convinced Borders that SALON could add value to their existing business. As a result, the regular SALON feature "Sneak Peaks" evolved. Borders does its own book reviews, as well, but having an independent third-party review its books, whether the review is favorable or not, gives the effort greater validity and Borders additional credibility.

SALON selects the books, selects the reviewers, and select the reviews that appear in the zine. In return, Borders contributes financially to SALON, advertises, and takes the reviews it wants to use and merchandises them throughout their stores. The relationship between Borders and SALON is likely to continue and evolve into other alliance activities.

Another alliance partner, Adobe, is more of an investor. In their search for capital, Talbot and Zweig approached companies who had similar interests. Adobe obviously has an interest in books and the printed word.

The CEO of Adobe, John Warnock, is himself a bibliophile and book collector. He liked the zine concept and had an investment fund, so Adobe Limited Partners invested in SALON. For the most part, the relationship has been one of Adobe's investment in SALON, but the relationship is beginning to expand. SALON now appears in *Adobe Magazine*, and Adobe tools are used to create the zine.

The third alliance partner is Apple Computer, Inc., which is mostly a marketing relationship that may someday evolve into an investment relationship. Apple contributed money for the first SALON prototype. The quality of that prototype was critical in helping SALON build other business relationships. Also, beginning in June of 1996, the Apple Performa line will include three screens for SALON featured quite prominently in the Internet section of the digital tour of the machine.

Initially what Apple hoped to do was use SALON as a communications and marketing medium that would bolster Apple's relationships with its core market group. Education, home, home learning, creative community, and entertainment were the specific markets. They were seeking strategic content investments upon which they could piggyback other marketing efforts for their now defunct Internet effort. SALON was perceived as one of those content investments.

Zweig believes that for now, looking to make money offline to support your site makes more sense than online efforts. For example, SALON is getting into article syndication. The hope is that syndication will give SALON a strong presence on other Web sites and bring revenue strength to the zine. Eventually, SALON would like to offer a subscription price for online readers, but there are no immediate plans for launching a subscription service yet.

SALON does have ad banners sprinkled throughout the site, but Zweig believes it is important to pursue alternative revenue sources in addition to ads. The general fee for a banner on the zine is approximately $40 per thousand hits; consequently, lots of thousands are needed to generate serious revenue. Zweig believes that most of the serious ad banner money is going to popular search engines and companies such as Netscape.

From the outside, it appears that SALON has no difficulty in securing good writers, but it's harder than it looks. Talbot says that it is difficult to bring well-known established writers from the print world to the online world, because, as a group, they are often conservative about technology, and many of them are not online yet. They are aware of the Internet, but they typically don't pay it much attention. From time to time, SALON editors will find themselves typing in copy that arrives on paper, because the contributing authors have no modem capability. Some writers don't even have a fax. As a result, it's a challenge to convince these particular writers that the Internet is worth their time and that they should be involved.

Talbot explains that writers are often a shy lot, so getting them to participate in the Table Talk area has been difficult for SALON. To date, only one or two writers have taken the leap. In the future, Talbot would like to

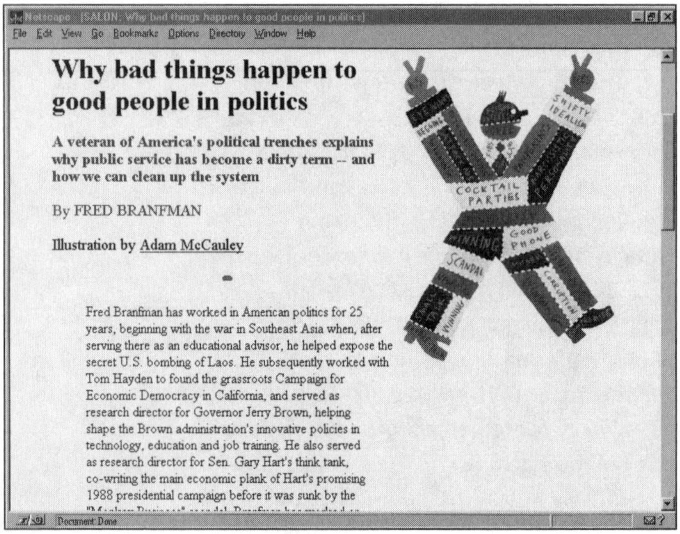

Figure 5-3
SALON has a strong pool of columnists.

feature more writers in the live chat area to stimulate traffic.

Many of the staff members at SALON worked for years at prominent newspapers and magazines, and through long-standing relationships brought many of the writers with them to SALON. Because of the high quality of the editorial staff, the zine quickly established a reputation within publishing circles of treating books and writers with seriousness. Writers are beginning to realize that it is a good place to showcase their work, which is probably why they are willing to accept pay at a fraction of the rates paid by the top magazines in the country.

Recently SALON went from being a bi-weekly publication to a daily schedule for some features, and the number of hits has since tripled and are continuing to rise. It appears that the audience really wants SALON to be a daily habit.

TECHNOLOGY BACKBONE

SALON's servers, two Apple Macintosh 6150s, are presently located offsite and are maintained by the third party that owns and operates a server farm of considerable size. When SALON started, it had no full-time technical people and determined it would be unwise to try to deal with hosting and running a Web site in addition to all of the other issues involved with being a start-up online company.

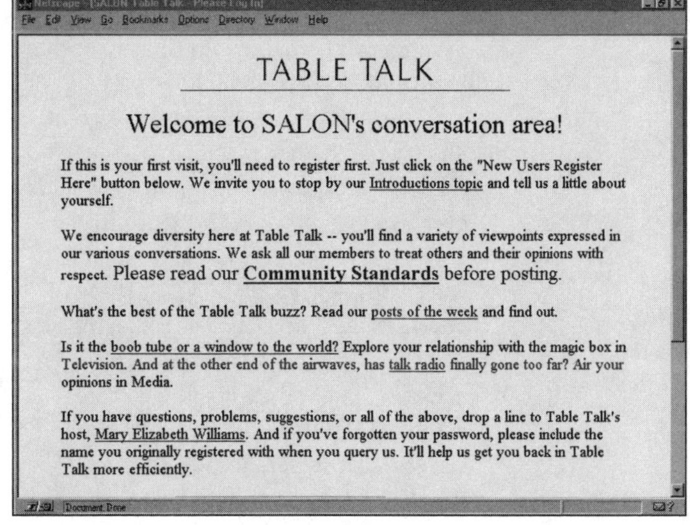

Figure: 5-4
Table Talk, the live chat area on SALON.

The initial software supporting the Table Talk area was slow, unreliable, and impossible for the editorial staff to maintain. Even minor changes had to go through the third-party software vendor who supplied the technology. Because the Table Talk section was viewed by the editorial staff as crucial to the mission of SALON, a search began for a better solution.

Web Crossing was that solution, because it addressed many of the concerns with original software. At this writing, more than 12,000 people have registered to participate in the forums. SALON integrates Table Talk into the SALON issues as much as possible, creating links to topics, starting new topics when new articles get written, and so on.

Mignon Khargie, the Art Director, and her staff do 95 percent of the HTML coding—the editors do the other five percent. Khargie tries hard to maintain the rule that no single page download for a user should ever be larger than 60K. The goal is to have the magazine feel very fast and readable while also being graphically rich. The staff has created a collection of its own templates that are used to create new pages by copy-and-paste methods. In the future, more automated HTML tools may be employed, such as Microsoft Front Page, Adobe PageMill, Netscape Navigator Gold, or another similar tool that creates HTML pages on the fly.

SALON believes that good textual content in simple but elegant layouts (bearable even at 14.4K) are important to its success. But the technical folks are always on the lookout for new technology that will add value to the zine. They have recently begun using GIF89a animations sparingly, and a small number of audio clips that are more of the sound bite variety.

According to Dan Shafer, Director of Technology and Senior Webmaster, some experimentation is going on with JavaScript, and SALON is getting ready to deploy some small Shockwave objects. Down the road, it may offer some proprietary Java applets to enable readers to play interactive word games. The fancier stuff, such as VRML, is probably farther into the future.

Currently, a search engine is not being used on the site, but it is on the list of things to do. Excite is also a strong possibility, because Web Crossing has plans to implement it.

SALON is an all-Mac shop, both on the site and on the local network, and the staff is very happy with the technology. According to Shafer, the Mac is an incredibly powerful Web server and doesn't require a separate full-time person just to maintain it. Very few server problems arise that cannot be fixed remotely and quickly. Schafer uses Frontier for all of the CGI applications that are created in-house because he feels it has the advantage of being elegant, fast, and powerful. He also likes WebStar, the server software, because, according to Schafer, it is rock-solid and does everything he needs it to do.

LESSONS LEARNED AND HELPFUL SUGGESTIONS

The following are summaries of some of the lessons learned by the folks at SALON:

- Solicit opinions from your readers and be responsive. When Table Talk was being redesigned, a de facto committee of avid Table Talk users was formed to solicit suggestions for improvement, and as a result, the software and the interface were improved.

- Don't try to lock people into your site. The very nature of the Internet is that people want to move in and out of various sites at will. Keep your business model with that core understanding in mind. Keep people interested, but don't try to coerce them into staying.
- Revenue from ad banners will probably not support the cost of your site. Look for other opportunities for generating money.
- Take risks and try features that you may not think will be successful. For example, SALON's poetry feature did much better than expected, so they are planning to do it again.
- Find a niche where you can develop more cross-marketing relationships. It can be profitable to be the middle man and bring two companies together through the medium of your Web site.
- Have a good prototype in order to get serious investors interested, and invest as much money as possible developing it. People will not put down money for a only vision. The prototype must give people a sense of the look and feel of what you are trying to do.
- Understand that most of the metrics you use in print fall away with an online publication. Issue number, length of story, page count, and date of issue all become meaningless.
- Be important to your host. Make certain that the third party hosting your server sees it as its mission to maintain servers, so your site is always up and running.

FUTURE

Eventually, SALON would like to become a subscription service, but the online marketplace and the competition will dictate to some extent when that will happen. Immediate future plans are to go completely daily after more staff is added. Also, some plans exist for future spin-offs of SALON. One in particular is the creation of Global SALON—a publication similar to SALON but with a more international perspective.

If you want to know anything about food, wine, dining, or entertaining, Epicurious (**www.epicurious.com**) is your online destination.

The textually rich site offers plenty of information by using unique features that take full advantage of the interactive nature of the Net. Even though Epicurious has a bank of information available from well-respected print publications such as *Bon Appetit* and *Gourmet* magazines, the online zine creates its own original features and articles to give the site its distinct personality and voice.

The creators of Epicurious believe the online world requires a fresh approach and avoided the temptation to simply take existing publications and put them online with little or no modifications. They wanted to employ the full interactive nature of the Web. Consequently, a strategic business decision was made to create CondeNet, a separate business entity created to house Epicurious and other online publishing efforts within the parent publishing company Conde Nast.

Online users of Epicurious can do all of the following:

- Discover what is fresh at their local farmer's market
- Learn where to invite clients for dinner when traveling to various cities
- Follow along step by step and prepare a gourmet meal for friends and family
- Peruse recipes
- Get advance notice of upcoming culinary events

Epicurious has searchable databases on all kinds of food topics, offers tips on entertaining, and has special articles from *Bon Appetit* and *Gourmet*. The extensive online forums give food lovers plenty of opportunity to share recipes and communicate with online friends.

The modest fourteen-person staff of Epicurious is shared with Conde Nast Traveler (which is in the process of becoming Epicurious Travel). Even though Epicurious is successfully generating advertising revenue, the online product is still in the growing phase and an expensive process, so it is not yet profitable.

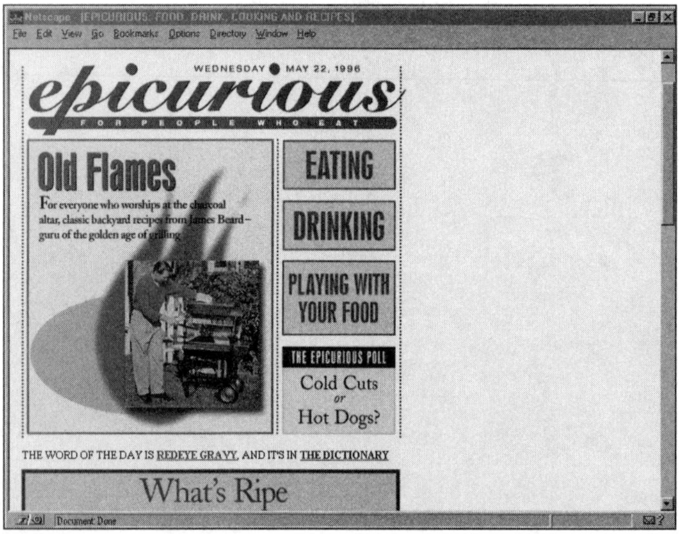

Figure 5-5
Epicurious covers eating and drinking with flair.

Epicurious At-a-Glance

The Product	Food and wine destination zine
URL	www.epicurious.com
The Company/ Owners	Conde Nast
The staff	14 employees
Software/Hardware	Recipe forum is created from a fully customized version of HyperNews augmented with the Verity search engine; other features were developed through in-house software development.

COMPANY BACKGROUND

The original idea behind Epicurious was spawned by Rochelle Udell, one of the true pioneers in the business of online publishing and now the editor-in-chief of *Self* magazine. For several years, she prodded Conde Nast to consider producing online publications before receiving the green light for Epicurious. She chose the title, "Epicurious," because she wanted to play with the idea of an Epicurean—someone who is concerned with all matters of taste, but particularly tastes involving food and wine. Epicurious seemed to capture her original intent, as well as offer something bigger with even more latitude.

Beginning with Udell's original idea, Joan Feeney, the current editorial director, further developed the idea into where Epicurious is today. Feeney began with a very basic question, "What do I want this computer to do for me on the subject of food?" An obvious question, but not one Feeney believes many online publishers initially consider. Often the thinking is, "What do I have, and how much of it do I want to put online?"

Feeney wanted to begin with the features that took advantage of the available technology and utilized the unique presentation power of the medium. And so she did. She started with the idea of a recipe database that linked directly to a food dictionary, so that the two worked together with the speed and flexibility impossible in print form.

Forums were another obvious choice. She knew that people like to talk to other people about food and swap recipes, and Epicurious was the logical place to make that happen. With those two basic ideas as a starting point, the rest of Epicurious evolved to where it is today.

PRODUCT DESCRIPTION

The editorial staff spent quite a bit of time thinking about everything they might want to do in the publication before they structured the site's architecture. They structured it in such a way that the areas could comfortably encompass virtually anything having to do with food. Currently, the core departments are "Eating," "Drinking," "Playing with

Your Food," and the imprint magazine areas, *Bon Appetit*, and *Gourmet*. The categories are general enough to offer quite a bit of editorial license in terms of what to include, and specific enough to give readers a clear sense of where the links are likely to take them. The other online features include the searchable recipe database, food dictionary, forums, and e-mail capability for feedback to Epicurious.

At present, users do not have to pay to visit the site, and Epicurious does not trouble its readers with registration and passwords. The site is very easy to navigate because it offers a Sit-Down or Drive-Thru option from the home page. Choose the Sit-Down option if you want the full graphical experience, or Drive-Thru if you are in a hurry and don't want to wait for the graphics to download.

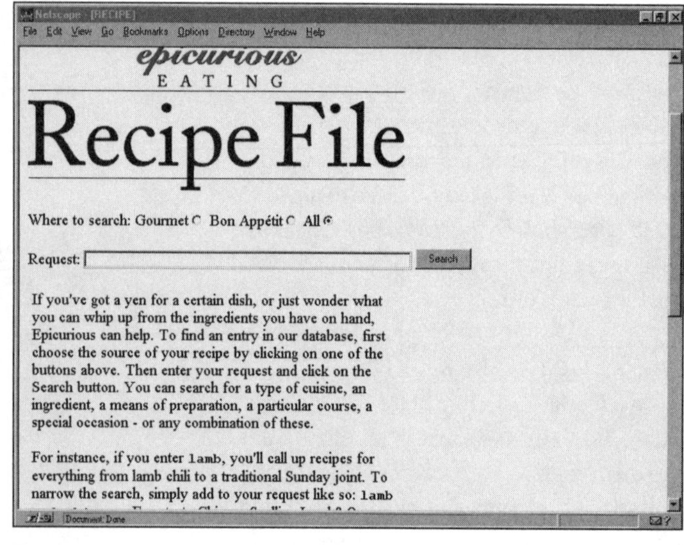

Figure 5-6

Users can search for recipes in previous issues of *Gourmet* and *Bon Appetit* magazines.

PRODUCT FEATURES AND BENEFITS

The editorial staff has made a concerted effort to make the voices of *Bon Appetit, Gourmet*, Epicurious, and the various other information sources on the site distinct, yet harmonious. In order to maintain Epicurious's unique style, some of the writing for Epicurious is done by the editorial staff, and the rest is done by freelance writers.

The latest issue of Epicurious (as of this writing) features the late James Beard as the first Hall of Fame inductee. Rather then stopping with just an article about Beard and his foundation, additional links are provided to his *Barbecue Cook Book*, other barbecue links on the Web, Beard recipes from the recipe database, and a complete Beard bibliography from the Library of Congress. If you want to double check the accuracy of the bibliography yourself, follow the link directly to the online version of the Library of Congress.

The section entitled "What's Ripe" is a fairly recent addition to the electronic publication that gives readers a weekly status of what is fresh in their geographic area. By clicking on a map of the United States, they can find out what is currently available in their region of the country, as opposed to just finding out what's typically ripe the first week of May. Based on the available ingredients, they can choose appropriate recipes they like and print them out before leaving the house.

Feeney got the idea for Farmers' Market during her walks three mornings a week on her way to work through Union Square's Farmers' Market in New York City. She usually buys whatever is in season and builds her cooking around the fresh produce. Because everyone does not have the option of walking to work, she thought that putting Farmers' Markets online would be an excellent service Epicurious could provide its readers.

Other sites also have farmers' markets online, but they basically just describe how to shop at farmers' markets and then list them around the country. Feeney wanted to do something more meaningful. Offering timely information on the seasonal availability of food is an important part of eating and food appreciation, and something that would encourage regular site visits.

Using the Farmers' Market Association as a starting point, the staff at Epicurious used traditional journalism skills to find the biggest markets in terms of size, history, and volume. The next step was to contact the managers of the markets to see if they would be interested in participating. The staff took the idea even one step further. Because shoppers often don't recognize certain kinds of produce, like kumquats, let alone have the first clue what to do with them, the staff thought it would be a great idea to link the

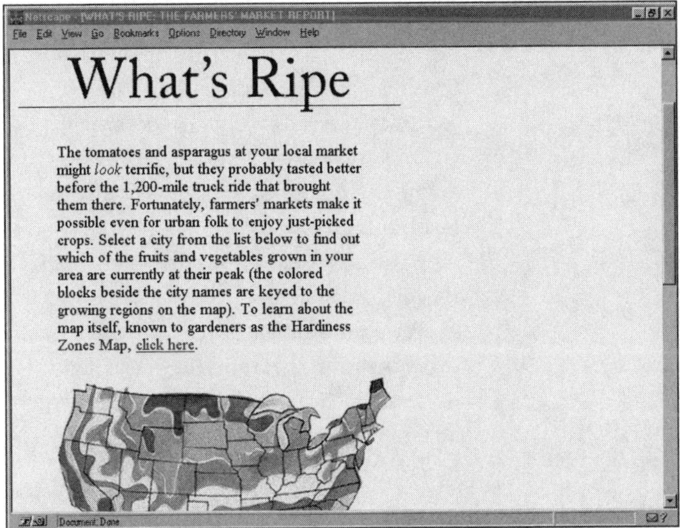

Figure 5-7
What's Ripe provides weekly updates of fresh produce across the country.

Farmers' Market to the recipe database and food dictionary. People could then look up the item, print out a couple of recipes, and take them to the market. Shoppers could then get all their ingredients in one trip as opposed to buying this and that at the market, going home, looking up recipes in cookbooks, and then realizing you don't have everything you need to make the recipe.

Farmers' Market is a good example of how the staff is constantly looking at ways to use the power of hypertext to not just add to the site but enhance it. Whenever a new idea is generated for Epicurious, the first thing the staff does is look carefully at the entire site and determine how it can best be used to enhance the other existing features. For example, after acquiring the food dictionary, *The Food Lovers Companion* by Sharon Tyler Herbst, not only was it put it on the site, but it was integrated with other features such as Farmers' Market. The dictionary also continues to be integrated into the recipe database.

A very useful feature on the top of every recipe pulled from the searchable database is a little box where you can enter an e-mail address and mail the recipe to a friend. The Epicurious URL accompanies the e-mail, so the friend can visit the site directly if they desire—a clever marketing strategy helpful in spreading the word about Epicurious.

In order to avoid problems with copyright infringement in the forums with recipe sharing, rules are posted that all participants must read in order to participate. Although not foolproof, a concerted effort is made to make people read the rules that are explained in a very clear, understandable manner. Epicurious also makes a clear distinction between the recipes that are put up by the editors, which are tested and warranted, and those posted in the forums, which Epicurious cannot warrant. User to user information does not go through the editorial process.

Epicurious also offers plenty of opportunity for readers to talk to each other. A number of forums and live chat sessions are available on a variety of topics. Users can discuss great restaurants, swap recipes, discuss wine, or they can even search the forums for previous discussions.

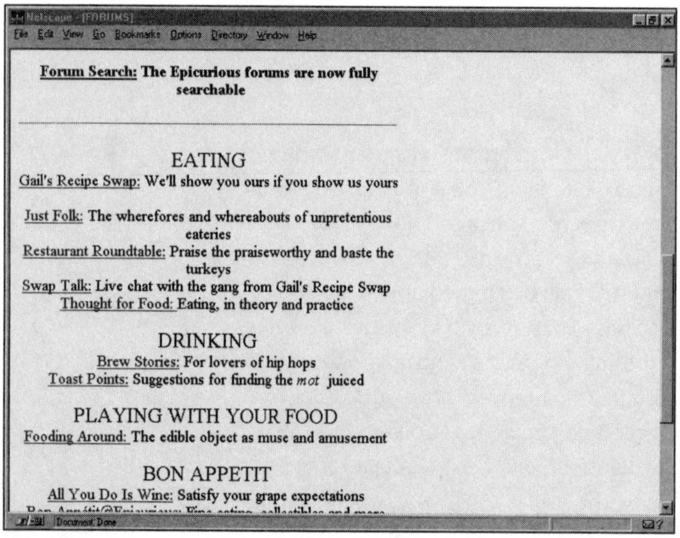

Figure 5-8
Users can participate in a number of discussions about eating and drinking.

BUSINESS/MARKETING MODEL

Feeney tries to link intelligently and amusingly to other sites by using editorial rigor and skill, which is why all of the people she hired to work on the site have journalism backgrounds. The staff is small and works very closely. Most of them came from such publications as *The Wall Street Journal*, the *New York Times*, *Conde Nast Traveler Magazine*, and other magazines. According to Feeney, they all share the ability to think like editors—they know how to package material in a way that makes it meaningful to people.

In terms of managing a budget, the online publication poses particular challenges because it is not a finite medium. In some respects an online product is a living, breathing thing. For example, if you see a mistake, you can correct it immediately. Or if you have a new idea today, you can sometimes implement it within ten hours; consequently, running a business from a cost management standpoint is quite different. Basically, very little precedent exists, and something that is not a finite product is being created on an on-going basis. According to Sarah Chubb, Director of CondeNet, figuring a cost model for producing really good content online is a difficult challenge.

CondeNet is run on a tight budget, but it is not reflected in the quality of the product—something for which Chubb gives the staff a great deal of credit, even though trades often have to be made for budgetary reasons. Also, keeping up with the latest Web technology is an expensive proposition. New technology may come along that wasn't budgeted for six months ago may prove critical for the site. In the online world, a budget can be a very fluid thing.

Epicurious operates from the belief that what a computer user wants differs considerably from what a magazine reader wants, because they are two totally different experiences. Online, people want to be able to search, sort, and customize information. They also appreciate sites that are easily navigable.

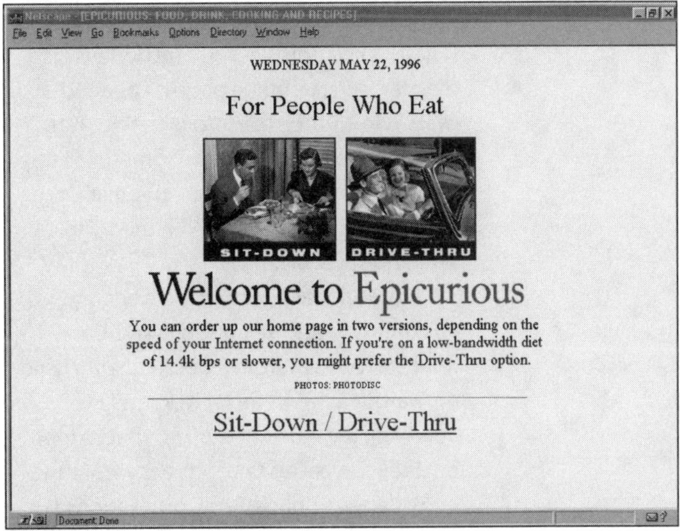

Figure 5-9
Navigation is not a problem at Epicurious—the first page offers the option of full graphics or the quick drive-thru version.

A magazine reader is more passive and expects the editor to tell him or her what to eat, buy, wear, or drink in the current issue. The online publication is user-driven, as opposed to editor-driven, because the user has much more control in the electronic environment. As a result, parts of Epicurious are updated daily to keep readers interested. For example, you can participate in the whimsical daily poll, often a play on words and food experiences, and see the results immediately. Check out the "Word of the Day" plucked from the food dictionary. Also, the menu on the home page is changed every two or three days. Cover stories turn over about once a week and sometimes stay longer if they are particularly popular. Other features are updated as well, although on a less rigid schedule.

Promotional arrangements enable Epicurious to add value to the site. Currently, an excerpt from a book is being used online, but it has been repackaged creatively by the editorial staff, so that it does not look like pages taken directly from the book slapped online. Book promotions are negotiated with both the publisher and the author.

In terms of selling advertising space on Epicurious, a charter program was in effect during the launch to draw in advertisers. Now open rates are available, and at the publishing of this book, they are $7,500 a month for a three month commitment and a banner that will run through the top six traffic areas. For a six month commitment, the price drops to $6,000 a month.

Deeper advertising spots are sold as well along with more custom designed packages. For example, on the recipe database, Robert Mondavi Winery currently has a custom advertising package. When the user prints a recipe from the database, the Robert Mondavi Winery banner appears on the top of the recipe that you take to the store. If the user, while still online, clicks on the Mondavi banner, a little interim area appears about pairing wine with food rather than taking the user directly to the Mondavi site. The interim area enables the winery to do a little more direct advertising. This strategy helps Epicurious close advertising sales, and keeps advertisers happier because the marketing is more targeted.

Although there was some concern that the online site would compete with the print subscriptions of *Bon Appetit* and *Gourmet* magazines, the concern turned out to be unwarranted. In January, the *Bon Appetit* and *Gourmet* areas were added to the Epicurious site with a subscription offer to the publications tucked deep into those sections. Within three months, 1,000 subscriptions were sold. According to Chubb, the cost to acquire a first-time subscriber is usually more than the subscription cost itself; whereas, online, the subscribers were acquired free of charge.

When Epicurious first launched, the division ran print ads in some of the Conde Nast magazines that are mentioned on the site. But most of the attention given to Epicurious happened word-of-mouth. Because the site was both large and content-rich, it found its way onto many "Cool Site" lists.

TECHNOLOGY BACKBONE

Epicurious is in the process of a major re-engineering effort in terms of server hosting and software applications. The recipe forum is created from a fully customized version of HyperNews augmented with the Verity search engine. Live chat comes from a simple, practical, easy-to-use Web chat that was written in-house with C. Farmers' Market was created using simple HTML page building. A team of HTML coders, as well as editors, work with HTML editing tools.

The technical staff at Epicurious are seeking to build sophisticated, personalized applications that provide useful functionality and leverage the site's unique content. Also, they are seeking to strengthen the sense of community with technologies such as Java-based user interfaces/application, more fully-featured forums (personalized to the users), and enhanced chat that enables one-to-one as well as many-to-many communication.

LESSONS LEARNED AND HELPFUL SUGGESTIONS

- Keep in mind at all times what your site is really offering to the online user.
- Make your site easy to navigate.
- Give your online site a distinct voice and personality from your offline publications.
- Create an environment where the technologists, designers, and content providers all work closely together so that the site works as a whole.
- Organize your site so that the user does not feel overwhelmed by the amount of information and links.
- Remember that content and organization is key to a successful Web site.

FUTURE PLANS

Future plans include making Epicurious bigger and better and ultimately creating a site where virtually every interest or curiosity a user could have about food or drink is satisfied. In addition, the staff is looking at agent technology and its potential to offer a more personalized experience for the user. From a revenue-generating standpoint, Epicurious plans to add more custom advertising opportunities for businesses.

CondeNet is just getting into its travel site. It hopes to offer transaction service in the near future, enabling users to book tickets and hotel rooms. The company is also exploring the possibility of charging subscription fees to access certain sections of the site.

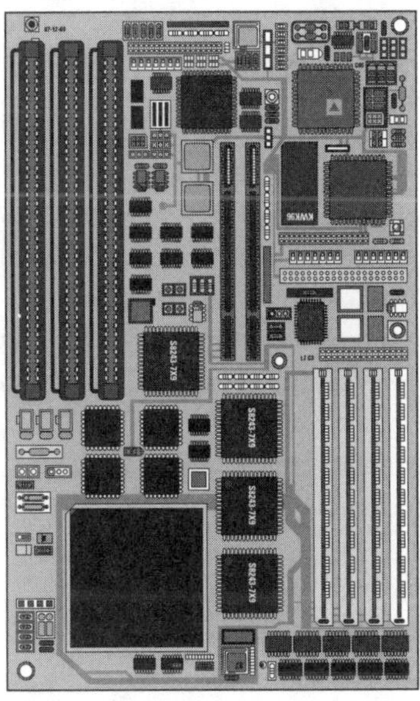

CHAPTER SIX

NEWS DELIVERY AND DIRECTORY SERVICES

In Chapter 5, we looked at some of the outstanding efforts at producing Internet-based publications. This chapter continues in that vein by looking at other ways in which information is being delivered electronically.

We will take a close look at three case studies. The first is C|NET, currently one of the premiere Web publications that has pushed the concept of what a publication is well beyond the limits of well-designed content. Second, we check out Newshare, a company that is developing technology to implement new models for buying and selling news and information. The third case study we spotlight is BigBook, an Internet business that has expanded the traditional yellow pages directory concept to embrace new technologies for finding information.

C|NET (**www.cnet.com**) represents one of the strongest examples of a growing number of publishing companies that is attempting to weave together publishing and broadcast information services by using a combination of print and electronic media.

In the case of C|NET, the combination includes a weekly TV show called "C|NET Central" and the C|NET Web site, C|NET Online. Both TV program and Web site provide featured information about the computer industry and Internet development. In its own words, C|NET is "an integrated information source devoted to computers, multimedia, online services, and the ongoing digital revolution."

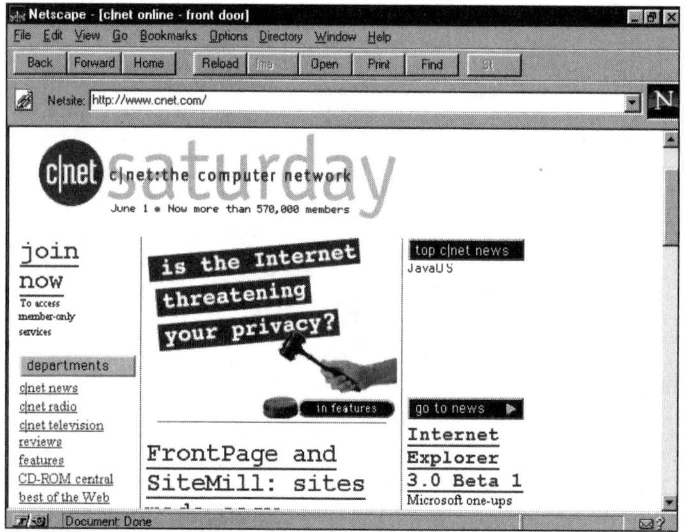

Figure 6-1
C|NET's home page.

C|NET Online is a superb example of a second-generation, content-based Web site. Rich in dynamic media content, and elegantly designed with ample doses of multimedia, C|NET demonstrates a sophisticated understanding both of Net technologies and of user expectations. Currently C|NET has three parallel Web sites (with more planned): C|NET Online (**www.cnet.com**), Shareware.com (**www.shareware.com**) and Search.com (**www.search.com**).

COMPANY BACKGROUND

Currently, the C|NET-produced weekly television show, "C|NET Central," is seen on the USA Network, the Sci-Fi Channel, and KPIX-5, the CBS television affiliate in San Francisco, California. It is hosted by Richard Hart and Gina St. John.

According to the C|NET press releases:

"The half-hour program is filled with in-depth features, multimedia reviews, stories about the Internet and on-line services, and demonstrations of compelling real-world uses of digital technologies. C|NET central is uniquely tied to C|NET Online; each story featured on the television program is expanded in greater detail online, where viewers can access additional information and resources on every topic."

C|NET Online, officically launched on June 24, 1995, has rapidly made a name for itself as one of the fastest-growing communities on the Internet. C|NET Online was initially developed in only two months, a

C|NET At-a-Glance

THE PRODUCT	C|NET Online, Search.com, Shareware.com
URL	www.cnet.com
THE COMPANY	C|NET
OWNER	Jonathon Rosenberg
THE CUSTOMERS	computer users, especially those interested in the Internet; watchers of the C|NET TV program
START DATE	June 24, 1995 (initial development was completed in only 2 months)
LESSONS LEARNED	Had to face numerous low level O/S specific bottlenecks; tuned low level TCP/IP parameters like MTU size to optimize performance
SOFTWARE/HARDWARE	4 multi-processor SunSparc20s, Solaris 2.4, Netscape Communication Server, Listserv for NT from LSoft
SUBSCRIBERS	300,000 users on mailing list, "Digital Dispatch"

remarkably short period of time considering the complexity of the project. And as of this writing, C|NET claims more than 500,000 registered users.

In addition to C|NET Online, C|NET: The Computer Network also produces Shareware.com, a software library boasting more than 210,000 titles from both public and corporate archives; and Search.com, a collection of Internet links to more than 250 Web search engines and databases.

PRODUCT DESCRIPTION

C|NET Online is an extensive undertaking, offering more than 30,000 pages of original Internet-only content, much of which is updated on a daily or weekly basis. It is a free, advertiser-supported service, and although C|NET encourages users to complete a brief registratration form, registration is entirely voluntary. C|NET's focus is community news and information. Its home page looks like a magazine, and it has daily updated news stories, weekly features, and reviews.

In addition, C|NET provides a wealth of functional services. The two most prominent of which are Search.com, an Internet metasearch engine, and Shareware.com, a database of shareware software available on the Internet. Other functions include hot deals, posting and polling for members, a computer industry product finder, and a "Best of the Web" review of over 350 top Web sites.

Figure 6-2
C|NET's Product Finder.

PRODUCT FEATURES/BENEFITS

C|NET online is composed of five major sections: "Departments," which contains the news and information content; "Resources," which provides software and technical directories and a glossary; "Search Services," which features C|NET's two additional sites: Search.com and Shareware.com; "Community," where members can partipate in online discussion forums or take part in polls; and "Marketplace," which offers hot deals and a list of C|NET sponsors.

DEPARTMENTS

Departments is the principal content section of the C|NET site. It consists of computer industry news that is updated throughout the day; "C|NET radio," informative audio broadcasts using RealAudio; schedules and information drawn from "C|NET Central;" as well as a wide variety of feature articles and reviews. A Personalities section provides columns from well-known industry writers, including Christopher Barr, Robert Seidman, Raphael Needleman, and John C. Dvorak.

In addition, there are several specialized departments including:

- CD-ROM Central, an informational guide to CD-ROM software
- GameCenter, the place to find out about the latest in computer games, unofficial game hints, and game industry news
- Product Finder, an extensive database of computer products and vendors
- Best of the Web, a frequently updated collection of reviews of the top Web sites

One personal favorite is the PC Comparative Review section, which features four different interfaces to help consumers identify the PC hardware appropriate for their particular needs. The most impressive of the four is a Java-based application that asks consumers to rank the importance of various consumer criteria, (price, performance, service, and so on) and then produces a scatter chart of the systems that best matches these requirements. As of this writing, there are 50 PCs included in the reviews.

SEARCH SERVICES

This section of the C|NET site contains the two recently acquired, technology-based sites, Search.com and Shareware.com. Search.com advertises "over 250 ways to search the Net." It provides direct links to a wide variety of general purpose and specialized search tools and directories, and is composed of multiple CGI scripts, one for each of the search engines that Search.com queries.

Shareware.com is the place to go to search for, browse, and download software available on the Internet—including freeware, shareware, demos, fixes, patches, and upgrades.

Shareware.com has no files at its own location; rather, it serves as a global metaindex of the FTP sites where specific software is located. Shareware.com has a search facility that allows you to locate the software package you are looking for via keywords. This alone puts it a couple of notches above the many excellent repositories of software that are either bare FTP sites or have FTP sites accessible through the Web but without keyword-based indexing.

In addition, Shareware.com rates the FTP sites. When you choose to download a piece of software, Shareware.com gives you a list of sites where the software is available, accompanied by a reliability rating that tells you which sites are the best to try.

C|NET also participates in an effort to standardize FTP archiving called "VSL" or "Virtual Software Library." At present, a standard format for desribing the contents of an FTP archive does not exist—those who maintain FTP archives have their own, different formats for describing the files they have. VSL, by standardizing the format, also makes it possible to search across FTP sites more simply.

RESOURCES

The Resources section of C|NET features several directories of information. There is Software Central, which, in addition to being a pointer to Shareware.com, contains informative guides and directories related to the task of obtaining software online. Info Source boasts information on over 100 vendors of computer-related hardware, soft-

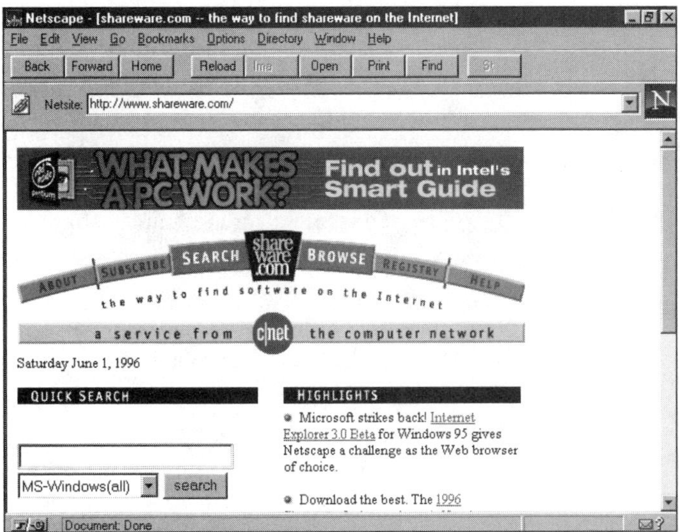

Figure 6-3
Finding shareware on the Internet can hardly get any easier than this.

ware, and peripherals, as well as an Internet resources guide. In Tech Central, you can find links to facts and FAQs on technical issues. Also quite useful is a virtual phone tree for locating contact numbers for hardware and software vendors. Other resources in this section include the Tech Advisor, which provides much needed Internet strategies as well as a glossary of Internet terms to aid the neophyte Web surfer.

COMMUNITY

The C|NET Community section provides information about C|NET—such as how to use it—and a description of the various services it offers its members. For a large site, C|NET is remarkably low-key about tooting its own horn. The About C|NET section is limited to a list of press releases and a brief corporate profile. You can get a live-action picture of C|NET by visiting the Studio Cam page, which is produced using a Sony 8mm video camera connected to a Macintosh running Shutterbug, an inexpensive shareware video capture application. One interesting feature of this section is a RealAudio tour of the entire site with your choice of tour guides—Brian Cooley, Gina St. John, or Richard Hart.

The heart of the Community section is made up of areas for *posting* and *polling.* Posting is a bulletin-board-like discussion forum, where users can communicate with one another or with the forum moderator. Polling features a new reader survey question every week or so, with members-only voting (though anyone can check out the current survey standings).

MARKETPLACE

The C|NET Marketplace is the one section of this site that is somewhat disappointing. Essentially, a showcase for C|NET advertisors, Marketplace contains two links, one to weekly updated "hot deals" from the sponsors, and the other to a page of information about the sponsoring companies themselves.

BUSINESS/MARKETING MODEL

The C|NET Web site operates as both an adjunct to "C|NET Central" and as a publishing enterprise. You can find information about the TV program in the C|NET TV section of the site, but there is also a wealth of information and a number of services aimed at both novice and experienced Internet users at the site as well.

Advertising is the main source of revenue for C|NET's Web site. Advertisers, also called sponsors of the site, are given a standard ad banner space on C|NET Web pages, which are linked to additional advertiser information and Web sites. C|NET is also moving toward offering advertisers the opportunity to conduct online sales transactions, of which C|NET would receive a commission on the transaction.

At the moment, sales opportunities are limited to the "hot buys" section of the site, which features discounted prices on selected sponsor merchandise.

TECHNOLOGY BACKBONE

All three of the current C|NET sites, C|NET Online, Search.com, and Shareware.com, are built on the same basic architecture. This consists of a network of four multiprocessor Sun SPARC 20s running Solaris 2.4 and a Netscape Communication Server. All three sites together serve an average of 1.3 million pages per day, 500,000 of which are served from the main site.

Much of C|NET's success may be attributed to its committment to maintaining a cutting-edge site. It has done this partly through the acquisition of technology, such as Shareware.com, as well as through the introduction of technology-based features, such as Search.com. Another prominent example of C|NET's technological innovation is its weekly newsletter, Digital Dispatch, which is e-mailed to registered users. Useful examples of Java programming are also beginning to appear on the site. In short, C|NET continues to demonstrate a command of Internet technologies as well as report on them.

C|NET CENTRAL

The initial site, which went online in June of 1995, was implemented in only two months—exceptionally fast for such a complex site. According to Jonathan Rosenberg, Vice President of Engineering at C|NET, the main reason for the ultra-fast implementation was that all of the principal developers already had substantial Internet expertise coming into the project. Although, they found they had to overcome a number of bottlenecks at the TCP/IP and operating system level.

In addition to the basic Web server environment, C|NET also operates a commercial Listserv application that is used to deliver Digital Dispatch, the e-mail-based newsletter. The Listserv application is developed and sold by LSoft and operates on a Windows NT platform. Digital Dispatch has a weekly distribution of 300,000, and C|NET's Listserv sends e-mail to the entire list within approximately two hours.

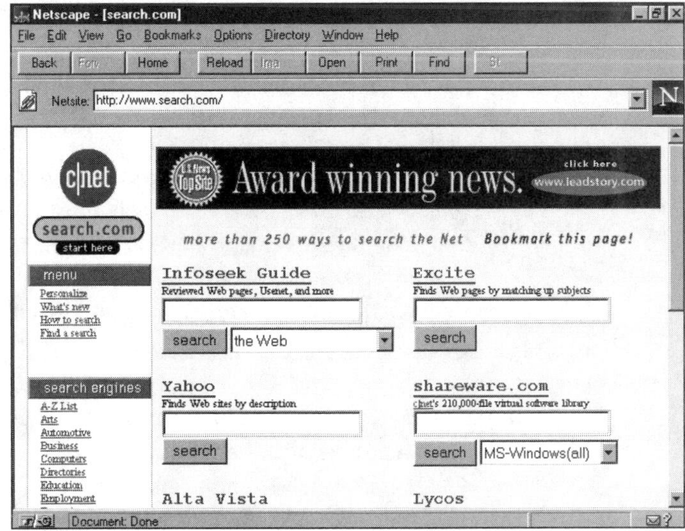

Figure 6-4
Search.com links to more than 250 Internet directories and search engines.

ELECTRONIC NEWS DELIVERY

Two elements distinguish electronic delivery of news and information from more traditional channels: personalization and incremental charges.

"Personalized" news generally means the news you read is pre-filtered based on criteria you have selected. At the moment most of the personalization services are unintelligent, meaning they do not analyze your preferences, but simply process them in a literal fashion. If you say that you are interested in rhinoceroses, the service sends any article that includes the world *rhinoceros*. It does not infer from your interest that you may want to read about other large animals in Africa. An example of an intelligent filtering agent would be one that asked questions to identify yourself demographically and then sent you targeted content appropriate to your demographic group.

The most common delivery mechanism for personalized news and information is e-mail. Such services draw its news from any of a number of newsfeeds or newswires and then filter and compose an e-mail newsletter. Alternative delivery mechanisms include fax-based personalized news and Web sites that provide online search engines to information.

One issue related to the development of a news delivery site involves the aggregation and distribution models used. Many information-based services still derive their content through established, non-network mechanisms. It is highly possible, however, to allow contributors to place content online with a minimal amount of effort on the part of the editorial staff. Allowing online contributions, however, always introduces questions of quality and control of the content.

If content acquisition is more smooth in the online environment, charging for content is somewhat thornier. At the moment, most of the information available on the Internet is free. Some sources charge a membership or subscription rate, usually to users who wish to take advantage of special features. Other sources, such as Newshare (see the Newshare spotlight that follows) are set up to work on an incremental charge basis.

Content management is performed using a proprietary infrastructure called PRISM, built by C|NET engineers over a period of five to six months. PRISM allows both dynamic and static content to be dealt with in a common framework. It has been used since the latest revision of the site, at the beginning of 1996.

SEARCH.COM AND SHAREWARE.COM

Search.com performs a metasearch of serveral of the major Internet search engines. It is composed of multiple CGI scripts, one for each of the search engines that Search.com queries. The site was built using proprietary tools and took two months to complete.

Created and developed by Dr. Ziga Turk, a professor at the University of Ljubljana in Slovenia, Shareware.com's Virtual Software Library was purchased by C|NET. Dr. Turk now works with C|NET and is part of the effort to create a standardized format for content submission from sites hosting shareware.

FUTURE PLANS

C|NET will undoubtedly continue to do what it has done so well to date, namely:

- Effectively meld reviews, information, and how-to guides with feature-based writing
- Extend its feature set with new technologies, such as Search.com and Shareware.com
- Reinforce its multimedia position by combining TV broadcasting and online publishing models
- Solidify its community approach with services such as Digital Dispatch as well as with features like the posting and polling sections.

Recently, C|NET and the San Francisco-based syndicator, Golden Gate Productions, announced a partnership to produce a new TV show to attract those hungry for Internet information. Dubbed TV.COM, this weekly series will also have its own Web site (**www.tv.com**) that will feature information from the show, and provide users with opportunities for communication and interactivity.

Currently, Newshare (**www.newshare.com**) is forming an online syndicate of content providers to market general interest news and advertising directly to consumers. Content providers will retain editorial and pricing control over the information they submit, although they will be required to uphold certain quality guidelines. Newshare is also seeking to form a coalition of non-traditional news sources from across the country, including freelance writers, Internet newsgroups, and small news organizations. By combining content from a wide range of sources, members of Newshare will be able to offer their customers a breadth and depth of information that is not always economically feasible today.

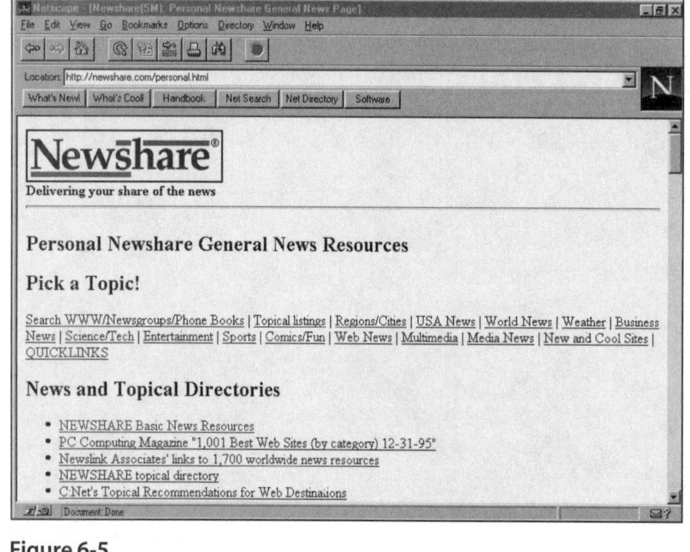

Figure 6-5
Newshare's home page.

COMPANY BACKGROUND

Newshare was co-founded in 1994 by Bill Densmore, Bernard Re Jr., and David M. Oliver, who envisioned Newshare as the Internet's first news brokerage service. Newshare is still in its formative stages; it has been a goal of Densmore's for many years. Back in 1979 Densmore had the original idea of bringing a variety of news sources together to create an electronic medium through which everyone would get their information, as opposed to the more traditional paper channels. But the vision did not come together until Oliver and another partner, Michael Callahan, brought the technology behind Newshare, Clickshare, to the table. Now with the right technology in place the group seeks to actively build a market for independent and small publishers and their customers.

PRODUCT DESCRIPTION

Newshare is a nationwide brokerage for the electronic distribution of time-sensitive news and information. Individual publishers and content providers contribute information, which is then resold by other members directly to consumers, who use technology provided by Newshare to select their own specific news topics. Newshare enables members to provide personalized news electronically rather than via traditional print distribution channels.

PRODUCT FEATURES/BENEFITS

Newshare offers small and non-traditional content providers a recognizable brand name to use when selling information. In the ever-expanding Internet world, where anyone can claim to be an expert, brand names will become an important part of getting and keeping news consumers. By enabling smaller organizations to band together, Newshare enables them to reach a larger market than they could have on their own. And consumers get a high-quality source of regional, national, international, and topic specific news tailored to their individual tastes.

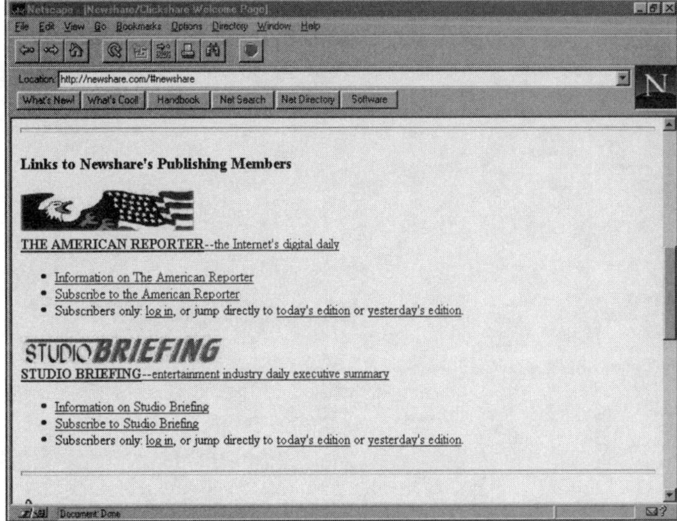

Figure 6-6

Newshare is currently conducting a pilot with two publishing members, The American Reporter and Studio BRIEFING.

BUSINESS/MARKETING MODEL

As Newshare is a news brokerage, independent content providers are paid when they contribute news and information, and charged when they resell information provided by other content providers. Newshare expects that it will be the primary distribution channel for its members, although not necessarily their exclusive outlet. Members are granted a geographic or topic area franchise when they join Newshare so that they are not competing directly against one other.

Also, content providers are responsible for all of their marketing and sales. Newshare does not directly market to consumers. The individual content providers are responsible for signing up customers, but are able to use the Newshare brand in their marketing. The bartering nature of the business model enables content providers to gain access to all of the customers signed up by every other member, even though they only need to manage and be responsible for their own customer accounts.

TECHNOLOGY BACKBONE

The Newshare concept relies on a technology called Clickshare. Clickshare is the system that makes it economically feasible for publishers to form online syndicates to package and resell information that resides on different servers scattered about the Web. Clickshare enables publishers to embed links to information on other Clickshare-enabled servers and track usage of the links.

Both the publisher providing the link and the ultimate provider of the information get paid when a user accesses information. The publisher sets the price for each piece of information accessed by its users, including information stored on other

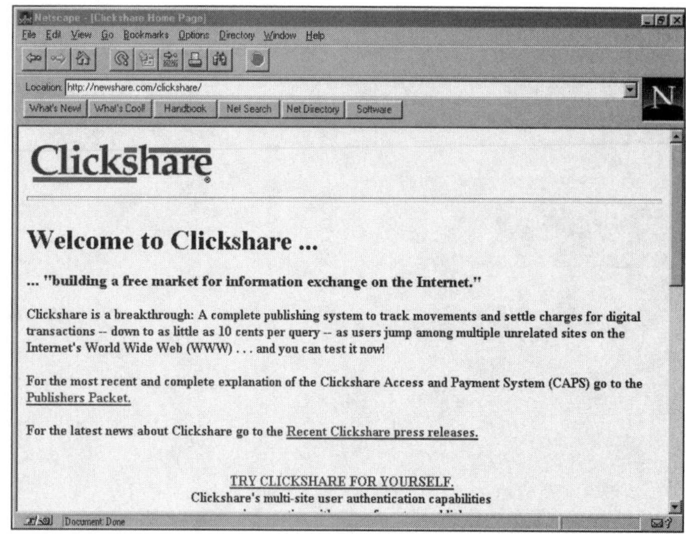

Figure 6-7
Clickshare also tracks accesses to links on the publisher's server.

servers. A publisher is charged for each access its users make to other servers, so most publishers charge a slight premium when its users access other servers. This need not be the case though. Publishers could make links free and rely on subscription and advertising revenue.

Publishers can, however, establish multiple pricing directories on their Web server, grouping similarly-priced content within directories. Theoretically, the Clickshare technology permits dozens of pricing directories. These directories are termed *value classes.* Items within a given value class can have different absolute prices to different end-users, depending on the pricing philosophy of the entity that owns the user's credit relationship. For example, one user might pick an article in Pricing Directory One on the foobar.com server and pay 10 cents for that article. The very next user may pay nothing for the same article, because his Clickshare Service Provider (the entity billing the user) offers access to Clickshare content for a flat, monthly subscription. A third user acquiring the same article may pay 15 cents, because her Clickshare service provider adds a 50 percent retail markup to information it sells.

Think of the Clickshare technology, which drives the Newshare business model, as a wholesale-retail distribution model. The content owner etablishes a wholesale information price, but the end user pays whatever his or her retailer charges for that information.

The customer relationship is completely controlled by the publisher who uses the Clickshare technology. User accounts are set up by each publisher, and each publisher is responsible for creating, updating, and canceling user accounts. No central administration of user accounts exists, so no large database of users and the information they have accessed is available. The central billing database tracks only user account numbers with no demographics attached, the URLs that have been accessed , and other information needed to bill users.

Every Clickshare user can purchase information from any Clickshare-enabled server, regardless of which publisher actually "owns" that user. This enables publishers to sell information all Clickshare users, even though that publisher may have had no prior contact with those users. By eliminating the need for each publisher to track all users, a significant roadblock to mass distribution of information is removed.

At regular intervals, every Clickshare-enabled publisher is billed for the accesses its users have made to other servers. Clickshare acts as a billing clearinghouse for all publishers who use the Clickshare technology. The Automated Clearing House (ACH) network, an electronic-funds transfer network maintained by U.S. banks that functions worldwide, is used to electronically debit and credit publishers for the purchase and sale of information. A publisher, paid by Clickshare for the sale of articles, finds an electronic ACH credit in the appropriately designated bank account. This process makes the system far more efficient. If a publisher's users access other servers more often than other users access the publisher's server, then the publisher will owe money to Clickshare.

The opposite is also true. If a publisher's site is accessed more often than its users access other sites, then the publisher receives an ACH credit. Essentially, each publisher is responsible for billing its own users, and Clickshare provides each publisher with enough information to do so. Because this information is provided periodically, information providers do not necessarily get paid immediately for accesses to their site.

The moment a piece of information is sold in real-time by a vending publisher, Clickshare assumes a responsibility to pay that publisher the wholesale price of that content. First, Clickshare must charge, through the ACH debit, the Clickshare Service Provider or the Publishing Member who "owns" the end user who purchased the information. This could be a maximum of 30 days after the purchase. Newshare's intention is not to "play the float." It also pays the vending publisher at that same settlement. Eventually, the system will have to move to more frequent settlements—daily or several times daily as the volume increases.

With Clickshare, users are able to buy information from any Clickshare-enabled server without needing to provide a different account and password at each site. The validation is performed by the Clickshare Authentication and Logging Service (CALS) of authentication servers. The request to authenticate a user comes from the vending publisher's Clickshare Web Server daemon, but the answer comes from Clickshare's backend technology.

Clickshare does not require the user to install special software to participate; however, Clickshare publishers must run the Clickshare Web server software, which provides a real-time connection to the Clickshare Authentication and Logging Service.

LESSONS LEARNED

- Promote your concept openly because that is what the Internet community expects.
- Seek to collaborate.
- Articulate your value to consumers clearly and concisely. Don't focus on competition, because it moves too fast to track. Focus on getting to market.
- Design technology in service of a vision or market need. Don't rely on proprietary or patented technology. It just invites competition to find a way around you and marginalize you. Avoid setting dates for delivery of a system until the system is running.

FUTURE PLANS

Newshare was put on hold while the Clickshare product continues to be developed and marketed. Although Clickshare is owned by a separate company, Newshare is dependent upon the Clickshare technology. Newshare will proceed with enrolling publishers as Clickshare becomes established in the marketplace.

Information Directories

Information on the Internet suffers from two key problems: there is far too much of it, and most of it is of appallingly low quality. Users desperately need to have some way to separate useful from useless information and to find what they want quickly.

Which is where the Internet information directories come in. These directories, which typically comprise both a search engine and some kind of indexing scheme, occupy some of the highest profile positions on the Internet today. Names like Yahoo!, Lycos, WebCrawler, and right behind them, Excite, AltaVista, Infoseek, and Magellan, are well known by even casual users of the Internet.

Some of these information directories have built themselves around the yellow pages model, both structurally and in terms of a business model. The following section examines BigBook, a recent arrival on the information directory scene that fits into that category.

BigBook, Inc., (**www.bigbook.com**) is giving the phone companies a run for their money by creating an information directory online that is more informative and user-friendly than the existing Yellow Pages. The directory covers more than 11 million U.S. businesses and offers much more than just providing a category heading followed by a list of businesses and their phone numbers. BigBook employs the full interactive nature of the Web to offer more detailed information about businesses, including maps of their locations, and other value-added information for the consumer.

The fast-growing company officially opened its doors on December 1, 1995, with just a few employees. Within six months it grew to 42 employees and plans to continue to add staff at a rate of five to seven per month in the immediate future.

Figure 6-8
BigBook provides comprehensive coverage of 11 million U.S. businesses.

COMPANY BACKGROUND

Kris Hagerman, the mastermind behind BigBook, first got the idea for the online directory while working as a Silicon Graphics project manager for WebForce, a family of computer systems devoted exclusively to helping companies get onto the World Wide Web. Hagerman was trying to convince telephone companies to use SGI machines for their Web servers. Unable to convince them, he decided to launch his own free competitor to the traditional yellow pages print product. Fortunately, his former employer agreed help Hagerman by donating the server hardware for BigBook.

The company is primarily funded with $1 million of seed captial from New Enterprise Associates (NEA), which is headquartered in Baltimore, Maryland, and has a remote office in Menlo Park, California. NEA has taken a number of prominent information companies, such as Silicon Graphics, public over the last several years. BigBook also received more than $750,000 worth of computer systems from Silicon Graphics of Mountain View, California, and database software from Informix of Menlo Park.

PRODUCT DESCRIPTION

Users of the traditional yellow pages may often get frustrated when they try to find a local vendor to provide a service or a product. Usually, under a general topic description such as "pizza," numerous business are listed. Using quality and proximity as basic criteria, consumers often have difficulty deciding which one to choose. This process can be particularly troublesome if you are from out-of-town.

BigBook's solution is to offer more useful business information. For example, if you are in Columbus, Ohio on business, and you want to order a pizza, you can use the Quick Search option in BigBook to find the closest Pizza Hut to your hotel. Simply enter "Pizza Hut, Columbus, Ohio," and the zip code of the hotel to find the closest location.

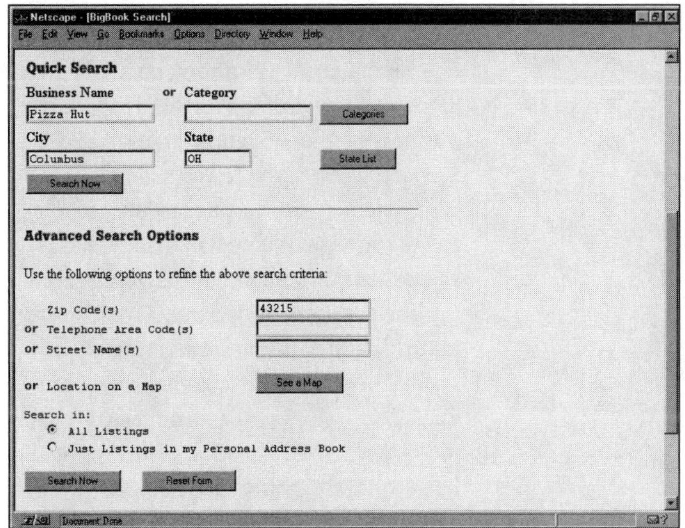

Figure 6-9
If you are out of town, you can use the Quick Search feature to find the closest Pizza Hut to your hotel.

The company combines a comprehensive U.S. business database with nationwide, street-level maps to provide users with a simple, graphical way to find the location of any business in the U.S. Also, users have the option of starting with a map of any U.S. city or neighborhood, zooming in or out until they have defined the area they want, and then searching that area for the types of businesses of most interest.

BigBook benefits businesses because the directory can provide more detailed information about a business's products and services without charging a fee. In addition, BigBook builds basic informational Web pages free of charge, so that businesses that are intimidated by the expense and difficulty of establishing a Web presence, can gain entry into the online world via BigBook.

Consumers benefit from BigBook because they can access more detailed information about businesses, and therefore make more informed choices. Once the consumer selects a vendor, he or she can view a map of the business location and determine if it is close enough or not. The user also can read third-party reviews from professional publishers and view the business rating determined by votes from fellow consumers.

PRODUCT FEATURES AND BENEFITS

With BigBook, users may enter the businesses they contact frequently into a Personal Address Book. BigBook is designed to be a personalized yellow pages—users can continually add or delete businesses at will.

In addition, non-biased third-party reviews of restaurants and hotels, and recommendations on shopping, entertainment, and points of interest are provided by business partners, Gayot Publications and Sasquatch Books.

Customers can participate in the interactive consumer forum where they can share their opinions about the businesses listed in the BigBook directory. They can also participate in BigBook's rating system—a scale of one to five for three variables: price, quality, and whether they would recommend the business to others. To encourage fair results, BigBook requires users to register before voting. Each user is permitted one vote per business, but they may change their vote as often as they like.

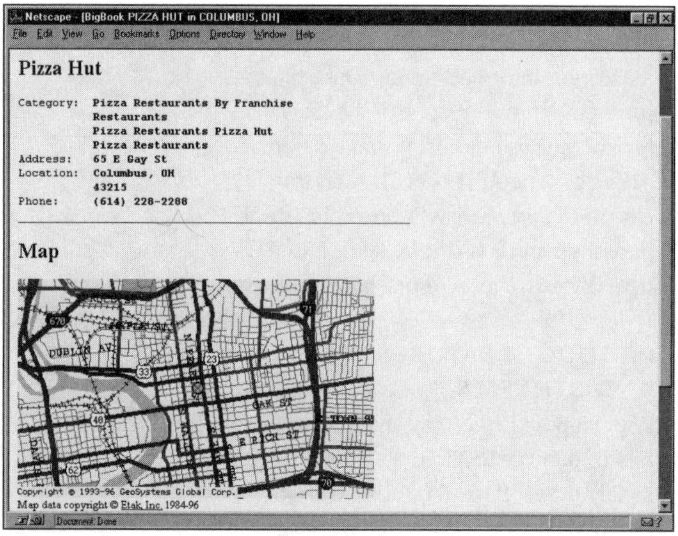

Figure 6-10
BigBook quickly locates the business you are searching for and provides a proximity map.

Businesses can update, modify, and enhance their Web page at any time, at no cost. They can even add audio clips that announce special features and prices by simply calling in and recording over the telephone the promotional message. The free audio message is automatically linked to their home page.

Custom settings enable users to conduct fast searches because BigBook automatically fills in the information each time they begin a new search. If a business already has a Web site, BigBook provides a free link to the site that will help attract more traffic. It also offers an e-mail feature for customer feedback.

BUSINESS/MARKETING MODEL

In order to produce a quality service, Hagerman worked to build both a strong engineering team and a strong business team. Also, the staff makes a concerted effort to listen to consumers to keep BigBook as user-friendly as possible.

Most of the 11 million companies listed in the BigBook directory were licensed from Database America. BigBook took the data and did a merge and purge to eliminate the duplicates, reclassify the businesses, and make sure that the data was as current and as accurate as possible. From there, it added new business classifications, added additional businesses, and added more content using GeoSystems' mapping software and Etak's digital map data.

With the existing data available from Database America, home pages were easily created for each of the businesses. In order to include other value-added information, special permission from each of the businesses is necessary, which is something the staff at BigBook is presently working on. An open invitation has been extended to the more than 11 million businesses in the database to update their information, provide current hours, list accreditations, and give directions. To make the process simple, businesses can either go directly to the BigBook Web site and fill in the form online or fax it back.

After businesses update their Web page, BigBook validates the information with them. In the future, BigBook plans to use a registration process and account numbers, so that it can be certain the information really is coming from the appropriate business entity and not someone else providing bogus information.

Competitors of BigBook are primarily the big phone companies; however, their models are significantly different. According to the staff at BigBook, the phone companies are basically building their online efforts around taking the content that they already have in the yellow pages and putting the information online. If a business wants to add information beyond just a straight line listing, it costs the business money. In contrast, BigBook is giving businesses an opportunity to offer much more information at no charge.

Revenue for BigBook is generated primarily by national advertising and banner advertising online. It sells banner ads on a cost per 1000 basis—the advertiser pays *x* dollars per 1000 users per 1000 people that see that banner. Basically, BigBook offers two kinds of ads: a general impression ad that is less targeted, which is what you see if you are in a general area (such as checking out your personal address book, registering, or looking at voting results); and a targeted ad, which you see if you conduct a specific search.

For example, if you did a search on hotels in the San Francisco area, you might see a Hilton ad banner on the search results page. Advertisers like the targeted ad banners because they cut through the clutter and reach desired audiences, as opposed to advertising on a popular search engine and hoping that a certain percentage of people will be looking for that particular product.

Because BigBook is a free service, businesses have to take responsibility for keeping their site updated; however, the company sends out quarterly reminders to remind them to do so.

BigBook requires personal information of its users so that it can maintain quality control, but the company policy is to never release the information for any reason.

In order to capture the market mindshare, BigBook has made an effort in the online world to let people know that it is out there. Also, Web users and key influencers on the Net have responded very positively to BigBook, the little upstart trying to go up against the phone company giants. There are plans in place for broader marketing programs that involve advertising on the

Net, and, very shortly, advertising in the real world through more traditional channels.

BigBook boasts some powerful business partners. Informix Software gave the company some of its cutting-edge relational database technology and also provides technical support in exchange for minority equity share. Because BigBook is performing some cutting-edge relational database management, it also functions in a loose sense as a premier research and development test center for Informix. BigBook also has strategic partnerships with Organic Online, which has developed Web sites for companies including Levi Strauss, MCI, and Saturn. Organic Online functions somewhat like a big brother to BigBook by sharing office space and helping the growing company with some of its engineering work.

Other business partners have an equity interest in BigBook in exchange for their contributions. The mapping software is provided by GeoSystems and the mapping data comes from Etak. All of the database information comes from Database America. Connect, Inc. and Progressive Networks provide the voice information systems and audio capabilities. Other business alliances that add value to BigBook include Yo Design (intuitive architecture and user interface design), John Grimes (cartoonist, humorist, illustrator), Gayot Publications (provider of reviews of restaurants, hotels, shopping, and points of interest in major U.S. cities) and Sasquatch Books (guides for restaurants, lodging, and touring in the Pacific Northwest).

TECHNOLOGY BACKBONE

Two T-1 lines come into BigBook, so it has plenty of bandwidth—the site is capable of shipping 3.0 megabits per second of information. BigBook uses Informix Software's Universal Server technology as its database of choice. GeoSystems provides the mapping software, and Silicon Graphics provides the computer systems.

FUTURE PLANS

In the future, as more and more people conduct proximity searches, BigBook hopes more opportunities will arise to overlay other kinds of databases, so that it can target users geographically, by business category, and psychographically (targeting based on lifestyle). For example, if BigBook can track a user conducting a search based on zip code and street address and note the "lifestyle neighborhood," an advertising banner can be served up that is much more targeted to the user's needs and wants.

By mid-1996, BigBook plans to cover businesses in Canada and Mexico and expand to Asia, Europe, and South America by the latter part of 1996 and 1997. BigBook also intends to develop a Custom Directory that users can build, enabling users to choose particular cities, neighborhoods, and even city blocks to search every time they access the site.

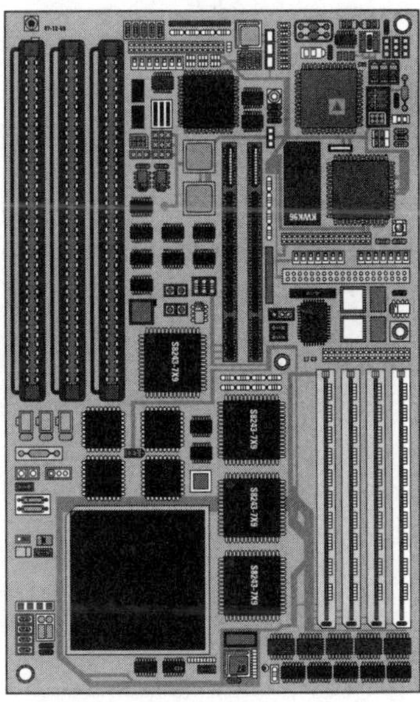

CHAPTER SEVEN

JOINING THE PUBLISHING REVOLUTION

More than a decade ago, the appearance of desktop publishing tools made it possible for small companies and individuals who could never have afforded to use professional equipment to publish and sell information. Desktop publishing tools have not necessarily "democratized" the publishing industry, but they have made it possible for a new publishing entity to spring to life with a smaller initial outlay of capital: a large percentage of the desktop publishing work done today is probably generated by corporate marketing communications departments. Desktop publishing has allowed businesses to publish *more*—and to publish a wider variety of messages to smaller demographic groups.

Similar things are happening in the online publishing world as a result of the introduction of the World Wide Web. There has been much discussion of how the Web allows "little people" to publish. Anybody who can afford an Internet account that provides Web space and who takes the time to learn some basic HTML can be a publisher, evidenced by the exploding number of small publications, mostly of the e-zine type, available on the Internet. But unlike desktop publishing, Internet publishing comes with a built-in distribution mechanism—all the individual publishers have to do is entice readers to their sites.

This new influx of "information" has several consequences:

- It increases the overall quantity of information. One of the first things any new user experiences on the Internet (after the frustration of slow or broken connections and the rush of globe-trotting at the click of a hyperlink subsides) is the overwhelming sense of information glut. How can you possibly tell what you want without weeding through a morass of outdated, irrelevant, or trivial verbiage?
- It decreases the overall quality of information. This is not to say that a big budget guarantees high quality information, but a big budget does at least force potential publishers to take into account how many people are likely to find the information useful or entertaining.
- It encourages an expectation that information should be free. Since this is a frequent observation about Internet publishing, it is worth noting that the Internet did not create this expectation. It inherited it from existing mass media, largely from television and the print media, which are principally driven by advertising. With this in mind, perhaps it would be more accurate to say that on the Internet there is an expectation that the cost of information should be underwritten by someone else, whether advertisers or the authors of the information themselves.
- It encourages an expectation that information should be fresh. Internet users crave current information. Partly this may be because Internet users in general hunger for what is new. Mostly though, this is the result of a desire to know that the information is still pertinent, given the accelerated rate of change brought about by the Internet.

These factors are unlikely to change in the near future. There will always be free information on the Internet, much of it created and maintained by vigilant individuals—those information shepherds in cyberspace.

These same factors also create the conditions that will enable revenue to be generated from publishing. The ability to provide high quality, user-customized information in an easily digestible form will command a premium price, as will up-to-the-second reporting.

The Basics

Since 1995, more than 3,000 publications have appeared on the Internet scene. Many of these, particularly in recent months, were derived from existing media in the print world.

These publishing efforts can be classified according to the publishing model they exhibit.

NEWS MAGAZINES The magazine is, at the moment, the most common publication model in evidence on the Net. The news magazines focus on presenting current news on either general or more specialized topics. Those that offer daily updated news resemble more a newspaper than a magazine, particularly when the information is obtained from a news feed source, which typically contains no graphics or other multimedia content.

The other major variation of this publishing model is the weekly magazine, which is usually divided into departments—feature articles, commentary, regular columns, and so on—that change on a weekly basis. In contrast to the e-zine which we discuss next, the emphasis of the news magazine is still on news and information for some target audience.

News magazines are often leveraged from (and in turn used to promote) existing news sources. When this is not the case, the magazine is typically constructed from a variety of third-party electronic news feeds.

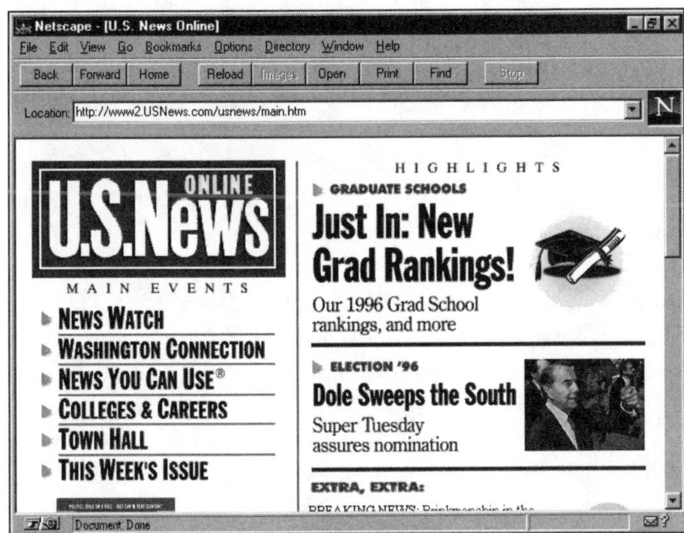

Figure 7-1
Home page from a typical news magazine.

THE E-ZINE Generally speaking, the term "e-zine," short for electronic magazine, may be used to refer to any electronic publication. In point of fact, though, "zines" are more community-oriented than news publications. A zine may provide information, but it does so within a more interactive context. The point of a zine is to cultivate audience identification with the zine, and to create a place where the target audience can meet and talk as well as read. As a result, zines (for better or for worse) tend to pay more attention to their own style than do the news publications.

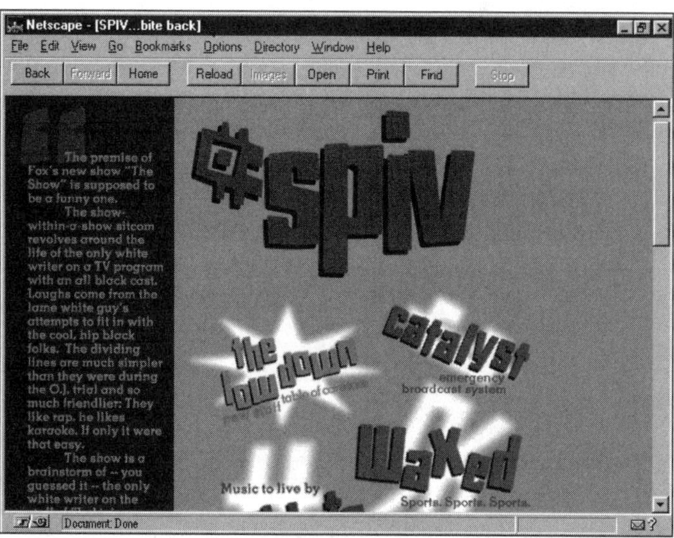

Figure 7-2
Home page from Spiv, a not-so-typical e-zine.

NEWS DELIVERY SERVICES News magazines and e-zines are typically not delivered to you. In order to read them, you have to seek them out by visiting their Web sites. This is fine if you are the kind who prefers to go looking for information when you want it.

There are times, however, when it would be more convenient to have the news delivered to you. That is the focus of the services in this category. Many of the rapidly increasing number of services, such as C|NET and HotWired, use a combination of conventional Web publishing and delivery to bring information to your virtual doorstep. When this happens, it is usually the case that the delivered information has been excerpted from longer stories available to anyone who wants to access the Web site (so that the delivery mechanism serves as a form of self-promotion).

Usually you register with these news delivery services by providing a profile of your interests. Then you are provided with only the information that matches your requests—so that the news is pre-filtered to your specifications. Trying to make these filters intelligent and reliable is one of the challenges facing the next generation of Internet publishers.

BROADCAST PROGRAMMING Until recently, Internet content was rarely event oriented. Information was posted to a location and left there for the perusal of all at their leisure. As an increasing number of audio and video technologies are introduced to the Internet, this is starting to change. Now it is not uncommon for sites to post a schedule of programs they sponsor, just as a radio or TV station would. In fact, it is primarily the radio stations and TV networks who have jumped on this technology as a way of re-broadcasting and promoting their content over the Internet.

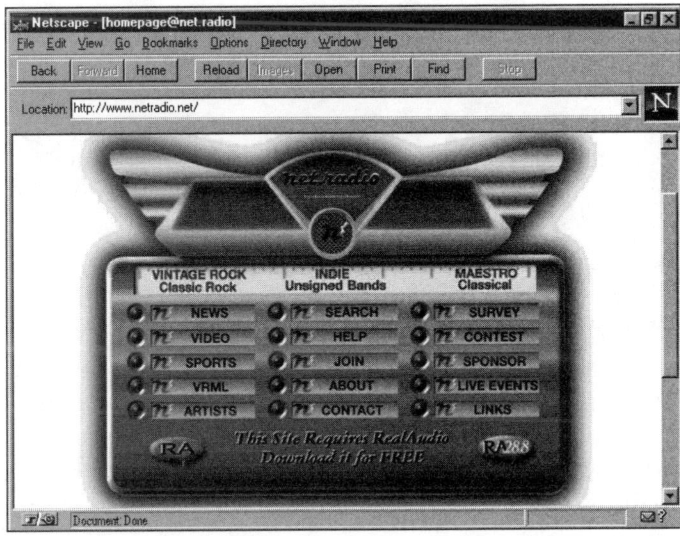

Figure 7-3
Shot from a virtual broadcast station.

DIRECTORIES, INDEXES, AND RATING SERVICES With all of this information, good and bad, floating loose on the Web, the biggest challenge facing a potential user is how to find anything of interest. The numerous directory and index services cropping up on the Internet are capitalizing on this problem in an effort to serve as the information brokers to Internet content.

There are two main ways directories are set up—either as search engines, capable of matching keywords contained in the text of documents, or as categorized databases, in which each entry is actually reviewed, labeled, and listed in a way that allows for easy browsing (or "drilling down" as some directories call this process). Many services, like Yahoo!, for example, provide both of these functions—and a whole lot more besides.

Key Components

All of the key components of a publishing system center around content: content acquisition, content conversion, editorial management, storage and delivery, and some mechanism for generating revenue.

Information Retrieval

There are several considerations that go into the crucial decision of how users will locate and view the information you make available to them.

1. What kind of data/information do you have? This question will dictate to some extent the options you have in designing your information retrieval system. Is the data highly structured or eclectic? Is it constantly updated or static? Is it text-only or multimedia? Is it contained in a single repository or in several different places? Examining these questions will help you determine if you need a state-of-the-art search tool, or just a simple keyword search engine.

2. How much direct access do you want to give users? There are many reasons not to allow users to browse your material. Browsing is not a particularly efficient means of presenting information. You may want to charge for access, for example, which is easier when access is allowed only via a search. Or you may want to limit the quantity of information a given person can access.

3. How readily will users be able to identify appropriate search parameters? One of the obvious limitations of a search tool is that the user has to be able to guess what words or phrases will unearth the content they want. If you choose not to provide a browsing mechanism so that users can familiarize themselves with the body of knowledge you have amassed or have access to, you may at least consider providing them with some helpful hints about what searches are most likely to produce successful results.

Information Retrieval Tools

EXCITE FOR WEB SERVERS Excite is the brand name of the search engine developed by Architext, Inc. This is the same search engine used on the Excite Internet search page (**www.excite.com**).

The distinguishing feature of the Excite search engine is its concept-based search mechanism. Unlike most search tools that build an index of all the words contained in a set of documents, Excite can search for words similar in concept to the specified terms without the necessity of an exact match. Users specify what they want to find using standard requests rather than a string of words separated by spaces or commas. This makes it a particularly user-friendly mechanism.

For example, suppose you collect antique automobiles and you want to find out if there are any resources on the Internet to support your hobby. If you conduct your search using a standard keyword search engine, you will get a list of sites that match one or both of the words "antique" and "automobile." With Excite, you may also locate sites featuring classic cars or vintage driving machines.

Other notable Excite features include:

- A ranking of relevant sites and color-coded results to highlight the best matches

- An automatic summary generated from each matched document
- A query-by-example feature, which allows users to find additional documents that resemble any designated document

To try out concept searching on the Internet, visit the Excite search page at **www.excite.com**. If you are interested in using Excite in conjunction with your own content, visit the Excite corporate Web site at **corp.excite.com**, or contact:

Excite, Inc.
1091 N. Shoreline Blvd.
Mountain View, CA 94043
Tel: 415.943.1200
Fax: 415.943.1299

VERITYTOPIC SEARCH PRODUCTS Verity provides a full line of information retrieval tools suitable for publishing, that involve the dissemination of information over multiple sources (including the Internet), an enterprise LAN, and on CD-ROM. The Topic product line includes the following components:

- **topicACCESS products.** These products provide access to information from numerous sources, such as databases, Internet servers, newswires, USENET groups, and file systems. Several topicACCESS products provide data synchronization, which keep the topic index up-to-date with sources that change continuously.
- **topicSEARCH products.** These products include Internet servers that support common Web standards, including CGI, NSAPI, and ISAPI. They also include Verity's full-scope client server enterprise retrieval solution, and CD-Web Publisher, for integrated searching across CD-ROMs and the Web.
- **topicAGENTS.** These provide users with personal agents to filter live information. The most relevant information is delivered to users automatically by their choice of delivery mechanism.
- **topicTOOLS products.** These development tools can be used to embed powerful full text search capabilities in stand-alone products. topicTOOLs are also suitable for internal development of large-scale systems and online services.

Learn more about Verity's Topic tools on their Web site at **www.verity.com**, or contact them directly at:

Verity, Inc.
1550 Plymouth Street
Mountain View, CA 94043
Tel: 415.960.7600

OPENTEXT Like Excite, OpenText Corporation sells Web search tools and maintains a Web site with an Internet-wide search engine to showcase its technology. OpenText offers two principal search tool components.

- **Livelink Search**—the basic search engine and indexing software
- **Livelink Spider**—automated agent software that locates documents on designated Web sites and brings them back to be indexed

OpenText's search engine is a standard keyword search tool, but it is robust and fast. It supports boolean searches and proximity searching (locating words close to the spelling of the requested word). Like Excite, it can do similarity searching ("find me items like this one") and it can allow users to search entire phrases. Users may limit a search to specific elements of a document and assign relative importance to each of their search terms.

The spider tool searches through an entire Web site hierarchy and builds a searchable index of the pages it finds. This spider is capable of indexing Portable Document Format (PDF) and Standard Generalized Markup Language (SGML) files, numerous document formats, as well as standard HTML files. It allows users to maintain an up-to-date searchable database of your Web site.

For more information about OpenText products or to try out their search engine, check out their Web site at **www.opentext.com** or contact them at:

OpenText Corporation
180 Columbia Street W. Suite 2110
Waterloo ON N2L 3L3 Canada
Tel: +1.519.888.9910
Fax: +1.519.888.0677
E-mail: info@opentext.com

RETRIEVALWARE Excalibur's RetrievalWare is a family of software components that enable developers to build information retrieval solutions for a wide range of digital information types, including text, document images, and multimedia data types.

RetrievalWare applications and multi-layered toolkits integrate Excalibur's APRP and Semantic Network technologies into information systems for workgroups, enterprises, and wide-area networks, including the Internet and the World Wide Web.

RetrievalWare provides profiling capabilities for integrating real-time and retrospective text searching, document imaging, combined full text and database searching, and content-based image retrieval in a wide range of applications.

For more information, check out the Excalibur Web site at **www.xrs.com** or call Excalibur at: 800.788.7758.

PROFILING AND USER TRACKING A successful online publishing venture must have the ability to report who its readers are and what content they are reading. The ability to track user activity is important both for building revenue and for determining future content.

All Web servers keep a log of basic site usage, but your publishing application may need something more involved. Perhaps you want to tailor the content to particular readers. Or maybe you want to present a reader with different information depending on whether this is the first time they have seen a given page or not. In this case, you may want to investigate a more sophisticated solution to your user tracking needs.

PWS One such solution is the Personal Web Site software by W3.COM. PWS is a development application that allows you to track your Web site visitors and tailor site content and advertising to their individual needs. Its administration functions let you identify individual "surfing" patterns for site customization, manage your membership base, and interact easily with any member through powerful, direct marketing e-mail functions.

Features of the software include:

- Tracking visitors to your site
- Visitor specific site customization
- Membership and pay-as-you-go capabilities
- Web site conversion in minutes
- Narrowcast to very specific segments of your audience
- Records where visitors leave your site—great for advertising
- Profile-specific e-mail lists

For two examples of publications using PWS software, check out PC World Online (**www.pconline.com**) and New Media Magazine's HyperStand. (**www.newmedia.com**).

For more information as well as a demonstration of PWS in action, visit the W3.COM Web site at **w3.com** or contact them at:

W3.COM
459 Hamilton Avenue #202
Palo Alto, CA 94301
Tel: 415.323.3378
Fax: 415.323.2420
E-mail: info@W3.COM

Content Production, Delivery, and Management

If you are planning to build an information-based Internet application, chances are you have existing content that will have to be reconditioned before it is delivered online. Even if you have assembled a team of content creators to produce new material for your enterprise, you will have to think about the form in which the content will be delivered to you—since it is rare, particularly among larger projects, that all of the providers will submit content in the format you will need for displaying or delivering it.

DOCUMENT FILES VS. DATABASES The first consideration is whether to store information in document (or other content) files that can be easily indexed with common indexing tools, or to place the information in a database that can be used as the basis for querying the content.

If you are putting together a conventional text-based publication, you will probably keep the content in text files. If the information source you plan contains smaller chunks of similarly structured data, then a database is the obvious choice.

The advantage of information kept in a database is it flexibility. It is easy to assemble the parts of a given data record in any of a variety of ways, which simplifies the task of building multiple views of the data with varying levels of detail.

Keep in mind, though, that traditional relational database systems are not particularly adept at dealing with sizable text documents or multimedia elements, such as graphics, video, or audio. If you want to build your publication information into a database, you may want to consider one of the larger database systems that have specific facilities for such elements.

For example, Oracle Corporation, producer of the Oracle relational database system, offers a Media Server product line, designed to meet the needs of interactive, multimedia publishing. It has components for storing, retrieving, and managing movies, music, photographs, and text articles. It is also capable of providing customer tracking and billing information for commercial publishing services. For more information, visit Oracle's Web site at **www.oracle.com**.

Illustra Corporation, now owned by Informix, Inc., makes and sells an object-oriented database management system. This system is composed of a core database and extensible objects, called *datablades*, for dealing with user-definable elements, such as text, graphics, and multimedia elements. With these datablades, a publisher could create a sophisticated Web site with highly customizable, easily updatable, content. For more information about the Illustra database, check out the Illustra Web site at **www.illustra.com**, or contact the Illustra offices directly at:

Illustra Corporation
1111 Broadway, 20th Floor
Oakland, CA 94607
Tel: 510.652.8000
Fax: 510.869.6388

SGML TO HTML An alternative that combines the flexibility of data records with the simplicity of text-based systems is to use the SGML to mark up the documents. SGML, of which the World Wide Web's HTML is a fairly primitive application, is designed for identifying the structural elements of a given type of document. The basic idea of SGML is to mark up your documents using markup tags based on an appropriate document type definition. Having done so, you would then be able to extract from the document any of the structural elements, such as the author's name, chapter headings, or bulleted points, you wished to display. In this way, SGML offers a means of storing documents in text format while still retaining some of the advantages of a database system.

EBT'S DYNAWEB DynaWeb is commercial-grade Web server software that serves large SGML documents to Web browsers for rapid navigating and searching. DynaWeb enables remote Web browsers to fully exploit DynaText-like functionality on the Web, but requires only minimal effort on the part of publishers to set up and maintain. The DynaText/DynaWeb environment provides publishers with the ability to perform cross-platform publishing via the Web, CD-ROM, and LAN/WAN.

Publishers can adjust the DynaWeb server to fit special requirements, such as which electronic books are available for Web browsing (managed access to material), the TOC auto-generation threshold (the maximum number of bytes DynaWeb will send in reply to a single client request), and the default TOC depth (how many levels into the TOC hierarchy DynaWeb displays during TOC auto-generation), as well as some cosmetic settings like the default icons.

Once the DynaWeb server is installed and configured, and a stylesheet is set up to handle the SGML-to-HTML transformations, your DynaText electronic book collections become instantly available to all Web clients on the Internet for browsing and searching.

DynaWeb connects Web client browsers to the full functionality of the DynaText search engine—end users can locate relevant information quickly with searches that span multiple electronic book collections.

DynaWeb automatically generates a TOC on-the-fly directly from the SGML structure in the electronic book, and users can expand and contract the TOC as desired. Navigating DynaText books via DynaWeb's auto-generated TOC is the same as navigating ordinary HTML documents on the Web. High-end users will want to consider this option seriously as a means not only of easily displaying complex data/information sets, but also as a means of efficiently managing and updating that content.

For more information about Dynatext, other EBT products, or SGML in general, you can visit EBT's extensive Web site at **www.ebt.com**. or contact EBT directly at:

Electronic Book Technologies (EBT)
One Richmond Square
Providence, RI 02906
Tel: 401.421.9550
Fax: 401.421.9551
E-mail: info@ebt.com

ADOBE ACROBAT EXCHANGE (PDF) Another document format is the Portable Document Format (PDF), mentioned previously, pioneered by Adobe Corporation. PDF technology allows users to view a document in its original format without needing the application, fonts, and so on, used to create the document. It is especially useful as a way to quickly capture print documents without the trouble of using Optical Character Recognition (OCR) software to convert the scanned page image into text characters.

To read a PDF file, you only need the Adobe Acrobat reader, a browser-like application specifically for PDF file viewing. You can download a free copy of this application for Macintosh, Windows, or UNIX from Adobe's Web site at **www.adobe.com**. Also available from the Web site is a Netscape plug-in version of the PDF viewer called Amber.

To create PDF files, you will need to purchase Acrobat Exchange, a commercial product that imports several common document formats, including word processor documents and desktop publishing formats and spreadsheets, and generates a PDF file.

PDF works best in situations in which you have a large body of print documents you want to make accessible to people while retaining the documents' original formatting. It is also useful as a way to make available documents, like complex forms, that the user needs to print in their original format.

The Internal Revenue Service, for example, has made available all of the tax forms and publications in PDF format. The *New York Times* Web site delivers many of its articles online in PDF format. And Fidelity Investments has a growing number of its fund prospectuses in PDF format.

One disadvantage of this system is that the contents of the document remain fixed—they cannot be divided and displayed in multiple configurations. There are also fewer ways to search these documents. One solution is to associate a database record with each file and allow searches on the database. Another is to use VerityTopic, which is capable of searching PDF as well as HTML files.

To try out some examples of PDF documents, check out Adobe's Web site at **www.adobe.com**.

From the U.S. or Canada, you can contact Adobe directly at: 800.628.2320 for customer service or 800.83FONTS (800.833.6687) for sales information.

MULTIMEDIA BROADCAST TOOLS Until recently, the prospect of audio and video transmission over the Internet was unheard of. The biggest problem was that services such as the World Wide Web are built on a "stateless" environment. This means that each time a request is made of a server by a client application (your Web browser), it waits until the request has been fulfilled and then disconnects itself from the server. The server retains no information about the "state" of the client when it made its last request.

Recently, however, several companies have begun to develop "streaming" technologies that can be integrated into this environment. Streaming files do what you normally think of radio or TV as doing—they are "beamed" to you and play on and on and on. Similarly, in the Web environment, streaming audio or video files are initiated by downloading them, but they begin to play almost immediately after the downloading begins and continue to play as the download continues. No long waits while megabytes of information creep slowly across the wires to your desktop.

Here are some of the most promising streaming technologies currently available:

RealAudio RealAudio is a client/server-based application that enables users to listen to streaming audio, either live or re-broadcast, on demand. The player is optimized for low bandwidth connections (as in 28.8 dial-up access), and plans have been announced for a version that will actually adjust the quality of the sound to the available bandwidth. Also in the near future developers will be able to synchronize audio files with their Web pages (**www.realaudio.com**).

Xing Streamworks Streamworks is an Internet-based client/server application that delivers streaming audio and video over the Internet using the MPEG standard. This architecture supports both on-demand and live video and audio delivery. It easily supports "multicasting" and "unicasting" of live or on-demand content to multiple simultaneous users over local as well as wide area networks (**www.xingtech.com**).

VDOLive VDOLive is another technology that enables real-time video applications on the Internet. The VDOLive scaleable technology enables the VDOLive Video Server to play audio and video to users at all Internet connection speeds, from 28.8 dial-ups to T1 connections. The VDOLive Video Server optimizes the quality of the video depending on the network speed available throughout the connection. The VDOLive Video Player can be used with any browser as a helper application, or as a plug-in with Netscape Navigator 2.0, to play back video online. According to VDOLive marketing information, "VDOLive enables 10 to 15 frames per second of motion video with only a 28.8 Kbps dial-up modem connection" (**www.vdolive.com**).

Generating Revenue

If you anticipate a need (or a desire) to build a publishing site that generates income for you or your company, you should give careful thought to this well before you launch your venture. There is not yet any guaranteed method of making money by peddling information, particularly in a medium from which most users have come to expect free access to information.

But there are several established methods of generating revenue, either directly or indirectly, from a publishing application.

ADVERTISING This is probably the most potentially lucrative means of generating income. Advertisers at the high profile Web sites, such as Yahoo!, Netscape, and HotWired, may pay upwards of $30,000 a month for the privilege of displaying the thin little ad banners that have recently become standard fare for commercial Web sites. (Look for these to grow as users grow increasingly accustomed to their presence.)

But before you start multiplying the number of pages on your site by $30K, consider that there is something of a conundrum involved with using advertisements to fund your publishing efforts. No one is likely to pay top-dollar to advertise on your site until you can show impressive user statistics. You cannot show these statistics unless you have a top-notch site up and running long enough to generate traffic. Advertising dollars may make your venture self-sustaining, but you should probably investigate other resources in order to generate the money you need to get you up and running.

SUBSCRIPTION/MEMBERSHIPS This is a familiar model to the magazine publishing world and does not bear a great deal of explanation. As you might suspect this model works best when the application involves delivery as well as presentation of the information. On the Internet, delivery of content looks like a service that people might be willing to pay for. When they have to hunt for the information themselves, it feels like it should be free, like going to the library (without the late return fees!).

Basically, it is feasible to consider charging a subscription price if your application offers some value-added service above and beyond the information itself. To date, this usually means either delivery service or some customization of the content based on user profile information—or both. It is also fairly common among subscription-based services to have a tiered-system. Some access to their information is usually available for free. Detailed information or custom services require payment of a monthly fee.

CLICK-CHARGES In the membership model, you pay for the privilege of access to the information source. Once you are in, it's a smorgasbord of "all you can read." The problem with the subscription model is that membership pricing has to be done based on some anticipated average usage. This may make the price look to high to a casual user, someone who would like to access some small amount of information but who is not ready to shell out the money for a full-fledged subscription.

If your information lends itself to the casual or one-time reader, you might want to consider a payment model that charges on a per-view basis. Users only pay for the content they actually want. To work, this system requires the ability to charge customers in very small increments, in amounts of less than a dollar, for instance. Another consideration is how to present enough information to interest the user enough to ask for more without giving away too much beforehand.

SERVICE-ORIENTATION FOR SALES This is not so much a method of generating revenue as a justification for why you might not care. It is a common observation among Net pundits that the Internet has forced businesses to adopt a service-oriented attitude. Even companies who only wish to use their Web site for marketing purposes find that their goals are best served if they position their marketing efforts within the context of providing or fostering some service to the Internet community.

In this spirit, then, it may be possible to justify a newsletter or other information-based publication as part of a larger sales objective of positioning your company as an industry leader or knowledge expert. For example, a health insurance company might sponsor a newsletter featuring helpful health and fitness information, or a sporting goods store might publish a runner's guide. In these cases the publishing venture serves as indirect advertising for the business that sponsors it.

Tools to Facilitate Ad Revenue Generation

ADSERVER (www.netgravity.com) NetGravity's AdServer provides a means of managing advertising on an Internet Web site. AdServer software consists of a database and scheduling software for the placing, rotating, tracking, targeting, and reporting of advertisements.

The AdServer is configured to display the correct advertisement in the right ad space at the right time, and for collecting statistics vital to ad planning.

AdServer includes numerous advertising and promotions management features, including:

- **Online Interactive Ad Calendar**—Accessible from any Web browser, the online calendar automates ad placement, eliminating manual error and reducing administration costs.
- **Key Reports**—Ad statistics are easily accessible by Web administrators and remotely by advertisers.

- **Impression-based Scheduling**—AdServer's scheduling system allows Web sites to deliver a guaranteed number of impressions to their advertisers and increase sales by selling unused impressions to other advertisers.

- **Grouped Ad Categories**—AdServer enables sites to simplify the process of selling ad blocks to advertisers by categorizing ad spaces within a Web site according to criteria such as popularity, subject matter, or viewer demographics.
- **Keyword-based Ad Targeting**—AdServer provides Web sites the means to sell targeted ad displays by delivering ads on the context of a search or a news feed.

DOUBLECLICK (**www.doubleclick.net**) Doubleclick.net is a targeted advertisement service. Web sites wishing to generate ad revenue list with doubleclick.net. Then they make a provision for the ads in the HTML of their site pages, and Doubleclick activates the site.

Advertisers in turn register with Doubleclick by filling out a profile form indicating the target audience for their ads. Payment is by "page impressions," and advertisers can indicate a maximum number of impressions for which they are willing to pay. When a user accesses a Web site that is a member of doubleclick.net, doubleclick.net dynamically displays the ad that best matches the user's or organization's profile.

BROADVISION (**www.broadvision.com**) Broadvision One-To-One is a comprehensive application system that enables companies to establish direct customer connection and attain higher profit margins by dynamically marketing and selling goods and services online on a personalized one-to-one basis.

Using the product's Dynamic Command Center feature (for which the company has a pending patent), marketing, advertising, and Web content managers can:

- Personalize editorial content, advertising, and incentive programs based on individual consumer demographics, psychographics, and usage patterns
- Observe consumer interactions in real-time
- Foster virtual communities by integrating electronic mail bulletin boards and online forums with One-To-One applications
- Establish collaborative online dialogues with customers

Dynamic Command Center allows marketing, advertising, and editorial managers to exercise real-time control over their online applications. Any business rule that dictates editorial content, advertising placement, product pricing, or promotional incentives can be modified directly through a point and click interface, without programming.

Table 7.1 Featured Applications

NAME	URL	SUB-TYPE	SIZE	COMMENTS
NewsPage	www.newspage.com	news/delivery	XL	headline news from over 600 news sources
Pointcast Network	www.pointcast.com/	news/delivery	L	application for ordering personal news items
Word	www.word.com	e-zine	L	cool content galore
Conde Nast Traveler	www.cntraveler.com	e-zine	L	excellent example of an online zine that goes beyond its print counterpart
Discovery Channel Online	www.discovery.com	broadcast/e-zine	L	proof that good things *can* happen when TV programming goes interactive
San Jose Mercury News	www.sjmercury.com	news	L	subscription-based online newspaper
Electric Library	www.elibrary.com	directory/reference	XL	a virtual research source; still green but with definite promise

NewsPage is a daily news service that provides access to full-text information culled from over 600 business and computer industry-related publications. The NewsPage contents is divided into 20 main categories and more than 2,300 total categories.

NewsPage offers three subscription levels.

The basic subscription is free with registration. You can view headlines from news items even without registering. As a basic subscriber, you have access to full text stories from all "basic sources." You can also use the straightforward search function, which allows searches on just today's news or on all news items.

For $3.95 a month, you can get a Premium subscription. This provides all the features of the basic membership, and you can read full-text versions of all "Premium Sources." You also have access to all "Pay Per View" sources, which require an additional charge to read.

With a NewsDirect subscription for $6.95 a month, you can also have a personalized edition of "NewsDirect" sent daily to your e-mail account.

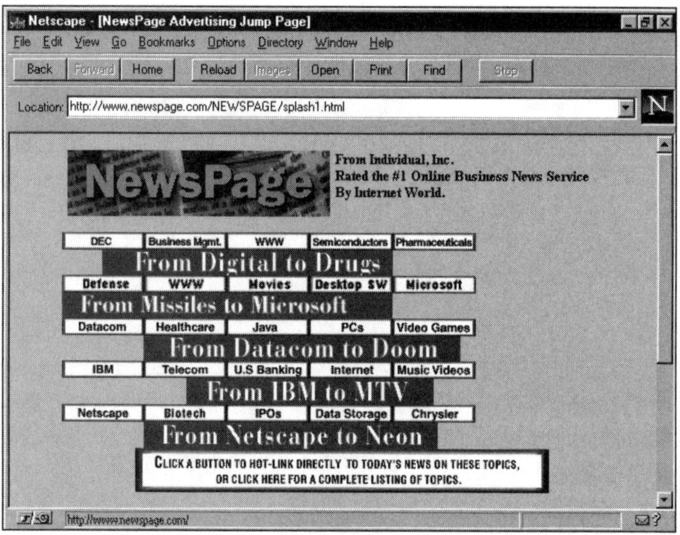

Figure 7-4
The NewsPage home page.

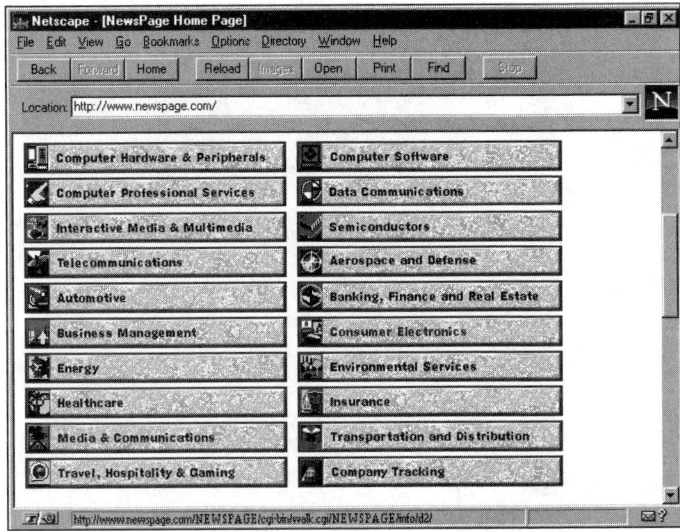

Figure 7-5
The NewsPage category list.

The Pointcast Network is a news service that uses a separate application to download personalized news and information to your desktop. News items, including general news, politics, and international stories, as well as sports, weather, business, and horoscopes, can be retrieved on demand or in the background.

Pointcast has a variety of "channels" that can be personalized according to individual preferences using the ChannelViewer application.

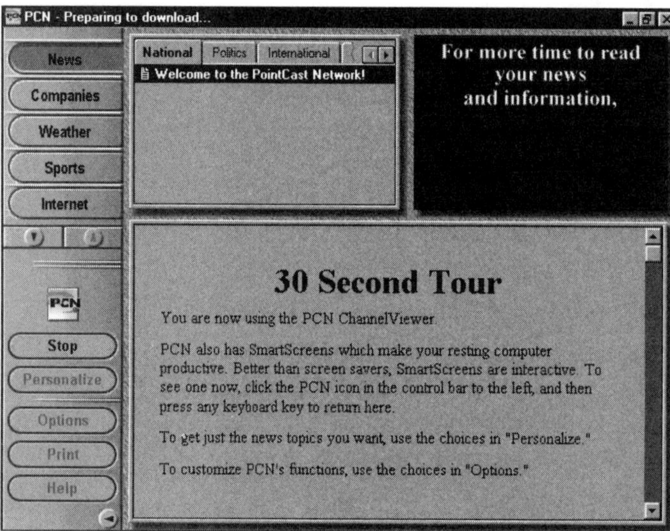

Figure 7-6
Pointcast ChannelViewer interface.

- **News**—From Reuters, national, international, business, and political news headlines are available.
- **Companies**—Users can view charts with six weeks of stock price and volume data along with recent news from PR. A scrolling ticker provides the latest stock price information for the selected companies.
- **Weather**—From AccuWeather, forecasts, satellite images, radar maps, the Ray Ban UV index, and national weather maps are available for viewing.
- **Sports**—SportsTicker news and schedules are available for Major League Baseball, NFL, NBA, NHL, college football and basketball, golf, and tennis.
- **Internet**—This section features a built-in Web browser, an interesting toy, but unlikely to be of real use to most Internet users.
- **Industries**—News and information is available on more than 35 industries.
- **Lifestyles**—Reuters NewsMedia delivers the latest in entertainment news covered by Variety. Users can also personalize the Lifestyle channel to receive their daily horoscopes and the winning lottery numbers for the states that interest them.

One of Pointcast's most ingenious features is what the company calls "SmartScreen Technology." When your machine is idle, Pointcast software displays headline news on your screen, arguably the first ever practical application of screensaving technology.

Another aspect of the software is its ability to perform automatic updates to the client application. The user is automatically informed when an update is available and the upgrade is performed easily and painlessly. No need to download new software, reinstall, and then remove old files.

Pointcast appears to have poured its energy into its application and interface. It is well designed, and easy to set up, use, and navigate through news stories. The quality and breadth of news stories, all of which are distilled from Reuters, is less compelling, however. The application might do well to increase the news offerings and subordinate some of the more frivolous information.

A great deal of what makes Pointcast work smoothly takes place behind the scenes. Pointcast is built on a client/server architect, optimized for low bandwidth, high-traffic environments. It is designed to use few computer resources.

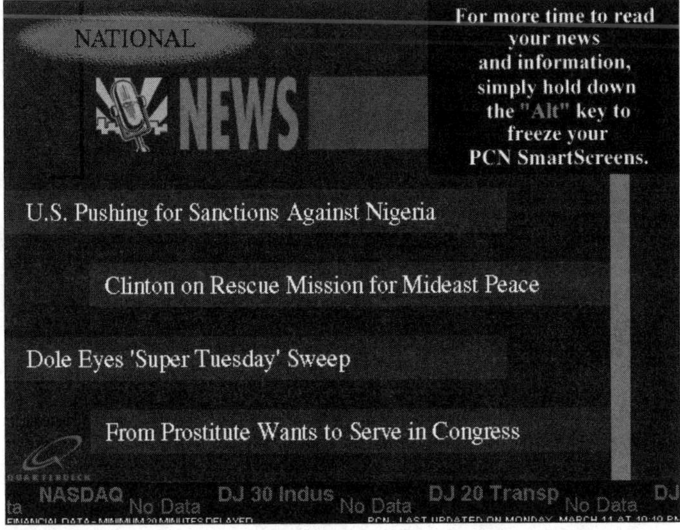

Figure 7-7
SmartScreen—at last, an intelligent screensaver application.

Word is a highly designed e-zine for the culturally hip, literati crowd. It is not a Web site to be accessed when you are in a hurry. For best viewing, hook your 21" monitor to your T-3 (Word does offer a "Words only Word" for the rest of us...). Interface issues aside, Word is both graphically appealing and chock-full of slick, articulate essays and editorials. A great deal of energy has gone into presenting the words in off-beat, visually engaging ways. The designers have also gone to great lengths to keep the interface "state of the art" with push/pull animations, Shockwave, RealAudio, and the like. But all that froth can get to you after a while.

Content is divided into eight main sections: Habit, Gigo, Money, Travel, Machine, Work, Place, and Desire. Each section contains several articles, some heavier on text, some on design, loosely tied to the topical section name. As near as I can tell, "Habit" is hip-speak for "Features"; I have no idea what "Gigo" is supposed to mean.

A more or less random sampling of the titles from the March issue: Superdyke, Laura Perry vs. the dorks; Antisocial and Insecure, in which Devon Jackson explains why Social Security's about as secure as a hole in your pocket; Sahara, Sand, Sand, Sand, Existentialism and Sand, By John Bowe; E Pluribus

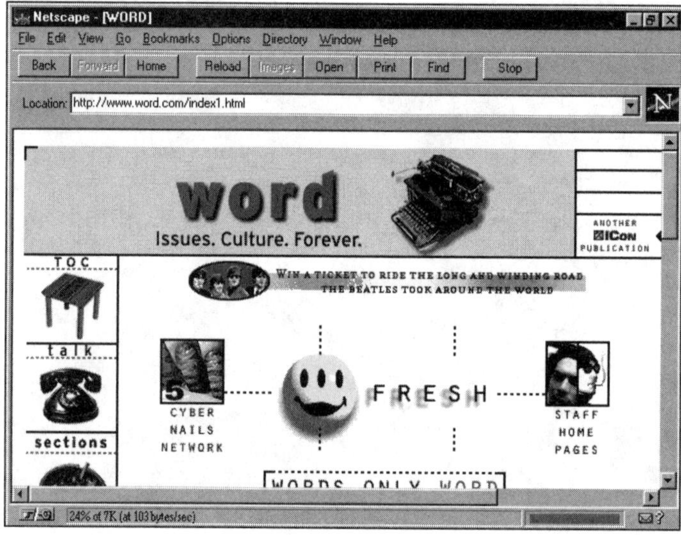

Figure 7-8
A small corner of the Word home page.

Unum, There are those for whom the idea of a single self does not apply, By Jim Baumbach; The Life and Times of the Miracle Compound, How freon brought you frozen dinner rolls and major ozone holes, By Philip Dray; Mano a Mano (or My Life in the Collection Racket), Jack Thorn is a collection agent—he'll get you to pay, even if it hurts. Viva Las Vegas, Debbie Reynolds, and a sparkling, disembodied brain massage. Who could ask for more? By Jim Servin.

There is enough attitude in one issue to last most of us a lifetime. Except for the briefest hints of advertising support, Word seems to be entirely self sustaining. There is a section called "Commerce" which lists (as of this writing) two progressive commercial enterprises. An awful lot of volunteers? Published by ICON Net.

The online version of CN Traveler is a superb example of a print publication transformed in the new medium of the Internet. To begin with, the Traveler contains stunning photography, making it a natural for the World Wide Web. There are feature articles in the "Stop the Press" section as well as previews of the upcoming print edition. In addition, the producers of the site have developed an impressive array of interactive features. These include:

- **Great Escapes**—This section provides a global map to click on, a text index of locations (index), and a "sophisticated search engine" (the concierge) for finding particularly fine vacation spots. There is also a standard search mechanism—by location or by descriptive keyword—to help you find the right place to go.
- **Photo Gallery**—The Photo Gallery is just what it says—a vast collection of stunning photography, organized by location. For those of us who make decisions intuitively, there is even a feature here called "Snap Decisions." You are presented with a random selection of pictures and asked to select the one that strikes your fancy. Then learn about the location you have seen—or "travel on" to see more photos.
- **Readers Choice Awards**—This section offers readers the chance to search through a database culled from 30,000

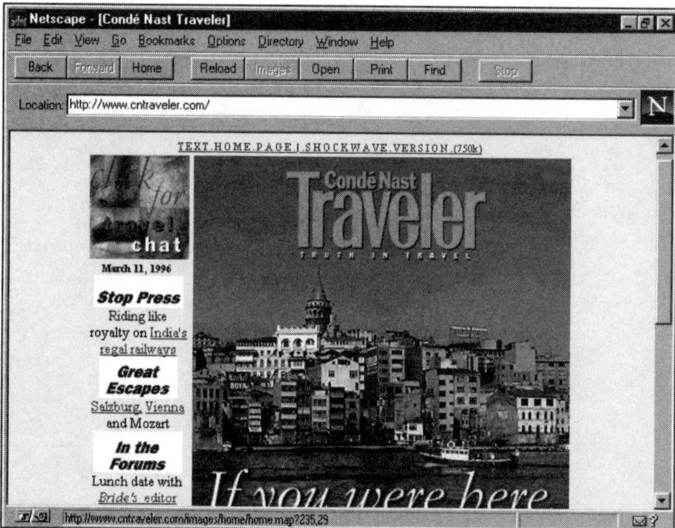

Figure 7-9
CN Traveler home page.

CN Traveler readers. Find out what they think are the top rated cities, islands, hotels, spas, car rentals, resorts, airlines, and cruise lines.

- **Forums**—Forums are organized by geographical reason. There is also a section on "Know How" and a newly added "Traveler's Chat" that offers specified times in which users can come and participate in conversations about designated topics.
- **Concierge**—This is my favorite feature. By answering a few pointed questions about your vacation dreams, the concierge will indicate the priority of your interest on a list of criteria. You select your preferences for region, hotel, cost, and climate. At each stage, the concierge informs you how many locations match your criteria and offers you the option of viewing the matches or continuing to refine your search.
- **The Arcade**—This section has to two diverting activities. One presents you with a photo and invites you to guess the location. The other, "Seven Characters in search of an island," divides the world into personality types and finds you the perfect island based on your preferred lifestyle. It can accommodate combination types as well.

Clearly there is enough interactivity here to keep you planning and dreaming for hours.

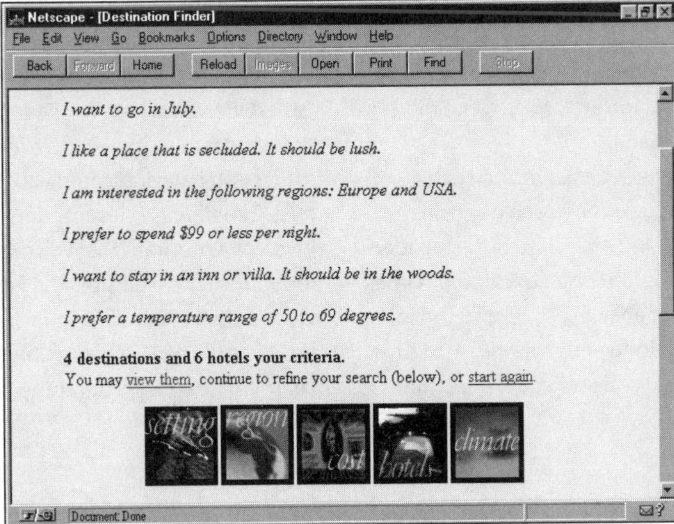

Figure 7-10
The Concierge.

The Discovery Channel Online extends the reporting and activity orientation of the cable television station of the same name. The site is a well-organized collection of information, clearly presented with clean, inviting graphics. Content is neatly arranged in a table structure that minimizes the necessity to scroll. Highlights are prominently displayed so that the user always has the impression that new and exciting things are happening on the site.

Discovery World is the heart of the site. It is divided up by days of the week and each day is associated with a topic—history Monday, nature Tuesday, science Wednesday, people Thursday, exploration Friday, technology Saturday, your story Sunday, and a special event section. Each section also has a section in the bulletin board (housed on a separate server) associated with it that contains numerous forum topics (some more active than others).

There is a Newsdesk, with science-related stories gathered each day from news services, and a weekly contest to identify a photographed object. Winners' names and the correct answer are posted the following week, along with hyperlinks to sites loosely related to the object in question.

Discovery Pavilion is the fancy name for the store. It has three areas: "Multimedia" describes the CD-ROMs available for purchase from the Discovery Channel; "Catalog" has the full product offerings complete with order forms (no secure transaction method is mentioned); and "School" is a window into a whole world unto itself (and a separate server).

School contains a Video Vault, Subject Area Managers (SAMS) with advice on teaching the topics related to Discovery Channel programming, links to other learning communities, and a professional support area for teachers to interact with other teachers.

The third section, Discovery on Air, is devoted to information related directly to the television programming. In addition to the requisite program schedule, there is a "smart viewer" which will send you an e-mail message reminding you to tune in to programs you have indicated you don't want to miss. Cyberlife is a new section which involves a program that will draw on user input from the Web site. And FanZone provides detailed "how it's done" information for some of The Discovery Channel and The Learning Channel programs.

Figure 7-11
Discovery Channel Online's clean, well-lighted home page.

The Discovery Channel Online contains a search mechanism and also a nifty feature they call the KnapSack. Registered site users can issue search requests that are stored in their knapsack. When they check back, the knapsack will be filled with items matching their request. Basically, it is offline searching with the ability to repeat the search an indefinite number of times. Search results can be delivered via e-mail or picked up manually when you visit the site.

The Discovery Channel Online is a carefully conceived and maintained site. My one reservation is that there is perhaps too much emphasis on promoting the television programming. There are many interesting articles to read, but the site doesn't quite feel like it has a life of its own.

A recently introduced but already impressive collection of information can be found in the Electric Library, which archives the full text of over 900 magazines, 150 newspapers, 2,000 books, encyclopedias, and 20,000 photos and maps. Designed for both children and adults, the Electric Library bills itself as the first usable Internet site for conducting research.

The search engine is the heart of the library. Results are returned to a user ranked in order of relevancy, displaying the document title, source type, date of publication, size, and reading level. Using the advanced search parameters, you can limit results to works published within a given time period or by actual publication titles.

The contents of the Electric Library are somewhat eclectic (it is too early to abandon the old fashioned physical library as a resource), but the Electric Library brings together a wide range of sources and makes it easy to find them in minutes. I look forward to seeing the content list grow.

The Electric Library allows users to set and retain "power" settings for search queries. These settings remain in effect each time the user logs on to the library. It could benefit from some additional ancillary features to round out its offerings and to make it feel more like a resource library and less like a search engine.

At the time of this writing the Electric Library was still available as a free service. At the end of the trial period, the published price is $9.95 per month for "virtually unlimited" searching and retrieving (**www.elibrary.com**).

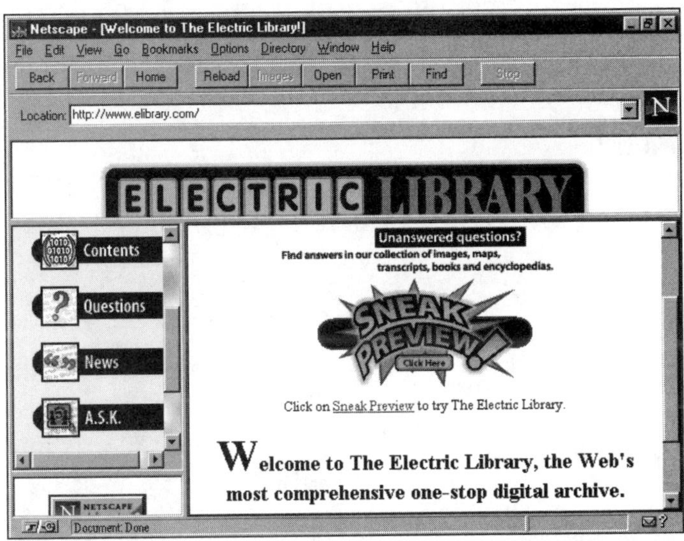

Figure 7-12
The Electric Library interface.

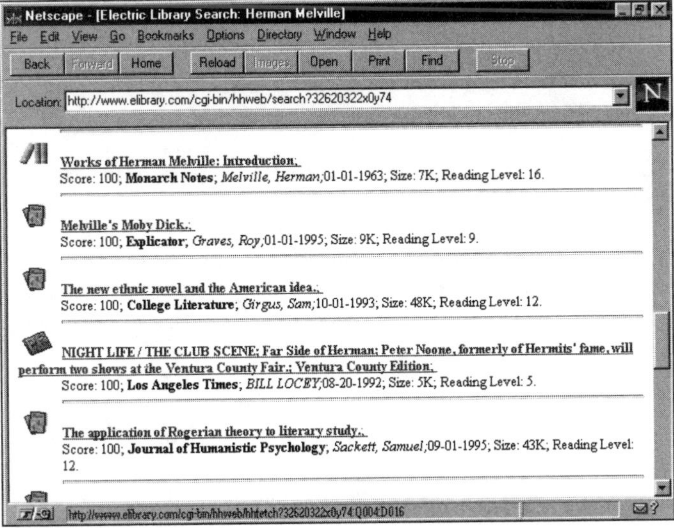

Figure 7-13
Sample search results.

The Short List

What follows is a list of additional sites related to online publishing. This list is intended to be representative rather than comprehensive. For more directories of publishing sites, see "Additional Resources" that follows.

TABLE 7.2 THE SHORT LIST

NAME	URL	SUB-TYPE	SIZE	COMMENTS
NewsBytes	www.nbnn.com	news	L	covers the computer and telecommunications industries
Digital Delivery	delivery.reach.com	news delivery	na	agent technology for delivery of formatted publications
InfoSeek	www.infoseek.com	directory/search	L	searches the Web, newsgroups, and newswires
Farcast	www.farcast.com	news delivery	L	personal news retrieval software
Crayon	crayon.net	news	L	acronym for CReAte Your Own
Z-DNet	www.zdnet.com	news/e-zine	L	features Personal View
The Electronic Telegraph	www.telegraph.co.uk	news	M	a top news daily from the UK
U.S. News Online	www.usnews.com	news/magazine	M	online version of print weekly big sponsor buttons
Pathfinder	www.pathfinder.com	news/e-zine	XL	enough content to last a lifetime
CNN	www.cnn.com	news/broadcast	M	CNN on the Internet
ESPNet Sportzone	espnet.sportszone.com	news/broadcast	L	ESPN on the Internet
USA Today	www.usatoday.com	news	M	USA Today on the Internet
Epicurious	www.epicurious.com	e-zine	L	combines cuisine magazines with online fun
Salon	www.salon1999.com	e-zine	M	upscale literary zine
iWorld	www.iworld.com	magazines	L	computer publications
Spiv	www.spiv.com	e-zine	L	hip e-zine funded by Ted Turner
The MOJO Wire	www.mojones.com	e-zine	M	*Mother Jones* online

(continued)

TABLE 7.2 THE SHORT LIST (continued)

NAME	URL	SUB-TYPE	SIZE	COMMENTS
National Public Radio	www.npr.org	broadcast	M	uses RealAudio
NetRadio	www.netradio.net	broadcast	L	24 x 7 live audio broadcasting
GNN	www.gnn.com	directory/e-zine	XL	another mega-site
NYNEX Yellow Pages	www.niyp.com	directory	XL	business directory offering free listings
PointCom	www.pointcom.com	directory	XL	ratings and reviews for Top 5% of web sites
Magellen	www.mckinley.com	directory	XL	index, ratings for web sites
ABC RadioNet	www.abcradionet.com	broadcast	XL	uses RealAudio

Additional Resources

News Collections

THE ELECTRONIC NEWSTAND (**www.enews.com**) This newstand includes a "monster" list of over 2,000 publications, some Net-based, some not. For ease in browsing and searching, the entire collection is divided into categories. Discount subscriptions are offered on the print publications.

ZINERAK (**www.zinerak.com**) ZineRak is a hipper, but humbler collection of e-zines that covers a dozen general categories.

THE NEWSTAND (**www.web-newsstand.com**) This newstand is focused directly on news sources on the Net (as opposed to magazine publications). It includes links to some more recent broadcast-type productions.

JOHN LABOVITZ'S LIST OF E-ZINES (**meer.net/~johnl/e-zine-list/index.html**) This site lists over 900 e-zines.

Meta-Search Engines

These search engines can send queries to multiple search engines simultaneously. They all operate in essentially the same fashion: compose your search request, indicate which of the search engines you wish to include in the search, wait awhile (these search engines are actually remarkably fast if you think about what they are doing), and then see the results collated and ranked. No more surfing around from site to site in the hopes of finding some elusive reference. (Note—these sites are to be distinguished from several "all-in-one" type pages which have amassed links to multiple search engines on a single form page.) Some examples of meta-search engines include:

- SavvySearch: Parallel Internet Query Engine (**cage.cs.colostate.edu:1969**)
- MetaCrawler Multi-Threaded Web Search Service (**metacrawler.cs.washington.edu:8080/index.html**)
- ProFusion (**www.designlab.ukans.edu/ProFusion.html**)

Future Directions

See Chapter 10, "The Malling of Cyberspace" for additional discussion of agent technologies.

In the future, online news and information will divide increasingly into online e-zines that will focus on clearly delineated markets (or reader communities) and news delivery services that will provide highly customized news and information on a continual basis.

The e-zine Web sites will focus increasingly on producing sophisticated, interactive, user experiences, incorporating multimedia technologies like streaming audio and video, as well as programming technologies like Java and VMRL 3-D environments.

Both the e-zines and the news delivery services, though, will depend increasingly on the ability to dish up information tailored to the interests of specific users.

PART THREE
Electronic Commerce

In Part Three, we look at companies developing applications in the domain of electronic commerce. Each takes a slightly different approach to this emerging market. Together, they demonstrate that there is more to online commerce than virtual shopping malls (although, of course, that is one model).

In Chapter Eight, "Online Shopping," we look at three consumer-oriented applications—an online catalog system, a mail-order operation, and an automated procurement service.

In Chapter Nine, "Transaction-Based Services," we consider three cases that make possible more complex transactions than the simple exchange of credit card numbers.

In Chapter Ten, "The Malling of Cyberspace," we discuss issues related to developing a transaction-based Internet application and describe the tools you can use to conduct electronic commerce.

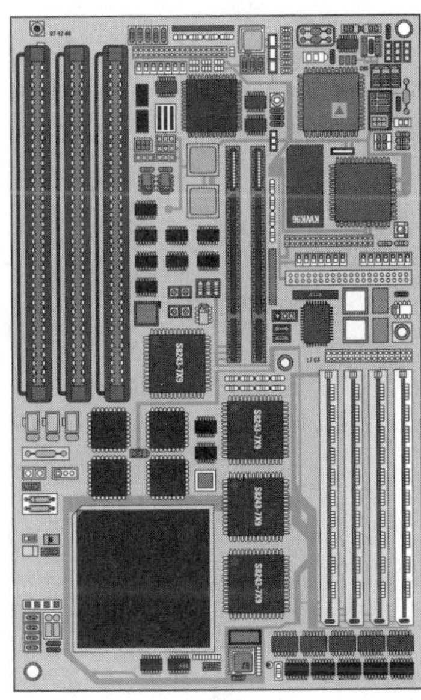

CHAPTER EIGHT

ONLINE SHOPPING

The vision of an Internet marketplace, where customers let their fingers do the buying, is a major force in bringing businesses online. At the moment, however, hype still outruns actual development by a wide margin. To a casual observer, widespread commerce on the Internet still appears to be the holy grail of business application development.

Not that there aren't businesses conducting profitable trade online today—there are. But the price tag can be high, and the results are not guaranteed. On January 15, 1996, *Interactive Week* reported the results of a survey of 20 major companies that had developed Internet transaction systems. The average price tag: $1 million, three to four times what some companies had budgeted. This is a sobering statistic, but it is tempered somewhat by the fact that in spite of the hefty price tag, most of the companies surveyed were happy with the results. But there are notable exceptions—small companies that have augmented their sales by adding an online channel—and these exceptions are likely to become more common, even as the cost of the major commercial ventures drops significantly.

In addition to the cost factor, attracting customers and inducing them to buy online continues to be a challenge. Potential shoppers are still reluctant to send their credit card numbers over the Net, and they are still somewhat suspicious about online businesses. Obviously, name-brand companies who take to the Net will have the advantage here. Smaller enterprises and start-ups will have to prove their reliability the hard way.

Also, some products lend themselves more readily to online commerce than others. Products that can be easily sampled and delivered electronically are obvious candidates for online transactions. Other goods will have to demonstrate that buying them online offers real advantages over buying in person.

All these issues are likely to be overcome with time, as technologies mature and users become more comfortable with technology. When banks started to install ATMs, nobody used them at first. Now, for many, they are indispensable. It is quite clear that, although the market is still young and the models still largely untested, the Internet is destined to be a principal channel for business into the 21st century.

What Is an Electronic Commerce System?

In earlier sections we defined a *communication system* as one that facilitates the sending and receiving of messages, either between individuals (one-to-one) or from an individual to a group (one-to-many). Communication systems transfer data with little or no packaging. In contrast, *information delivery systems* are characterized by highly packaged data, which may be aggregated from a single source or from many sources and then distributed to many people—either in standardized form, or personalized.

In both of the aforementioned systems, the thing being transferred—talk or news—is the thing of value. In a *transaction-based system,* a transfer is made—as in the case of a transfer of funds—to initiate some additional exchange of goods or services. In the case of electronic goods and some services, the thing itself may be delivered over the Internet. But the transaction is simply the carrying out of the agreement to perform the delivery of something else.

The quintessential version of the transaction system is, of course, the electronic "shopping center"—which usually resembles a shopping catalog more than it does a store. But transaction systems may extend far beyond catalog status. At the moment, one of the most successful uses of transaction systems is in the financial world. Today, several companies perform investment transactions, complete with clearing and reporting functionality. And electronic banking services are not far behind.

Turn to Chapter 10,"The Malling of Cyberspace," to learn more about the nuts and bolts of building an electronic commerce system.

Likewise, subscription services, reservations, and ticket sales all lend themselves well to this environment. Another area being developed is the ability to submit authorization forms—health care policy applications and claims, for example. Even tax forms could be delivered and processed electronically.

Founded in 1994 by Peter Granoff and Robert Olson, Virtual Vineyards (**www.virtualvin.com**) is a successful, purely online shop that sells specialty wines and foods. Since it first appeared on the Web in early 1995, Virtual Vineyards has continued to define itself as an exemplary model of online catalogs.

Virtual Vineyards is a privately held company and will not release exact figures, but it claims to have strong sales and continues to grow. Net Contents, the parent company of Virtual Vineyards, has one other division called Merchant Services Division that is launching other online ventures because of the success of Virtual Vineyards.

With its relaxed and unobtrusive style, multiple avenues to content, and an impressive catalog selection, Virtual Vineyards has many characteristics that other online purchasing systems seek to emulate.

COMPANY BACKGROUND

Robert Olson's desire to start the online venture spawned from his strong interest in Internet commerce as a general business concept.

At first, all Olson, the President of Net Contents, knew was that he wanted to market something on the Internet, but he wasn't exactly sure what product he wanted to sell. He ended up discussing the idea with his brother-in-law, Peter Granoff, who was in the wine business, and jointly they decided that wine was a product that could potentially sell well on the Internet. They believed that one of the reasons wine is an appealing option for online sale is that

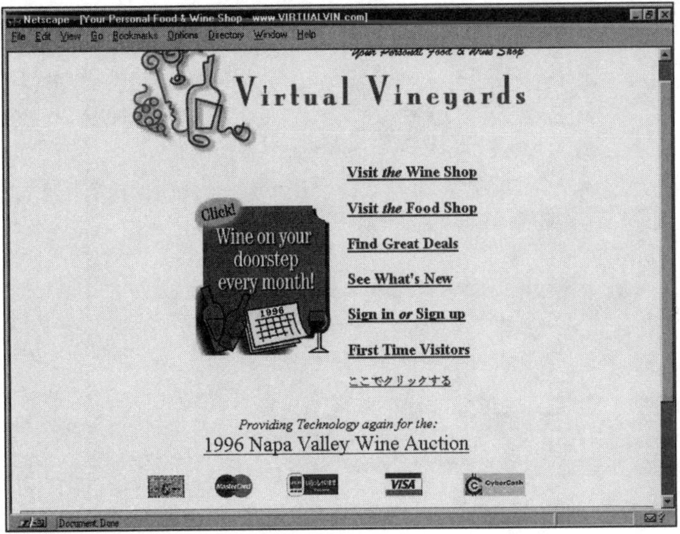

Figure 8-1
Shop at the virtual winery and pay for your purchases online with a major credit card or CyberCash.

Virtual Vineyards At-a-Glance

THE PRODUCT	Online wine and specialty foods shop
URL	www.virtualvin.com
THE COMPANY	Net Contents
OWNER	Robert Olson and Peter Granoff
THE CUSTOMERS	15 employees
START DATE	January, 1995
SOFTWARE/HARDWARE	SGI Indy and custom software development

through the medium they could provide people with helpful information about the wine that could significantly impact what they purchased. Granoff knew from his experience in the wine industry that the more information customers had about a particular bottle of wine, the better prepared they felt to purchase it.

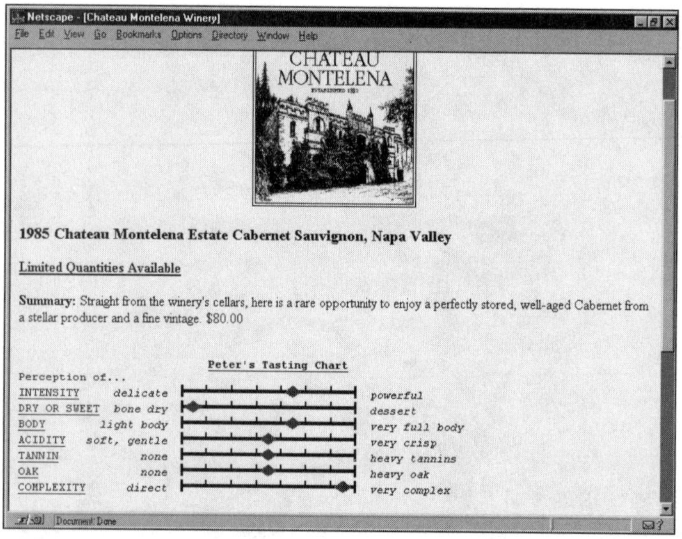

Another reason they felt wine made a desirable product to sell online was that it had an element of scarcity. They figured that if you're going to sell on the Internet, you need to give people a reason to seek you out as opposed to selling something that they can easily purchase from the corner store.

Granoff and Olson decided to feature small wine producers whose wines customers are unlikely to find at the local wine shop. Another plus was the fact that Granoff had been in the wine business for more than 20 years. He was familiar with the California wineries, so he was able to find small producers who created exceptional wine, but because of limited productions, struggle to get wide distribution. Those producers immediately saw the business potential of selling their wine online.

Figure 8-2
Virtual Vineyards' Granoff draws on his vast experience with wines to create tasting charts.

The company was officially formed in late 1994; however, before it went online, several key issues had to be resolved: the legal issues surrounding the business of shipping wine, the developing of the technology backbone, and the initial content and graphics development, which took about six months to complete.

PRODUCT DESCRIPTION

The wines sold at the site include wine from small, well-respected producers along with limited production bottlings from larger wineries. All of the wines are carefully chosen by the Virtual Vineyards wine expert Peter Granoff, the Founder and General Manager. In addition, Virtual Vineyards sells specialty foods that are also created by small producers. It is often difficult for small companies to be visible in the crowded food and wine marketplace. Thus, Virtual Vineyards is a good vehicle for them to get their products to market.

Complementing Virtual Vineyards' wine selection is a rich information source that offers tasting notes for each wine, graphical representation of the wines' flavor profile, additional information about the wine-makers and food producers, and recipes that offer advice on pairing wine and food.

PRODUCT FEATURES AND BENEFITS

More than 50 wineries supply Virtual Vineyards, and the online shop offers between 150 and 200 wines. Also, approximately 25 food producers sell their products at the site—the food shop carries about 125 to 150 items. Additional products are continually added to keep up wtih growing demand.

Virtual Vineyards began selling a limited number of specialty foods in the fall of 1995. Recently, they hired someone with a retail background in specialty foods to expand the food offerings and establish a separate food shop. This new food shop with many more products and a new look opened in July of 1996.

At the site, customers can create a Personal Virtual Vineyards Account. This feature reminds customers which items they liked by maintaining a history of previous pur-

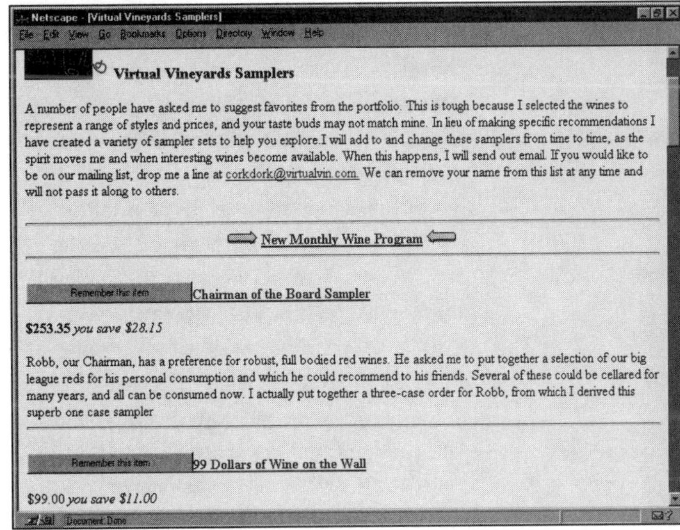

Figure 8-3
Sampler packs enable customers to try a variety of wines within their price range and broaden their wine experience with the help of a wine expert.

chases, as well as keeps records of their own tasting notes about favorite purchases, and tailors the presentation of products to meet their specific preferences.

Virtual Vineyards Samplers is another popular feature for the online business. It evolved after so many people asked Granoff to recommend favorites from the wine portfolio. In response, he created a variety of wine sampler sets to help customers explore different styles of wine from several price ranges. Many customers order these samplers, as the samplers offer a good chance to try new wines that the customers might not necessarily have tried on their own.

During the fall of 1995, the Virtual Vineyards Monthly Program was launched, which also evolved into a popular feature at the site. Customers select from several options to specifically tailor the program as much as possible to meet their individual preferences. Customers can choose the type of wine they prefer—red, white, or mixed—and the number of bottles to receive monthly—two, four, or six. Prices are set based on the number of bottles the customer receives.

The recipes at Virtual Vineyards in the Food and Wine Pairing feature come from a variety of sources: wine-makers, Square One Restaurant, well-known cookbook authors, and the Virtual Vineyards "Kitchen," a feature of the new food shop. The recipe ingredients often include items sold in the Specialty Food Shop and a wine from the portfolio is recommended as a complement to the meal.

You can also link to *Wine and Spirits* magazine sampler housed on the Virtual Vineyards server where Interneters can read a couple of sample articles and subscribe to the publication if they like what they see.

Sometimes customers get confused by some of the wine terms on the Web site, so Granoff created "The Glossary of Terms"—a short, easy-to-use glossary to assist customers as they peruse the site.

Easy ordering saves the regular customers time. Rather than having to go back and forth from winery to winery, they can click to a very basic menu and immediately order the products they want by checking them off as they move down the list.

Virtual Vineyards accepts a number of different credit cards and CyberCash—a new payment system designed specifically for online transactions.

BUSINESS/MARKETING MODEL

A few of Virtual Vineyards vendors have their own Web sites, but most of them use Virtual Vineyards as their marketing vehicle on the Internet. Essentially, the vendors enjoy the advantages of being on the Internet without having all of the upstart costs, not to mention the learning curve associated with the technology. From their perspective, Virtual Vineyards is a retailer that happens to sell over the Internet. They provide their product to the online retailer as they would to someone who operates a physical store. And all of the technical issues, all of the problems of getting visibility in the Internet world, and all of the online selling issues are Virtual Vineyards' problems, not theirs.

Virtual Vineyards works closely with its suppliers. For example, descriptions of wineries on the site are written by the Virtual Vineyards staff, who also include a description of the winery written by the wine-maker. The result is that the customer gets Virtual Vineyards' view as well as a more personal perspective of the winery.

The relationships with the participating vineyards have been developed and nurtured over time. Many of the relationships stem from Granoff's twenty-year experience in the wine business. For example, Granoff was a wine buyer for the Stanford Court Hotel in San Francisco, and the Director of Wine for Square One, a highly regarded restaurant in San Francisco. His professional experience in evaluating wine and figuring out what appeals to customers has contributed to the product quality and the depth of information available at the Virtual Vineyards' site, and ultimately to its success.

Granoff tastes and chooses all of the wines for Virtual Vineyards. His selection criteria include quality and value of the wine, track record of the winery, and whether the wine adds to the many styles, varieties, and prices Virtual Vineyards tries to offer. Along with this job, he performs some of the content development with a few other writers. The technical staff helps him with such tasks as scanning images and HTML coding.

For each winery appearing on the site, Virtual Vineyards includes a description, an objective assessment about why the wine is good enough to be sold at Virtual Vineyards, along with a tasting chart that describes and profiles the wine. The tasting chart is designed to help consumers determine whether or not they are actually going to like a particular wine.

Virtual Vineyards offers a guarantee that covers any problems a customer might have with a product by either replacing the product or offering a credit. If a product should break in transport, the customer is covered, or if the customer simply didn't like the wine because he or she felt the description didn't match his or her expectations, Virtual Vineyards will offer to replace the bottle or give the customer credit. The company tries to be flexible, recognizing that when trying to sell something remotely, customer service is critical.

Every couple of weeks, a newsletter is sent out to customers who sign up to be on the e-mail mailing list. Sometimes it highlights new features and products added to the site, such as a special offer, a new winery, a new food producer, or a new wine from an existing winery. Sometimes the newsletters are purely informational. For example, a recent newsletter featured a collection of menus that used some of the food products sold at Virtual Vineyards to generate more interest in the Food Shop.

Virtual Vineyards has generated quite a bit of press since its initial launch in 1994.

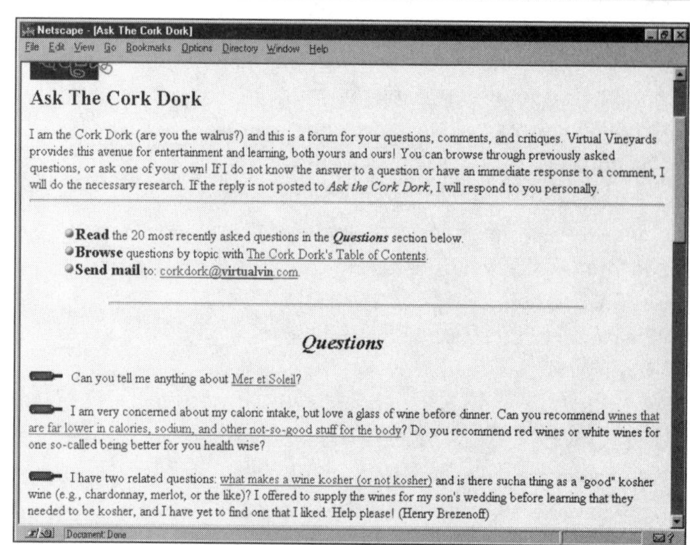

Figure 8-4
The Cork Dork is a popular feature that adds a personal touch to the online shopping experience.

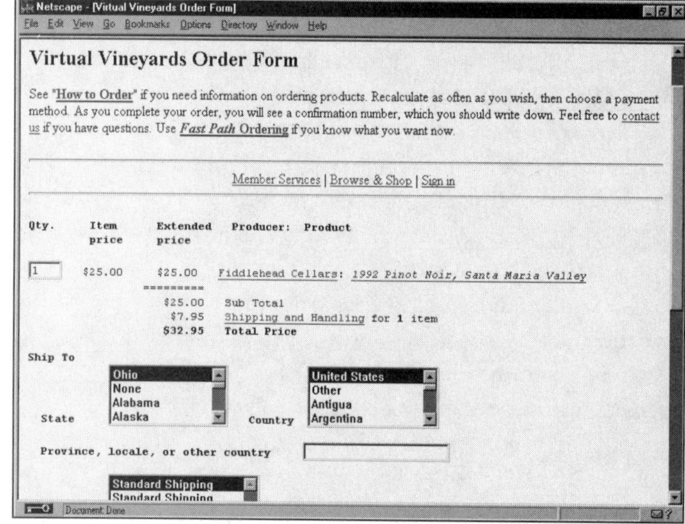

Figure 8-5
Virtual Vineyards' ordering process is quick and uncomplicated—all shipping and tax charges are automatically calculated.

Some of its publicity resulted from being one of the first online businesses to actually make transactions. Also, Peter Granoff and Robert Olson, the two founders, are articulate and personable businessmen who tell the an interesting story about building the online business and the problems they faced.

Japan is a good market for Virtual Vineyards, but overall probably less than 10 percent of the orders are international. Business overseas is slowly increasing.

One of the most important criteria to Olson and Granoff is that the content on the site is meaningful and useful. They believe that if all they provide is a list of products and the opportunity to buy, people will get bored quickly. Solid content keeps customers back for more; however, now and then it can cost a few sales as well. Sometimes customers comment that they use the site for helpful information and then go down to the local liquor store to purchase a wine. Even so, customer contact is taken very seriously at Virtual Vineyards. Last year Granoff received an estimated 10,000 e-mail messages through the Cork Dork feature, and he responded to every one of them.

Virtual Vineyards does not get in the way of a sale. It makes customer registration optional. Although, many customers choose to register because it makes online ordering easier. By registering on the site, they can avoid entering all of their billing and shipping information every time they want to make a purchase.

Until recently, Virtual Vineyards focused on getting the word out about its site to the Internet community. Most of their public relations efforts focused on the technology press and the business press. They also purchased banner ads at certain key sites. Now they are beginning to focus on "food and wine" people in general whether they are online or offline.

TECHNOLOGY BACKBONE

Virtual Vineyards maintains its server on site, because they are committed to keeping it running 24-hours a day, seven days a week. Virtual Vineyards uses an SGI Indy as its server platform.

As of yet, Virtual Vineyards has not ventured into the arena of online forums or searchable database software; however, such ideas are being considered, and the technical staff is currently researching chat/forum software.

Most of the HTML coding is the responsibility of the technical staff, as well as any coding involving Perl, Java, and other higher-level tools.

Virtual Vineyards does not use shopping-cart software for its online transactions. Rather, the software developed in-house relies more on a shopping list—it remembers items on the list as opposed to placing them in a shopping cart.

The technical staff at Virtual Vineyards strives to put the customers' needs first, in contrast to the many Web site developers that put the Web site first and the customers second. They believe that site development should be the result of customer feedback, and sales and marketing data.

LESSONS LEARNED

- Recognize that the text and the graphics alone do not make a successful online business.
- Advertising with banner ads on other online sites is a challenging process. Sometimes the sites that seem to be obvious choices have disappointing results. For example, some of the other food and wine sites that you would expect to be naturals for Virtual Vineyards, are less effective than some of the sites that appeal to a more general audience. No one at Virtual Vineyards is entirely certain why that is the case.
- Have lots of money. You can't just set up a few Web pages and expect people to beat a path to your door. Technology is critical to a successful Web site and it is expensive. For example, if you are going to enable customers to conduct transactions online, you must have the secure capabilities to accept credit cards. Also, if your fulfillment of orders occurs at a separate site from where you are operating your online business, you need the technology in place to make that process happen as smoothly as possible.
- A responsive customer service center is very important to running a successful online business, and the technology behind having effective customer response center takes time to build.

- Easy navigation is very important. Think through your Web site very carefully so that the customers coming to your site feel like they are doing what they want to do, while you guide them to do what you want them to do—buy something.

FUTURE PLANS

The creative minds behind Virtual Vineyards are always looking for ways to make the site more visible and information-driven, in addition to being a good place to shop. Forming additional cooperative business relationships with businesses both online and offline is another priority.

Future plans include expanding the existing product line. Some consideration is being given to adding new products that are likely to appeal to the same audience as the Virtual Vineyards audience.

The parent company, Net Contents, is also looking at ways to leverage the technology and the tools developed for Virtual Vineyards to help other people do business effectively on the Internet.

SPOTLIGHT: SMOKIN' JOES

Smokin' Joes (**www.smokinjoes.com**) is riding the wave of the recent cigar smoking craze. Smoking dens are popping up like coffee houses across the country, restaurants are offering special cigar dinners, and many prominent Hollywood celebrities have become cigar aficionados.

J.D. Jenkins, owner of Smokin' Joes, the first and largest online supplier of premium cigars and cigar accessories in the world, made money from his online investment not long after its initial launch in 1994. Smokin' Joes offers products that fit well with the Internet culture—the products are easily recognizable, popular, sell for less than $200, and are easy to order sight unseen. This profitable site, essentially run by three people, benefits from purposeful planning, financial commitment, fresh ideas, and strong demographics.

The demographics of Smokin' Joes are every online business owner's dream. The site appeals to males between the ages of 20 and 40 with high discretionary incomes and credit cards. As a bonus, more female shoppers in the same age bracket and financial situation are becomming interested in cigar smoking.

The Jenkins family owns three separate autonomous cigar businesses—a wholesale operation, retail stores, and the online business. The cigar business operates in a demand-exceeding-supply marketplace. The retail ordering from the Internet is very profitable, and the regular retail shops continue to be profit-generators.

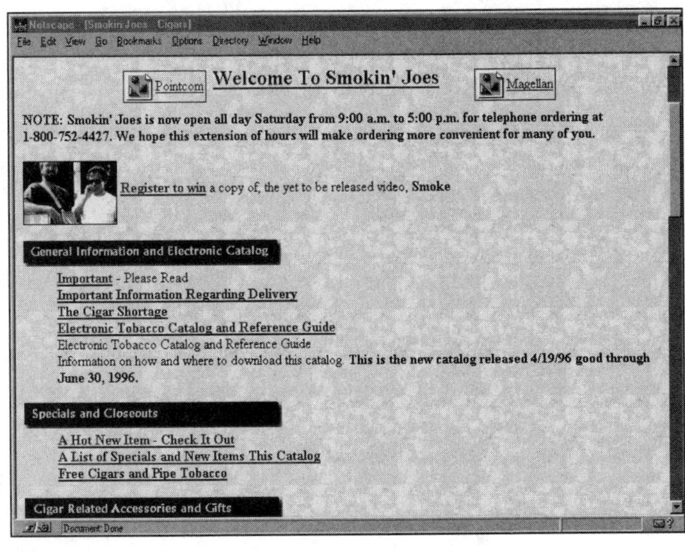

Figure 8-6
Smokin' Joes is a successful online mail-order operation that sells cigars and cigar accessories.

COMPANY BACKGROUND

The company has been in business since 1980 and employs 27 people between the wholesale business, retail business, and online business. The wholesale operation provides products to more than 200 retailers across the country, including sales to Jenkins' own retail shops, which operate as autonomous entities from his wholesale operation.

Smokin' Joes At-a-Glance

THE PRODUCT	Online retailer of premium cigars and cigar accessories
URL	www.smokinjoes.com
OWNER	J.D. Jenkins
THE STAFF	3 employees are dedicated to the online business
SOFTWARE/HARDWARE	Secure commerce server and offline catalog software program
VOLUME	Offers 1,350 different premium cigars in various accessories

Jenkins also wholesales to some of his online competitors.

Before entering the online marketplace two years ago, Jenkins spent roughly three months planning the launch of his Web site. The online store marked the launch of his first retail mail-ordering operation directly to consumers. Prior to the site's launch, Jenkins had never been involved in mail-order retail either online or offline.

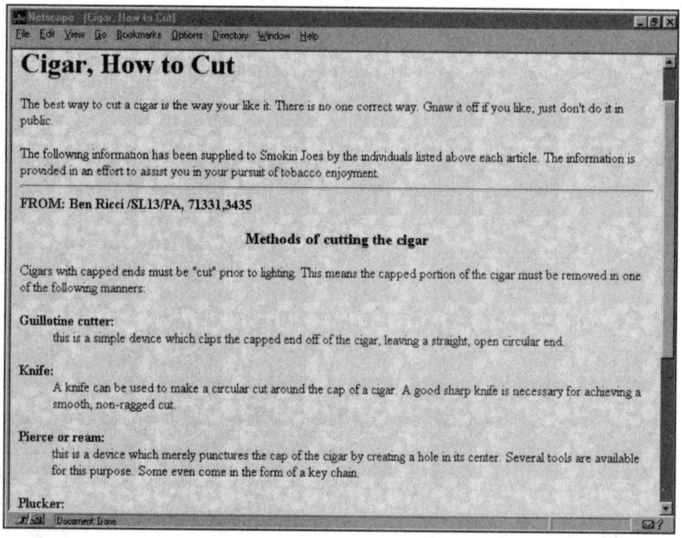

Smoking Joe's online mail-order business officially came into existence when Jenkins contacted Sally Elliot, who was launching an online mall called the Internet Business Connection. In order to attract potential customers, Elliot was advertising an initial free Web page design promotion that attracted the attention of Jenkins. The creation of Smokin' Joes' free Web pages led to a much-expanded Web site—400-plus pages at present—and a close working relationship between Elliot and Jenkins, a relationship that continues today.

Netscape - [Cigar, How to Cut]

File Edit View Go Bookmarks Options Directory Window Help

Cigar, How to Cut

The best way to cut a cigar is the way your like it. There is no one correct way. Gnaw it off if you like, just don't do it in public.

The following information has been supplied to Smokin Joes by the individuals listed above each article. The information is provided in an effort to assist you in your pursuit of tobacco enjoyment.

FROM: Ben Ricci /SL13/PA, 71331,3435

Methods of cutting the cigar

Cigars with capped ends must be "cut" prior to lighting. This means the capped portion of the cigar must be removed in one of the following manners:

Guillotine cutter:
this is a simple device which clips the capped end off of the cigar, leaving a straight, open circular end.

Knife:
A knife can be used to make a circular cut around the cap of a cigar. A good sharp knife is necessary for achieving a smooth, non-ragged cut.

Pierce or ream:
this is a device which merely punctures the cap of the cigar by creating a hole in its center. Several tools are available for this purpose. Some even come in the form of a key chain.

Plucker:

Document: Done

Figure 8-7
The Cigar Information Center provides general information of interest to cigar smokers.

PRODUCT DESCRIPTION

Smokin' Joes sells everything from cheap cigars to the most expensive cigars you can buy in the U.S. At present, Smokin' Joes offers more than 1,350 different premium cigars. The online business also sells plenty of cigar-related accessories, such as air purifiers, 100-percent silk cigar ties, humidors, lighters, humidifiers, rolling papers, and so on. The most popular items with customers are the cigars and the humidors.

PRODUCT FEATURES AND BENEFITS

Many of Smokin' Joes' customers are serious and experienced cigar smokers, but quite a few are new smokers who nevertheless take their cigar-buying very seriously. The newer cigar smoker can find help with some of the finer points of cigar smoking from The Cigar Information Center, which includes such topics as, "How to Light Cigars," "Cigar Storage/Humidity Requirement," "Who Smokes What: Celebrities and Their Smokes," and "Cigar Database." Smokin' Joes leverages useful information about cigars and cigar smoking so that customers learn to trust the business as an information resource as well as a top supplier of cigar products.

Jenkins believes that offering information to the customers adds to the success of the Web site. The information on Smokin' Joes' Web site focuses on product information and related cigar-smoking interests of the customers. This site avoids the "yes I have it, here it is, and here's my price" mentality of many quickly thrown together online businesses. The site was carefully designed to be both a place to buy products and a place to come for information. Consequently, people are frequently referred to the site from newsgroups because of the site's combination of products and information.

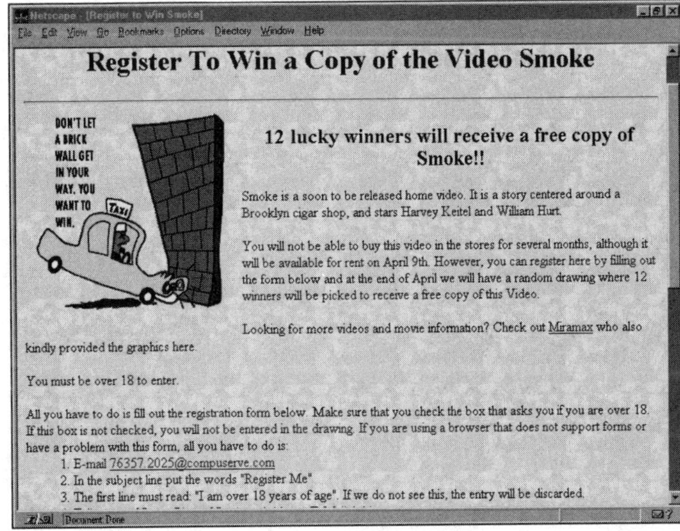

Figure 8-8
Through strong business partnerships, Smokin' Joes is able to conduct special promotions.

Customers can e-mail questions, suggestions, and general comments directly from the Web site. Smokin' Joes responds within 24 hours. If for some reason a problem exists with a customer's e-mail address, an attempt is made to fax or send information through regular mail when the appropriate information is available. Jenkins believes that getting back to customers in a timely fashion is critical to online business success. Don't forget: If you get unhappy customers on the Inter-

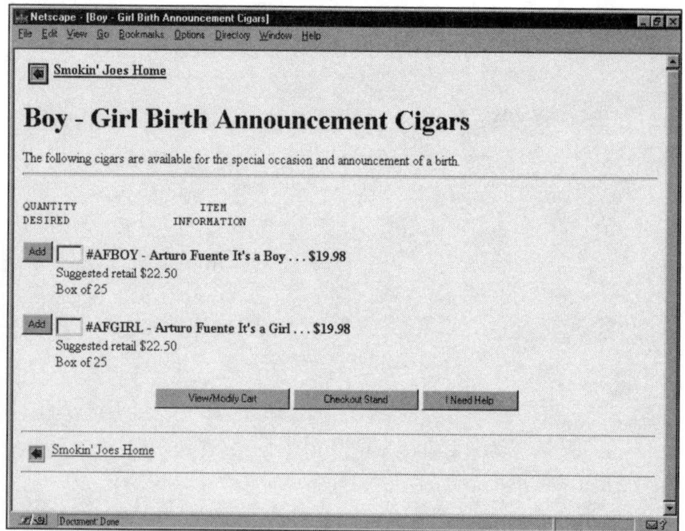

Figure 8-9
Smokin' Joes offers a special cigar box for birth announcements.

net, they can tell the world in a matter of a few seconds.

A concerted effort is made to keep minors from ordering cigars online. All marketing efforts are directed at adults, not minors. Smokin' Joes requires an adult signature for mail order deliveries even though this slightly increases shipping costs. Jenkins believes that the increased cost is worth the effort to keep tobacco out of the hands of minors. Also, packages are no longer left outside unattended by the carriers. This standard policy eliminates theft of the merchandise and the customer's credit card information, which is on the receipt in the box. Presently, they are the only online cigar shop with that requirement. They work very closely with their carriers and all packages contain stickers reading: "Adult Signature Required."

BUSINESS/MARKETING MODEL

Smokin' Joes maintains a presence on America Online, CompuServe, and the Internet. All marketing and promotion is done online. You can access Smokin' Joes presence on AOL by using keyword *SJI*. You can also find information about SJI using the keyword *cigars* and follow the direct link from there to the SJI Web site. They actively participate in cigar newsgroups on the Internet as well as the discussion groups on AOL and CompuServe.

Instead of viewing the entire Smokin' Joes catalog online, customers have the option of downloading the entire electronic catalog, which is a stand-alone computer program. Because the program is downloadable, it resides on many sites across the country. This stand-alone feature was added to save people time and money by making it possible for them browse the catalog offline. Also, once it is downloaded, people can pass the catalog to their friends who may or may not have Internet or online access. The program is like a printed catalog complete with an order form. You select the items you want, and the program transfers you to the order form. You have several options for placing your order: e-mail the file, print a hard copy and mail it with a check or credit card information, or print a hard copy and fax it to Smokin' Joes.

Through negotiated arrangements with other online businesses, Smokin' Joes offers links to other online businesses that in turn offer links back to the Smokin' Joes site. Because of the high level of traffic on the Smokin' Joes site and its desirable demographics, some businesses pay Smokin' Joes for including its links.

Due to the success of the site, other companies have approached Smokin' Joes with promotion opportunities. Currently the site offers a contest to win the video, *Smoke,* a promotional venture with Walt Disney Company, which owns Buena Vista Home Videos, Touchstone Home Videos, and Miramax.

Smokin' Joes' What's New section is a marketing strategy that encourages customers to try new products. Everyone has a favorite cigar, but because demand often greatly exceeds supply in the cigar marketplace, a customer may not be able to get his or her favorite but are likely to still purchase a cigar anyway. The What's New section is designed to serve as a guide for that kind of customer. Also, many customers are on a continued quest for that ultimate cigar. They may have their favorite brand, but they are always looking for something better and are willing to try new things.

TECHNOLOGY BACKBONE

HTML coding, creative design, and graphics are provided by Sally Elliot of Internet Business Connections (**www.intbc.com**). She is the primary creative person for Smokin' Joes and operates out of Ormond Beach, Florida. In addition to Smokin' Joes, she provides Web site construction and maintenance for other companies as well.

Virtual Networks provides the secure commerce server for Smokin' Joes secure online credit card transactions.

LESSONS LEARNED

- Treat your online business as a separate entity from your other business or businesses. Running an online business takes as much time and energy as running any business. If you want to be successful, count on investing money and hiring the right people to help you with your effort. It is not a part-time effort.
- Have a plan for processing the hundreds of e-mail messages you might receive in a day. People expect instantaneous responses, and they expect their orders to be filled very promptly. If for some reason a product must be back-ordered, customers expect to be notified immediately. It takes one person full-time just to communicate with people. In addition, the phone must be answered, and boxes have to be packed and shipped out promptly.
- Plan on investing considerable time in promoting the site—networking, spending time on newsgroups and discussion groups, and looking for creative ways to differentiate yourself.
- Avoid too many graphic-intensive images unless you give people a viewing option. You don't want slow-loading graphics to slow down access to your site.

- Make a commitment—go as far and as fast as your pocketbook and ability will enable you to go. People will pay more attention to you and take you seriously.
- Develop good relationships with people in the appropriate newsgroups. Sometimes people will develop an interest in your site and participate in its development. Word-of-mouth can be a powerful marketing tool.
- Stay open to unique business partnerships. For example, a supplier may want to get involved with your site from a monitory or a product standpoint. These kind of relationships can help you fund the continued development of your online business.

FUTURE PLANS

Smokin' Joes plans to add more products to its online shop and to add some Java-animated graphic technology. Jenkins also has more domain names registered and plans to launch other purely online businesses that will be totally autonomous from the cigar business.

Online Brokerage Systems

The Internet was originally designed for distributed computing in which elements of a particular application, databases for example, are maintained in multiple, remote locations. This capability encourages a "brokerage" model on the Internet—one company that builds an application capable of drawing on the functionality of several existing applications in order to aggregate information.

In the first wave of commercial Internet development, the most prominent illustration of this principal has been the countless online shopping malls. Most of these facilities do not actually broker the products of the entities they "house." They are merely directories, providing categories of shops and a convenient link to disparate catalogs. It does not take a very vivid imagination, however, to envision the next step, in which a company would help users locate actual products from the catalogs, comparing prices and availability.

The FAST Electronic Parts Broker Project (**info.broker.isi.edu/1/fast**) is a prototype automated procurement service developed at the University of Southern California. Arguably the first instance of real electronic commerce on the Internet, FAST is operated from the Information Sciences Institute at USC. This research project was funded by the Advanced Research Projects Agency (ARPA) of the U.S. Department of Defense, the same agency that funded the early research and development of the hardware infrastructure and protocols of the Internet.

The FAST project operates as a brokerage for customers and vendors of electronic parts, components and products, test instruments, and laboratory equipment. Customers are primarily research institutions, universities, and federal agencies, although anyone, including individuals, can be customers.

While the pundits are attempting to predict when electronic commerce will take off on the Internet, the FAST project has already conducted over $15 million of business since 1988. Long before the World Wide Web was a gleam in the eye of its creator, the FAST project had already conducted over $10 million of business in electronic parts using electronic mail—the workhorse of the Internet. The FAST project recently added a forms-based interface on the Web to its infrastructure.

COMPANY BACKGROUND

The Informational Sciences Institute (ISI) conducts a wide variety of research related to information processing at the University of Southern California. It also participates in the development of advanced computer and communication technologies and provides networking services to the University and community.

The Institute's research divisions are directed by nationally recognized research scientists. ISI has close ties to the School of Engineering, particularly the Departments of Computer Science and Electrical Engineering. ISI benefits from its interaction with the faculty of USC and other local universities, and in turn provides opportunities for research and thesis supervision to graduate students.

PRODUCT DESCRIPTION

The FAST project provides brokerage services, including price quotes, order processing, and procurement for electronic parts, components and products, test instruments, and laboratory equipment. Customers use FAST e-mail templates, the X12 industry standard for Electronic Data Interchange (EDI), or, more recently, a World Wide Web form to request a price quote or place an order. In addition, the FAST project goes beyond the usual EDI technology and has built business relationships that operate over the older fax and dial-up BBS technologies.

When FAST receives an electronic quote request, it obtains quotes from its vendors and returns them to the customer via e-mail. Customers may instruct FAST to place an order for a part found at a given price, or

FAST At-a-Glance

THE PRODUCT	FAST parts brokerage for electronic components
URL	http://info.broker.isi.edu/1/fast
THE COMPANY	Information Sciences Institute at the University of Southern California
OWNER	ARPA-funded research project originated at USC/ISI
THE TEAM	6 staff and 1 team-lead/project manager; 4 programmers; 3 buyers; 1–2 management staff
THE CUSTOMER	Universities, federal agencies, research institutes and others
SOFTWARE/HARDWARE	Sun server, Oracle database, X12 EDI

customers may order specific products through FAST via e-mail. FAST places the order with the vendor, who ships directly to the customer. FAST then bills the customer and pays the vendor.

PRODUCT FEATURES/BENEFITS

FAST's customers send messages via the Internet or commercial networks. Communications use either standard e-mail forms (templates) developed by FAST for quotes, orders, and so on, or the industry standard for Electronic Data Interchange (EDI), X12. More recently, FAST has added Web-based forms accessible only to registered customers.

Of the request forms available, the most commonly used requests are Attention, Quote, Order, and Quote and Order. With an Attention request, you can send free-form text to FAST. FAST manually processes your message, and you receive a customized response. The Quote request generates a FAST e-mail response with price information from all applicable vendors. The order requests places an order and initiates the FAST billing process. Quote and Order requests allow customers to supply FAST with simple criteria-based rules for placing orders automatically based on quotes received. Multiple requests can be included in the same message to FAST.

FAST also provides an optional Quote and Order capability. To use this feature, customers submit a request made according to simple rules set down by FAST. If the quote responses obtained by FAST meet the criteria provided by the customer, FAST will, under this option, order directly, without returning the quote to the customer. Quote and Order is quick and reduces the customer's effort in purchasing to a minimum.

The FAST Broker is particularly advantageous for small quantity purchases, since the automated system constructed for FAST can easily handle a large volume of small requests.

BUSINESS/MARKETING MODEL

The primary added value of the FAST brokerage is the rapid procurement, even in single unit quantity, of a wide range of products from a large number of vendors via competitive bidding in a quote and order framework. The FAST project personnel proudly claim that it is possible, in many cases, to have a part ordered and delivered within an hour or two.

For this high value service the FAST project charges a premium of eight percent over the quoted price. Although that may seem reasonable to most, it gets even better. Due to the volume of business conducted by the FAST project, the prices quoted by vendors to FAST brokers is usually lower by such a margin that the eight percent premium is often only a one to two percent premium over what the vendor would quote directly to the customer.

To use the FAST service, customers must become members of the FAST brokerage/market by making a sum of money available up front. Purchases are charged to this amount and the amount needs to be replenished at regular intervals. The actual amounts and the details of the customer-FAST relationship are not cast in stone and depend upon the volume of business to be conducted by the customer.

TECHNOLOGY BACKBONE

The FAST Electronic Broker operates on computers at ISI in Marina del Rey, California, where it is connected to standard commercial networks and to the Internet.

FAST runs on several Sun workstations and a Sun server, which houses the Oracle database at the heart of the FAST system. The FAST project has developed a large set of programs, which reference more than 70 database tables, holding information about customers, vendors, quote requests, orders, and more.

FAST maintains more than 20 custom interfaces to vendors' proprietary mainframe terminal software.

- FAST uses e-mail templates, X12 EDI, and automated fax.
- FAST automation software queries remote databases through dialup or Telnet interfaces originally designed for human use.
- When all else fails, FAST uses the telephone.

LESSONS AND FUTURE PLANS

As presently constructed, FAST does not support a negotiation between buyer and seller, such as would occur for large volume purchasing contracts. Nor does it support negotiating complicated delivery arrangements. For purchasing that consists of obtaining multiple quotes, followed by orders against these quotes, however, FAST is appropriate.

For articles about the FAST project, check out **info.broker.isi.edu:80/fast/articles**.

Additional Resources

THE BARGAINFINDER AGENT (**bf.cstar.ac.com**) A prototype built by Andersen Consulting to demonstrate the possibilities of using agent technology to provide price quotes for queried products.

ELECTRONIC COMMERCE RESOURCE CENTER (**www.ecrc.ctc.com**) The mission of the ECRC Program is to promote awareness and implementation of Electronic Commerce and related technologies in the industry.

ELECTRONIC COMMERCE ASSOCIATION (**www.globalx.net/eca/**) A voluntary organization, the association provides a forum for sharing information and discussing ideas and initiatives related to electronic commerce.

PREMENOS ELECTRONIC COMMERCE RESOURCES (**www.premenos.com/Resources/guide.html**) This developer of EDI software provides links to a wide variety of electronic commerce and EDI information.

EC/EDI AND OTHER NAFTANET INFORMATION (**www.nafta.net/ecedi.htm**) Another resource page, sponsored by Key Software Solutions.

THE CATALOGER (**www.hummsoft.com/hummsoft/The_Cataloger.html**) The Cataloger contains information, trends, sites, and activities concerning product catalogs used in support of Electronic Commerce. Sponsored by Hummingbird Software Corporation.

COMMERCENET (**www.commerce.net**) CommerceNet is a substantial quantity of information related to Internet business development; also a commercial directory.

OPEN MARKET'S COMMERCIAL DIRECTORY (**www.directory.net**) Open Market develops commercial Web servers and products. This is their directory of commercial services, products, and information.

THE ALL-INTERNET SHOPPING DIRECTORY (**http://www.webcom.com/~tbrown**) Links to 3000+ select shopping sites on the Internet. Includes a biweekly list of the top 10 sites found during that period.

HALL OF MALLS (**nsns.com/MouseTracks/HallofMalls.html**) This is the site that asks, "What will online shopping be like when there are more tee-shirt shops and more malls than can reasonably fit in anybody's bookmark file?" A long list of catalogs and mall sites.

THE SHOPPER (**www.hummsoft.com/hummsoft/shopper.html**) Sponsored by Hummingbird, Inc., The Shopper provides links to other top-rated malls and shopping facilities. Check out the "Top Ten Tips for On-Line Malls and Merchants."

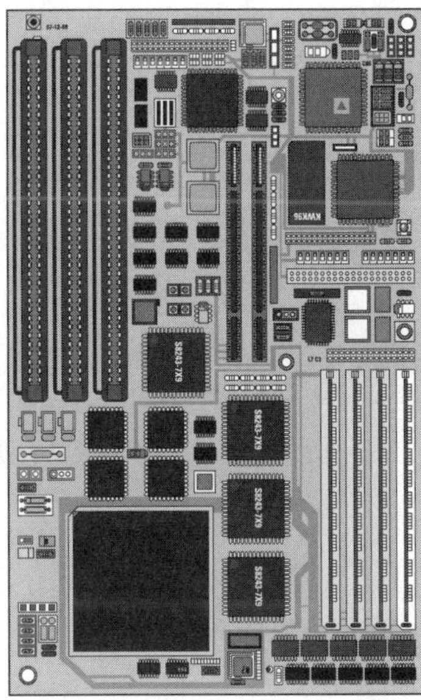

CHAPTER NINE

TRANSACTION-BASED SERVICES

Mention the words *electronic commerce,* and most people think of the online catalogs and malls discussed in Chapter 8. In this view, commerce is limited to the buying and selling of merchandise.

In fact, though, a great deal of the transaction-based systems currently appearing on the Internet are service-oriented rather than product-oriented. The main reason is simple: You can deliver a service—whether the ability to select a mutual fund, book an airline ticket, or take an order for your next meal—online. That means that there is a quantitative advantage to using the Internet for ordering such services. For example: few busy signals, no waiting on hold, and not having to deal with less-than-gracious telephone sales staff. Online systems make it easy to conduct your transaction quickly, painlessly, and at your convenience.

The case studies in this chapter examine several variations of the theme of offering service-based transaction systems on the Internet. In all cases, the most important element is the ability to hook the Web application to a back-end order-processing system.

In effect, all electronic commerce involves transaction-based systems. In the preceding chapter, we looked at two Internet applications dedicated primarily, if not solely, to the direct exchange of goods for money. In some cases, as with Virtual Vineyards and Smokin' Joes, the goods are physical products, shipped to customers via traditional channels.

Many of the transaction-based systems currently under development involve a more complex set of transactions. The basic model for these applications, like the catalogs and secure shopping environments we examined in Chapter 8, is to generate revenue. However, these transaction-based applications typically feature an enhanced set of functions, which are often designed to aid customers in their purchase decision-making.

Others have extended the ordering model to become a brokerage system for products, which is a variation of the mall concept. In this chapter, we look at three such examples: the first is the Lombard Center, a notable example of online financial investment services. The second is Travelocity, a travel reservation and booking service. The third application described, Waiters on Wheels, is an online ordering service for meal deliveries.

Many people understandably equate *transactions* with the exchange of goods for money. However, there is a rapidly growing segment of Internet applications that offer the transaction as part of a service function. This would include any reservation service, ticketing agency, subscription service, enrollment services for insurance, health care, among other applications. Any operation that involves submitting information through a form is a candidate for online transactions.

The hottest service-based transaction remains the one dealing with money—investment services. In part, this is an ideal candidate for online treatment because investment data is so volatile. It is also an ideal candidate because allowing people to perform for themselves some of the services typically performed by brokerage firms provides a means of cutting costs a service—allowing individuals to take greater control over their finances—is being rendered.

SPOTLIGHT: LOMBARD INSTITUTIONAL BROKERAGE, INC.

Lombard's Real Time Trading and Research Information System (**www.lombard.com**) is an extension of the investment services offered by Lombard Institutional Brokerage, Inc. The system is designed to provide users with a reliable and secure means of receiving stock market information and placing trades.

To the general public, Lombard offers the ability to obtain delayed stock and mutual fund information and to plot graphs of the stock activity. In addition, customers with accounts at Lombard can use the Internet system to provide fully-developed account reporting and a portfolio management function. They can also place and track orders to buy and sell stocks and mutual funds online.

PRODUCT DESCRIPTION

The Lombard site has a no-nonsense look that is appropriate to an investment tool. Tastefullly designed icons with a decidely money-green tone add visual appeal to the layout. From the home page users can select from two main options: to proceed directly to the investment center if they have previously registered, or to check out the public access information if they are still considering registration. For those who would like to register (a free process), they can do so from the home page. There is also a help function organized as a Frequently Asked Questions (FAQ) document, for those unsure what to do.

Current Lombard account holders can use the Investment Center to make trades, access quote services, graphs, and charts, as well as to secure 24-hour transactions and portfolio management services. The recently added Quote Basket allows the user to make use of the Net's real-time updating capabilities to track up to ten favorite stocks around the clock.

LOMBARD AT-A-GLANCE

The Product	Lombard's Real Time Trading and Research Information System
URL	www.lombard.com
The Company	Lombard Institutional Brokerage, Inc.
The Customers	holders of Lombard investment accounts, potential investors
Lessons Learned	underestimation of cost; difficulty of integrating proprietary data and systems
Software/Hardware	Unix, Sybase

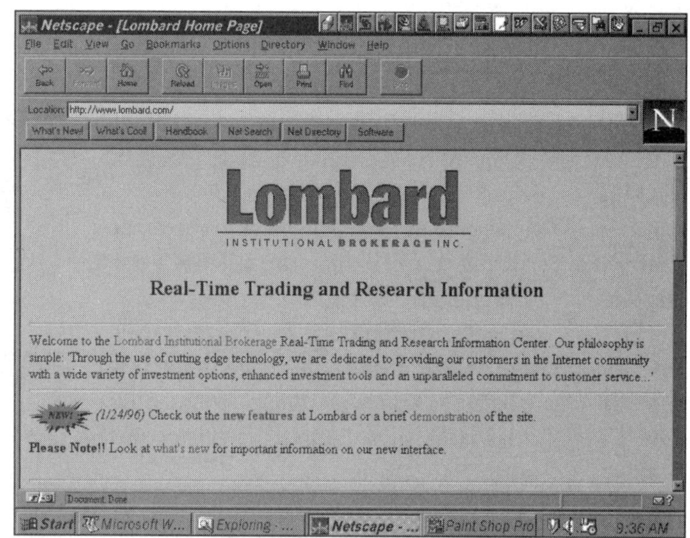

Figure 9-1
The Lombard home page.

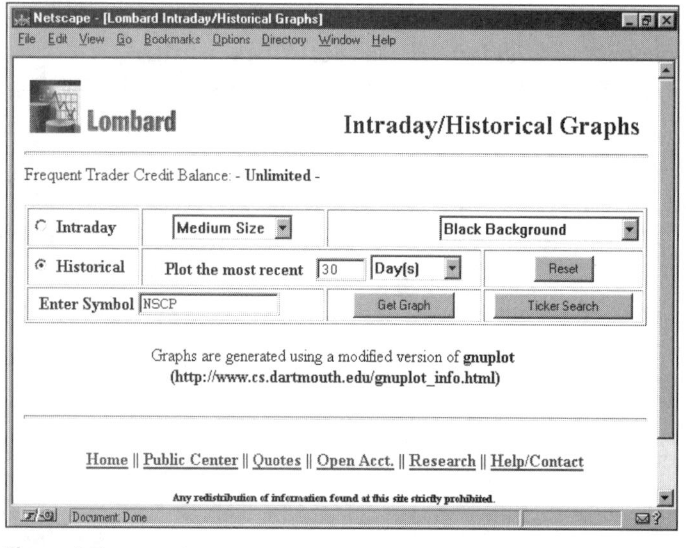

Figure 9-2
The Lombard search form.

PRODUCT FEATURES/BENEFITS

The prospect of online, real-time tracking of stocks, the placement of orders, and reporting/portfolio management functionality offers several benefits to investors. Some of these benefits include:

- The ability to make trades when and where customers want
- No commisions on trade activity
- Access to real-time information any time or place
- The ability to generate flexible reports and portfolio management

Lombard's Internet site is designed to appeal to two different audiences: guests and clients.

GUESTS

The first is the potential client. To these *guest* users, Lombard provides access to its stock search engine and stock activity graphing facilities. Stock prices and information are delayed 20 minutes to guest users. In many regards these functions are the most impressive functionality of the site (if we overlook the ability to do live trades, which clearly was the most difficult feat to accomplish).

Guest features include:

- 20-minute-delayed stock and mutual fund quotes
- Graphs showing trading activity for a given ticker symbol
- Historical graphs showing activity for a 30-day period

Part of Lombard's goal is to hook guest users by giving away a fairly sophisticated search tool. Interested users can of course fill out an information request form to be e-mailed back to Lombard for processing.

CLIENTS

To existing Lombard customers, the Lombard Account Holders, the Internet application offers an entirely new level of service. First and foremost, customers can access real-time stock quote information. But even more important, clients can execute trade orders, track orders, and manage their portfolio using Lombard's imressive array of reporting capabilities. Customers can even pick a basket of stocks to follow in real-time, with prices that are updated to the browser screen every two minutes.

Lombard Account Holders have full access to a broad range of services:

- Order Entry—Lombard Account Holders can fill out an order ticket for real-time trading or for options order entry.
- Portfolio Management—Account Holders may view and price their current holdings.
- Trade Executions and Open Orders—Account Holders can access information on their trade orders.
- Intraday and Historical Graphs—Account Holders can chart over 7,000 stocks, 61,000 options, and 5,000 mutual funds.
- Real-time Quotes—Account Holders can access real-time stock prices on more than 7,000 stocks and 5,000 mutual funds.

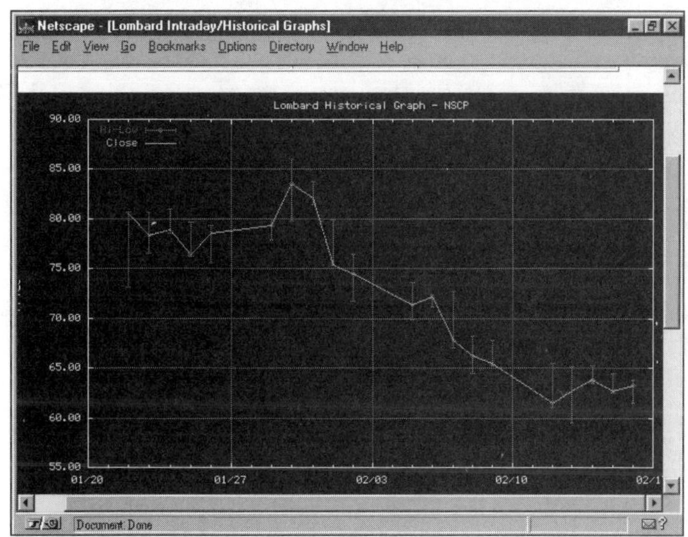

Figure 9-3
Example of a Lombard historical graph.

Lombard's site is still evolving as facilities are added. Its current content is dynamic; real-time feeds constantly feed into the Lombard database. Visual updating is done on demand by users when they graph their portfolio and/or track certain stocks.

BUSINESS/MARKETING MODEL

Lombard offers conventional investment services plus many unique online services (real-time ticker and graphing, for example) to the public for free. Lombard's intention is to use the easy accessibility of the Internet to broaden its customer base and generate revenue via conventional commissions on trades.

No fee is charged for the online services unless a user decides to trade. Thus Lombard sees the Web site as another channel to reach customers, and therefore, considers the cost of the Web site a cost of doing business. In the short time it has been online, the site has generated over 15,000 new accounts for Lombard—at a significantly lower cost per new account than conventional marketing methods. In addition, the short time frame in which Lombard generated these new accounts—and generated at much lower overhead—translates to significant bottom-line savings.

Lombard is also looking to generate revenue from advertisers who can place an ad banner on any of several screens.

TECHNOLOGY BACKBONE

Lombard's greatest technical challenge was interfacing the Web server to the many different proprietary and archaic data formats coming in. In addition, a number of interfaces to non-TCP/IP network protocols like SNA (proprietary IBM) had to be created in order to connect the service to the many back-end financial systems.

Lombard also has an interface to ADP's financial network to move the money that changes hands during trades. ADP, a computerized transaction processor, has an internal connection to U.S. Clearing, a clearing house that performs the financial settlements.

In addition, Lombard uses a database search engine and a modified version of the freely available graphing application called *gnuplot* to produce the stock search and graphing capabilities.

LESSONS LEARNED

- It is difficult to build parsers for the proprietary data—one engineer was occupied full-time as a data format parser specialist.
- It is also difficult to find people with the range of skills—Sybase database, UNIX networking, Web real-time data feed interfaces, proprietary network protocols—to set up and operate the business.
- Underestimated the budget by a factor of 2 ($400K vs. $800K).
- Underestimated the hardware budget by a factor of 4 ($55K vs. $200K).
- Underestimated the time needed by a factor of 2.5 (4 months vs. 10 months).
- The complexity of predicting schedules was higher in areas where multiple programming languages had to be used and where newly released technology components ("bleeding edge") were used, such as with beta software.
- In spite of the actual cost and time being significantly higher than anticipated, Lombard management still believes that the project was well worth the cost due to the magnitude of the returns. They could never have reached so many new accounts without the Internet application.

FUTURE PLANS

Lombard intends to upgrade the design of the site. They will soon add a database of mutual funds and bonds to the collection of instruments to buy and sell. Lombard also has plans to include news information and alerts associated with the stock quotes and graphs.

Travelocity (**www.travelocity.com**) is a one-stop travel site on the Net managed by SABRE Interactive, the leading provider of online travel reservation services, and Worldview Systems Corporation, the leading publisher of interactive and online destination information.

Travelocity enables users to access one service to reserve and purchase airline tickets, find travel and entertainment information, purchase travel guides and other unique travel-related products, and to share travel experiences with fellow travelers through online bulletin boards, chats, and forums.

COMPANY BACKGROUND

Prior to Travelocity, SABRE and Worldview Systems Corporation previously developed online relationships to appeal to the unmanaged travel market. SABRE Interactive's easySABRE product has been available to frequent travelers and online computer users for ten years, and Worldview has offered a consumer product line since September, 1993.

Several years ago, Worldview envisioned creating an interactive online site that would provide users concierge-type services as well as transaction capabilities through the Internet, or through private and public networks. At this time, Worldview and discovered that they were remarkably similar, so they decided to create a one-stop shop that integrated travel, planning, and reservations. Together they started to build the architecture, infrastructure, and create the management and operations needed to bring their ideas into reality. The work was divided up and teams traveled back and forth between the two businesses, World-

Travelocity At-a-Glance

The Product	Comprehensive online travel reservation and destination information service
URL	www.travelocity.com
The Company/Owners	SABRE Interactive and Worldview Systems
Start Date	March 12, 1996
Software/Hardware	SABRE Interactive's Silicon Graphics, Inc., WebFORCE CHALLENGE servers and Worldview System's Sun Microsystems SPARC servers
Volume	Schedules are available for more than 700 airlines, and reservations and tickets for more than 370 airlines. Travel guides are available for more than 160 featured destinations, 140 activity and interest areas, as well as over 1,700 maps, photos, video clips, and sound clips.

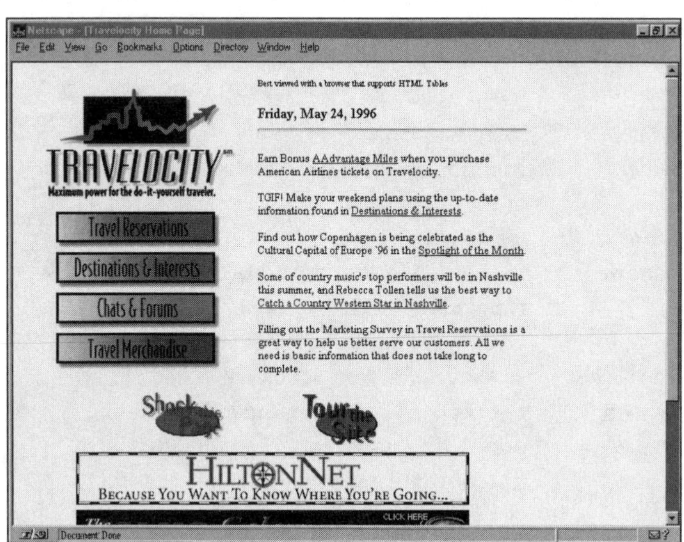

Figure 9-4
Travelocity's home page.

view in San Francisco, and SABRE in Dallas. A strong interactive and online communications system was put in place to manage the project. Budgets and forecasts were set. Finally, the large, comprehensive site was built and launched on March 12, 1996.

PRODUCT DESCRIPTION

Travelocity is essentially a free online service designed to attract the do-it-yourself travelers who want to take control of their travel plans. At present, much of the site has free access with the exception of minimal charges to access premium content, such as videos, some full-text articles, and photo albums. Major purchases such as airline tickets, hotel reservations, and travel merchandise, are made through a secured, personal member profile and charged to the user's credit card.

PRODUCT FEATURES/BENEFITS

Travelocity offers schedules for more than 700 airlines and reservations and tickets for more than 370 airlines, all provided by SABRE, which represents close to ninety-five percent of all seating capacity in the world. FlightFinder, a SABRE exclusive, automatically searches for the lowest fare available between multiple cities, and displays the three lowest-cost itineraries. In addition, users can retrieve existing reservations made in easySABRE. The site also has airplane diagrams in standard configurations for the most popular commercial aircraft.

Customers can enter their credit card information and purchase airline tickets online. If they are uncomfortable sending their credit card number over the Internet, they can call and give the information offline. At the customer's request, tickets can be sent via an overnight delivery service, delivered through a travel agency, or arranged to be picked up at the airport or ticket reservation center.

The Customer Service Center is staffed with professionals specially trained to meet the needs of online travel shoppers, and are available toll-free between 6 A.M. and 1 A.M. Central Standard Time, Monday through Friday; and between 8 A.M. and 1 A.M. Saturday and Sunday.

Worldview contributes the majority of the information on the site. Travel guides are available to more than 15,000 destinations worldwide with in-depth profiles of more than 160 featured destinations. Online users can also browse over 140 activity and interest areas. Regular travel columnists are also featured. The site has many graphics, offering more than 1,700 maps, photos, video clips, and sound clips.

Users can search the entire site by keyword, phrase, destination, or interest, or shop for travel-related merchandise, order products, and purchase them online. They can also find out what essentials they need for special destinations by following the Packing Essentials link, as well as pick up a few tips from the packing pros.

Travelocity's Business Information feature offers tips on business and recreational services offered in cities around the world. You can find out everything from where to rent laptop computers to the location of the hottest shopping districts. Also, the Foreign Protocol Etiquette provides helpful information to prevent any cultural faux pas.

Also available are several online forums and live chat sessions about various travel

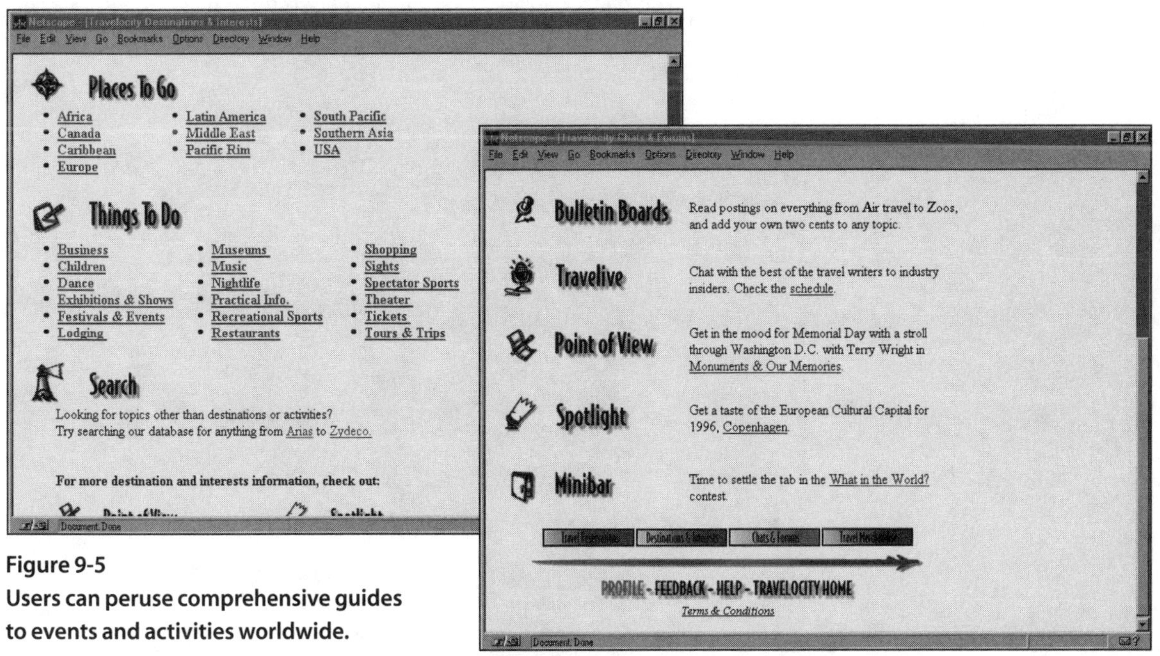

Figure 9-5
Users can peruse comprehensive guides to events and activities worldwide.

Figure 9-6
Fellow travelers can interact with each other and discuss a variety of travel issues.

topics. Users can visit bulletin boards to swap ideas, ask questions, and touch base with fellow travelers on a broad range of travel topics. Traveline offers regularly scheduled live chats and conversations with travel experts. Point of View features places, people, travels, and trends around the world. Spotlight profiles a special destination or a topic of the month. And the Minibar features games and contests to challenge the wits of the travel-savvy.

The Travelocity Merchandise department carries plenty of travel accessories that customers can order and pay for online, and then arrange for shipment directly to their doorsteps. The Product Directory enables users to scan an entire product category for a special item. They can also review a complete list of merchants providing travel products, such as Magellan's travel accessories, IVN travel videos, and Lanier Publishing International.

BUSINESS/MARKETING MODEL

Travelocity was not designed to compete with travel agents. Both SABRE and Worldview offer products and services to travel agencies and have no desire to alienate their clients. At Travelocity, they believe that there are two distinct markets: the independent traveler and businesses that have substantial travel needs.

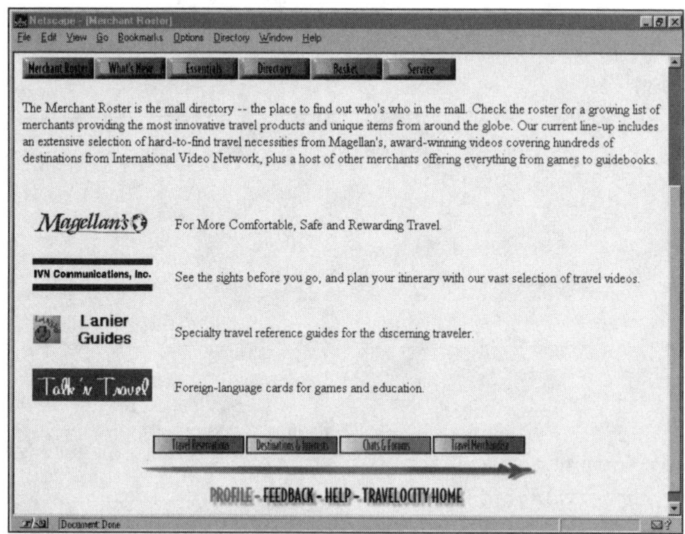

Figure 9-7
After ordering their tickets, travelers can shop and buy specialty items from Travelocity's online travel mall.

The company is targeting a class of users that will find Travelocity to be more appealing, more enthralling, more entertaining, and more efficient than a travel agency. Today, that is a small subset of the overall traveling population. Over time, Travelocity believes that another class of users will evolve who will use Travelocity for certain transactions and travel agents for others.

Currently, revenues are meeting initial projections. Travelocity is deriving revenues from all of the sources anticipated; however, in some cases, the reveune is generated in slightly different proportions. Travelocity is able to meet its revenue projections because the traffic and retention rate on the site is growing at the rate expected.

Worldview provides a large amount of the content to the Travelocity site, but other content providers contribute destination information, photos, videos, maps, and multimedia products. Freelance travel writers and photographers contribute travel destination essays and photographs. Some of the larger content providers include HOTELogic, Lanier Publishing International, and Corel Professional Photos.

Also, strategic distribution business partnerships have helped contribute to the depth and breadth of the site. Partners include GE Information Services, Inc., Infoseek Corporation, Star Text, Prodigy, *USA Today,* and WOW! from CompuServe. These business relationships are also varied. Travelocity believes that volume is the key to success regardless of which economic model will evolve, so it is important to create a number of distribution partnerships.

Even though some airlines and hotels are accepting reservations through their own independent Web sites, Travelocity does not view this as direct competition to its more comprehensive efforts. By design, Travelocity is a centralized booking agency focused on bringing in additional customers to travel businesses that may or may not already be online.

Because no one is entirely certain of the best way to generate revenue on the Internet, and what the future of the medium and a business opportunity may be, Travelocity by design has made provisions to derive revenue from as many sources as possible. The site sells airline tickets, travel products, banner advertising, as well as some content. And future plans include experimenting with everything from subscriptions to pay-per-view.

Another revenue strategy is to create a travel utility that can be privately branded, or that can be incorporated into someone else's Web site. For example, Travelocity recently developed a version of Travelocity that is branded for *USA Today*.

USA Today's Web site has a significant amount of online traffic—several million users per day. Based on a poll of its users, *USA Today*'s online editors discovered that information on travel is a strong magnet and retention device in the Life section of the newspaper. Rather than build travel information into their own page, *USA Today* approached Worldview and requested help with generating content that would draw and keep people at their site.

In response, Worldview created a small private version of parts of Travelocity and branded it as a *USA Today* travel guide. The users now had a choice of either using the travel information at the newspaper's site, or going directly to Travelocity. The hope is that more content partners and distribution partners will want to provide this kind of specially packaged travel information to their users.

Worldview's editorial staff of aproximately 30 people keep the content on the site current. The staff also manages a correspondent network around the world that varies between 80 and 134 people, and manage a network of 3,500 discreet sources worldwide that provides information to Worldview. Each month the staff translates the information into several languages, abstracts it, puts it into the database, and the production staff actively links and tags it, and attaches photos, maps, and videos. SABRE maintains real-time connections to 700 airlines, which are continuously updating fares, schedules, and availability. Both operations have developed these legacy systems over time and have attached them to the Internet through Travelocity.

TECHNOLOGY BACKBONE

Travelocity uses some of the proposed HTML 3.0 standards, such as tables, centering, and alignment of images, that are supported by most current Web browsers.

SABRE Interactive's SGI WebForce Challenge servers and Worldview System's Sun Microsystems SPARC servers provide the reliable hardware for the site. The system is protected in an underground concrete bunker and can operate for three days without electricity or water. It is one of the largest privately-owned real-time computer systems in the world—it handles more than thirty percent of the world's airline reservations booked through reservation systems.

Travelocity incorporated the ability to handle transactions with a user database, and a publication and product management capability that is built into the Netscape application. One of Travelocity's early partnerships was with Netscape, which gave Travelocity a leg up in terms of time to market. (Travelocity is also the case study for the use of Netscape's Internet Commercial Applications Suite.) Travelocity built on Netscape's platform as well as did additional custom engineering work, and it was from Netscape where Travelocity licensed its commerce server, merchandise server, community of interest server, and its publication server.

Because Travelocity has not seen widespread use or general acceptance of the electronic cash systems, it is currently supporting credit card transactions.

LESSONS LEARNED

- The Internet is a vibrant and exciting business, but because the market is moving fast and changing rapidly, no one has any idea what the future holds. It is too early to tell what models will or will not work.
- Continually enhance the product and deliver new and better material all the time.
- Be flexible. Explore as many revenue streams and partnerships as possible. If you can't be flexible, you may create a nice niche on the Internet, but you will not become a category killer.

FUTURE PLANS

The next step for Travelocity is to increase the amount of traffic on its site through attraction and retention programs. New development is being done to entice, entrance, and enlighten users so that they have a good experience at the site and want to come back. More promotions and compelling content will be offered as well as a better interface and a more personalized experience for the user. Travelocity wants to more fully integrate bulletin boards into the content areas, and it is already planning its second, third, and fourth generations of the project that are largely based on user feedback.

Soon Travelocity will offer reservations and purchase capability for 28,000 hotels and 50 car rental companies. They are working on turning their maps into real-time interactive features with geo-location functionality. At present, a few hundred thousand pages comprise the Travelocity site; the goal, within several months, is to have close to a million pages that are even easier to use.

Travelocity is aware that some content holes and navigation paradigm problems exist within the site, so new and better ways for the user to find information are being designed. Plans include employing everything from agent technology to customized views of the database, so that individual users will have more control over their own Travelocity experience. This challenge is not only providing users with information that is tailored to their interests, but also enabling Travelocity to learn more about the users so that its system can become more proactive.

World Wide Waiter (**www.waiter.com**) is the first online service to enable customers in the San Francisco Bay area, to place take out and delivery food orders over the Internet free of charge. Currently, 200 restaurant locations participate in World Wide Waiter's online ordering. World Wide Waiter officially opened its doors on December 4, 1995, and serves the San Francisco Bay area with plans to extend its service to other metropolitan areas.

World Wide Waiter is an entrepreneurial effort that operates under the official company title of Maverick Solutions, Inc. While online orders may be placed around the clock for take out and delivery during a restaurant's hours of operation, customer service representatives are available daily between 9:00 A.M. and Midnight (Pacific time), to handle inquiries or to provide user support.

COMPANY BACKGROUND

Craig Cohen generated and explored the concept of World Wide Waiter with his partner, Michael Adelberg. Cohen and Adelberg have a long history together. They both attended the same junior high school, graduated from MIT together, and then went off to study at the Stanford Business School.

While working at Sun Microsystems, Cohen started to get the beginnings of an idea that eventually evolved into World Wide Waiter. Cohen was intrigued by some of the tools his colleagues developed that made it possible to order burritos online from the local burrito place. Essentially, someone just hacked together the program, and people used it to place real food orders. "Burrito Tool" was not the most robust software program in history, nor was it particularly reliable, but Cohen thought that it was some-

World Wide Waiter At-a-Glance

The Product	Online ordering, takeout, and delivery service for local restaurants
URL	www.waiter.com
The Company	Maverick Solutions, Inc.
Owners	Craig Cohen and Michael Adelberg
Start Date	December 4, 1995
Software/Hardware	Sun workstations, NCSA 1.4 Web server, and custom software
Volume	200+ participating restaurants

thing that had tremendous business potential, given the growing availability of the Internet. Thus he decided to create an environment where all kinds of individuals and companies could have a common, reliable way of ordering food from their favorite restaurants, without needing to have a menu handy or use the telephone.

Funding for World Wide Waiter came primarily from the investment of the two business partners, and private money from their families. They plan to do another round of financing this year so that they can expand the business.

PRODUCT DESCRIPTION

World Wide Waiter focuses almost entirely on fast, efficient service. When customers come to World Wide Waiter, they can review complete menus from a large number of restaurants, place an order, customize it, pay for it, and have it ready for pick-up or delivered to their doorstep (where available). Customers can also search World Wide Waiter by city, cuisine, and whether or not the restaurant offers catering.

Once a customer selects his location, he can review the various available restaurants. For example, once a customer selects a city, a chart appears that has all of the participating restaurants in that area arranged by type of restaurant—bakery, Chinese, Italian, and so on, and whether or not they offer take out, sit-down, and/or delivery options.

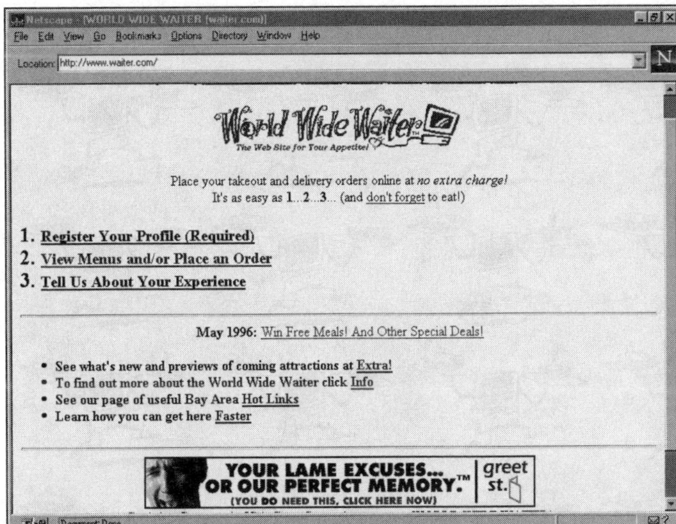

Figure 9-8
World Wide Waiter offers convenient online ordering of food from various Northern California restaurants.

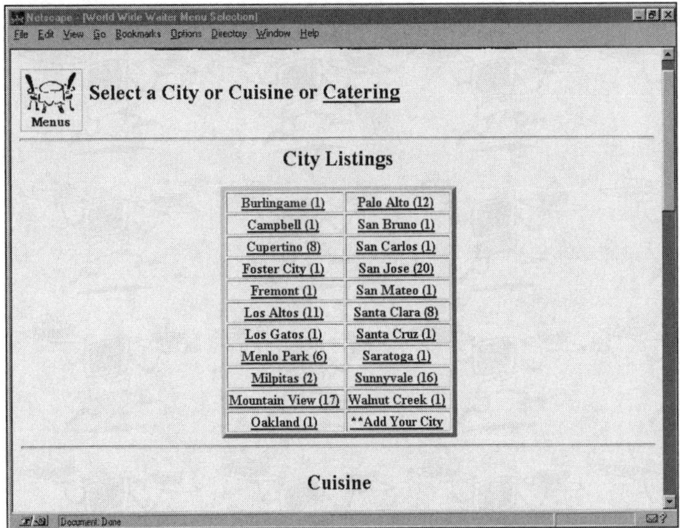

Figure 9-9
The chart lists each city and the number of participating restaurants in the area.

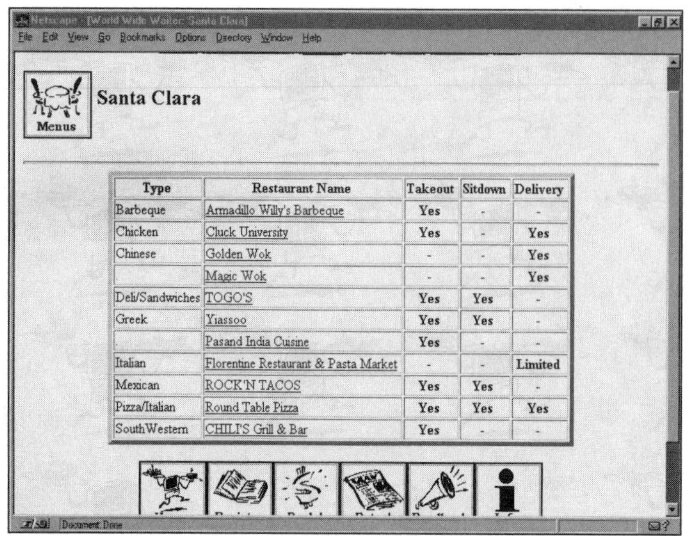

Type	Restaurant Name	Takeout	Sitdown	Delivery
Barbeque	Armadillo Willy's Barbeque	Yes	-	-
Chicken	Cluck University	Yes	-	Yes
Chinese	Golden Wok	-	-	Yes
	Magic Wok	-	-	Yes
Deli/Sandwiches	TOGO'S	Yes	Yes	-
Greek	Yiassoo	Yes	Yes	-
	Pasand India Cuisine	Yes	-	-
Italian	Florentine Restaurant & Pasta Market	-	-	Limited
Mexican	ROCK'N TACOS	Yes	Yes	-
Pizza/Italian	Round Table Pizza	Yes	Yes	Yes
SouthWestern	CHILI'S Grill & Bar	Yes	-	-

Figure 9-10
This chart presents all the restaurants doing business through World Wide Waiter in the Santa Clara, California area.

[Home] [Register / Replay] [Menus] [Deals] [Extra] [Feedback] [Info]

Register

Registration / Replay System

Welcome to the World Wide Waiter Self Registration / Replay Facility.

Register as a New User

Modify Existing User Profile

Remove Yourself as a User

Replay Directions: To retrieve a previously saved order, enter your UserName and Password below, and then hit the **[Retrieve Orders]** button. This will bring up a page which lists all your Saved Orders, from which you can chose which one you want to use.

UserName: **Password:**

Retrieve Orders | Reset Form

Figure 9-11
You only go through the registration process at World Wide Waiter once.

Essentially, World Wide Waiter serves two markets: the individual who wants to order a sandwich, pizza, or more complete dinner, and companies that want to bring in food for a large group of people.

PRODUCT FEATURES AND BENEFITS

When customers come to World Wide Waiter, the first thing they do is register and create a profile, which takes about one minute. The customer is assigned a password that enables him to select a menu from any of the 200 available restaurants and place an order online. World Wide Waiter checks the order and makes certain that the customer has allowed enough time for the order to be filled. Finally, the customer clicks Send and the order is automatically transmitted to the restaurant.

The World Wide Waiter's Web server receives the order and converts it into a fax that is sent automatically to the restaurant in approximately 60 seconds or less, and the restaurant prepares the order. If it is a delivery order, the restaurant is responsible for getting the food to the customer.

Also, when customers order they can enter their credit card information, so that by the time they go to the restaurant to pick up their food, the order is already run through and paid for. The credit card information only travels over the Internet one time when the customer registers—after that, the information is sent offline to the restaurants each time an order is placed. World Wide Waiter also provides the option of letting customers call in or fax their credit card information directly.

With World Wide Waiter, customers can create and save customized orders that can be recalled with just a few mouse clicks. For example, if a customer wants to customize his own pizza, he can select the size, crust, toppings, and add any special requests right on the online menu. He can then send the order directly to the restaurant and add it to his "hotlist" of saved orders, or he can save it without having to send it first. The next time he orders, he can simply replay the previous order and send it on to his favorite pizza place in a matter of seconds.

The graphical nature of the Web makes the use of maps very practical, and World Wide Waiter provides two kinds of maps at its site. Location maps illustrate how to find restaurants designed specifically for customers new to the area, or are unfamiliar with a specific location. They can simply print out the map and take it with them.

Delivery maps are even more helpful, because they chart whether or not you are within a restaurant's delivery area. Some of the restaurants that work with World Wide Waiter are franchised and have different delivery zones. With the delivery maps, the user can easily determine the franchise in his zone.

World Wide Waiter features special discounts and promotions offered by the participating restaurants. The Deals link takes

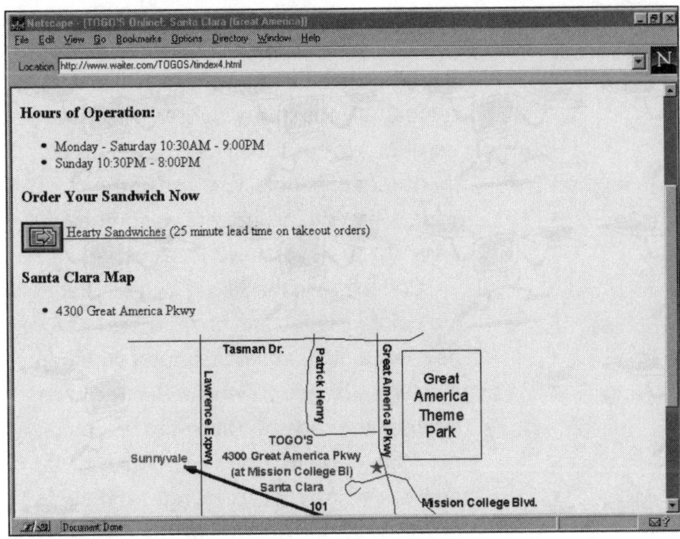

Figure 9-12
World Wide Waiter makes it easy for customers to find restaurant locations.

you directly to the monthly specials list. Also, with every online order, customers are automatically entered into a drawing for a free meal at one of the restaurants from World Wide Waiter.

The staff at World Wide Waiter is conscientious about customer service. Customers can send feedback, comments, and suggestions, and request to add their favorite restaurant to the service via e-mail directly from the Web site.

BUSINESS/MARKETING MODEL

The first goal of World Wide Waiter was to get the software working and the restaurant network built to prove that the online ordering concept was a viable business opportunity. Now that the service is up an running successfully, the staff is focused on marketing efforts to build their user base. Tens of thousands of people have visited the World Wide Waiter site, an impressive number given that it serves only a local market.

Cohen chose the Silicon Valley as a starting point for launching his business because he knew that his initial customers would most likely be people who understood the Internet and had good access to the Internet. Many people in the Silicon Valley have high-speed Internet access right at their desktop at work; whereas, in other parts of the country that is still the exception rather than the rule. However; Cohen believes that over time more cities will become ripe for a business like World Wide Waiter.

The personal information World Wide Waiter collects during the registration process is not shared with anyone outside of the business. In the future Cohen and Adelberg may look at the collected information in aggregate in terms of assessing restaurant trends, for example, but said they will not exploit specific personal information.

The general purpose behind the registration process is to provide a contact number and e-mail address in case there is a problem with a customer's order. Also, if a customer wants a delivery order, the restaurant needs to know where the customer lives; however, once the customer is registered, the information never has to be entered again. The customer just needs to know his password and the rest of the process is automated.

In some respects Cohen is cautious about adding additional site enhancements too quickly. He plans to stay focused on the service aspect of the business—the fast ordering and delivering of food—and take a more of a "wait and see" attitude toward some of the new technology coming along. Things are happening quickly, however, and there is no guarantee of a return on investment with each new feature added to the site. The staff at World Wide Waiter tries to judge the market and launch the right technology at the right time.

The staff also tries to strike a balance between having both an attractive and functional site. A fair number of users are accessing World Wide Waiter through dial-up, so it is better to have the menu come in quickly with a snappy ordering process than add too many pictures on the page that can slow the process down.

To join World Wide Waiter, restaurants are required to pay a setup fee. Depending upon the plan they choose, the restaurant can either pay a per-order charge or a monthly fee to be part of the system. The fee is affordable for the restaurants, as World Wide Waiter adopted a long-term approach in developing relationships with participating restaurants. World Wide Waiter is also doing more than just giving the restaurants a presence on the Web—they are bringing business directly to the restaurants. In order to increase business opportunities for the restaurants, World Wide Waiter is enhancing their catering section to be more responsive to those restaurants that offer those services.

Online, the site is listed in all of the relevant directories, and are featured as one of the "cool site" picks on Yahoo! and a three-star pick on Magellan. World Wide Waiter lists all of the restaurants' sites individually as well as its own site.

Offline, all of the restaurants participating in World Wide Waiter have an in-store display that tells people how they can order online through World Wide Waiter. Along with the display are business promotional cards that people can take with them. World Wide Waiter also drops flyers around the San Francisco Bay area to direct market the site.

To stimulate traffic, World Wide Waiter offers free food to customers who use the site frequently, refer a restaurant to the service, or who help spread the word about the site. For example, the user who places the largest total dollar amount of orders in a given month wins $40 in gift certificates.

World Wide Waiter is aware that many restaurant guides are popping up on the Internet, and they intend to differentiate themselves by focusing on the ordering aspect of their online business.

TECHNOLOGY BACKBONE

World Wide Waiter uses Sun workstations for its servers, which share a T3 (45 Mbps) network connection, and is currently using the NCSA 1.4 Web server. The company built much of its own custom software for online ordering.

Director of Software Engineering, Shakil Chunawala was forced to create a "shopping cart" style ordering system, to solve problems that arose from bugs in various Internet browsers, and bugs in the Windows 3.1 operating system. The first release of the World Wide Waiter software used long HTML forms to allow users to specify and customize each item they wanted to order. While this led to long menus in some cases, it had the benefit of sending the user the entire menu with all the options in one transfer. The user could then take his or her time while working on the form, and then transmit it back to the World Wide Waiter Web server when it was complete.

There were two major problems that arose with this approach. First, Windows 3.1 would typically run out of "stack space" on long forms, and either fail to display all the menu items or worse, simply crash the browser. Browsers such as Netcom's Netcruiser or America Online's brower had difficulty handling big forms, or reliably sending all the data across to the Web server. This lead to confusion and frustration on the part of end users.

Second, long menus that contained many customizable options, such as selections (pull down menus) or check boxes, would take a long time to display on other browsers, and slowed down the scrolling process.

These problems led World Wide Waiter to implement a so-called "shopping cart" interactive ordering model, which gave users a simplified list of a restaurant's menu items that they could then click through to gain additional information about a particular item or customize the item's quantity and options. This made the top level menu much shorter and faster, but had the side effect of increasing the amount of browser/server interaction required. (World Wide Waiter upgraded its server hardware to improve the performance.)

World Wide Waiter had hoped to find "off the shelf" software to help it implement its shopping cart system, but none existed that could handle customizing individual food items and correctly calculate the price of the item.

They offer the following advice to others considering building real-time transaction system business on the Web: Consider server co-location on a fast network, rather than having your own slower dedicated link, as users tend to be sensitive to latency as well as bandwidth. Design your screens to be incredibly intuitive, as users don't tend to be willing to read more than a few words online, and prefer to start clicking buttons. Be prepared to staff a customer support line, as users will get into all kinds of interesting problems that you never imagined.

LESSONS LEARNED AND HELPFUL SUGGESTIONS

- Take marketing efforts seriously and plan to invest in it continuously.
- People need to see your URL repeatedly and know what you do.
- It takes a while for people to learn about your site, and even more time before they actually log-on and come to your site.
- Expect the implementation of plans to take sometimes two or three times as long as you expect.
- Try to offer something of value on your site. Give users other things to look at and do on your site than simply purchase the product or service you are offering, as this will build interest in your site and encourage return visits.
- Have patience and be creative in promoting your site.

FUTURE PLANS

Immediate plans include adding more restaurants to the service and expanding service to the rest of the San Francisco Bay area. Eventually, the company hopes to expand to other Internet-savvy cities that are responsive to online business. It is also exploring more traditional advertising venues such as print and radio, and is currently in the process of buying lists of Internet users. Finally, World Wide Waiter plans to barter with other sites to encourage cross-marketing as a means to further increase traffic.

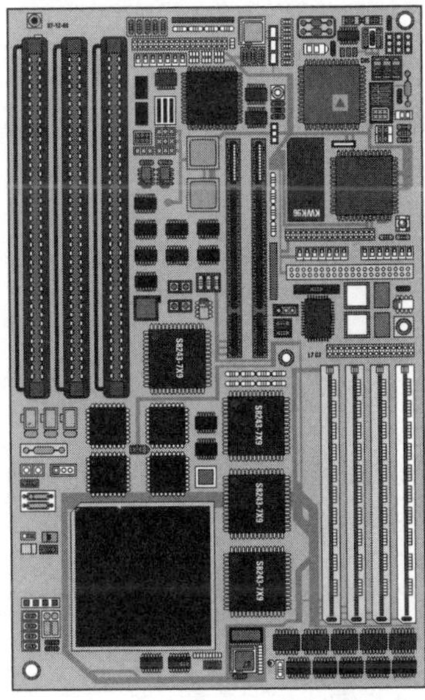

CHAPTER TEN

THE MALLING OF CYBERSPACE

You are thinking about investing in an electronic commerce system. You understand all the issues involved, and you want to know, "Should I dive in now and take a risk with online transactions, or should I just dip my toes in to test the water by putting up a simple, low-cost, low-maintenance Web site?"

Good question. It is definitely safer to start small in a risky business. It may also be wise to start small if it will take you some time to divert staff and resources to an Internet project.

But keep in mind that migrating from an HTML-based Web site to a transaction-based system is not a small undertaking. You will have to upgrade to a secure server. You will need to add a good deal of programming functionality to your site, and you are likely to have to reformat and reorganize much of your data. It will undoubtedly save you time in the long run if you start out with a transaction-based system design in mind, even if you don't plan to offer electronic transactions immediately.

Don't forget, too, the speed with which things change on the Internet. Pushing off a transaction system implementation for six months to a year could quite possibly put you behind the competition.

If you would like to implement an online catalog with order-taking capabilities but are unable or unwilling to invest in an in-house solution, consider listing with one of the growing number of cybermall services that offer complete application development services (several of which are discussed in this chapter). Working in this way will allow you to build a basic application that can be ported to an in-house system later, and will still provide the incentive to begin developing the in-house resources needed to manage such a project.

The Basics

When most people think of Internet electronic commerce, they picture either an online catalog or a cybermall. These entities go by a variety of names. In fact, The Shopper (listed in "Additional Resources" later in this chapter) has created a table for help in selecting a name for these things.

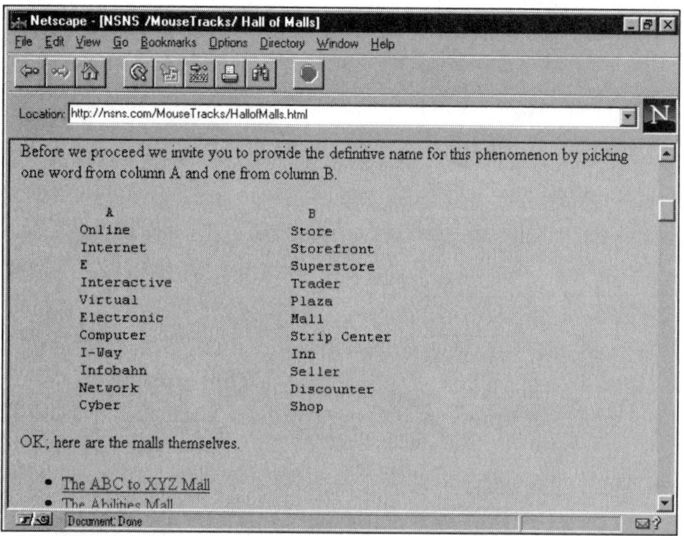

Figure 10-1
Name that shop—from the Shopper.

But naming contests aside, sites offering electronic commerce typically fall into one of three camps.

1. **Online Catalogs**, which consist of product information. Catalogs usually include a brief description of the product, vital details such as price, and often a thumbnail illustration of the product. Increasingly, catalogs are being built around a larger set of functions billed as "customer services." Such features may include games, giveaways, consumer information and resource links, chat rooms, and other "community" promoting services.

These super-catalogs look to be the wave of the future, offering value-added services as a way of attracting customers, building brand loyalty, and fostering a corporate "service" orientation to the commodity market.

Figure 10-2
A typical catalog page.

2. **Cybermalls**, which are essentially catalogs of catalogs. Some malls provide space for their "shops" and manage them internally. Other malls are simply directory services with pointers to vendors who have listed with them. Still others do both. These services look to have to fight to compete either at the name recognition level with individual vendors or on the value-add level with super-catalogs on the one hand and the village complexes (described below) on the other. Look for these to coalesce into strict directories, such as the Yahoo! model; consumer brokerages, which will locate the best price from a set of vendors; and discount "warehouses," which will offer low prices on a range of goods the company stocks and delivers.

3. **Virtual Villages**, which typically incorporate cybermall complexes into a larger set of "community" service offerings. Modeled very much like the big commercial online services (AOL, CompuServe, Prodigy) these entities are essentially the inverse of the super-catalogs described above. They offer a range of services first and particular name-brand products second. This approach is likely to appeal to the casual "window-shopper," who just wants to browse around the mall before playing a game on the Net, checking the weather, sports, or the stock market, or chatting about current affairs.

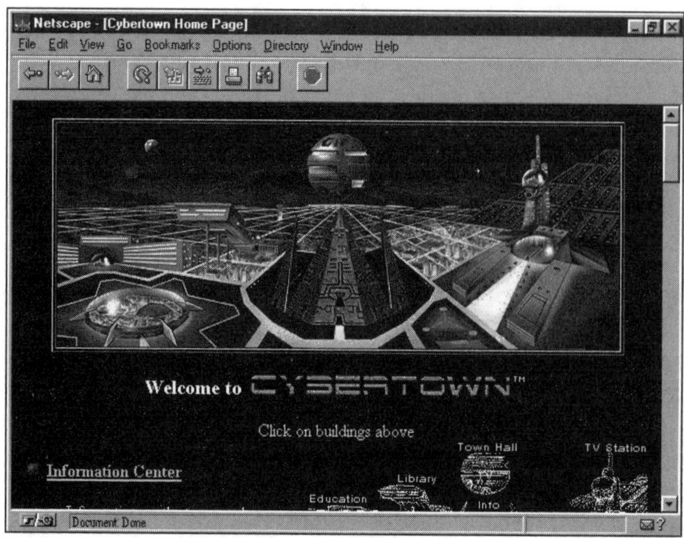

Figure 10-3
Life in a Cyber Village—from Cybertown.

Beyond these shopping facilities, all clearly modeled on real-world analogies, other applications loom on the horizon. These applications will emerge as electronic commerce goes from a way of sending flowers, candy, and novelty products, to a robust mechanism for conducting real business. As this happens, other commercial activities will also find their way onto the Internet. Such activities include directory services, like the current *Yellow Pages* models, consumer services, which help consumers make intelligent economic choices, and brokerage services, which connect suppliers and retailers.

At present, the majority of catalogs, malls, and village shopping complexes do not provide a method of purchasing directly over the Internet. Instead, they offer information and invite customers to contact them in any of a variety of ways—e-mail, phone, or fax—in order to initiate and/or complete the transaction. Many, too, are built exclusively from hard-coded HTML pages. These companies are soon likely to discover that this is an unprofitable way to deliver their product information and to generate sales.

In the following sections, we examine the key components of commercial-grade electronic commerce in the near future.

Key Components

At the moment, the most important consideration for electronic commerce is to provide a secure environment for transactions. In this section we will discuss some of the basic technical aspects of Internet security. In addition, we will call attention to some interface issues as well, since the more comfortable users become with buying and selling online, the more they will come to demand interesting and satisfying shopping experiences.

Security

People sometimes imagine that security on the Internet is an all or nothing proposition: either you have it, in which case you needn't worry, or you don't. Unfortunately, there is only one way to ensure that your operations are secure from Internet hackers: keep your operations off the Internet (but even then you need to establish appropriate internal, corporate security policies). Short of unplugging the computers, you will always be vulnerable to some degree. The key is to decrease your vulnerability to the point where the small risk is far outweighed by the advantages to you; and for the would-be hacker, the large effort involved to breach your security far outweighs the possible rewards of attempting it. It is basically the same calculus you would use when planning an investment in security measures for physical property.

The Internet is like a large, open-air market—throngs of people milling about, usually without a clear destination in mind, just out to see what's happening. There's not a lot of crowd control, just a general carnival mood. It's a great place to set up shop to hawk your goods. You have plenty of exposure—established customers can find you easily and a constant stream of newcomers can wander by and check out your wares. But the same environment that encourages commerce also makes prime pickings for thieves, pickpocketers, shysters, and other less-than-legitimate operations that rely on anonymity for their success. From their perspective, your "exposure" makes you an open target.

Should you stay away from such an environment? If you deal in small, easily cancelable, hard to trace, high-value goods, you might think twice about it. Maybe keep the inventory at home, and bring some full-color brochures instead. Or put the merchandise in locked glass cases and keep the only key around your neck. If you do set up a booth, would you pack up the accounting department records, all the customer contact information, and company financial records and bring them along with you? Highly improbable. If you had to check any of the information before making a sale, you would probably figure out some way of getting the information quickly without making it accessible to the general public.

A similar mentality is needed when constructing an Internet site. Here are some general guidelines to keep in mind:

1. Move all sensitive data that is not essential to conducting business offline.

This is common sense, but you'd be surprised how often convenience wins out over common sense. If you have a corporate LAN attached to the Internet, any sensitive information should be kept off the LAN, or at the very least behind firewalls. If it is information necessary to conduct electronic commerce, it should be set up with a staging system. Setting this up may require increasing the real-time response of your ordering system, however. You could either confirm orders via e-mail, or, make a copy of the data you need to access and make it accessible to your system (though this requires some method of transaction control).

2. Take all reasonable precautions to secure your host computer and network on which your application is running as well as the application itself.

This, like the suggestion above, is largely a question of intelligent network design and "good housekeeping." The following is a list of the basic security issues to consider.

- Keep the number of user accounts to a minimum
- Minimize use of other Internet services, like FTP and Telnet
- Institute a firewall
- Test the computer for potential security holes
- Eliminate security holes in any application that processes input from users
- Institute an alert mechanism for system malfunctions
- Configure your Web server for appropriate security

3. Use an established method of securing the transaction itself.

Several methods of securing online transactions are available today, ranging from encryption technologies to various methods of replacing credit card information with user-specific passwords. These methods include:

- Secure Web servers that provide various means of data encryption
- Credit holding companies, with which users and vendors can establish accounts
- Cybercash mechanisms, which are developing electronic forms of "e-cash" accounts
- Online checking systems, which allow vendors to draw checks directly from customer bank accounts
- Do-it-yourself encryption mechanisms (such as PGP, which is discussed later in this chapter)

Tools to Provide Secure Transactions

Currently there are two principal, widely supported schemes for providing secure transactions over the Internet. The first, called Secure Hypertext Transfer Protocol, or S-HTTP, was originally developed at EIT in conjunction with CommerceNet. The second system, called Secure Socket Layer, or SSL, is the system championed by Netscape Communications. In this section we will first provide a brief overview of how encryption mechanisms work and then discuss some of the more common commercial servers available.

SECURE SERVER TECHNOLOGY Secure servers must tackle the problem of hackers waiting to steal credit card information as it passes across the Internet using a process of encryption and authentication.

First a word about how encryption works. Most everybody is familiar with a system of encryption called "single key" encryption, even if they don't know it by this name. In single key encryption, a normal message is encrypted using a designated algorithm.

Say for example you want to encode the message "Call me tomorrow at five." You could decide to change each letter by counting 13 letters forward in the alphabet (circling around to "a" after you reach "z"). In this case, your encrypted message would read "Pnyy zr gbzbeebj ng svir." This encoding scheme is called "rot 13" and is commonly used in USENET groups wishing to render their messages unreadable at a casual glance. This is frequently done, for example, in groups that post potentially offensive jokes.

The problem with single key encryption methods, even those somewhat more sophisticated than the above example, is that they are just too easy to crack. Thus, a new method, called "double key", or "public key" encryption, was devised in 1976 by Whitfield Diffie and Martin Hellman. With double key encryption, every sender and receiver of messages has two keys: a private key, which he or she keeps to his or herself; and a public key, which he or she can make available to anyone.

How does the public key system work? Essentially, the public and private keys together "negotiate" a complicated single key that actually encrypts of the data.

Imagine that Joe and Jane wish to exchange a secure message. First, they exchange public keys. Then, if Joe wants to send a message to Jane, he encrypts it using Jane's public key. The only way the message can be decoded is with Jane's private key, which she alone knows. Likewise, when Jane communicates with Joe, she uses his public key to encrypt message which only his private key will unlock.

Security Standards

Most everyone agrees that a dependable means of securing sensitive data is absolutely necessary, but there is no clear agreement yet as to what the best mechanism is to do this. At the moment there are two competing standards.

1. **Secure Hypertext Transfer Protocol** (S-HTTP) is an application-level protocol that extends the functionality of normal HTTP to include a variety of security enhancements for the Web, such as:

- Authentication—which assures that the right client and server are speaking to one another
- Encryption—which renders it impossible for data to be stolen and misused

- Digital signatures—which prove that data sent were not tampered with
- Non-repudiation of data—which means the receiver of the data can prove the sender really sent the data

S-HHTP is currently implemented in the secure version of the NCSA server and in OpenMarket's Secure Server.

2. **Secure Sockets Layer** (SSL) is a transport layer security technique. It works below the level of the actual Web server so that it can be applied to HTTP as well as to other TCP/IP-based protocols. SSL provides authentication, encryption, and data verification. It cannot, however, provide non-repudiation of individual requests. SSL is the security method favored by Netscape Communications and is included in its Commerce Server.

SET

In February of 1996, VISA and MasterCard agreed to develop a joint open standard for security. Called SET (Secure Electronic Transaction), this standard would combine elements of both S-HTTP and SSL.

The SET specification incorporates the use of public key cryptography from RSA Data Security. Cardholders would have software on their personal computer to encrypt and transmit data. The merchant's network computer would accept this data and pass it to the bank for verification. In addition, the merchant's bank would have technology to decrypt the financial information and then return the results to the merchant's system.

Secure Servers

Several companies offer secure servers. The following are four commercially available secure servers currently available:

- Netscape's Commerce Server—which incorporates SSL encryption on both Unix and NT platforms
- OpenMarket's Secure Web Server—a Unix-based server that can employ both S-HTTP and SSL security features
- Microsoft's Internet Information Server—which uses SSL security and the NT operating system's native security features
- The Internet Factory's Commerce Builder—another NT server that uses SSL

All four servers operate as standard HTTP servers with the added ability to accept a signed digital certificate, or key, that enables the server's encryption capabilities. This digital certificate, which must be purchased separately from an authorized key issuing entity, provides a unique seed number that enables the encryption process to work.

Keep in mind that in order to work, these servers require the user to have a client browser application that also supports secure transactions, such as Netscape Navigator or Microsoft's Internet Explorer.

Encryption

There are a handful of operating cybermalls that rely on PGP for encryption credit card transactions. PGP, or Pretty Good Privacy, is a public key encryption application written by Phil Zimmerman.

Zimmerman inadvertently cast himself into the middle of a glaring spotlight when he posted his software on the Internet as freeware. According to the U.S. Commerce Department, Zimmerman's actions were in violation of export laws. (It seems that the U.S. government does not want anyone in this country making encryption techniques that they cannot crack available, in case they fall into the wrong hands.) In mid-1996, though, the government dropped its case against Zimmerman, and the software is freely available in the U.S. and in popular use by those who prefer to keep prying eyes away from their e-mail.

In a similar fashion, some cybermalls make their public keys available to customers. When you send a credit card number, you must first run it through encryption. The business then decodes it with its private key. This may only be a "pretty good" solution, but it is pretty easy on your capital resources as well.

Holding Companies

If you don't want to lay out the cash necessary for a secure server, you can solve the security problem by obtaining credit card information offline through some means other than the Internet, and then providing customers with an identification number when they place an order. This means, of course, that potential shoppers must fill out a registration form or dial an 800-number to register with your service before placing an order. This makes spontaneous buying somewhat more difficult for first-time shoppers at your site, but once they have an established account, the process is as seamless as any other online transaction.

FIRST VIRTUAL (www.fv.com) A company called First Virtual has solved this security dilemma by setting itself up as the keeper of credit card information for online merchants. Your customer can simply enroll with First Virtual, then make purchases at any business that also subscribes to First Virtual. One form, lots of buying.

For more information about First Virtual, see the First Virtual Spotlight in Chapter 9, "Transaction Based Services."

In the First Virtual scheme, designed for low- to medium-priced software sales and fee-for-service information purchases, the user signs up for a First Virtual account by telephone. During the sign-up procedure the customer provides his or her credit card number and contact information, and receives a First Virtual account number in return. Thereafter, to make purchases at participating online vendors, the user provides his or her First Virtual account number in lieu of credit card information. First Virtual later contacts the customer by e-mail, at which time he or she has the chance to approve or disapprove the purchase before his or her credit card is billed. First Virtual is in operation now and requires no special software or hardware for either the user or the merchant.

Electronic Cash/Electronic Wallets

A somewhat more ambitious approach to electronic transactions, which in the long run is likely to be more successful, is to eliminate the credit card number from the transaction altogether. All you really need is for some company to vouch for your ability to pay for whatever you are ordering.

This is the basic notion behind electronic cash: create an alternative form of money that can only be spent by the holder of that money.

There are many companies already implementing a version of this approach. For example, banks offering electronic cash are beginning to appear on the Internet. In our discussion, we will focus on DigiCash, the creators of the "e-cash" concept and CyberCash, which uses a digital "wallet" model.

DIGICASH (**www.digicash.com**) DigiCash, a product of the Netherlands DigiCash company, is a debit system something like an electronic checking account. In this system, users make an advance payment to a bank that supports the DigiCash system, and receive electronic cash, or e-cash, in return. Users then make purchases electronically and the e-cash is debited from their checking accounts. To make a purchase, users install special client software, which is available for Windows, Macintosh, and UNIX computers, to keep track of and authorize their expenditures. DigiCash calls this software the user's "wallet." You might think of it as a militant accountant!

Digicash does not plan to operate its own e-cash systems. Rather, it has begun to license its software to a number of banks, financial institutions, and other organizations. DigiCash currently follows a non-exclusive licensing policy, allowing multiple parties to issue e-cash with their own competitive pricing structure. The First Mark Twain Bank in St. Louis was the first (and of this writing, the only) bank to offer actual e-cash accounts over the Internet on a trial basis.

For more information on DigiCash and the e-cash concept, check out the DigiCash Web site at **www.digicash.com**. DigiCash's main offices are in the Netherlands and may be contacted at:

DigiCash
Kruislaan 419
1098 VA Amsterdam
The Netherlands

Tel: +31.20.665.2611
Fax: +31.20.668.5486

In the United States, DigiCash can be reached at:

DigiCash
55 East 52nd Street, 27th floor
New York, NY 10055-0186
Tel: 212.909.4092 or
Tel: 800.410.ECASH (800.410.32274)
Fax: 212.318.1222
E-mail: office.ny@digicash.com

CYBERCASH (www.cybercash.com) The CyberCash Secure Internet Payment System, invented by CyberCash, Inc., facilitates the purchase of goods and services on the Internet by providing a secure environment for transactions between consumers, merchants, and their respective banks.

Merchants who wish to use the CyberCash system first set up a merchant account at a participating bank. They then install the (free) CyberCash merchant software on their Web site, connecting it to the bank through CyberCash's servers.

When a consumer wants to make a purchase at a site with CyberCash, they must first obtain a specialized client application called a "wallet." They configure this wallet application with information about any credit card they wish to use online. When they are ready to make a purchase, the merchant server simply sends a message to the customer's wallet, asking them to indicate which card they will use for the purchase. The CyberCash system then records the charge to the selected credit account and credits the merchant's bank account.

The whole process requires six steps, as explained in this excerpt from the CyberCash Web site:

1. The consumer indicates desire to make a purchase by selecting a product from the merchant site.
2. The consumer clicks on the "Pay" button which launches the CyberCash wallet, chooses which credit card he or she wishes to pay with and clicks "OK" to forward the order and encrypted payment information to the merchant.
3. The merchant server receives the information, strips off the order and forwards the encrypted payment information to the CyberCash server.
4. The CyberCash server receives the information, takes the transaction behind its firewall and off the Internet, unwraps data within a hardware-based crypto box (the same ones the banks use to handle PINs as they are shipped between automated teller machine networks), reformats the transaction, and then forwards it to the merchant's bank over dedicated lines.

5. The merchant's bank forwards the authorization request to the issuing bank via the card associations or directly to the American Express or Discover card companies. The approval or denial code is then sent back to CyberCash.

6. CyberCash finally returns the approval or denial code to the merchant who then passes it on to the consumer.

For more information on setting up a merchant account or to download the CyberCash wallet software, check out the CyberCash Web site at **www.cybercash.com**. CyberCash can be reached at:

Tel: 703.620.4200
Fax: 703.620.4215
E-mail: info@cybercash.com

Virtual Checking

Another method of transferring money across the Internet is the use of "virtual checks." In this scenario, a customer authorizes the vendor to draw up a check to the amount in question, which is then sent to the bank for clearing much in the same way as a normal check.

This is in fact similar to the First Virtual method since it involves first setting up a pre-arranged account with the vendor in question.

Some companies offering this service include:

- Checkfree (**www.checkfree.com**)
- Intelli-a-Check (**www.icheck.com**)
- Net Chex (**www.netchex.com**)
- Checkmaster (**www.checkmaster.com/internetchecks**)

The Eclectic Approach

At the moment there is no single solution to the security issue and no clear standard for electronic commerce. As a result, the best solution seems to be for a business to cover as many bases as possible. This strategy is effectively exemplified by Spiegel catalog's site, which is described later in this chapter. It offers not one, not two, but six methods of payment. These include:

- Secure sockets through Netscape's commerce server
- Secure keypad—Spiegel's name for its offline registration
- Fax
- Callback
- 800-number
- Snail mail

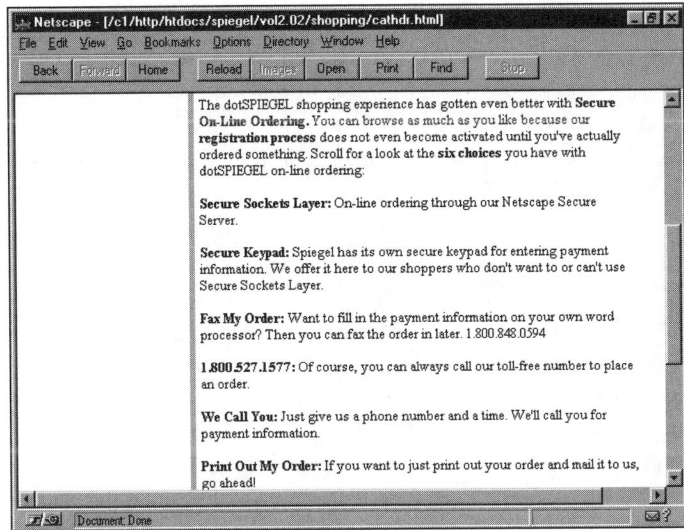

Figure 10-4
dotSPIEGEL offers a plethora of purchasing options.

It is an open question whether so much choice is impressive or befuddling, but perhaps any catalog company trying this hard to take your money deserves at least a small portion of it.

Integration with Existing Back-end Systems

Between the excitement of the Web's "cool," hypermedia environment and the paranoia about computer break-in artists, it is easy to forget that a large part of the work involved in setting up a transaction system involves the "back office" operations, from inventory management to fulfillment.

If you are starting a business that will have an Internet component, you will need to incorporate a back-end, management system. If you have an existing business, you undoubtedly already have a working system. The trick is how to build a bridge from your existing system to the Internet operations. In "technobabble," the question is, how will you integrate your legacy systems?

Either way you will need to outlay a large portion of your budget to satisfy this need. Functions you may need to provide include:

- Clearing and settlement
- Sales tax and shipping calculations
- Order notification and invoice tracking
- Order fulfillment or conveyance
- Inventory updating
- Invoice statements
- EDI links

Tools for Managing Electronic Commerce

Developing an Internet application for conducting electronic commerce can be an expensive and time-consuming process. Equally difficult, however, is the process of managing and updating the application once it is operational. In this section we will look briefly at two tools designed to help with this process. The first is Netscape IStore, a software application that helps you quickly set up and add to your catalog or cybermall. The second is Open Market's OM-Transact, which focuses on the back-office transaction functions.

NETSCAPE'S ISTORE Netscape's IStore is content management software that assists merchants in setting up and maintaining a shop on the Internet. It is designed to sell merchandise and includes an easy-to-use interface for creating and updating product information, generating merchandise displays, and managing the daily tasks of operating an Internet store.

IStore also includes a set of display templates as well as a sample storefront that can be easily customized to reflect a merchant's distinct identity. Based on industry-standard protocols and integrated with Netscape Commerce Server's security features, IStore includes a built-in credit card gateway that processes credit card transactions over an encrypted channel.

IStore also includes an integrated relational database for the accurate tracking, management, searching, and updating of product information; as well as reliable billing and order processing.

For more information, visit Netscape's Web site at **www.netscape.com** or contact Netscape at:

Corporate Sales: 415.937.2555
Personal Sales: 415.937.3777
Federal Sales: 415.937.3678

OM-TRANSACT Open Market's product, OM-Transact, is a transaction management application that helps to secure Internet commerce. When combined with a content management system, OM-Transact provides all of the features necessary to build an Internet-based transaction system. Its features include:

- Support for both S-HTTP and SSL security mechanism
- Online, real-time transaction records for merchants
- Order reports and transaction activity audit trail
- Account-based or one-time purchase models for order management
- Shopping cart technology for cross-merchant order aggregation
- Online account statements and customer service
- Online order status for hard goods
- Secure transaction and payment processing—it automatically calculates shipping charges

- Flexible payment models for paying in installments, by subscription, or through a one-time charge

OM-Transaction also has several optional modules:

- Sales Tax server—sales tax for U.S. and Canada automatically computed
- Fax server—hard good order reports faxed to merchants
- EDI server—electronic messaging back-end to facilitate order fulfillment, status, and other transaction activities

Open Market information is available at their Web site at **www.openmarket.com**, or by contacting them at their east or west coast offices:

Open Market
245 First Street
Cambridge, MA 02142
Tel: 617.621.9500
Fax: 617.621.1703
or
535 Middlefield #250
Menlo Park, CA 94025
Tel: 415.614.3400
Fax: 415.614.3409

Complete Merchant Systems

In addition to application products, both Netscape and OpenMarket offer high-end, multi-component packages that provide turn-key solutions for all of a business' transaction needs..

THE NETSCAPE MERCHANT SYSTEM To tap into this rapidly growing marketplace, Netscape Merchant System provides firms with the ability to set up and manage their own storefronts on the Internet and other IP networks. It also allows enterprises to set up online electronic malls for hosting hundreds of stores and managing the sales of thousands of products. This software solution appeals to a broad range of firms, including large, mail-order catalog companies and retailers, as well as telecommunication service providers looking to expand and complement the services they provide.

OPEN MARKET MERCHANT SOLUTION Open Market's Merchant Solution provides all of the software needed to set up a secure Web site, build a store, process orders in real-time, deliver soft goods online, produce activity reports, provide outstanding customer service, and more.

Merchant Solution's uniquely distributed architecture allows you to focus on your store, while Open Market's Integrated Commerce Service (ICS), a comprehensive customer service and electronic transaction processing center, seamlessly handles back-office operations. Merchant Solution's front-office tools allow you to create and manage compelling content for your online store, enable your store to sell both hard and soft goods, and track and use customer data to refine your product offerings.

For back-office support, Merchant Solution customers subscribe to the Integrated Commerce Service. Because the ICS is an open, standard-based solution, Merchant Solution can easily take advantage of other back-office services (based on these standards) as they become available on the Web. Additionally, as new features (such as new payment methods) become available on the ICS, merchants can immediately take advantage of them. And as your business grows, Merchant Solution's scaleable architecture allows you to easily add more Web content servers (store locations) or even assume management of your own back-office transaction system, providing a complete solution for your operation, now and in the future.

Developing Gateway Applications

If you are planning to build a sizable database as part of your catalog, you *could* do it all by hand. This would mean designing and constructing the database itself as well as writing the CGI programming and the HTML forms that customers will use to query the database.

This is fine as long as time is not an issue.

An alternative, however, if time is an issue, is to invest in one of a growing number of Application Development Tools that allow you to design and build these components much more quickly.

BLUESTONE'S SAPPHIRE/WEB Sapphire/Web is a visual application development tool designed to build access to UNIX databases, such as, Oracle, Sybase, and Informix. In using this tool, the steps for building your Web database application are greatly simplified. The steps are as follows:

1. Use any HTML editor to create HTML forms and templates for the information returned from database queries.
2. Select an appropriate object from the list of Sapphire/Web database and application objects and bind it to the form using the drag and drop Object Bind Editor.
3. Add any custom processing.
4. Test and generate C or C++ code.

You can try out a demonstration of Sapphire/Web on Bluestone's Web site at **www.bluestone.com**. For more information, contact Bluestone at:

Bluestone
1000 Briggs Road
Mt. Laurel, NJ 08054
Tel: 609.727.4600
Fax: 609.778.8125

VISUAL PROGRAMMING ENVIRONMENT, INC'S (VPE) WEB BUILDER Like Bluestone's product, VPE Web Builder is a "Rapid Application Development" (RAD) tool. In addition to providing a visual development environment that allows developers to bind HTML forms to Web Builder's rules-based programming, Web Builder can be used to maintain session information across extended data transactions. Web Builder also incorporates a networking capability that allows an Internet application to be run on one CPU while accessing production data on another CPU. This capability provides an additional layer of security for enterprise databases.

VPE has a demonstration of its product on its Web site at **www.vpe.com**. You can contact VPE at:

VPE
601 Madison Street, Suite 200
Alexandria, VA 22314
Tel: 703.684.3700
Fax: 703.684.3727
E-Mail: info@vpe.com

SAQQARA SYSTEMS STEP SEARCH Unlike the previous tools, Saqqara's Step Search is really a search engine that provides a unique front-end query format for catalog-based searches.

With Step Search, users can browse a product catalog by selecting a desired feature and then progressively narrow the results until they have a list of products that match their original product criteria. This mechanism is particularly suited to large databases of products that have similar characteristics. (See the AMP product catalog Spotlight later in this chapter.)

Application development is conducted with the Step Search Builder. The designer determines a list of features to be used as selection criterion. Each feature is then associated with a list of possible feature values. For example, if the feature selected is "color," values might be red, green, blue, or rainbow. Each product is then associated with the appropriate feature values. This information can be updated remotely at any time by an authorized administrator of the system.

A Step-Search demo is available on the Saqqara Web site at **www.stepsearch.com**. And the company may be contacted at:

Saqqara
1230 Oakmead Parkway, Suite 314
Sunnyvale, CA 94086
Tel: 408.738.4858

Enhancing User Experience

As security technologies continue to stabilize and become more reliable, consumers will eventually become acclimated to buying and selling in an electronic environment. But their next question will be, what advantages does the online world offer over my existing methods of making purchases?

Some advantages are obvious: 24-hour convenience, no long check-out lines, no crowds or surly sales clerks, no parking tickets. These are counterbalanced, however, by the absence of anyone to provide advice or encouragement as well as the obvious lack of the physical presence of the goods being considered for purchase. It is difficult to test drive a new car or try on a pair of jeans in cyberspace.

Does this mean that cars and jeans will never be sold online? Not at all. It does seem likely, though, that online stores will never entirely replace the physical analogs. Instead, online stores should strive to augment the services available in actual showrooms and shops, and take advantage of the features of the electronic medium that are difficult to replicate elsewhere.

To be successful, however, an online shopping "environment" should be enticing, comfortable, and fun on the one hand, and efficient and easy-to-use on the other. At the moment, most online stores are limited to catalogs arranged hierarchically by category with possibly a keyword search function. These are a poor substitute for the experience of walking into a store and taking in the product displays while one searches out items of interest. But there is no reason to try to replicate the real-life experience in the virtual world. By the same token, shoppers are unlikely to settle for an experience that is less satisfying than the "real" thing.

A growing number of online stores are supplementing the shopping experience by devising *super-catalog* sites. Super-catalogs do more than list products available for purchase. They provide news information, contests, and chat rooms (where customers can discuss product-related matters), among a host of other services. These services do not directly translate into increased sales, but they are designed to draw curious newcomers, support the return customer, and lend a sense of community to the overall tone and feeling of the online environment.

As online store development continues to mature, we should begin to see stores offer a wider variety of support services for potential customers. These services may start to appear as companies work to integrate their online component more fully into their existing operations.

For instance, imagine that you could conduct your search for an automobile online. Let's say you could simply answer a questionnaire about your budget, your general preferences, your personality type, and so on, from which certain cars would be suggested to you. From there you could examine the various models, in 3-D of course, so that you could walk around them, sit in the driver's seat, even tour the inside of the engine if you like, without worrying about grease stains. You could experiment with how the car might look with various colors and options, and see the retail price of each option totaled as you went. Finally, once you had narrowed your choice, you could locate the nearest dealers who currently have those cars in stock, or who offered the best prices, and book an appointment to test drive the car you had selected.

Sure, you would still have to see the car in person before you bought it, and the salesperson might still have to make his or her pitch to you before you were sold, but from your perspective, you have performed most of the shopping around you would normally do in a fraction of the time. From the sales side, you have prequalified yourself so that when you walk in the door there is a far greater chance you will walk out the proud owner of a new car. Once this level of user experience can be built into online shopping, electronic commerce will have arrived at its maturity.

Table 10.1 Featured Applications

NAME	URL	SUB-TYPE	SIZE	COMMENTS
dotSPIEGEL	www.spiegel.com	catalog	M	the Spiegel catalog on Prozac
DealerNet	www.dealernet.com	catalog	L	comparison shop for automobiles
AMP Connect	connect.ampincorpated.com	catalog	XL	huge parts catalog with unique search engine
DreamShop	www.pathfinder.com/ DreamShop	mall	M	beautiful interface, no online orders
1Mall	www.1mall.com	mall	S-M	a small mall with big feature set including content management
CyberTown	www.cybertown.com	cybervillage	L	way cool 3-D city with shopping center

Spiegel is practically synonymous with the catalog business, and dotSPIEGEL is a noteworthy example of a print catalog effectively redesigned for the Web environment. But if the print catalog is fairly straight-laced and matter-of-fact, dotSPIEGEL is Spiegel with its hair let down and its suspenders loosened a notch. It is breezy, chatty, splashy, and net-hip without being pretentious or icy cool. It just seems to have caught the Internet feeling.

Features of the site include a magazine section with upbeat articles on topics such as personal fitness, home care, better living, and recipes. Another section called "Loose Lips," is, in the site's own words, a "community center, front stoop, and corner park all rolled into one." (Elsewhere it is described as a "water cooler and backyard fence all in one"—amazing how easily virtual reality morphs!) This section provides a forum for visitors to share gossip, stories, or views via e-mail. There is also an advice column where you can "Ask Babs,"—one of the "dotEXPERTS" featured at the site—all of your customer service questions.

Spiegel's catalog appears to be built from hard-coded HTML pages. A user simply browses the catalog by category and subcategory, which then leads to a list of products, and then finally to a detailed product page. From the product description, a customer can page through the other products in the same category. Currently there is not any search mechanism available. They do have, however, a basic shopping basket technology built into their ordering system.

dotSPIEGEL uses Netscape's Secure Server and accepts online credit card information in encrypted format. In all, dotSPIEGEL boasts six methods of making a purchase, from printing out the order form and mailing it in to sending your encrypted credit card number. It is hard to say whether this many options is reassuring or daunting to the potential customer, but at any rate it is a prime illustration of the need for online catalogs to hedge their bets in the absence of any clearly preferred method of purchasing.

See dotSPIEGEL for yourself at **www.spiegel.com**.

Figure 10-5
The dotSPIEGEL home page.

SPOTLIGHT: AMP CATALOG

AMP is a large developer and manufacturer of electronic/electrical interconnection devices. Founded in 1941, AMP employs over 40,000 people in 45 countries and has 1995 sales exceeding U.S.$5.2 billion. It produces electronical parts for several products, including satellites, aircraft, automobiles, trucks, trains, ships, computers, telephone equipment, outside plant equipment, consumer electronics, and household appliances, to name but a few.

The AMP placed its catalog, called "AMP Connect," online. This catalog provides information on many thousands of parts and it is maintained in six different languages. The AMP catalog search mechanism uses Saqqara Software's Step Search technology to build its user interface. Search options include picture search, part number search and alphabetical search. One additional feature is the ability to search by part "family." A fairly long page shows a graphical representation of each product family with its name and a pop-up menu list of all the family members.

Once you select a product, the search process gets interesting. Instead of seeing a list of all matching products, you are given a list of distinguishing criteria and asked to select what type of feature you want. In this way, you narrow your search (a step at a time, hence "Step Search") according to the features you want rather than by guessing at some cryptic part name.

AMP Connect provides an impressive example of a next-generation catalog in which the interface is designed to help the customer locate what he or she wants from a vast array of data, whether the customer starts out knowing how to ask for what he or she wants or not. It is fast, easy-to-use, and cleanly designed. It manages to make the search for odd-looking electrical parts and gizmos almost pleasant.

Users can register to use AMP Connect free of charge at **connect.ampincorporated.com**.

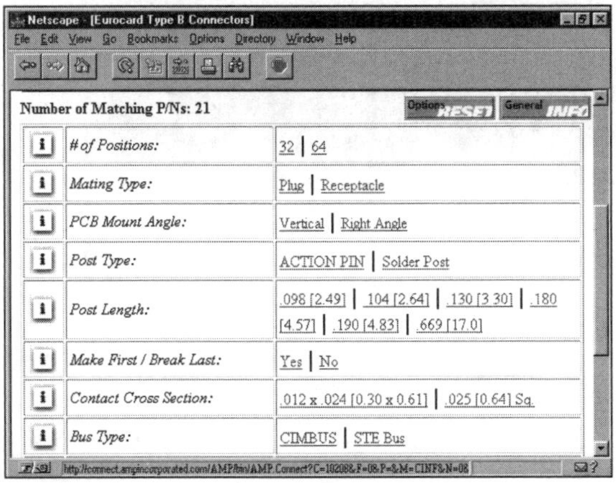

Figure 10-6
AMP's parts catalog with Step Search engine.

Fresh from a major design overhaul, DealerNet, sponsored by Reynolds + Reynolds in Seattle, is one of the Internet's most complete resources for online automobile shopping. In addition to its slick design, DealerNet has an impressive set of features to offer a potential car buyer. In addition to a well-implemented search mechanism, DealerNet provides informational pages for each of its registered dealers as well as a featured "Dealer of the Day" section, a section on "pre-owned" cars, another devoted to boats and RVs, and reviews from *New Car Test Drive* magazine. There is even a link to a service that (for a nominal fee) will obtain a copy of your credit rating for you.

Figure 10-7
The DealerNet home page.

The most useful aspect of the site, however, is the search form. You are prompted for basic information regarding the car you seek: brand names, vehicle types, price range, and your zip code (so it can try to match you with a nearby dealer). From the list of automobiles the search returns, you can view a neatly formatted page of detailed information and photos. You can also add cars to a "shopping list." Currently the shopping list is not used to make a purchase, but rather to generate a detailed comparison page for the selected cars. This is a useful feature, although for some reason you can only add one car at a time to the shopping list. If you want to add another, you have to return to the list, and then go back to the shopping list page before building the comparison chart.

DealerNet includes dealer representatives from over 40 different automobile brands. However, there are usually only three or four dealerships represented for each brand. For instance, the closest Toyota dealership to me in California was in Texas. Although impressive as a catalog, DealerNet is not really a viable system for serious shoppers (a fact it acknowledges indirectly on its search page). Rather, it is a harbinger of things to come in the retail automobile industry.

Check out DealerNet at **www.dealer-net.com**.

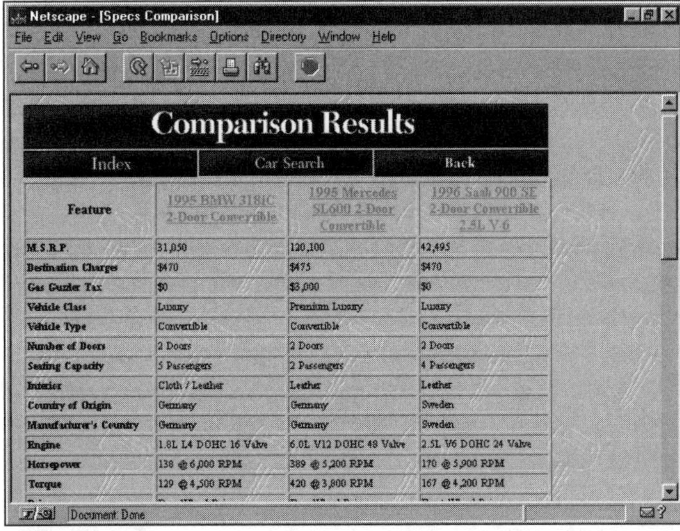

Feature	1995 BMW 318iC 2-Door Convertible	1995 Mercedes SL600 2-Door Convertible	1996 Saab 900 SE 2-Door Convertible 2.5L V-6
M.S.R.P.	31,050	120,100	42,495
Destination Charges	$470	$475	$470
Gas Guzzler Tax	$0	$3,000	$0
Vehicle Class	Luxury	Premium Luxury	Luxury
Vehicle Type	Convertible	Convertible	Convertible
Number of Doors	2 Doors	2 Doors	2 Doors
Seating Capacity	5 Passengers	2 Passengers	4 Passengers
Interior	Cloth / Leather	Leather	Leather
Country of Origin	Germany	Germany	Sweden
Manufacturer's Country	Germany	Germany	Sweden
Engine	1.8L L4 DOHC 16 Valve	6.0L V12 DOHC 48 Valve	2.5L V6 DOHC 24 Valve
Horsepower	138 @ 6,000 RPM	389 @ 5,200 RPM	170 @ 5,900 RPM
Torque	129 @ 4,500 RPM	420 @ 3,800 RPM	167 @ 4,200 RPM

Figure 10-8
The DealerNet Search Form.

Like most of the specialty areas connected to Time-Warner's Pathfinder site, DreamShop is strikingly beautiful, elegant, and inviting. From a functional standpoint, DreamShop is your basic mall, with all of the features of a cybermall you would expect: specials, featured stores, shopping cart technology, and secure server encryption of purchase information. DreamShop doesn't do anything spectacular—It just does what it does flawlessly.

DreamShop also boasts an impressive list of upscale catalogs, including Eddie Bauer, The Horchow Collection, The Sharper Image, Spiegel (not the same as the dotSPIEGEL catalog described above), The Bombay Company, Time Warner Viewer's Edge, Book-of-the-Month Editors' Choice, Caswell-Massey, and Williams-Sonoma. In addition, there are several specialty sections offered as part of the "Personal Shopper." Upon last checking these sections included "Indulge Yourself," "Feel at Home," "New Year's To-Do's," and "Grown Up Toys." The search mechanism returns a thumbnail image of each matching item drawn from the entire selection of catalogs. My quest for "chocolate" retrieved six scrumptious-looking items, though all (fortunately) out of my price range.

DreamShop does not currently support its own online means of ordering products. Instead, it relies on an 800-number system, with separate extension codes for each of its vendors.

Visit DreamShop at **www.pathfinder.com/DreamShop**.

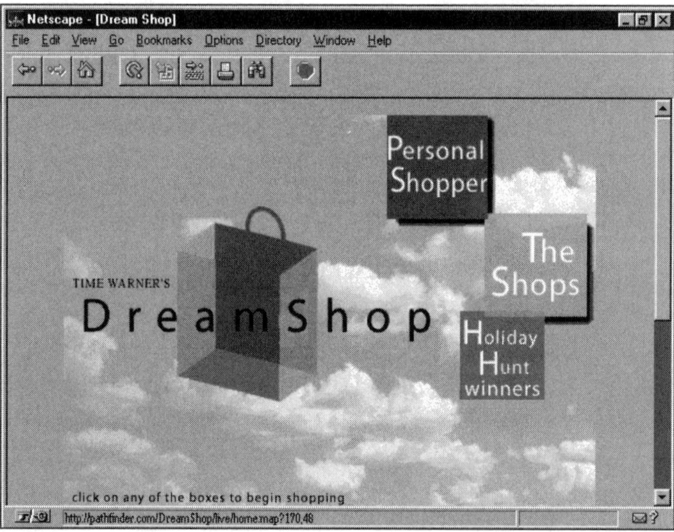

Figure 10-9
DreamShop home page.

SPOTLIGHT: CYBERTOWN

Cybertown would be just another virtual city in cyberspace except that it seems to be taking the metaphor more seriously—at least more literally—than most places. It is aided in this regard with some fine 3-D graphics work, accompanied with a growing repertoire of Shockwave and VRML content (including a cool VRML freeway!), making Cybertown a fun place to shop and play.

In addition to the shopping area, Cybertown consists of a long list of content areas: an entertainment complex, an education center, a cyberbroadcasting TV station, "CyberNews," "CyberPark," "Le Cafe," the "Health Center," and a large number of neighborhoods—from up-scale to outland. Most of these areas are comprised of links to other resources.

The shopping mall consists of roughly 40 stores, mostly small businesses and services, representing nearly 20 product categories. The mall has a simple search engine, and stores are built in hard-coded HTML. The mall has one noteworthy feature—a virtual automated teller machine that provides registered users with discounts with participating merchants. The CyberTown information notes that there are plans to offer ways to earn ATM credit toward discounts as you navigate around the city. A creative marketing idea, but not yet implemented at the time of this writing.

You may enter CyberTown at **www.cybertown.com**.

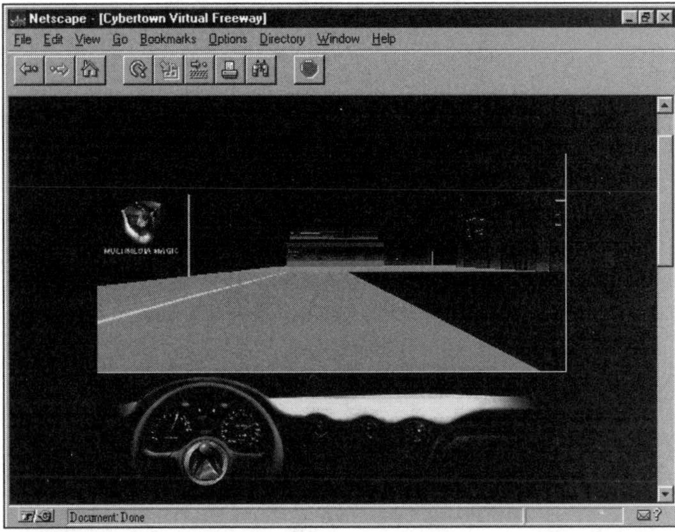

Figure 10-10
Cybertown from the freeway.

The Short List

What follows is a list of additional examples of applications making use of electronic commerce. This list is intended to be representative rather than comprehensive. For more complete directories of sites offering electronic commerce, see "Additional Resources" that follows.

TABLE 10.2 THE SHORT LIST

NAME	URL	SUB-TYPE	SIZE
Access Market Square	www.amsquare.com	mall/directory	M
Catalog Live!	www.cataloglive.com	mega-catalog	L
Downtown Anywhere	www.awa.com	cybervillage	L
eMall	emall.com	mall	M
Empire Mall	empiremall.com	mall	L
imall	www.imall.com/homepage.html	mall	L
Internet Shopping Network	www.internet.net	mall	XL
Land's End	www.landsend.com	catalog	S-M
marketplace MCI	www2.pcy.mci.net/marketplace	mall	M
Infotique's MegaMall	infotique.lm.com	mall	XL
NECX Direct	www.necx.com	catalog	XL
Netshopper	www.netshopper.com	mall	S-M
Shopping2000	www.shopping2000.com	mall	M
shops.net	shops.net/shops	mall	M
The Branch Mall	branch.com	mall	L
The Internet Mall	www.internet-mall.com	mall/directory	XL
The Internet Shopkeeper	www.shopkeeper.com/shops	mall	M
The Sharper Image	www.sharperimage.com/tsi	catalog	M

Additional Resources

COMMERCENET (www.commerce.net) CommerceNet provides a substantial quantity of information related to Internet business development; also a commercial directory.

THE SHOPPER—BY HUMMINGBIRD, INC. (www.hummsoft.com/hummsoft/shopper.html) Sponsored by Hummingbird, Inc., The Shopper is a TCP/IP software development company that provides links to other top-rated malls and shopping facilities. Check out the "Top Ten Tips for On-Line Malls and Merchants."

CONSUMER WORLD (www.consumerworld.org) Consumer World has gathered over 900 of the most useful consumer resources on the Internet. It includes everything from checking airfare prices to comparison shopping for bargains and clipping electronic coupons.

THE ALL-INTERNET SHOPPING DIRECTORY (www.Webcom.com/~tbrown) This directory contains links to 3000+ "select" shopping sites on the Internet. It includes a bi-weekly list of the top 10 sites found during that period. Other features include "Bargain Bonanza."

HALL OF MALLS (nsns.com/MouseTracks/HallofMalls.html) This is the site that asks, what will online shopping be like when there are more tee-shirt shops and malls, than can reasonably fit in anybody's bookmark file? It includes a long list of catalogs and mall sites.

OPEN MARKET'S COMMERCIAL DIRECTORY (www.directory.net) This is Open Market's directory of commercial services, products, and information, which includes an alphabetical list of all business sites as well as a daily listing of new sites. It is very comprehensive and informative.

Future Directions

Brokers, Agents, and Narrowcasting

If 1996 was the year electronic commerce hit the Internet, 1997 is shaping up to be the year the hype becomes real. Sorely needed application development tools that will greatly reduce production costs and speed development are starting to show up, and better search engines and interfaces continue to mature. Security should standardize, allowing sensitive transactions to become more accepted. All these factors will foster the growth of electronic commerce.

In addition, the development of brokerage services, using agent technologies, and narrowcasting marketing techniques built on smart profiling engines loom on the horizon. Consider the following scenario:

You walk into your car repair shop, announce that your car's whozzit hose valve is broken, and ask how long it will take to fix and how much will it cost. The attendant taps a few keys on the trusty computer that is linked to an Internet parts broker, and then informs you the part is available at a store 30 miles away. It can be delivered, installed, and you're back in business for $349.98 plus labor. Or, if you are willing to wait until next Tuesday, they can get the part from a discounted for $75. less. You make your decision, and after a few more keystrokes, the part is on its way, and the supplier's inventory database is updated.

Or, imagine receiving the following e-mail message from your favorite CD outlet:

```
   Dear Bradley,

   Thank you once again for your most recent purchase of
three Todd Rundgren CDs on December 14, 1996. Based on our
analysis of your purchases, we would like to suggest you
check out the following artists whose music we feel you
would like:
   —
   <a list of CDs featuring musicians who company profiles
reveal are favored by Todd Rundgren fans>
   —
   Because you are a valued customer, we are offering you an
opportunity to purchase any of the CDs listed above at a 30%
discount if you make your purchase before midnight on Janu-
ary 31, 1997! Use our convenient Internet ordering system to
make your purchase and receive additional discounts on
future purchases.

   Bradley, this is a personal offer redeemable only by you.
It is our way of thanking you for your ongoing patronage of
our store.

   The CyberCD Hut Staff.
```

Two trends are beginning to emerge as Internet commercial transactions become a common reality. The first is that the Internet will become increasingly used for business to business transactions, taking over and consolidating the current means businesses use to order parts and merchandise that they need to serve their customers. This is not the sexy part of the Internet development, but as it happens, it will be a sign that the Internet has matured beyond its pre-adolescence.

BARGAINFINDER In effect, projects such as FAST offer brokerage services to vendors who need parts. A similar service will eventually emerge at the consumer level, offering consumer advocates price information for goods and services. Currently, Andersen Consulting, a Silicon Valley consulting firm, has assembled a prototype of this kind of service. Called BargainFinder, Andersen's service compares CD prices at various online outlets and allows you to select the one you want to buy. To try out BargainFinder, go to **bf.cstar.ac.com/bf**. We suspect that this kind of service will meet with some resistance from vendors who would rather price comparisons not be simplified in this way. For example, when I tested BargainFinder, it informed me that several of the CD outlets had blocked access to its agent! Who will win the battle—consumers or vendors? Stay tuned....

As an example of things to come, consider the FAST project, described in Chapter 9, "Transaction-Based Services."

The e-mail scenario above indicates one way in which businesses can increasingly use information gleaned through online transactions to solicit and retain customers using "micro-demographic" techniques. We will leave it to the marketing experts to figure out exactly how to profit from individualized discount offers. It is highly likely, though, that profiling will become a routine part of the online sales and marketing spiel.

Already, development applications are appearing on the scene with built-in profiling and "narrowcasting" abilities. As further signs of the direction things are headed, consider the experimental Firefly project described below.

See Chapter 6, "News Delivery and Directory Services" for more information about these tools.

PERSONAL AGENTS, INC. Another company currently promoting the development of software agents for electronic commerce is Personal Agents, Inc. At their Web site, **www.yourcommand.com**, Personal Agents provides a guided tour of what agent software will do for both consumers (what they call decision agents) and businesses (demand agents).

FIREFLY Firefly is a Web site for music lovers that features a "Personal Music Recommendation Agent." Using software technology developed by Agents, Inc., the sponsors of Firefly, the PMRA prompts you to rate a number of musical artists. From your responses it recommends musicians you might enjoy. You can then tell the PMRA what you think of those artists, and it will continue to refine its knowledge base of you.

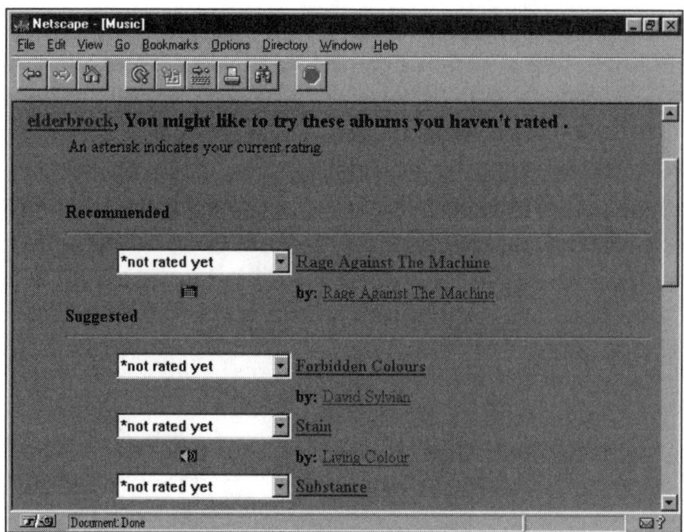

Figure 10-11
Your Personal Music Recommendor recommends music for you, personally.

Of course, Firefly is much more than just a place to get automated music recommendations. It is very much a community. Here the PMRA can help again—by linking you to other members who share some of your musical interests. There are moderated and open chat rooms, and users can write and share music reviews as well. At the time of this writing, Firefly was promising, but did not yet have, a mechanism for purchasing the music it recommends to you. Which leads one to wonder, can software agents be bribed?

PART FOUR

Managing Your Project

So far we examined Internet businesses that fall into three main categories: communication services, publishing and information delivery systems, and electronic commerce applications. In Part Four, it is time to turn to what you will need to get started on your own project.

In the remaining chapters we provide a basic road map of some of the major issues you will need to consider, the decisions you will need to make, and the challenges you may have to face. We also offer practical tips based on several years of watching businesses try to get their Internet presence off the ground.

In Chapter Eleven, "Harnessing the Vision," we provide an overview of the entire process of starting an Internet business, from identifying an initial opportunity to planning for future growth and enhancements.

In Chapter Twelve, "Assembling Players and Parts," we focus on the province of the project manager. We examine all of the key decisions that have to be made and the participants who need to be procured in order for the project to proceed smoothly to a successful completion.

In Chapter Thirteen, "The Essential Applications," we survey some of the major software products available to help you build, run, and manage your project.

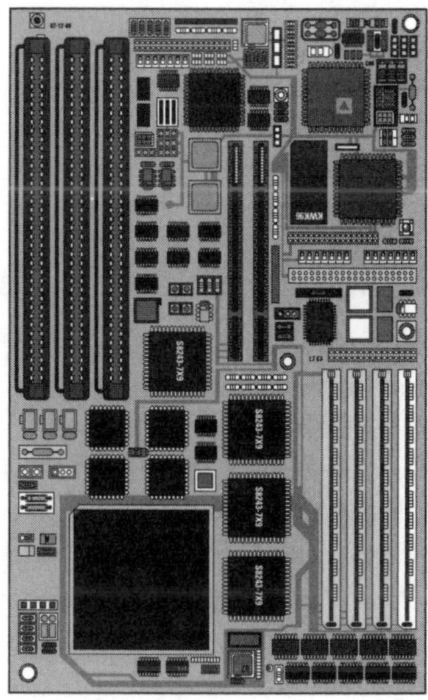

CHAPTER ELEVEN

HARNESSING THE VISION

It is increasingly difficult to avoid the Internet in one's daily life. Newspapers, magazines, and now television talk about the topic incessantly. URLs appear on billboards, TV commercials—even radio commercials. For anyone setting out to develop an Internet project, this kind of visibility is a mixed blessing. It certainly helps to generate interest and enthusiasm, but it also conveys a somewhat false impression that everybody is already engaged in a productive Internet enterprise.

The fact is, a fair amount of what passes for enterprise on the Internet is more sound and fury than a solid, substantial business. The Internet is a new frontier where there is an abundance of opportunity. In such an atmosphere, some projects will survive, and others will not. Our goal in this section (and in the whole book) is to make sure that your Internet project has the qualities to make it a success.

In this chapter, we describe the major stages involved in establishing and running an online business. The stages are presented more or less in chronological order, with the caveat that the process is not purely linear. You may still be refining your understanding of the opportunities or exploring new marketing possibilities as you develop, maintain, and expand your business.

For each stage described we illustrate the main issues involved as well as offer general tips and advice. In addition, we follow the course of two hypothetical businesses as they build their successful Internet presence. These two fictional cases include:

- Jay Danmyer, who owns and operates a small chain of resort hotels in the southwestern U.S.
- Norma Mailer and Jean Conners, who are interested in setting up a retail import partnership.

Note that these examples are entirely fictional case studies used only to exemplify some of the general issues brought up in the chapter. We invented cases that are typical in some regards and probably unrealistic in others. Perhaps they will have as much entertainment value as merit as real businesses. (And besides, if we had invented a really good business opportunity, would we just give it away like this?) The fictional case studies are an amalgamation of our experience with a little creative license mixed in. Any resemblance to existing Internet applications is entirely a coincidence.

Further note that we advise against attempting to model a business directly on either of these hypothetical cases. We encourage you enjoy the examples and to learn from the way they present and address the same kinds of issues you are likely to encounter as you develop your own business.

Identifying Internet Business Opportunities

The first step in analyzing an Internet business is to identify a viable business opportunity. This may sound like an obvious statement, but in an atmosphere thick with hyperbole, common sense is sometimes forgotten.

Currently, just about everything looks like an opportunity on the Internet. Unfortunately, some of the opportunities turn out to be better than others.

In general, there are two classes of opportunity afforded by the explosion of interest in the Internet.

- **The Internet-augmented business.** This type occurs when you have an existing business and you see a way to either improve upon or expand that business through the online medium.
- **The Internet-based business.** This type is more entrepreneurial in that you see an opportunity afforded by the Internet itself and proceed to develop a completely virtual company.

The Continuum of Internet Businesses

One way to distinguish an Internet-augmented from an Internet-based business is in terms of how and to what degree you use existing assets, including current business functions, content, resources, services, and so on, and incorporate them into your Internet business. In the case of the purely Internet-augmented business, nothing new in the way of products or services is added. Content is redirected; functionality is replicated from existing operations. Conversely, the Internet-based business generates all new content and functions for the purpose of the business.

It is convenient to classify all Internet businesses as one type or the other. In practice, though, businesses usually fall somewhere along a continuum between a purely Internet-augmented business and a purely Internet-based one. Identified below are the major degrees of Internet involvement that your business might have.

- Extension of current business functions and content, such as
  - Marketing
  - Customer service
  - Interdepartmental communications
- Supplement to current business services
- Supplement to business content
- Independent spin-off of the current business
- Entirely new, Internet business

Pros and Cons of Using Existing Assets

Obviously there are pros and cons to trying to re-deploy existing assets as opposed to creating or purchasing new ones. In a moment we will look at an example of each type of approach, but before we do, it is worth thinking about some of the strengths and weaknesses of each approach.

Pros

- Using existing assets will save development time and money.
- Using existing assets allows you to operate within a more familiar business environment.
- Using existing assets allows you to build productive interchanges and economies of scale between Internet and non-Internet businesses.

Cons

- Existing resources may not lend themselves well to Internet orientation.
- The cost of conversion may be higher than starting from scratch.
- When using existing resources there is a greater tendency to ignore the specific strengths and weaknesses of the Internet as a medium.
- An Internet-only business may be a cleaner structure and easier to manage.

Generally speaking, if you have existing resources you will find it easier to convert them to the Internet medium than if you had to start from scratch. However, you may have difficulty "retro-fitting" existing content to this medium. Those who start from scratch may find that their end result is more suited to the Internet community and makes better use of Internet technologies.

In either case, one goal should be to develop an *Internet-centric* approach. By *Internet-centric* we mean that you ask yourself two important questions about the type of business you are producing:

1. Does the structure and content of your application take advantage of the strengths of the Internet as a communication/information delivery medium, or could the same effects be achieved just as effectively (perhaps even more effectively) in another medium?
2. Does the structure and content of your application take into consideration and attempt to foster the unique culture and characteristics of the Internet community?

The Case Studies

At this point it is time to introduce our hypothetical case studies as examples of these two types of Internet businesses.

Rest Easy Resorts (Internet-Augmented)

The first case involves a small chain of resort hotels, the Rest Easy Resorts, owned and operated by Jay Danmyer. Jay has a staff at each of the four establishments in four different cities in the southwestern U.S. His central administrative offices are in Phoenix, Arizona.

Jay sees a few ways in which the Internet could be of use to his current business:

- Improve communication channels among offices
- Provide marketing for his resorts
- Supplement his reservation systems

He also identifies an additional Internet opportunity for his business: providing a vacation planning service to those contemplating trips to the four cities in which his resorts are located. He already has a network of contacts in the related vacation industries and he thinks he could generate some advertising revenue for his service from these contacts. Jay's plan fits under the classification of an *Internet-augmented* business, although his vision of a supplemental service could easily spin off into a business unit of its own.

Exotique Virtual Imports (Internet-Based)

The second case involves two associates, Norma and Jean, who have for several months been discussing a shared interest in starting a retail import business. They are quite excited about the idea, but have been unable to put together the capital necessary to get them started in retail. Then it occurs to them that perhaps there is an opportunity for an Internet-based service focused on the import business.

They decide to call their service Exotique Virtual Imports and identify the following two goals:

- To develop a consumer service for locating desired imports
- To build the service by brokering for retail businesses

To Norma and Jean, the main attraction of the online import brokerage business is that it allows them to enter the import arena without the initial outlay of cash required to acquire and maintain a product inventory, or the overhead involved in setting up a shop. They will still get to deal with the merchandise they enjoy, make contacts in the industry, help to satisfy customers, and learn a great deal as they go. And maybe they will even make some money. Their goal is to reach profitability faster than they could if they borrowed the money to capitalize a retail shop.

Exotique Virtual Imports is an example of an Internet-based business. It is quite possible, however, that Norma and Jean might decide to take any profits they earn and apply them toward the purchase of a retail store.

Devising an Internet Business Plan

Once you have identified the opportunity that the Internet affords you, the next step is to create a reasonable plan for seizing the opportunity. This is a crucial step. With all of the media attention currently given to the Internet, it is easy to get caught up in the apparent immediate need for every company to have an Internet presence. If you let such instincts drive your Internet strategy, however, you stand a fairly good chance of ending unsuccessfully.

Without clearly defined direction and goals, it will be all too easy for your project to change each time something new and exciting appears on the Internet horizon. On the other hand, if you agonize too long over the details of just the right plan, your project runs the risk of being outdated before it even launches. Try to balance clear, achievable goals with a flexible development plan.

Develop a Business Model

Base your decisions about how much of an Internet presence to establish on sound business models. This book will help you select an appropriate model. If you cannot find a business justification to proceed, don't. Working out a model is likely to take time, but it will be time saved in the long run.

To get started, ask yourself the following questions:

WHAT IS YOUR BUSINESS GOAL? Generally speaking, there are two answers to this question: (1) increase revenues by generating income, and (2) increase productivity and thereby realize a cost savings. More specifically, we offer a list, by no means exhaustive, of possible reasons for wanting to develop an Internet-based business application.

- To provide a means by which you can leverage your existing business to new customers
- To serve customers more effectively and efficiently
- To increase internal employee productivity
- To deliver electronically or provide online samples of a product or service
- To develop a new business idea you have for this emerging marketplace

In many cases, the achievement of these goals is likely to be sometime in the medium to long term. If you are undertaking this business as an investment in the future, be sure to project how long into the future you will have to wait before you see some return. If revenue is your goal, don't settle for a vaguely defined notion that if you get online now, you will beat the competition and be better positioned when the money starts to pour in. If productivity is the goal, calculate how long it will take before people will be using the new system efficiently.

WHO IS THE INTENDED AUDIENCE? The main reason to ask this question is to ensure that the application you do develop effectively targets your market. Another reason is to consider whether this intended audience is likely to use the Internet or not. You may have a brilliant business model worked out, but if the people you expect to use the application are not connected to the Internet and don't regularly use computers, your model is probably useless. (If your target user base is not composed of Internet users, it may be premature to develop a full-scale Internet application today.)

HOW WILL YOU GAUGE YOUR SUCCESS? Now there's a good question! One of the things that plagues many businesses that currently have an Internet presence is their inability to accurately determine the effectiveness of their efforts. Most are smart enough to collect usage information, but it is not always clear what to make of the fact that there were 2,340 hits on their home page last week. Is that a lot or a little? How does it translate into a business objective? People came and saw, but did it have any effect?

Part of answering this question involves setting up measurable, meaningful benchmarks for your business application, and then figuring out how you will collect the measurements and what you will measure them against. Partly, too, this question implies the need to design an application that lends itself to measurable results. Advertisers know that if a certain number of people see an advertisement a given number of times, some percentage of those people will buy the advertised product. Keep similar statistics for your Internet application and then compare them with target projections.

A Note About Experimenting

Insisting on a good business rationale for your plans does not mean that you should never undertake anything experimental, especially because that would rule out quite a bit of the activity on the Internet. With good sense, though, you would probably want to hedge your bets against any of the riskier, unproved undertakings. Don't make new technologies the core of your applications, for example. Try out experimental technologies in a test bed environment before you present them as a central part of your site. Be prepared to abandon them without jeopardizing the integrity of your application as a whole. In a volatile technical atmosphere, you don't want to put all of your digital eggs into one basket, unless perhaps you have a hefty amount of venture capital.

The Rest Easy Model

When Jay examined his goals, he realized that he wanted the Internet both to improve one aspect of his company's efficiency and to realize some additional revenues. Initially, Jay had imagined that he would improve productivity simply by connecting all of his establishments to an e-mail system. When he looked at the costs involved, however, which included upgrading technology as well as training his employees, he at first decided that the costs were too great compared with the benefits. Phones and fax machines could get them by a little longer.

At the same time, he realized that he had already been investigating a database system that would connect all of his establishments to a central network, instead of having each handle report its accounting separately. He felt that if he could build this system into an Intranet, he could add e-mail as an added justification of the expense. In addition, he wanted to explore the cost of providing a secure method by which online users could make, cancel, and confirm registrations directly. This, he knew, was a long-range plan, so he set about gathering the information he would need to make an intelligent decision about if and when to implement such a system.

Jay recognized that a large percentage of Internet users take vacations in the four cities where his resorts are located. He feels there is a large incentive for him to use the Internet for advertising purposes now. In addition, he designs a searchable database of vacation-related services near his resorts. He arranges a referral fee with the services he includes and then offers a discounted price on room rates for anyone who uses the database to locate a service. In this way, he projects that his efforts will more than pay for themselves, and he will not only make a small income, and increase his name recognition among vacationers, but also get his own advertising for free.

The Exotique Model

Norma and Jean already calculated what it would cost to open a retail establishment. Setting up a virtual import brokerage "mall" will require much less capital. They are somewhat concerned that their target market is predominantly women while Internet users are predominantly men. However, the general economic bracket of the target market is a good fit, and with some creative marketing (described later in the chapter) they believe they can overcome this challenge.

Norma and Jean decide to charge each retail business that lists with them a nominal, per item fee to cover the cost of inputting content into the system, and another fee for handling any transactions that occur. They set up a secure transaction system as well as other offline methods of transacting business in order to allay the fears of those users still uncertain about security. They prearrange with five retailers to put their content online, and project that they will break even within four to six months.

For the time being, Norma and Jean decide to keep the service free to users in order to increase the volume of traffic. Looking to the future they intend to add a content-based service describing the locales from which the items are imported, and perhaps even some cameos of the artisans. Once volume of usage increases, they plan to institute a member-based user fee for the full-featured service.

Take Into Account Your User Base

In keeping with the notion that good business sense should rule your decision-making process, you should consider whether you really need the Internet at all. You may have good reasons for *not* wanting to develop an Internet application at this time. Many of those reasons revolve around who you would potentially serve by adding this presence.

Collect Research to Support Your Model

You don't need to be an expert on the Internet to envision and oversee the construction of an effective Internet application, just as you don't need to have ever traveled to a foreign country to conduct business there. But it frequently helps. It does not take very much experience on the Internet to begin to get a strong sense of its limitations as well as its virtues. The frustrations you encounter are the ones you will want to try to avoid in your own development efforts.

By the same token, the more accustomed you become to the Internet, the more you assume the "when in Rome" mentality, the more you will design a site that will also appeal to the Net-savvy crowd.

Create a Realistic Budget and Timeline

Many projects begin with a grandiose vision and then run up against the reality of a limited budget and time frame for completing the project. Part of the problem stems from the fact that there is still not a great deal of evidence that investing large sums of money in a project will yield profitable results (although the body of that evidence is growing). Yet there is usually the pressure to have something up and running on the Internet quickly.

SOME PRETTY GOOD REASONS NOT TO DEVELOP AN INTERNET PRESENCE

Deep in our hearts, of course, we believe that everyone should have an Internet presence. We are willing to entertain the possibility, however, that some companies may not be quite ready to appreciate that presence. So, in the spirit of objectivity, we present some reasons why you might want to think twice before starting your Internet project tomorrow:

- **You and your company employees do not use, plan to use, or ever care to use the Internet for business.**
- **Your target customer base does not use, plan to use, or ever care to use the Internet.**
- **You do not have the time, resources, staff, or money to devote to the project.**
- **You have a business that depends more on privacy than on publicity.**

If yours is this kind of environment, it may be best for you to adopt a phased approach to your Internet application. Keeping the grand vision as the target, develop a smaller piece of that vision immediately, while you hold the more expensive, cutting-edge parts of the project for Phase II. This is a good approach, too, when your company needs the time internally to become familiar with the Internet, such as how it works and how it can work for you. In the process you are quite likely to discover new avenues of development.

One word of caution about the phased approach, however. The key is to build enough elements of interest in Phase I to ensure that there is momentum to carry you into Phase II. Once you begin to divide the task up, it is tempting to do in Phase I only what is comfortable and familiar, which is likely to mean a marketing Web site. Starting this way could make it harder to make the leap to the next phase, especially if the Phase I site is less successful than predicted. Try to build enough functionality into Phase I to get a feel for what your full-fledged application would be like.

Developing the Product

The main challenge faced at the development stage of your Internet project will be deciding who will do the development. Internet development is a wide open field. There are many ways to accomplish the same tasks, and very little agreement about how development should get done, what tools should be used, or how much it should cost. In this chapter, we focus on some general words of advice about how to get what you want at the end of the development phase.

For more information and detail about the development phase of your Internet business, see Chapter 12, "Assembling Players and Parts."

Do Your Homework

Because there is so much variation between the recommendations and bids you will receive, it pays to research as much as possible in advance of requesting bids for your project. You should get some sense of the prices different outfits charge (not always an easy task) and what they are charging for. It also pays to have some sense of the development options available to you (again, this book will help here) so that you can intelligently assess the proposals put in front of you. Similarly, the more focused you can make your request for proposals, the more you will be able to distinguish the experienced developers from the novices.

Finally, be sure to check the track records of any contract workers you hire. Weigh for yourself the value of a less expensive bid by an independent consultant versus the probably higher prices of a larger, funded firm. It is usually preferable, where possible, to hire a group that can hand you a complete solution rather than jobbing out pieces of the project to several entities.

In-house Versus Outsourced Work

One of the biggest questions you will struggle with is whether to use existing personnel to produce your application or to hire an outside group on a consultant basis. Consider the major pros and cons of doing the work internally.

Pros

- By doing the work internally you will retain tighter control over direction.
- You will save time in logistics.
- You will save money.

Cons

- Doing the work in-house diverts staff from core responsibilities.
- The in-house staff may have less expertise in given areas.
- It may be more difficult to organize an in-house team to cover all needs.

All things equal, you would probably prefer to do the work yourself, but this is frequently not a viable option. In this case, you might consider jobbing out the more demanding aspects of the project and doing some of the labor intensive, but less technical, work in-house. This is a particularly good approach if you plan to have one or more staff members maintain the site once it is developed. Their participation in the development phase can help familiarize them with the application as well as with the technology.

On the other hand, splitting the project between staff and consultants does not always lend itself to a smooth development process. Another approach is to let the contractors develop and maintain the project initially, and then gradually bring the maintenance functions in-house. Often development houses will offer training services to assist in the transition process as part of a package deal.

Prototyping and Specifications

Because most Internet interfaces are built using HTML, and because developing in HTML is relatively easy to develop and easy to change, development groups working on a small- to medium-sized project typically do not attempt to build a prototype of the project. More commonly, the development group will first build and test the basic interface in HTML before implementing the more content-heavy or programming-intensive components.

Even if you do not go to the trouble of building a complete prototype model of your project, you will at least want to design a schematic diagram of the branching and linking within the interface. It is also sometimes helpful to construct a storyboard with sketched versions of the interface.

Also, take the time to put into writing all of the specifications for your project, including as many technical details about hardware, IP addresses, application configurations, and so on, as possible. In an environment as volatile as the Internet development world, maintaining an institutional memory is vital. Sooner or later, probably months after the project is ostensibly finished, someone is going to want one piece of this information, and the one person who knows it will have just left to do something else.

Setting Standards

Another document worth taking the time to produce is a standards document. The purpose of this document is to provide a level of consistency to your application as it is being developed and a road map to later development. It should contain information about:

- Interface design elements
- HTML code specifications and conventions
- Graphical design styles

Putting this information in writing is difficult during development, when just getting the job done feels like a much bigger priority. Particularly if you have any intention of transferring responsibility for the application from a contract group to in-house staff, you will save yourself a lot of grief if you take the time to produce this document.

Testing

For a while on the Internet, everyone marked their projects "under construction." After a while, this concept became stale as more and more sites became perpetually under construction. Now, everything is in "beta," and Internet users have become, like it or not, de facto beta testers.

Part of the reason for this is the ease with which a Web site can be updated or corrected. Also, part of the reason is the perceived need to get products out quickly. However, it is one thing to solicit user feedback for a new product so that you can adjust it to the user's needs. It is another thing to foist an unfinished product on an unsuspecting user just to get your press release out a couple weeks earlier.

Build some opportunity for user testing into the project timeline. In the best case, there would be some time for testing different levels of the interface design and functionality throughout the process. Otherwise, invariably, someone will say two weeks after the graphics have been completed, "I just don't like that color somehow...."

In addition to testing for usability and for programming bugs, be sure to test the application in as many different environments as possible—different platforms and configurations, different monitors, different access speeds, different browsers. Things that work well in one situation may bomb in another, and it is better to find this out yourself.

Avoid Using Technology for Technology's Sake

It is fairly common for businesses to clamor to their developers, "We want Java! We want VRML! We want streaming 3-D animation and real-time video conferencing!" Why? Just because it's hip?

There is no doubt that there is an abundance, perhaps a wee overabundance, of hipness on the Internet today. If your purpose is primarily marketing, this may not be a bad thing, especially if your target market identifies with hipness. However, cool technology has a way of getting in the way of an otherwise very useful application. This is not because new technology is useless, but because typically people start "playing" with the technology before they have discovered a use for it.

By the same token, don't shy away from technologies just because they are not tried and true (a criterion that would eliminate seventy-five percent of Internet activity anyway). In effect, the advice here is the same point we made earlier—let your decisions be driven by reasonable business motives: will the use of this technology allow your users to accomplish what they want to do more efficiently or in a way that they find more satisfying?

The Case Studies

THE REST EASY DEVELOPMENT PLAN

Jay knows that he does not currently have the staff to both develop and maintain his site, so he decides to use a development group that can offer him a package deal: design, implementation, hosting, and maintenance. They are more expensive than some of the other options he explored, but they have a good deal of demonstrated experience and can deliver what he wants quickly. Also, it makes him feel better to know that he only needs to call one number if he needs to request a change or correct a problem. In the meantime, as he plans for his network plans, he builds into this arrangement a provision for maintaining his own site. He also asks the Internet development team to present a plan for transitioning the site into his control.

EXOTIQUE'S DEVELOPMENT OPTIONS

Norma and Jean consider two options. One development group they contact offers to build all of the pages for their service and includes a maintenance contract for doing subsequent work. The other group proposes to design a database-driven system that will allow Norma and Jean to make updates themselves. The bid on this is significantly more for the initial development.

When Norma and Jean make some assumptions about the number of products and retail outlets they plan to service, however, they realize that the second option will be far more economical. They have done some market testing and have decided not to scrimp on graphic design, though, since they found that an artistic presentation vastly improves the sale of imported goods.

To offset some of the cost, Norma and Jean decide to learn HTML on their own and have the development group focus on the technical solution and graphic design. This way, they tell themselves jokingly, if their import business fails, they can always find employment as developers!

Launching the Application

How you market your Internet business depends very much on its function and target audience. For example, if you are building an Internet application that will streamline your customer service, it will better serve your interests to focus on how to encourage existing customers to use the Internet service and on a plan to phase-out other, less effective means of doing customer service.

Alternatively, if you are launching a new Internet service, you will want to put most of your energy into a marketing scheme that encourages existing Internet users to take a look at what you offer.

Transitioning An Existing Customer Base

This applies to two different scenarios. In the first scenario, your goal is to encourage your customers to use an Internet-based service either as an extension of the current services you offer, or as a replacement for current services that use other media. Some examples of this might include:

- Customer or technical support
- Replacement for phone-based services
- Replacement for purchasing systems

The second scenario is one in which the users you are transitioning are not your customers but your employees. If you are undertaking an Internet—or increasingly, "Intranet", project and you think you will not have to conduct a marketing campaign, you are likely to be in for a rude awakening. Just like your customers, those who work for you are accustomed to getting things done in certain ways. Even if they are not the most efficient or most effective ways of working, they are familiar. Old habits die hard, especially when the execution order comes from above (it is altogether possible that the employees of a company have spear-headed the change efforts, in which case the marketing efforts are probably similar, but in an opposite direction).

In either case, the marketing efforts required take a similar shape. The main points include the following:

- Offer incentives
- Provide additional support
- Solicit feedback
- Use the older medium to promote the newer
- Duplicate services for a time

Getting the Word Out on the Internet

Now let's examine the more prevalent case, in which you have developed a new consumer-based Internet application and you want to drive traffic to your site. Take a three-step approach.

1. Get the customers to your site.
2. Keep them there.
3. Bring them back again.

Listed briefly, here are some ideas for accomplishing each of the preceding goals. For more ideas on marketing your Internet business, consult one of the growing number of books devoted to marketing-oriented Web sites.

Getting Them There

- List your application with the major Internet search engines.
- Get your application noticed by the growing number of Internet "best of..." rating services.
- Advertise your application on other Web sites.
- Advertise the old-fashioned way, in print, radio, TV, billboards, and so on.
- Feature promotions as incentives to attract users.
- Conduct a link exchange with related sites.

Keeping Them There

Obviously, keeping users on your site once they arrive is not exclusively a marketing concern—good content and satisfying experience will keep them there. But this is also partly a question of good presentation methods—which is something marketing folks are more attuned to.

The biggest problem faced by people on the Internet is that surfing is so easy and so tempting that the problem is how to keep people from doing the equivalent of channel surfing—hit the home page and on to the next thing. Here are just a few words of advice:

- Create a balance between enticement and information—at every step give them something and keep them wanting more.
- Have new content in several places—many sites will have one page that they update, which effectively means you only have to revisit that one page. A better approach is to spread new items around the site, where people who like to browse will wander into them and then create a master list of these new elements for those who like to know what's new. In effect your list of new elements will serve as a springboard into all of the nooks and crannies of your application.
- Hide Easter eggs on your site—in software development, an "Easter egg" refers to a semi-secret treasure that a programmer builds into the software and then hides. To find the Easter egg, you have to know the special key combination to press or the special sequence of menu items to access while holding down a special key. This concept may not be easy to replicate exactly in the Internet environment, but the idea of enticing the user on a "treasure hunt" is a useful way to have them surf through your pages.

Bringing Them Back

There are several good ways to bring users back: provide a function that they need to use regularly, convince them that the next time they return they will find something new of value which was not there before, or provide so much enticing content that they have to return to see more of what they missed.

Some of the principal ways to entice users back, include:

- E-mail newsletters sent as a service to valued, registered users (be careful not to make this a nuisance!)
- Promotions that require users to do something and then return at a later date to see the results
- Scheduled events (described in more detail in Chapter 12)

The Case Studies

Now back to Jay, Norma, and Jean.

REST EASY'S TRANSITION PLAN

In the short term, Jay's Rest Easy Internet site primarily targets existing Internet users, so Jay submits a description of his site to all of the usual locations. He offers some creative incentives on the site to users, partly as a way to encourage business and also as a way to measure the level of interest in the service.

At the same time, Jay is planning a fairly major network installation, including an Internet-based reservation system. While he is still working out the plan for this, he decides to install a simple Internet-connected kiosk in the front lobby of his most popular resort. From the kiosk, guests can access

A COUPLE OF SUGGESTIONS DERIVED FROM EXPERIENCE

It can be very useful to have a "demo" version of the product that can be loaded on a laptop computer and shown on the road in presentations whenever Internet connections are unavailable or inconvenient. This can take some planning, particularly if there is, say, a database with lots of CGI programming at work. One solution is to create an HTML-only version to demo with. Another solution is to run an actual Web server on the laptop, although many of these require an Internet connection to function, thus defeating the purpose. Whatever you do, plan ahead and build the creation of the demonstration version into the project scope.

Another bit of advice is to think ahead about where and how you might wish to reuse some of the design elements from this application. Frequently, businesses will decide to create some print collateral to show off their new Web application. We have seen home pages put onto business cards, into annual reports, even on T-shirts. The problem, however, is that most graphic design work done for online display is done at screen resolution not print resolution. Make sure that you reserve the right to reuse design elements and then obtain high-resolution versions of the graphics if you have any thought of producing future marketing materials from them.

the site to locate information about nearby restaurants, night clubs, theaters, museums, parks, and special events.

At first, the resort's concierge is not pleased with the intruder. He discovers, however, that guests use the system to find information and still ask him for his recommendation. Jay offers to pay the concierge a bonus to write out some of his recommendations to implement in the next version of the Internet service. Thus, Jay finds a way to prepare his guests for the next phase of his Internet plans, and converts at least one member of his staff to the project (he is prepared to provide training to the rest). Plus, a new feature of the site (and a new working relationship) is born.

EXOTIQUE'S MARKETING COUP

One of Norma's and Jean's primary concerns about their Internet enterprise is that not enough women, the primary target market for import goods, use the Internet. It occurs to them, though, that one of the chief reasons men frequent import stores is to look for gifts for the significant woman (or women) in their lives.

In order to tap this opportunity, Norma and Jean invent the Gift Box, a special section of their service that features five different products each week and offers them at a discounted price. Users can even select from a variety of gift wrappings, right online. For an additional fee, users can even join a gift-of-the-month club, which allows them to pre-select 12 items to be sent to a special someone each month.

The service proves successful, so much so that they are even featured the local newspaper, eager to offer its readers anything to do with the Internet.

Sustaining the Momentum

In our experience as developers, the one aspect of developing an Internet business application that is most often underestimated if not altogether ignored is what it will take to keep the application alive and well. According to one recent report, sixty percent of the current corporate Web sites will be "stabilized" in the near future. In this context, *stabilized* does not mean *made more stable*—it means something closer to *put out to pasture.*

What does it take to prevent the stabilization of your Internet business?

- A continual source of fresh content (content/interfacials/event-driven)
- Active user involvement
- Sufficient staff to support the application

The ideal Internet presence, at least from the business standpoint, is the one that causes its users to exclaim, "I just can't get through my day without that!"

The Case Studies

So, how are the fictional cases going to sustain momentum?

REST EASY

Ultimately, Jay plans to have his Internet application revolve around a reservations system, which will allow users to check the availability of rooms and reserve them online. Such a system will need to be connected directly to a central database, which Jay has yet to install.

In the meantime, he sends content updates to the development company with which he has a maintenance agreement. This system seems convoluted to him. Most of the new content he wants to add comes from other businesses who agree to be part of his vacation services database. They send him content, he sends it to the developers, they put it online and notify him, he notifies the original company. Sometimes this works smoothly, but if there are delays or the content doesn't seem right to the owners, Jay is caught in the middle. He longs for a way to allow these other companies to input their content directly.

He also institutes his virtual concierge reviews, with new featured reviews every week. He invites his guests to contribute their comments on various services as well, and this proves to be a popular feature for users. He has some other ideas for generating fresh content, but decides to hold off until he has a chance to see whether his efforts are paying off or not.

EXOTIQUE

Norma and Jean maintain their application by adding new items as often as possible. They format all of the content themselves, and use a simple data entry, content management system that was custom-built for them as part of the programming of their application. This works well for the time being, but they do not have the ability to change the format of their catalog of import items. This is not significant at the moment, but they are beginning to have ideas about adding other kinds of information.

Their Gift Box marketing idea (described earlier) gives them a way to change a set of featured products on a weekly basis, which helps lend freshness to the site. They have some other ideas for adding content to the site, perhaps soliciting comments from users, but that will have to wait until they hit their revenue targets.

Growing Into the Future

Most businesses that decide that the time has come to develop an Internet presence begin with a grand vision. After they confront the realities of trying to develop a full-blown project in the midst of a still-developing environment, after it realizes the dimensions of the changes that this presence will demand of the company's resources and staff, and once it acknowledges the learning curve for this new market, it decides that the best plan is to use a phased approach and start a little less ambitiously.

Scaling back the initial development does not mean that you should forget about the grand vision. It does mean that the grand vision needs to provide for the time and energy necessary to get the project up to speed. How fast the ramp-up is done depends on urgency of demand and pressure from possible competitors as well as on the existence of readily available funds.

No matter how large or small the initial project, however, it should provide for the future. One aspect of this is to design the plan from the business perspective—scale the project based on its success. Use a certain amount of revenues generated to add to the project. Make further development contingent on quantifiable results: a certain level of response from users, a certain level of usage, and so on.

What are appropriate lines of development for the future?

- Increase the level of customer personalization (content/interface)
- Increase the quantity of multimedia content
- Increase the quantity and frequency of new content
- Increase the vigor of the delivery mechanism (infrastructure)
- Increase the level of interactivity

The Case Studies

Let's check in on our made-up businesses to see how they plan to build on what they have.

REST EASY'S RESERVATION SYSTEM

Jay's big plan is to install an Intranet-based network among his five locations in order to centralize his reservation system and improve the flow of communication among his staff. However, he is concerned with the security of his reservation data, and a friend pointed out to him that if he makes his room availability public knowledge, his competition will know how well he is doing. He is pretty sure there are ways to protect himself, but he is not certain it is worth the effort.

His alternative is to participate in a large scale reservations system that would link all of his offices via dial-up modems to the central server of the reservations system. Given how little computers are used currently in his operations, he suspects that he will probably opt for the latter option, even though the idea of guests being able to make reservations on their own still appeals to him.

EXOTIQUE'S ACQUISITION

After they were featured in the newspaper, Norma and Jean received a phone call from the president of the largest of the import retailers in town with an offer to buy their service. They were not actually pulling a profit yet, though were within their targeted projections, but since the price was right, they decided to accept the offer. The retailer has kept the Internet business alive, but uses it exclusively to showcase its own content.

Norma left to find a job with a major retail store as its company Web site administrator. Jean accepted a job as vice president of marketing with the company that purchased her application. The two are still friends and, now that they have the capital they needed, are contemplating opening a new retail store called The Gift Box.

Checklist for Getting Started

Here, by way of summary for this chapter, is a checklist of the eight most important points to keep in mind as you begin to plan your Internet business.

1. Base your decisions on a clear, realizable business model.
2. Stick to your core competencies.
3. Weigh the pros and cons of in-house versus outsourced work.
4. Avoid the impulse to use technology for technology's sake.
5. Be prepared for frequent changes in Internet technologies and for the delays that come with working in a less than stable development environment.
6. Design your application in keeping with your user base.
7. Don't underestimate what it takes to operate your project after it is up and running.
8. Plan for the long term, but build what is reasonable in the near term.

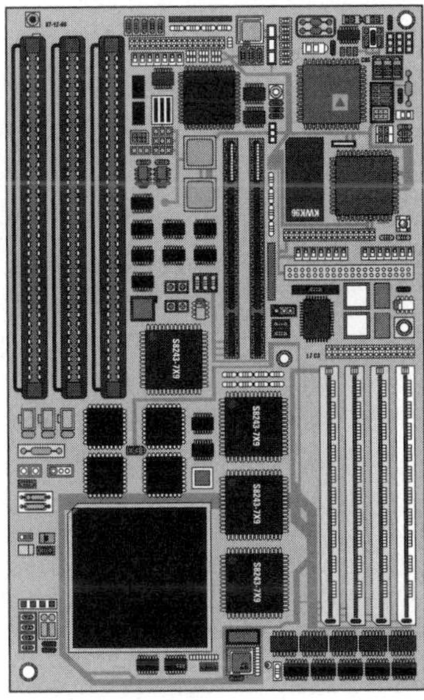

CHAPTER TWELVE

ASSEMBLING PLAYERS AND PARTS

In Chapter 11, "Harnessing the Vision," we looked at the development process from a business level appropriate for anyone who will participate in envisioning how the business will operate. In this chapter, we focus on the details of project development. This chapter is intended for project managers, those people who will be responsible for selecting and overseeing the production team for the project as well as making recommendations related to equipment purchases.

We organized this chapter according to the sequence of tasks that are likely to confront the typical project manager. We start with some general responsibilities that fall into the domain of project management. From there we look at some of the particular decision points of the project—hosting options and providing for system administration and maintenance; the application development team and its tasks; and the management of the content that will be part of the application.

Organizing the Project

In our experience, most of the people assigned the task of managing an Internet project are quite skilled in management issues but have had the Internet thrust onto them without a great deal of advance warning.

Perhaps your boss came to you with a "great idea" about how the company can make a killing, or at least a big wave, on the Internet. Or maybe the boss only came with a demand. The clock is ticking and you need an Internet gambit today, yesterday, next Monday at the latest. You have a reputation for getting the job done, and now your neck is on the line again.

Or maybe you stuck your own neck out and boasted that you could be the one to lead your company or your client into the 21st cyber-century. Now the bait has been swallowed and you need to deliver the goods. However it happened, you are now responsible to make your Internet project a success.

For the purposes of this chapter, we assume that most project managers who read this book already have some experience with managing teams of people and with coordinating projects. We will not bore those people with detailed advice about basic management techniques. However, before turning to the specific challenges associated with Internet development, we will briefly review some of the record-keeping techniques that are helpful in these circumstances.

Keeping Track of the Project

Almost by definition it seems, projects are hectic, driven by impossible deadlines and unrealistic expectations. This is certainly the case for Internet projects, if anything more so than other similar kinds of projects due to the level of attention the Internet is currently receiving and the feverish pace of change.

One element of Internet development that is especially challenging is the combination of deadline pressure and the impression (sometimes illusory) that anything can be easily changed anytime in the process. This phenomenon is partly the culture of the Internet—everything is always unfinished or subject to daily improvement. It is partly the result of unstable development within Internet technologies themselves. Standards are constantly evolving and exist simultaneously in two or three versions in order to keep up with demand for new functionality. Competing companies are tauting their own versions in an attempt to gain market share and to control the direction of the standards themselves. And development tools are in various stages of prerelease status.

All of this flux means that the need for setting project milestones and keeping records of the process is especially challenging and crucial. If your project, like most, involves the participation of contractors, this will add another level of difficulty to the task.

Keeping Project-Related Records

You should at a minimum keep the following records:

- Technical specification document, including component descriptions and schematic diagrams
- Design specification document, including an interface look and feel definition, style guidelines, design standards, and any template formats

- Project timeline with milestones, including deliverables, review sign-offs, and contingencies

Facilitating the Flow of Communication and Project Deliverables

- Keep written records of deadlines met and sign-offs as well as revision or change order requests.
- If you are dealing with multiple departments or separate companies, identify who will be the contact person at each level, how reporting will be handled, and how often the whole project team will meet.
- Create a plan for how existing content will be delivered to the developers and how they will deliver the application for review.

Ensuring Project Survival Beyond the Completion Date

Even after you reach a project's completion, you will find there is still a lot to do, especially when dealing with Internet projects.

- Make sure the project takes into account the operation and maintenance of, and updates to, the application after it is completed.
- Identify staff training requirements for the ongoing support of the application.
- Include an open-ended (as opposed to rigidly defined) future vision and direction in the initial design of the project.

Selecting a Host and Server

One of the first major decisions you will face in your project is how and where to run your Internet application. The principal questions are:

- Where will the application be located and how will it be connected to the Internet?
- Who will provide network and system administration?
- On what hardware platform will the application run?

A number of factors will affect your choices when deciding on host and server, including:

- The size and complexity of the project, especially the level of custom programming
- The degree to which keeping the application running is critical
- The need for particular supplementary server-based applications
- The time frame and budget for the project
- Existing network resources, equipment, and personnel within your company
- The selection of a development team

Hosting and Administration Options

Although there are a myriad of options for hosting your Internet application, they all break down into the following three categories:

- Installing your application on an Internet host that someone else owns and maintains at their location
- Installing your application on a host computer you own but which is connected to the Internet and maintained by a third party at their location
- Installing the host at your own location, connecting it to the Internet and maintaining it yourself

Later in this chapter, we will look at each of these options in detail. First, however, we will discuss the intricate world of Internet Service Providers (ISPs), the companies who are in the business of providing Internet access to individuals and businesses.

To understand what an Internet Service Provider (ISP) does, it is useful to have in mind a general conceptual picture of how Internet access is made available.

A Bit of Internet History

The Internet began as a project within the Advanced Research Projects Agency (ARPA), which made it essentially a military project. The idea was to link several existing government and university research computer networks using long-distance, high-speed data lines. The ARPA folks strung multiple lines between each of the points, producing a level of redundancy that would ensure that if one of the networks went down, or worst case, was destroyed, the others would still be able to communicate with one another.

There needed to be a way to identify any computer on the network, and also an easy way to let every computer on the Internet know any time a new computer was added. The only catch was that this information could not be kept in one central place, because if the central "brains" of the network went down, so would the entire network.

The Addressing Challenge

To solve this challenge, an addressing scheme was devised that not only identified every network as a domain, but also provided the ability for a domain to subdivide itself into sub-networks and provide a specific address within the domain to each computer. This scheme is roughly equivalent to the way the post office deals with addresses.

Each domain, or postal region, is assigned a unique number called a ZIP code. Within each ZIP code region, thanks to nine digit ZIP codes, there can also be sub-domains. Each location in the scheme, in this case a residence, has a unique identifier, such as street name and number. To make the analogy closer, imagine that instead of street numbers, the post office assigned every residence within a ZIP code region a unique number, sort of like a P.O. Box number. The result would be that each ZIP code domain would have a list of numbers it could assign as P.O. numbers to any new residences. The P.O. number assigned to you would not be unique in the world—someone in another ZIP code region could have the same number. But nobody could have the same ZIP code and P.O. number combination.

The virtue of such a scheme is that the central post office would not have to worry about assigning individual P.O. numbers. That could be the job of each ZIP code district. All they need is a way for all ZIP code regions to receive any updates to the list of local P.O. numbers.

Enter the ISP

In essence, the preceding describes what happens with domains in the world of the Internet. A given domain is provided with a set of numbers that it can assign as it wants to individual computers (and subnets if the domain is large enough). In contrast to the post office analogy, however, there is no reason that all of the computers or subnets within a domain need to be within the same location as the domain. They can be virtually anywhere.

On the Internet, owners of large blocks of domain addresses sell Internet connectivity to a another entity, and with that the second entity receives a certain number of the addresses belonging to the original owner. The second company can in turn (assuming the second company has permission), resell a block of its addresses to a third entity, and so on. In general, the farther "downstream" you are, in other words, the farther from the Internet backbone, the less expensive your Internet service should be. It is also the case that the farther downstream you are, the smaller the entity providing the service is likely to be, which can mean the entity has less bandwidth shared by more people, and less invested in network operations and support.

The point is that not all ISPs are created equal. Whether you choose to run your Internet application in-house or contract it out, you are going to need an ISP. Check carefully into such questions as:

- Who provides their Internet service?
- At what speed and with how many lines are they connected?
- What percentage of uptime do they guarantee? What provision do they make for getting down servers back online?
- What do they provide by way of system administration?

Also, you should check with current customers to see how satisfied they are with the service. If they are dialing in, do they always get a connection or are the phone lines frequently busy? Do they see degradations in speed from the service provider? Are they happy with the level of technical support from the provider? How responsive is the provider to new requests?

Gateway Providers

One question that comes up frequently in connection with Internet access is where do the major online services, such as America Online and CompuServe, fit into this picture? In effect, these online services also offer Internet access, but there is a difference worth recognizing.

American Online, CompuServe, Prodigy, and the other online services are first and foremost *proprietary networks.* That means that they have their own collection of cables running around the globe, connected at various points for user dial-up access (called *points of presence,* or POPs).

Until recently, these proprietary networks were completely separate from the Internet. When the Internet began to gain popularity, these networks realized that providing a way for their customers to access the Internet was going to be vital to their continued success. So they built gateways that would allow a computer connected to their networks to communicate with a computer on the Internet.

Connecting a proprietary network to the Internet is no mean accomplishment, and these networks provide many valuable services, but it is important to recognize the distinction between what they offer and what an ISP provides. Whenever you access the Internet via a commercial online service, you are doing it via a special gateway. Your computer is never directly connected to the Internet as it would be if you were connected via a standard Internet Service Provider.

ISPs and Internet Servers

In the beginning, ISPs provided Internet access only. You used your service provider only as a point of connection to the Internet. All of your access would pass through the provider, but the provider was essentially invisible to you.

With the increased interest among Internet users in setting up their own servers, especially Web servers, ISPs have begun offering hosting services as part of their package deal. Most ISPs offer a business access package that includes the following:

- Dial-up access with an unlimited number of hours
- Registration of a company domain name (in most cases you will still be responsible to pay the annual fee now charged by the InterNIC, the entity responsible for assigning IP addresses)
- Disk space allotted for your Web server documents (or FTP files)

In addition to the service provided by ISPs, a new breed of service providers has emerged. Usually referred to as *Internet presence providers,* these entities feature hosting services for Web server applications, but do not provide connectivity to the Internet as does an ISP.

If you are looking for a place to house your Internet application and you don't need Internet access yourself, a presence provider may be an appropriate choice. Price can be an important determinant here, since typically a presence provider will undersell a full-service access provider. However, prices, pricing structure, and service offerings vary dramatically. For example, some companies charge a fee for disk space that you will occupy. Others charge per volume of traffic that you generate. Still others do both. It pays to shop around.

In addition to price, there are several factors to consider when making this decision, since some entities are set up to handle only basic Web sites rather than full-fledged Internet applications. Be sure to ask the following questions:

- What kind of computers and operating system do they provide?
- What additional services does the provider offer, including server add-on applications for chat or electronic transactions, and so on?
- What do they charge to register a domain name for your company's application?
- What ability do you or your developer have to add custom programming to the site?
- What access to the account do you have? Most services allow Telnet and FTP access, although some restrict you to FTP access.
- What level of security via firewalls do they provide?
- What level of redundancy is built into the network?
- What technical support do they provide?
- How often do they perform backups? What is involved if data needs to be restored?
- What access to log files or statistics does the service provide?
- What kind of bandwidth and what level of uptime and turnaround time can they guarantee if the server goes down?

Selecting and Colocating a Server

In general, the more standard your application, the more likely that either an Internet service provider or a presence provider will meet your needs. The more custom technology or third party applications you need to add to your Internet application, the less likely this option is to work for you.

If you need full control over the host computer for your application, but you don't have the resources to administer the server internally, another option is to investigate *colocating* a server that you own.

Colocating means that you purchase a computer for your application which resides at the location of your Internet Service Provider and is attached to their network. This means that you will have full control over the server, since you own it, but almost all of your access to the computer will be accomplished remotely. Usually the ISP contracts to provide some basic system administrative responsibility for the computer, including UPS or other power backup, file backups, and even rebooting if necessary (since the one thing you cannot do remotely is completely power off the computer). Keep in mind, though, that not all ISPs offer colocation services (in fact most do not), so you will have to check around to find one that does.

The advantage of colocating is that it allows you to take advantage of the infrastructure of an existing ISP, which should mean a more physically secure, temperature controlled environment and better bandwidth than you may be able to provide yourself. At the same time, you will have full authority over the content of the server, so you can add programming to your heart's content. Furthermore, if you foresee a day when you may want to migrate the server in-house, this may be as simple as unplugging the computer bringing it home.

Platform Options

If you colocate, your biggest decision will be to decide what computer to use for your server. Sometimes ISPs that provide colocation services will dictate your options to you. Otherwise, you are on your own. Below, we will briefly examine the various options, as well as the advantages and disadvantages of each. In the next chapter, we discuss in detail the major Web server applications that run on each platform.

UNIX

Several years ago, most of the major servers on the Internet were UNIX-based. UNIX is an operating system that was designed with the Internet in mind. It is a multiple-user, multi-process, crash-resistant environment. The first two major World Wide Web servers were written for UNIX, one from the National Center for Supercomputing Applications (NCSA), the other from CERN (a research physics lab in Switzerland).

Although UNIX is a standard operating system, it comes in a variety of more or less compatible flavors. Some of the more popular makers of UNIX-based computers include Sun Microsystems (which makes the relatively affordable Netra server in addition to its Sun SPARC servers), Silicon Graphics, Inc. (SGI), Digital Equipment Company (DEC), International Business Machines (IBM), and Hewlett-Packard.

In addition, there are several varieties of UNIX-based computers designed to run on Intel-based PC computers. The most popular commercial Intel-based UNIX system is BSDI UNIX, from Berkeley Systems Design, Inc. For the cost-conscious company that is less concerned about technical support, there is also a freely available version of UNIX called Linux, which has a great deal of support within the Internet developer community.

UNIX PROS

- Very robust and scalable
- Excellent performance
- Well-supported within the Internet development community

UNIX CONS

- Very expensive (except Linux)
- Fairly steep learning curve

UNIX WEB SERVERS

- Netscape—Popular commercial server, standard and secure versions
- Open Market—Another commercial server, comes in standard and secure versions
- Apache—Freely available server, an extension of the original NCSA source code
- NCSA—Freely available, one of the earliest web server applications

Windows NT

Ever since Microsoft began to taut its Internet strategy early in 1996, there has been a flurry of Windows development, both within Microsoft itself and among the multitude of third-party Windows developers. Prior to that period, anyone attempting to set up a Windows-based server would have been at a sore disadvantage in terms of both performance and supporting software. Now things are leveling out, and once version 4.0 of Windows NT is available (by the time this book is published it may be released), the competition is going to be fought as much over price as performance.

WINDOWS NT PROS

- Relatively inexpensive
- More familiar, user-friendly environment
- Growing range of support applications and tools

WINDOWS NT CONS

- A world ruled by Microsoft
- Somewhat less robust than UNIX
- Software still mostly beta

WINDOWS NT WEB SERVERS

- Netscape—NT version of its standard and secure commerce server
- Microsoft—Microsoft Internet Information Server (IIS)
- O'Reilly—O'Reilly WebSite
- Several others

Macintosh

Apple Computer, Inc., has only recently woken up to the fact that they need a more visible Internet strategy in order to compete with the likes of Microsoft. As a result, Macintosh development efforts have lagged behind the PC community.

Interestingly enough, though, one of the earliest Web server applications to appear was MacHTTP. Once shareware, the source code was most recently purchased by Star Nine Systems and the application was renamed WebStar. Thus, although at this writing the Macintosh is not yet a strong contender in the Internet server market, it has much to offer, including a history of strong networking and multimedia capabilities.

Recently, Apple has begun to promote its own Internet server solution package, which consists of a high-end PowerMac file server and a CD-ROM filled with a variety of support tools and server add-ons.

MAC PROS

- Very user friendly, easy to set up
- Relatively inexpensive

MAC CONS

- Fewer options for additional software
- Less support among developers

MAC WEB SERVERS

- Star Nine's WebStar—Commercial product based on the source code from MacHTTP

Bringing the Application In-House

There are two typical circumstances under which companies consider running an Internet application from within their own establishment. The first is when they already have the infrastructure in place and the support personnel to maintain it. The second is the case in which a company would like to build such an infrastructure and plans to migrate their application in-house after that is accomplished.

In either of these scenarios, a project manager is likely to have only peripheral decision-making authority when it comes to building the infrastructure. In a best-case scenario, however, you would like to have input into what gets done to ensure that what gets set up will be adequate to the needs of the project you are developing. One thing you want to avoid is a case in which the infrastructure group, typically an IS department in a larger company, is making decisions about software, about user access, and so on, that impact your ability to produce the application you have designed. In effect, you are still involved in a relationship much like that of the Internet service provider, except hopefully you will be able to influence decisions that affect your ability to perform. These decisions encompass the following:

- **Network and system administration**—Who is watching the server and what provision is made for a problem?

- **Access levels**—Will you have the ability to add custom programming or additional server-based applications?
- **Reporting mechanisms**—How and in what form will you get usage information for your application?

These questions also help indicate at a minimum what players need to be involved. Typically, you would have at least one person responsible for network operations and possibly system administration as well, depending on the size of the network. In addition, you will want to assign a *Webmaster*, someone whose responsibility it is to make sure that the Web server is running properly and all of the files are linked and working as they should.

It is possible that if your company is large enough to bring an Internet server in-house, it may also be large enough to allow your project to have a dedicate computer to run its service. In terms of the level of control you would have over the server, this might sound ideal. Often, however, a company that allows multiple Internet servers within its walls will also begin to define company-wide policies and standards for design and development, which introduces a whole new can of worms.

Developing the Application

Selecting a team of developers to build your application is one of the most crucial decisions you will make in the process of managing your Internet project. In some ways it is even more critical than the choice of a service provider. You can always change providers later, without a large sacrifice. If you have to start over with a new development team, however, you will have lost both time and money.

The selection Process

In this section we describe two general procedures for finding and selecting a team to do the development for your Internet project, one formal and one informal. Of course, there are countless ways to find a development team, so these two are meant only to be representative. The method you choose will depend partly on your personality or your company's personality as well as on the size and circumstances of your project. A more formal approach works best when you already have a clearly defined working plan. The informal process is more suited to circumstances in which you are still exploring various possibilities.

Whichever method you follow, you will want to include the following questions in your checklist of things to inquire about development companies:

- Do they have experience with the kinds of tasks required for your project? By all means, examine prior Internet projects to see if they are of a similar level of difficulty.

- Do they have examples of different kinds of interface treatments? This is not absolutely necessary, of course, if you like the work they have done. But the ability to create different kinds of applications shows both a breadth of talent as well as the ability to adjust creatively to the demands of different clients.
- Do they have any proprietary software that they can contribute to the project? Again, not a necessity but worth asking about.
- Can they show evidence of their management of a project? This one is a little tricky, since a development team is not just going to show you the documentation from their last job. These would be confidential. But it doesn't hurt to ask them to describe the process they used, or the general procedures they follow. This is a good way to gauge the professionalism of the team—a very important criterion.

Generally speaking, hiring a single team to implement your whole solution is easier to manage than hiring a number of independent contractors. Usually these teams have worked together on other projects, so they may be more efficient than a team of people who have never met before your project. Not to mention the fact that it takes less time to recruit one group than several individuals.

On the other hand, there are some possible downsides to hiring a full team, which are worth considering as you assess your options. The first potential difficulty is that a consulting team is likely to provide a fair amount of its own project management services. This may in fact be an advantage to you and lessen some of your burden. Although, it can also add to the cost of the project.

The other potential drawback is that it can sometimes be difficult to assess the talent of the individual contributors who will make up the team. Many such groups have a pool of talent they draw from. In theory they will attempt to match their talent pool to the demands of your project, but in most cases—and unless you specifically stipulate—they are the ones who will make the selection. If you hire a number of individuals to work on the project, you will know exactly the capabilities of each one of your team members.

THE FORMAL METHOD This method involves circulating a written document that is called by a number of names, but is most frequently referred to as a *Request for Proposal,* or RFP. This document spells out the requirements of your project and asks for a formal response. Typically the request calls for background information on the responding group, including prior experience and the biographies or resumes of key members. In addition, it asks for a description of the approach the responding group will take in completing the proposed project. This usually entails a brief explanatory section, a timeline showing key project deliverables and their deadlines, and their price structure.

One of the chief advantages of using the RFP method is that it allows you to kick off the project with a much clearer formal description of what is to be done than is likely to exist after the informal method. This requires some pre-planning on your part of course, but it also forces you to be clear about what you want and expect from the development team.

Don't forget that it is important to have a feel for the development team as well as a formal understanding of their capabilities. Internet development projects can be intense experiences, and you want to know you have hired people you can work well with under stress. Most companies who circulate RFPs do so to a limited number of development groups that they prequalified, either by checking their references or by inviting them for a preliminary meeting.

THE INFORMAL METHOD It is somewhat of an oxymoron to pretend that there is one way to conduct an informal search. It wouldn't be informal if you could classify it so neatly. Still, the basic principle of the informal method is to identify one potential development group and meet with them on more than one occasion in order to make a decision about whether they can do the job.

Usually companies who proceed in this manner do so either because the team in question has come highly recommended from a trustworthy source, so they don't feel they need to shop around as much, or because they want to use their conversations with potential candidates as a way of refining what it is they want to accomplish.

This is fairly common practice, although most development groups are unlikely to be willing to attend meeting after meeting without a clear sense that things are proceeding towards a contract. If they sense that you don't know what you want to do yet, they may suggest that you hire them in the first instance to consult with you in order to produce the kind of formal documentation you need to formalize the project. This is not a bad plan for both parties, since it allows you to get to know the developers without being fully committed to them for a major project, and vice versa.

The Working Environment

How you establish your working environment,—where the project will be built and where and how it will be reviewed—depends a great deal on how you decide to host the site. The typical options include:

- Have the development team build the application at its location, where you will perform reviews, and then deliver the final product either to you or to the host computer.
- Have the development team build the application remotely on the actual host computer, typically either building it in a subdirectory or with password protection to keep it from the general public until it is completed.
- Have the development team work on site at your location.

A number of criteria can affect your decision. If your application requires a significant amount of custom programming, it may be most convenient to do the work on the computer where it will actually reside. If the application involves linking to existing network systems, it will almost inevitably have to be done on site.

Another criterion for making a choice is: who will be doing the reviewing and how comfortable is this person with online reviews? Sometimes remote reviewing is very convenient. Other times it can be a royal pain. Under any circumstances, the initial review sessions—when storyboards or initial graphic design directions are being presented—most likely need to be done in real-time.

CLEANING UP FOR THE WEB-CRAWLING SEARCH ENGINES

If you build your project online in a subdirectory of its final location, or maybe even in the same location, be sure to clean up draft versions of your files when you are finished. This is not easy to do, and you may wonder why you should bother since the extraneous files are not linked to anything and are not hurting anyone. The answer is: web-crawling search engines.

These robot agents are sent out across the Internet in search of Web servers. When they find one, they begin to chew through its Web pages, indexing as they go (actually they are smarter than this, but this is close enough to the truth to give you the idea). They don't care whether the page they index is actually in use on your Web site, as long as it looks like a Web page (here is a hint for making a smarter robot, if anyone is listening). Once, for example, we were searching for a relatively obscure set of keywords that turned up 15 documents from the same site. As it turned out, it was actually 15 versions of the site's home page, and all but one were outdated drafts of the current home page. You wouldn't have found them by going to the site, but the search engine found them.

Establishing Standards

In Chapter 11, "Harnessing the Vision," we discussed briefly the importance of establishing standards for the development process. Here we go into a bit more detail and mention some of the particulars of standards setting. Keep in mind that the development team may have (*will* have if they are good) some fairly strong ideas about how to define the standards. Listen to their preferences if they seem reasonable. Devise your own if they are not.

GRAPHIC SPECIFICATIONS The key concept when it comes to graphics is how to keep them small enough so that they don't bog down the application for those with slow, dial-up connections, yet rich enough that they give an appropriate look and feel to the pages. How large should the graphics be? That depends a lot on the application in question. So, rather than try to answer that arbitrarily, we provided a list of the kinds of elements to specify and standardize—with some advice when advice seemed appropriate.

FILE SIZE (IN BYTES) A good way to designate file size is in terms of an upper limit for the total file size for all elements on a Web page. The answer will give you a good indication of the time it will take to retrieve the whole page. 20K would be a pretty light-weight page; 40K is a good ballpark for medium graphics; 80K and up would be pretty graphic-intensive.

FILE DIMENSIONS (IN PIXELS) It is important to stipulate at least the standard width of all of the full size graphics on your page. The width of the longest graphic can influence the width of the user's window, so you want widths to be consistent. Also, it is a good idea to identify what minimum monitor size the graphics are to be designed for so that they can be viewed fully without forcing the user to scroll the page left to right. Typically, a 14–inch monitor is used as the standard. Beware, however, standard PC monitors and Macintosh monitors do not always have the same size browser windows.

COLOR RESOLUTION (IN DPI) Standard screen resolution is adequate here (72 dpi). Anything higher than 72 dpi is a waste of file size.

COLOR DEPTH (IN NUMBER OF COLORS) 256 colors is still the standard, although we have seen sites that recommend more for best viewing.

GRAPHICS FORMAT The de facto standard file format for Web graphics is GIF format (several versions are available, the most recent one is called GIF89a). Another popular format is JPEG, favored because of its highly efficient compression. JPEG is not universally recognized by browsers yet; however, Netscape, Microsoft Explorer, and most flavors of Mosaic can read JPEGs just fine.

In addition to standardizing these elements, it is important to create consistent standards for particular interface elements. Typical examples include banners and banner type, buttons, and icons. These should be defined for size, colors, type face, and placement.

HTML STANDARDS Deciding which HTML tag set to use in your application can become extremely difficult. As of this writing, HTML 2.0 is still the official standard, although HTML 3.0 is fairly well defined and most browsers now support at least some subset of the 3.0 tags. A revised (and greatly simplified) version of the HTML 3.0 standard, designated HTML 3.2, has been defined. However, the major browser developers—Netscape and Microsoft especially—have taken it upon themselves to lead rather than follow the standards by defining their *own* sets of recognized tags. In some cases, it is possible to create alternatives within the HTML itself so that browsers that recognize certain tags will display one thing and all others will display something else.

The result is a veritable HTML tower of Babel and a nightmare for trying to establish consistent standards. Partly your decision will depend on where on the spectrum between utilitarian and artistic your application falls. One popular solution is to create multiple versions of your application using various sets of HTML. Another solution is to pick a favorite version and issue a blanket warning to anyone incapable of taking advantage of the peculiarities of that version.

STANDARDIZING HTML PAGE LAYOUT In some respects, this is more the province of the graphic designer than the HTML coder, since the issue is similar to the need (discussed earlier) for consistency among graphical elements. Determine a standard for page design elements such as fill-in-forms, tables, lists, and so on. In the world of desktop publishing, such things fall under the category of creating a style sheet. As of this writing, it is not yet possible to define an HTML style sheet to standardize page layout elements. It is bound to happen, sooner or later, probably using a model similar to that employed in SGML applications today.

STANDARDIZING HTML CODING The other development standards concern the elements the user sees. If you have ever had to decipher someone else's HTML coding, you realize the importance of setting some style guides for HTML coding itself. Most of these items are familiar fare for programmers, but many HTML folks these days are not trained as programmers (in fact, we would guess that most are not). The following are some basic guidelines.

- Include meta information about the file, including the creator, creation date, and most recent update.
- Provide comments for particularly complex or unorthodox sections of HTML.
- Put separate elements on separate lines to improve readability.
- Use tags and attributes consistently, even though there are usually several ways to produce the same effect.

The problem of consistency and readability is somewhat compounded by the fact that more and more HTML is done with authoring tools, which take the formatting of the HTML itself out of the hands of the user. You would think that this would be good news, since presumably HTML that has been generated automatically would be cleanly formatted and consistent. Alas, it is not so. For that reason, we are not overly fond of authoring tools that hide the HTML from the user.

Frequently Confronted Development Issues

In this section we consider briefly some of the application design issues that are frequently confronted by companies contemplating an Internet application.

STATIC PAGES VERSUS TEMPLATED PAGES Static HTML is easy to produce and easy to serve up on a Web server. In cases where you have a lot of similar content to display, however, trying to create an HTML page for each item can be time-consuming and tedious. In addition, each time you want to change the format of the display, you have to make the change on every page.

If your application has this characteristic, you should seriously consider using some mechanism for generating a boilerplate template and filling it with content on the fly. This scheme, of course, requires a programming module capable of reading a template file, extracting content from a data source, and inserting the content in the appropriate places in the template.

DATABASE SEARCH VERSUS TEXT FILE SEARCH This issue is in some sense related to the preceding one. Several very powerful text search engines are available for providing keyword searches of the content on your Web site. These text search engines consist of two parts: an indexer and a search engine. Use the indexer to create a quickly searched index of the words in all of the documents on your site. When a keyword is requested, the search engine searches the index, finds matches and retrieves the files (or a reference to the files). This kind of search tool is very easy to set up and requires little effort on the part of the content owner.

An alternative to this mechanism is to put all of the content into a database and allow the database to be searched, with the help of one of many database search tools and gateways (many of which are discussed in the next chapter). In many ways, a database is a much more controlled search environment and much more flexible, because you can search for specific attributes of the data not just random text. If your content is not already in a database structure, however, it can be quite a task to get it there.

REGISTRATION VERSUS OPEN ACCESS Most simple Web sites do not require users to identify themselves in order to enter the site. However, an increasing number of sites are requiring users to register, even when there is not charge associated with access to the site.

There are several reasons a company might want to do this even though it is likely to decrease the traffic on their site. Usually these reasons revolve around the desire to capture user information. Such information is a valuable asset. If coupled with profile information, it can be used to create customized information for the user, a much sought-after feature of information delivery. By the same token, it allows the site to track the user more carefully and to offer targeted services.

Some sites institute a compromise. Registration is voluntary but encouraged. Sometimes the incentive takes the form of a competition for prizes. In order to enter the contest, you must register. How else would they know who had won? In this way, the registration process is made in exchange for some possible reward to the user for spending the time.

TO ADVERTISE OR NOT TO ADVERTISE This is a slightly more recent issue, as it seems every day another site decides to add advertising banners to the top of its pages. This decision depends primarily on the business model selected for your application. If you advertise, look into ways of closely monitoring the activity generated by the banner and by the page on which the banner appears. There are several applications that can help you to do this, one of the more popular being I/Pro. For more information, check its Web site at **www.ipro.com**.

What Gets Delivered?

The final topic in this section about the development process is pretty straight forward. The product gets delivered, right? Yes, but you may want to think up front about some other needs you may have in order to insure that the development process produces these as well. Some possibilities include the following.

A DEMO VERSION OF THE PRODUCT Frequently it is useful to have a version of your application that can be run locally, for example for presentations on the road. You might think that the best solution would be to dial in to the Internet server and access the live application, but experience says this does not always produce the kind of demonstration you would like to have. It may suit your purposes better to have a stripped-down version of the product that can be reliably accessed when occasion calls for it. Producing this version can take some planning, so if you think you will want it, be sure to build it into the initial proposal.

ORIGINAL, HIGH-RESOLUTION VERSIONS OF GRAPHICAL ELEMENTS Over and over again we have seen companies try to take their Internet graphics and use them in another medium where high resolution graphics are typically called for. Take a look, for instance, at many print advertisements for Web sites and you will sooner or later see an example of what we mean—grainy screenshots of Web pages.

If you think you want to reuse your Internet graphics, make sure you mention this in the beginning. In the first place, most design houses will not grant you unlimited use of the graphics they design, and if you try to use them somewhere else you may be infringing upon your agreement with them. Try to get higher resolution graphics at the same time the design house creates the Web graphics.

You probably also want the originals of the graphics in order to make revisions to the design later on, after the design team has finished its work. This is another reason to get the original graphical files, which often are easier to manipulate than the final versions.

SOURCE CODE FOR PROGRAMMING ELEMENTS This is similar to the issue of obtaining graphic files, except that you are unlikely to get the source code at all unless you stipulate this initially. And if you do get the source code you will pay for the privilege. One exception to this situation is if you have the programming done in an interpreted, scripting language like Perl as opposed to a compiled language like C/C++.

DOCUMENTATION It is a good idea to ask the development team to submit some documentation of the work they have done. This will of course need to be requested as part of the original agreement, because the preparation of the documents will take time and cost money. In the long run, though, when you try to get a second development team to implement your Phase II plan, you will be glad you asked for these documents.

TRAINING Another item to think about is training. You could implement training in lieu of documentation if it makes more sense for the development team to transfer its knowledge to an in-house staff. However, your training needs might be more involved than that, perhaps requiring some instruction for the people who will manage the content side of the application.

Quality Assurance Testing

It seems as if bug-testing has become the responsibility of users, since it has become standard to include a feedback link on your Web site to allow disgruntled users the chance to tell you what they found going wrong on your site. This is fairly acceptable behavior—just be sure someone is actually around to collect and field the feedback you get! It does nobody any good to collect feedback only to let the data go unused.

For this reason, we will not dwell much on QA testing, besides encouraging you to do some before you release your project to the general public. On the other hand, there are a couple of special cases of quality assurance testing that are specific to the Web environment and worth mentioning in this context. Details of these issues are covered earlier in the section on standards. Here we mention them from the standpoint of error-checking.

Check the Graphics On a Variety of Monitors

Most importantly, be sure to look at the graphics on both Macintosh and Windows monitors. Most graphic designers work on Macintoshes, but most Internet users have Windows-based PCs. Unfortunately, graphics that look stunning on the Macintosh may look down-right hideous on a PC unless they have been designed by someone who understands the difference between the Macintosh color palette and the standard Windows palette. Also, some graphics designers are used to their 21–inch, 16.7 million color monitors and sometimes forget about the rest of us with our measly 14–inch monitors. Try out the graphics on a variety of monitors, especially low-end VGA monitors. Don't bother with 16-color graphics cards. You can assume 256 colors, but no more than that, even though this remark will make the die-hard Macintosh users shudder.

View the Site From as Many Browsers as Possible

In theory there are standards that define how browsers are supposed to display the information they get from Web servers, just as there are supposedly standards as to what should be contained in the HTML coding. As you probably know, however, not all browsers are created equal, and some HTML can wreck havoc on certain browsers. Some designers will insist on using only standard HTML. Others, particularly those frustrated by the limitations of the current standards, will insist on designing to the best options, ignoring those who are unable to see their work properly. There is no best way here, but you should test to make sure that all users will be able to at least see something reasonable when they access your application. If there are persistent problems, you should consider creating dual (or multiple) versions of your site to accommodate different user needs—or at least warn people of the imminent danger.

Managing the Content

After your application is up and running, your principle concern will be to keep it that way. This means not only keeping it operational, but also adding to it in ways that keep it dynamic, alive, and growing. Three different types of content refreshing are mentioned below and are brought up here in order to emphasize that the tasks associated with them continue after the development is done. However, it should be obvious that any provision for adding this content should be made as part of the initial development plan. If your budget permits it, by all means have the development team include some management or administrative components to make the tasks of the content folks as painless as possible.

Adding Company and Third-Party Content

It has become a convention on Web sites to have a What's New? page even in cases where there really isn't much new to talk about. In point of fact, most of the information pertaining to a company is relatively static, unless they are in the business of producing new products on a regular basis.

One alternative to the What's New? concept is a featured highlights page, which can be used to rotate in and out regular content from the site as well as calling attention to any new items.

Another strategy employed by many Web sites is to offer to other entities an opportunity to display marketing information on the site. This third-party content can also require frequent updating. In these cases, the main duty of the content manager is usually to assist in the conversion of content, often in print format, into a format appropriate for the Internet.

Adding User-Submitted Content

One of the goals of Web site development is to enlist the help of users in creating information. User-created content can take many forms. It might be in the form of a request for feedback or comments, taken in as e-mail and added to a page of suggestions. It might take the form of a discussion bulletin board, with content archived over some period of time. It might also take the form of a database application in which users are invited to contribute to the data.

Whatever the format, user-submitted content can be accepted in one of two basic ways: without or without editorial review. Without editorial review would mean that the content submitted would be added to the data available for display immediately. There is something powerful for people in the ability to input data and see it in the system immediately. On the other hand, it can also create a strong temptation for someone to clog up the system with garbage.

The alternative is to build a review system. In this model the content is submitted online and an alert message is sent to the individual or entity responsible for reviewing the content. After it is reviewed, the content is added to the currently active data. This is a much safer system, in that it allows a company to catch bad data before it is entered into the system. However, it also requires a fair amount of time on the part of the content manager.

Managing Scheduled Events

A growing number of sites are adding to their dynamic quality by hosting time-sensitive events, usually in the form of guest speakers or columnists. Popular formats for this kind of scheduled programming includes RealAudio broadcast-style interviews, chat room-moderated forum discussions, and time-sensitive promotions.

The most elaborate of these currently are the growing number of cyber-soap operas. These sites follow the lives of some group of characters, just like a regular TV soap opera. However, these sites enable the visitors to interact with the characters, ask them questions, even talk to them in real-time. The idea is greater audience participation and a desire to return every day. Some of the more popular examples of this phenomenon include:

- **The Spot** (**www.thespot.com**) The original web soap.
- **Ferndale** (**www.ferndale.com**) A racy blend of pop pyschology and everyday life.
- **Techno3** (**www.bluepearl.com/entertainment/soap/**) Follows the lives of three hip, young New York women.

In the case of such scheduled events, the content manager effectively becomes more like a producer, responsible for making sure that events are orchestrated efficiently and that any content produced by the event is made available for later viewing (if that is part of the plan).

Maintaining Usage Reports

It is probably the responsibility of the Webmaster to generate basic usage reports. However, it is possible that this information may be incorporated back into the site, and thus become the provice of the content manager. One way in which this happens is if user information is linked to their usage information. This data could then be used to deliver customized messages, even customized content. Imagine a personalized newspaper that kept track of which articles you had read and presented you only with those which remained unread (much the way most newsgroup readers do already).

Summary Checklist

The following is a checklist of important items for project managers:

1. Document your application plans carefully and revise the documents as the project evolves.
2. Select an appropriate ISP based on your bandwidth and service needs.
3. Select an appropriate server platform, operating system, and server software.
4. Select a qualified development team.
5. Decide on standards for graphic design, HTML, and programming.
6. Decide what if any database functionality your site will have.
7. Decide what level of user-contributed content and event content your site will support.
8. Maintain accurate usage reports.

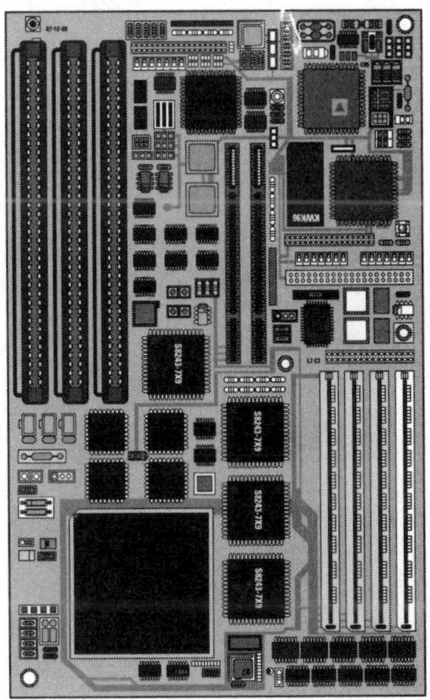

CHAPTER THIRTEEN

THE ESSENTIAL APPLICATIONS

In this chapter we provide an introduction to some of the software applications, tools, and utilities you may need to build and maintain your Internet business application. If your goal is to get started using your Internet business application, this chapter provides the detailed information to do so.

The primary audience for this chapter (as in all the chapters) is the decision maker. We provide a high-level survey of the kinds of software and tools currently available, including descriptions of the features and benefits of the products—all of the information essential to someone putting together a project plan or assembling a team to implement an already planned project.

For those who will be using the software, this chapter provides enough information to get you started—and enough information to help you decide which programs you or someone else should buy for your project. It was not feasible in this short space to offer detailed user guides for all of the products. Check the additional resources for more information. For help on installing the tools provided on the CD-ROM, see the Appendix, "Using the Companion CD and Web site."

How This Chapter is Organized

This chapter is organized by application function. First, we look at software that helps an application function: Web servers, database software, and text search engines. Next we examine site maintenance, usage tracking, and security tools. We then briefly survey design and authoring tools and utilities. At the end of the chapter we present some introductory information on the free, Intel-based version of UNIX called Linux and the Perl programming language.

This method of organization helps to give you a framework for thinking about the kinds of applications you will need for your project. One problem with this framework, however, is that an increasing number of products are combining several of these elements in a single package. For example, Web servers can be purchased with built-in databases or site management tools, or both. Databases may have built-in text search engines; rapid application development tools may have built-in databases; site maintenance tools may have built-in authoring abilities. The move is toward integrated environments.

Selecting a Hardware Platform

Before you can think seriously about what software you will need or want, you need to make a decision about the hardware platform you will use as the base of your application. In Chapter 12, "Assembling Players and Parts," we discussed in some detail the pros and cons of different hardware platform and operating system options. It is worth repeating some of those issues here, since it is just as likely that the price and availability of software products will be a heavy determining factor in your decision.

To summarize briefly, the major options for hardware are the following:

- **Commercial UNIX platform**—Very robust, good third-party support, very expensive.
- **Free Intel UNIX platform**—Unbeatable price, many third-party products available, more administration time required.
- **Windows NT platform**—Rapidly growing number of third-party products, less expensive than UNIX.
- **Macintosh O/S**—Easy to set up and maintain, currently fewer third-party products than other options, price competitive with Windows NT.

Your main considerations in making a selection are likely to be:

- Existing infrastructure, including applications and personnel (NT, UNIX, Macintosh)
- Budget (Macintosh, NT, UNIX)
- Scale (Macintosh, NT, UNIX)

In this book, we concentrate on UNIX and Windows NT applications, mainly because they currently dominate the market. A number of impressive Macintosh applications are appearing on the horizon. There are also many excellent applications available for O/S2, Novell, as well as the many flavors of UNIX. We concentrate here on the most popular business platforms. Even if you do not see your particular operating system mentioned here, you can still benefit from reading about the various kinds of applications described, as reading about other applications It will help you know what to look for.

Obtaining Software

For better or worse, the Internet has changed how software is developed and distributed. For many years, the non-commercial development community on the Internet has developed software collaboratively, through ongoing mailing list and newsgroup discussions and via e-mail. Source code was circulated freely, and everyone and anyone contributed to bug fixes and enhancements. The application was circulated to anyone interested in experimenting with it, and the experimenters became voluntary beta testers.

This spirit has infected even commercial vendors. Following the lead of companies such as Netscape, software developers have begun making prerelease versions of their software available and encouraging the software's wide circulation and use. In some cases, they are even giving away full-scale applications or supplemental utilities in order to enhance their market presence and image.

The good news is that a large quantity of useful software is available to the average developer. The bad news is that it is often difficult to determine when to use an application in a commercial project, since so many of the tools are in a perpetual state of beta testing. One cannot even simply ignore all prerelease software, since that would encompass most of the cutting edge technology that is defining the state of the art Internet today.

Perhaps the best advice we can give is to develop a two-tiered system, whereby the core of your application is always composed of stabilized software, and the more experimental *fringes* take advantage of any and every promising new tool. In this way you can avoid compromising the utility of your application while at the same time guard against your application going stale.

Web Server Applications

In the beginning, there were only two Web servers. One originated from NCSA, the other from CERN. Both were UNIX-based and both were free.

Then along came Netscape, and the Web server landscape changed forever. From the onset, Netscape's business model called for making browser software (now Netscape Navigator) readily available and charging for the server. Now, Netscape has begun to offer tiered pricing and functionality on its ever-expanding line of servers.

For more information about Open Market and Netscape commerce servers, see Chapter 10, "The Malling of Cyberspace."

Netscape's main competitor in the high-end UNIX market is principally Open Market. Both Netscape and Open Market commerce servers are discussed in depth in Chapter 10.

Netscape also developed a line of servers for Windows platforms, most notably for Windows NT. In this market, however, they encountered increasingly aggressive competition, primarily from Microsoft, but also from a host of other companies.

In this chapter, we will focus on three representative server products. The first is a freeware UNIX Web server called Apache. The Apache server, reputedly so named because it started as *a patchy server*, is the offspring of the original NCSA server code.

The second server we examine is O'Reilly's WebSite.

The third Web server product we discuss is the principal Macintosh Web server, WebStar. Currently controlled by Star Nine technologies, this Macintosh server began its life as MacHTTP, a once freeware server turned commercial product that was developed by Macintosh programmer Chuck Shotton and is almost as old as the original UNIX servers.

Immediately following the discussions of these three main servers, we take a brief look at two more specialized servers: the GNN Server and Hyper-G product. Both are attempts to combine basic Web server functionality with additional features. In the case of GNN, the extra elements focus on its built-in Illustra database engine. In the case of Hyper-G, the extras are a host of new features designed to improve information delivery in the Web context.

Apache (UNIX)

The Apache server is an extension of version 1.3 of the original NCSA server. (NCSA has continued to develop its own server, which is now in version 1.4 and contains some of the same enhancements.) The Apache project was initiated by a widely distributed group of computer programmers and server administrators who were interested in promoting the free availability of Web server software, and also in enhancing the functionality of existing software code.

Several of the members of the group had contributed software patches to NCSA's server. From this it was decided to create a separate product, dubbed Apache.

APACHE FEATURES According to its developers, the Apache code improves on the NCSA 1.3 server in several ways. In the first place, it responds to file requests more quickly; it improves server security; complies more completely to the existing HTTP standards; and it is still free.

In addition, Apache incorporates additional features into the server, a few of which are described here.

- **Multi-Homed Serving.** Frequently it is useful to run multiple Web sites from the same machine with the same server. This is particularly valuable for Web presence services, which maintain multiple client sites on a single computer. Apache has built-in ability to run several distinct Web sites from the same server. Each site can maintain its own server configuration files, document directories, access control information, and log files.
- **User Authentication Database.** The NCSA server provided for user authentication and access control via specially named plain ASCII text files stored within specified server file directories. This was an easy method to implement, but not particularly efficient for maintaining large numbers of users. Nor was it a particularly secure method of storing user names and passwords. The Apache server uses the DBM file format, a basic UNIX database structure, to store authentication information. In this way, large numbers of user records can be stored and retrieved efficiently. And because the data is not stored as a text file, it is somewhat more protected.
- **Customizable Error Messages.** Most Web surfers are intimately familiar with the standard Web server error messages, most of which consist of a number and a cryptic message. With Apache, it is possible to associate a customized HTML page with each type of error. In this way Webmasters can offer more user-friendly messages as well as maintaining error messages that are consistent with the look and feel of their site. One of the principal uses of this feature is the ability to redirect users who try to access restricted areas of a Web site without registering. Instead of being given a standard error message, these users can be redirected to the registration page, offering them the opportunity to complete the registration process.
- **Configuration Enhancements.** In addition to the major feature enhancements above, Apache implements a number of useful improvements to its configuration capabilities. The server can be set up to look for any of several default pages, so that in the event it does not find one named default, it will search for the next. This can be particularly useful in cases where more than one kind of default page is needed.

Apache also has the ability to perform content negotiation and to deal with clients of varying sophistication and HTML compliance, by serving them documents that present information that they are capable of accepting and displaying. This feature, however, requires implementation in the client software as well.

OBTAINING APACHE Version 1.0.3 of Apache is available on the CD-ROM in the back of this book. For information on installing Apache from the CD-ROM, see the Appendix, "Using the CD-ROM and Web Site."

Apache (version 1.1 beta) can also be obtained via the Internet. To locate an appropriate site to download current versions of Apache, go to the home page of the Apache Web site, **www.apache.org**. Here you will find information about the latest version of Apache, including current beta version availability and directions to FTP sites for downloading the software.

GETTING STARTED WITH APACHE Apache is distributed as C source code. It has been successfully installed and tested on IRIX, SunOS, BSDI, FreeBSD, HP-UX, Linux, SCO, Solaris, and NeXT. However, before you can use Apache, you must do the following:

- Compile the server software
- Configure the server
- Run it

The compilation process for Apache is designed to support the inclusion of optional modules, one of which is the DBM user authentication system. If you do not intend to use any of the optional modules, you can build the application by using a standard *make* command from within the source code directory. You may need to edit the stock Makefile before doing this.

In order to include any or all of the optional modules, you must first run a configuration script. The steps to do this are as follows.

1. Edit the `configuration` file. This is a text file that contains the configuration settings and indicates which optional modules to include. First, select a compiler and compiler options as appropriate to your computer. Then, uncomment lines that contain the optional modules you wish to install.
2. Run the `configure` script by typing **configure** at the command line prompt. This will generate a new Makefile and a custom C file. `modules.c`. If you wish to maintain several configuration files, you can specify which one the configure script should use. Include reference to the configuration file using the following syntax:
   `configure -file <myconfigurationfile>` replacing `<myconfigurationfile>` with the path and name of the desired file.
3. Type **make** at the command prompt to compile the code.

CONFIGURING YOUR SERVER Once you have compiled the Apache source code, you will have an executable named `httpd` residing in the `src/` directory. The next step is to configure the server for your Web site.

Apache provides three principal configuration files. In the source distribution, they are called `srm.conf-dist`, `access.conf-dist` and `httpd.conf-dist`.

First copy these files to `srm.conf`, `access.conf` and `httpd.conf`, respectively. Retain the original distribution versions, in case you need to return to the default settings. If you want to use a different naming convention for these configuration files, you will have to configure the server to reference them specifically.

Next, edit each of the files to your liking. The first file, `httpd.conf`, sets up general attributes about the server; the port number, server name aliases, the user it runs as, the e-mail of the server administrator, and so on. The second, `srm.conf`, sets up the root of the Web site's document tree, enables or disables special functions such as server-parsed HTML or internal imagemap parsing, allows you to establish directory aliases, and so on. The last configuration file, `access.conf`, is used to set up any access restrictions, either by requiring user passwords or by allowing or denying access by IP addresses.

Finally, move the Apache directories to their final location, typically in `/usr/local/etc/apache`.

To start the server daemon, invoke the `httpd` application, indicating the full path to the `httpd.conf` file as follows:

```
/usr/local/etc/apache/src/httpd -f
/usr/local/etc/apache/conf/httpd.conf
```

The `httpd` program may be set up to be invoked by the Internet daemon `inetd` each time a connection to the HTTP service is made. Alternatively it may run as a daemon that executes continuously, handling requests. Set the ServerType directive in `httpd.conf` to tell the server how it is to run.

The Apache server maintains several log files in the `log/` directory. By default, it records error messages in `errors_log`. It records each file request to `access_log`. If you are setting up your server to support virtual hosts, each virtual host can have its own set of log files.

FOR MORE ASSISTANCE Because it is not a commercial product, Apache does not have built-in customer support. However, as is the case with most products developed from within the Internet community, there are a number of places you may find helpful information. First, try the Apache Web site, at **www.apache.org**. There you will find basic installation and usage instructions as well as an Apache FAQ list.

For basic UNIX Web server configuration questions, you can also check the NCSA documentation at the NCSA Web site at **www.ncsa.uiuc.edu**. For other questions, try the **comp.infosystems.www.servers.unix** newsgroup, in which many of the Apache group members participate. Bug reports and suggestions can be sent to apache-bugs@mail.apache.org.

Database Tools

Connecting a database engine to a Web site is currently still considered something of an esoteric art. By the time the next generation of Web development has fully arrived, however, we predict that Web servers without some database engine will be the exception.

The need for database engines in Internet applications results from the fact that so much of what Web servers are good at center around the collection and dissemination of information. Static information is hard to update and forces users to tolerate a fairly high degree of noise in order to find the information they particularly want. In addition, most of the important tasks connected with managing and administering a Web site are much easier to do when driven by a database engine.

Database engines are sophisticated, more or less costly programs. Locating an inexpensive, relational database system that supports standard SQL is not an easy task. In this section, we introduce you to one such application, Mini SQL, and more briefly to a second, Postgres96.

Tip: If you are interested in a more complete list of free DBMS systems, check out **bunny.cs.uiuc.edu/databaseSoftware/**

Most of the rest of this section focuses on the software tools you will need to connect your database engine to the Internet. A number of such tools are freely available (though of course you will need to have a database to use them with). We describe two UNIX-based software tools: NeXT Software Inc.'s WebObjects and Sybase Inc.'s product, Sybase.web, as well as Cold Fusion and Spider for NT.

Before turning to the software itself, though, we consider some of the issues connected with choosing and using a database in this environment.

Selecting a Database

Deciding on a relational database application to connect to your Internet application is not an easy task. The high-powered databases, such as Oracle, Sybase, and Informix, are quite expensive.

Direct Data Access versus Staging

Another important question for building a database-driven Internet application is whether to allow users to have direct access to the database, either for submitting queries or, more critically, for adding or changing data. If you decide to allow this direct access, you will make real-time updating of information possible. At the same time, you create potential data management headaches, both in terms of transaction validity (what happens if two people try to change the same data simultaneously?) and also in terms of editorial control (how do you know that a user has not entered inappropriate information into the database?).

When the database in question is a corporate database, the issue of security becomes important. It is probably a better idea to safeguard that data by creating a staging scenario and deal with the logistical problems of synchronizing data.

Staging of data refers to introducing an intermediary step between the submission of data and the introduction of that data into the actual database application. A typical staging scenario would look something like the following:

1. At given time intervals, data from the database is exported in an appropriate data format.
2. It is then moved to another server, where it is imported into a database structure that is connected to a Web server.

3. When the user makes a query of the database, it sends the query to this secondary database. This data can not be directly changed by the user.

4. If the user has the ability to add or change information, any changes are stored, separated, and at given time intervals checked and imported into the primary database. (This is easier to do when adding new data than when updating existing data.) This data only becomes available to the user when a new export of this data is made and sent through the staging system as described above.

As you can see, the method just described provides reasonable guarantees of data integrity. It also increases the complexity of the system and increases the length of time between the submission of data and its availability to users. Much of the process can be automated and run at set intervals. However, the process of verifying the data can be difficult to automate and any automation of the process between the two databases will need to be able to pass through any existing firewalls, which can introduce new complications. There is no unilateral solution to these issues.

A NOTE ON LICENSING

One of the problems database companies struggle with is how to charge businesses for use of a database connected to the Internet. Client/server database licenses are typically sold by the number of users connected to the database at any given time. If you purchase a 10-user license, up to 10 people can be connected to the database. When the 11th person attempts to connect, they are told that there are no connections available and they must wait until one of the other 10 people disconnect.

When the database is connected to a Web server, however, as far as the database is concerned there is only one user—the Web server itself. This is because all requests made to the database pass through the server. It is as if your business bought a single user database and then hired one person to supervise all database operations. Everyone else who wanted to use the database would have to send their requests to that one person.

In the physical world, this is somewhat impractical. But it is perfectly reasonable in the Internet environment. Look for database companies to invent creative opportunities for themselves to get out of this apparent dilemma.

Mini SQL (UNIX)

Mini SQL, commonly called mSQL, is a commercial database management system developed by David J. Hughes and currently distributed and supported by the Australian company called Hughes Technologies. It was first released in June, 1994, and at the time of this writing was currently in version 1.0, patch level 14 (although the release history is current only through patch level 12).

Mini SQL is not freeware. You can download and evaluate the product for 14 days, after which time you must purchase a license to use the product unless you are a non-profit organization or educational institution. A version of mSQL is on the CD-ROM in the back of this book.

MINI SQL FEATURES Mini SQL is billed as a lightweight relational database that supports a subset of the ANSI SQL specifications. It is appropriate for use in relatively simple database applications that do not require overly complicated queries. Used in such circumstances, it is fast and requires a relatively small overhead of computer processing resources (database engines typically require a good deal of computer horsepower).

The mSQL package includes the database engine (msqld), a terminal "monitor" program (msql), a database administration program (msqladmin), a database dumper (msqldump) a schema viewer (relshow), and a C language API.

Mini SQL has a good deal of third-party support within the Internet development community. Users have contributed software for mSQL, including interfaces to mSQL from Perl, Tcl, REXX, Java, Python, WWW interfaces, and a Windows port of the client library.

OBTAINING MINI SLQ Version 1.0. patch 12 of mSQL is available on the CD-ROM that accompanies this book. For information on installing mSQL from the CD-ROM see the Appendix, "Using the CD-ROM and Web site."

mSQL can also be obtained via the Internet. To download the current version, go to the Hughes Technologies Web site at **Hughes.com.au**. There you can also obtain W3-mSQL, an interface between your Web server and the Mini SQL database.

Alternately, you can FTP the source code directly from **bond.edu.au in the /pub/Minerva/msql/** directory.

As of this writing, the current version of mSQL was 1.0 patch level 14. According to the FAQ, version 2.0 is under development. This release will incorporate more of the functionality specified by the ANSI SQL specification. It will also provide much greater performance for larger database and complicated queries. No release date was set.

GETTING STARTED mSQL was developed under Sun OS 4.1.1. According to the unofficial mSQL FAQ list, it was tested under Solaris 2.3, Ultrix 4.3, Linux, and OSF/1 (cc not gcc) and should "autoconf" and build on most BSD-derived systems, SVR4-based systems, or POSIX O/S's.

FOR MORE ASSISTANCE From the Hughes Technologies Web site, **Hughes.com.au**, you will find links to the unofficial mSQL FAQ list. There is also a complete HTML version of the user's manual, which contains detailed information about the supported ANSI SQL commands, as well as using the terminal "monitor" program, database administration program, schema viewer, and the API.

There is also a mailing list for discussing mSQL. To subscribe, send a message to:

msql-list-request@Bond.edu.au

An archive of mailing list discussion, maintained at Bond.edu.au, is available from the Hughes Technologies Web site as well.

Postgres95

Postgres is a database management system initially developed at the University of California at Berkeley under the direction of professor Michael Stonebraker. Started in 1986, the project sought to show that a relational database management system can be extended to include features of an object-oriented system and be highly extensible.

University development of Postgres officially ended with version 4.2. In the interim, a commercial company, Illustra, now a wholly-owned subsidiary of Informix, Inc., picked up the source code and produced a commercial version.

Postgres95 (developed by Andres Yu and Jolly Chen, former UC Berkeley Computer Science graduate students) is a revised and extended version of Postgres.

FEATURES The most notable change to Postgres introduced in the Postgres95 version is that the original query language, PostQuel, has been entirely replaced with SQL. In addition, the code was reworked to make it smaller and faster. Other enhancements include a tcl library for implementing tcl-based clients, support for GNU readline, and a SQL tutorial.

Postgres95 also has a Web gateway interface, called Wdb-p95. More information on this product can be obtained at **www.eol.ists.ca/~dunlop/wdb-p95/**.

OBTAINING POSTGRES95 Postgres95 is available free of charge. The current version as of this writing was 1.01, released February 26, 1996. You can FTP Postgres95 from s2k-ftp.CS.Berkeley.edu in the directory **pub/postgres95/postgres95-1.01.tar.gz**. Alternately, a list of mirror FTP sites can be found at:

http://s2k-ftp.CS.Berkeley.EDU:8000/postgres95/www/pglite4.html

Postgres95 was compiled and tested on Alpha (OSF 2.1, 3.0), DECStation (Ultrix 4.4), SPARC (SunOS 4.1.3), SPARC (Solaris 2.4), HP 9000/700 (HP-UX 9.0), Intel X86 (Linux and NetBSD), and IBM RS6000 (AIX).

In addition, ports are provided for Intel X86 (Linux, 1.2 kernel running ELF), BSD44_derived OS's (NetBSD, FreeBSD, BSD/OS), IBM RS6000 (AIX 3.2.5), and SGI MIPS (IRIX 5.3).

FOR MORE ASSISTANCE An HTML version of the Postgres95 user's manual is available at **www.eol.ists.ca:80/~dunlop/postgres95-manual/**

There is a postgres95 mailing list at postgres95@postgres95.vnet.net. For information about how to subscribe, send an e-mail message to majordomo@postgres95.vnet.net with the following lines in the body of the message:

help
info postgres95

Sybase web.sql (UNIX)

web.sql is a database gateway product specifically for Sybase database access.

FEATURES web.sql is designed to support in-line scripting and scripting calls rather than the separate scripting that is required for Common Gateway Interface (CGI) scripts. With web.sql, you can insert database instructions such as SQL statements and Perl scripts into the text of HTML pages. The result is better database access and response time.

OBTAINING WEB.SQL The Sybase web.sql product can be found on the CD-ROM that accompanies this book. For installation information on installing web.sql from the CD-ROM, consult the Appendix, "Using the Companion CD-ROM and Web Site."

Current information about downloading updated versions of web.sql can be found on the Sybase web.sql Web pages beginning at **www.sybase.com/products/internet/websql/**.

GETTING STARTED Sybase web.sql will run on Sun Solaris from Sun Microsystems, IRIX from Silicon Graphics, HP-UX from Hewlett Packard, and Microsoft Windows NT for Intel.

To install the web.sql product, first untar the tar file. Web.sql files will be placed in the `websql-home` directory. Next run the setup application by typing **setup** at the command line prompt.

The setup program will ask you for basic configuration information, including the path name of your server cgi-bin directory and document root directory. After recording that information, setup looks for a Sybase interface application. To run web.sql, you need to have a Sybase interfaces file in your `<websql-home>/sybase` directory. If you have an existing installation of Sybase Open Client v10.03, you can copy or link the interfaces file from that installation. Otherwise, you'll need to run `<websql-home>/sybase/install/sybinit -log sybinit.log` in order to generate an appropriate interfaces file.

To test the installation, open your Web browser and then point to the web.sql welcome page located at `/cgi-bin/websql/ websql.dir/welcome.hts`, assuming that you did not alter the default location of files during setup. You should then see the web.sql welcome page. At that point, you can proceed to configure web.sql, using the link to the administration page that is found on the web.sql welcome page you just loaded.

For more information about configuring web.sql, check the web.sql online manuals located at **www.sybase.com/products/internet/websql/docs/index.html**.

FOR MORE ASSISTANCE The web.sql web site is located at **www.sybase.com/products/internet/websql/**.

The downloadable releases are officially unsupported. However, there is a wealth of documentation and tutorials available from the web.sql Web site to help you use the product effectively. Check out **www.sybase.com/products/internet/websql/assistance.html**.

NeXT WebObjects (UNIX/NT)

WebObjects, created by NeXT, is a tool for the rapid development of Web applications. With WebObjects, developers can create dynamic Web applications capable of providing the information that is tailored to suit each user's needs. These Web applications are compatible with an organization's existing computing environment—heterogeneous hardware platforms, operating systems, databases, and so on.

WebObjects is currently available in three forms. The standard version is freely available for downloading. The professional version, WebObjects Pro, includes facilities for compiling custom Web Object code and implements dynamic distribution features. WebObjects Enterprise provides plug-in access to existing legacy data.

FEATURES WebObjects is a development tool designed to help corporations develop dynamic Internet applications that make use of existing corporate data in a variety of formats, residing in a variety of platforms. WebObjects is an example of open technology that works with products from many vendors, giving developers a wide range of tools to choose from when developing Web applications. Code generated by Web Ojbects is browser and Web server independent; database independent; and platform, operating system, and object model independent. In addition, WebObjects provides important security features, a scaleable application architecture, and a state management system to help manage dynamic data in the Web environment.

Applications created using WebObjects are typically generated from the following ingredients:

- **HTML templates**—Template files contain standard HTML markup elements that specify page structure and layout. Templates may also include WEBOBJECT markup elements that are replaced with dynamically-generated HTML code when the application is running.
- **Declarations files**—Declarations files specify components that dynamically generate HTML to substitute for WEBOBJECT markup elements.

- **Script files**—Script files include business logic specific to the application. Generally, they contain actions that define a response to user requests.

OBTAINING WEBOBJECTS A version of NeXT WebObjects is included on the CD-ROM that comes with this book. For information on installing WebObjects from the CD-ROM, consult the Appendix, "Using the Companion CD-ROM and Web Site."

You can also download a free version of WebObjects from the Next Web site at **www.next.com/WebObjects/**.

GETTING STARTED WITH WEBOBJECTS The WebObjects library of classes that define an infrastructure for Web applications is used to create a WebObjects application. A WebObjects application uses instances of these classes to respond to requests received from a Web browser. For instance, every WebObjects application contains an application object that receives requests and responds to them using application resources you provide.

A typical WebObjects application contains the following ingredients:

- Components that specify the content, presentation, and behavior of the application's pages
- An optional application script that creates and manages application-wide resources
- Optional compiled code that implements custom data and logic
- WebObjects classes that provide an infrastructure for the Web application

To write a WebObjects application, you provide components and, optionally, compiled code. Note that you can incorporate compiled code in a WebObjects application only if you have the WebObjects Pro or WebObjects Enterprise product.

Components are a part of each WebObjects application that you write. Each component defines the content, presentation, and behavior of a page or portion of a page. You can write scripted components in WebScript (the WebObjects scripting language) or compiled components in Objective-C.

Scripted components generally consist of three files.

1. **An HTML template** that specifies how the corresponding page looks. HTML templates contain markup elements that define the format for both static and dynamic page content.
2. **A script file** that implements application behavior specific to the component. Script files declare variables for managing dynamic page content and actions that define responses to user requests.
3. **A declarations file** that defines a mapping between the HTML template and script variables and actions.

Scripted and compiled components play the same role and are created in essentially the same way. However, instead of using a script file, compiled components use an Objective-C class.

The files of a component are organized in a component directory. The name of the directory has the same base name as the name of the component, but the extension `.wo`. For example, the HelloWorld example has a WebScript component named `Main` and a corresponding component directory named `Main.wo`.

The template, script, and declarations files in the component directory also have the same base name, and each file type has its own extension. Template files have the extension `.html`, declarations have the extension `.wod`, and scripts have the extension `.wos`. In addition to these three files, a component directory may also contain images and other resources used by the component.

The component for the first page of a WebObjects application is generally named `Main`. When a user starts a session with a WebObjects application, he or she can specify the name of the first page, but it is uncommon to have to do so. If no page is specified, WebObjects applications look for a component named `Main` to represent the first page.

Generally, you put the components of a WebObjects application in a directory with the same name as the application.

FOR MORE ASSISTANCE Consult the NeXT WebObjects Web site for a wealth of documentation and technical examples intermixed with marketing material at **www.next.com/WebObjects/LearnMore.html**

The Online Developer's Guide is located at: **www.next.com/Pubs/Documents/WebObjects/DevGuide.html.**

Search Engines

This section is devoted to search engines you may use in your Web application.

freeWAIS

freeWAIS is a freely available text search engine based on the Wide Area Information Server (WAIS), a distributed information retrieval system originally developed as a project of Thinking Machines, Apple Computer, Dow Jones, and KPMG Peat Marwick.

One of the project leaders, Brewster Kahle, formed WAIS Inc. to provide commercial WAIS software and services. Support for freeWAIS is currently provided by the Clearinghouse for Networked Information Discovery and Retrieval (CNIDR).

WAIS uses the Z39.50 query protocol to communicate between clients and servers.

FEATURES freeWAIS scores documents based on the number of times the query words appear in a document, the location of the words in a document, the frequency of those words within the collection, and the size of the document.

freeWAIS supports simple boolean searching. The words *and, or,* and *not* are interpreted to mean a request for a boolean search with the boolean operation being performed on the terms delimited by the operators.

WAIS is not limited to text documents. Other data types can be searched by using different search engines and parsers. It is still rather difficult to change search engines, but future releases of freeWAIS will provide a much better mechanism for this.

OBTAINING FREEWAIS Current versions of freeWAIS are available from the CNIDR FTP site at **ftp.cnidr.org.**

GETTING STARTED WITH FREEWAIS freeWAIS source code written for ANSI-C. GNU CC and non-ANSI cc's are supported through the addition of library routines that were not present in the early versions. It has been tested on a VAX, Sun-3, Sun-4, SGI, DECstation, Linux, HP/UX, AIX, Solaris, System V, HP-UX, BSDI, gcc, cc, ThinkC.

To install the software, first decompress and untar the distribution files.

To build the software, first modify the file `freeWAIS-0.5/Makefile` by setting the value of the variable `TOP`. Look over the options for compiling listed at the top of the `Makefile` to see if there are any you would like to add.

There are separate `Makefiles` for all of the supported systems, and you can build freeWAIS with one of the following commands:

```
make aix
make bsdi
make dynix
make hpux
make irix-cc
make irix-gcc
make linux
make osf
make solaris
make sunos
make ultrix-cc
make ultrix-gcc
```

FOR MORE ASSISTANCE There is a fairly active community of people on the Net who are interested in WAIS technologies. For more information, try the **comp.infosystems.wais** newsgroup, monitored by many of the people involved in developing WAIS. There are also several WAIS mailing lists, including wais-talk@think.com and zip@cnidr.org. You can join either of these by sending requests to wais-talk-request@think.com or zip-request@cnidr.org.

CNIDR currently maintains information about freeWAIS status, plans, and operational hints at its Web site, **www.cnidr.org**. This is perhaps the best way to get up-to-date information about freeWAIS.

For additional information, you might try a white paper available from Thinking Machines via FTP at **ftp.think.com** in the directory **wais/wais-corporate-paper.text**. There is also a WAIS FAQ maintained at the Web site:

www.cis.ohio-state.edu/hypertext/faq/usenet/wais-faq/getting-started/faq.html

Glimpse (UNIX)

Glimpse, which stands for *GLobal IMPlicit SEarch,* is a freely available search engine and indexing application. It was developed by Udi Manber and Burra Gopal of the University of Arizona, and Sun Wu of the National Chung-Cheng University, Taiwan. It is maintained at the computer science department of the University of Arizona.

Glimpse performs reasonably fast searches on large collections of text files. It creates relatively small index files and can be optimized for either index size or search speed. The application is easy to use and is highly configurable. There is even a Web interface, called GlimpseHTTP, that is available on the Glimpse Web site at **glimpse.cs.arizona.edu:1994/ghttp/**.

OBTAINING GLIMPSE The Glimpse source code is available for compiling on a variety of UNIX computers. You can also obtain binary executables for OSF/1 DEC Alpha, Sun Sparc Solaris and Sun OS 4.1.1, Linux, IBM AIX 4.1 and 3.2.5, SGI IRIX 6. and 5.3, HP UX, DEC Ultrix, and NeXT Mach 3.1.

You will find download information on the Glimpse home page on the Web at **glimpse.cs.arizona.edu:1994/**. You can also FTP the software directly from **ftp.cs.arizona.edu** in the **/glimpse** directory. The current version as of this writing was version 3.5.

GETTING STARTED WITH GLIMPSE The Glimpse package consists of the four following principal utilities.

1. `glimpseindex`, the file indexing tool
2. `glimpse`, the search engine itself
3. `agrep`, an improved version of the standard UNIX grep search utility
4. `glimpseserver`, a server version of the Glimpse searching package

Once you have compiled the Glimpse package, the first step is to use the Glimpse index to index the files you wish to make available for searching. To index all of the files in the directory tree beginning with the directory `<dir>`, type the following at the command prompt:

```
glimpseindex <dir>
```

By typing **glimpseindex ~** you will index your entire directory tree. You can set `glimpseindex` to create any of three different sized indices: a tiny one that is two to three percent of the size of all files; a small one, seven to nine percent; and a large one that is twenty to thirty percent. It is also possible to maintain multiple indices for different parts of your directory.

Once you create your index, you can search the document collection for the word `<keyword>` by typing:

```
glimpse <keyword>
```

Some basic search options include the ability to limit the search to particular files within the index, to allow for approximate matches (that is, misspellings), and to use multiple keywords. You can use boolean expressions in your search and simple expressions.

FOR MORE ASSISTANCE Check the Glimpse home page on the Web at **glimpse.cs.arizona.edu:1994/**. There you will find download information for the current version of Glimpse, links to demos and sites that use Glimpse, UNIX man page documentation, and information on the companion application, GlimpseHTTP.

There is also a Glimpse mailing list. Send e-mail to glimpse-request@cs.arizona.edu to be added to the list. Post messages—such as bug reports—questions, tips, and so on, to glimpse@cs.arizona.edu. According to the man page information, this list is used primarily for posting announcements.

Usage Tracking

analog

http://www.statslab.cam.ac.uk/~sret1/analog/

getstats

http://www.eit.com/software/getstats/getstats.html

wusage

http://www.boutell.com/wusage/

statbot

http://www.xmission.com/~dtubbs/club/cs.html

Site Maintenance and Security

The two tools we discuss here are Hahtsite and SATAN.

Hahtsite

Hahtsite is a two-component tool, designed to provide for multiple aspects of Web-based development, including visual page creation, graphics processing, team development, dynamic HTML generation, state tracking, debugging, and site management.

It consists of an integrated development environment (IDE) for the development and management of content and logical structure. This structure is then compiled and published on the Hahtsite Engine (application processor), which deploys the application.

Hahtsite, developed by Haht Software, Inc., and founded in June, 1995, aims to allow users of all levels—not just application development specialists—to build sophisticated, interactive Web pages and business applications quickly, easily, and effectively. Haht Software, Inc. is located in Raleigh, North Carolina.

FEATURES Hahtside features can be divided into the four following domains.

- Content creation
- Code development
- Deployment
- Maintenance

For content creation, Hahtsite features drag-and-drop placement, drag-sizing of text and images, URL generation, full HTML 2.0 support, integrated list and table support, form objects, text filters, graphics processing tools for palette reduction, scaling, transparencies, interlacing, and image mapping.

In the area of development, Hahtside offers a full-function application development language (HAHTtalk) with the Visual Basic syntax-compatible language; the ability to create, use, and share encapsulated, drag-and-drop code objects; and the ability to access any data source—via native API or ODB. It also contains built-in support for application "state" which allows applications to carry user-defined global variables, database connections, and file handles across pages.

Programming code can be built in at the following three levels.

- In the form of expressions, statements, or subroutines that reside on an HTML page with other Hahtsite elements/objects such as text, images and tables
- As subroutines that can reside on a Haht Code Page (a page containing only code), enabling the creation of libraries of routines that can be shared by all of the pages within an application
- As Intraprise Objects (I/O Widgets) that can be encapsulated into an object and made available to a developer as a drag-and-drop function via the project window

In addition, Hahtsite has robust data access capabilities. Applications can utilize any server-resident, including API, ODBC driver, .DLL, shared library, stored procedure, server-based OLE/OCX, ActiveX, and more.

For site management, Hahtsite uses a project window to manage all site and application resources, and for the ability to check-in and check-out shared objects and project definitions. The project window also contains incremental site/project updates with automatic URL resolution, and a built-in interface for a commercial version and source control system.

OBTAINING HAHTSITE Initial Hahtsite releases will support development under Windows 95/NT and Solaris, with the Hahtsite Engine, available on Solaris, HP-UX, IBM AIX, Windows NT, and Windows 95 (for prototyping).

Hahtsite is a commercial product. The Hahtsite development environment (IDE) is priced at $995 per user. Applications are built and deployed to the Hahtsite Engine, which is licensed at $2,495 per CPU.

FOR MORE ASSISTANCE For more information and product availability, check out the Hahtsite Web site at **www.haht.com.**

SATAN (UNIX)

SATAN, short for the Security Analysis Tool for Auditing Networks, is a UNIX utility program for systems administrators, developed by Wietse Venema and Dan Farmer. Its purpose is to identify system security problems and to provide help in correcting those problems.

The information gathered includes the presence of various network information services as well as potential security flaws, such as incorrectly configured network services or well-known bugs in system or network utilities. Having collected this data, SATAN can then either report it or use a simple rule-based system to investigate any potential security problems. Reports are generated in HTML format for easy access with any Web browser.

FEATURES SATAN identifies and reports several common networking-related security problems.

For each type of problem, SATAN provides a tutorial that explains the problem and what its impact can be. The tutorial also explains what can be done about the problem—correct an error in a configuration file, install a bug-fix from the vendor, use other means to restrict access, or simply disable service.

Some of the problems SATAN identifies include the following:

- NFS file systems exported to arbitrary hosts
- NFS file systems exported to unprivileged programs
- NFS file systems exported via the portmapper
- NIS password file access from arbitrary hosts
- REXD access from arbitrary hosts
- X server access control disabled

- Arbitrary files accessible via TFTP
- Remote shell access from arbitrary hosts
- Writable anonymous FTP home directory.

OBTAINING SATAN For information about installing SATAN, check the official primary FTP site at **ftp://ftp.win.tue.nl/pub/security/satan-1.0.tar.Z**

In addition, SATAN is mirrored on a large number of FTP sites. Check out the SATAN Web site or **www.cs.ruu.nl/cert-uu/satan.html** for a list.

GETTING STARTED WITH SATAN As of this writing, the current version of SATAN was 1.1.1, issued in April, 1995. This version represents a fix of a fix of version 1.0. To run SATAN, you will need root access privileges to the computer. The computer also needs to have PERL 5.000 or better.

SATAN was successfully tested on SunOS 4.1.3_U1, SunOS 5.3, and Irix 5.3. According to the documentation, it should work with "AIX, BSD types, IRIX5, HP-UX 9.x, SunOS 4 & 5, SYSV-R4, Ultrix 4.x, and maybe, just maybe, with a bit of tweaking, Linux."

In order get things up and running, you must first compile the source code by issuing the **make** command in the main source directory. After compiling SATAN, you will probably wish to edit the configuration file in `config/satan.cf`.

A NOTE ON LIMITING SATAN'S POWER SATAN is a very powerful tool. It is capable of scanning networks and hosts anywhere on the Internet regardless of whether you happen to be a part of the network in question. This fact has caused some alarm among network administrators who fear that, in the wrong hands, SATAN could in fact do more harm than good.

In the first place, this power means that you need to be careful when you run SATAN not to allow it to wander beyond the confines of the network you control and wish to secure. The documentation that comes with SATAN warns:

Not only is it an unfriendly idea to run SATAN against a remote site without permission, it is probably illegal as well. Do yourself and the rest of the Internet a favor and don't do it! While we don't know of anyone being charged with a crime or sued because they ran a security tool against someone else, SATAN could change that. Heed the warnings, limit your scans to authorized hosts, and all should be well.

As for the fear that SATAN could be used by network *crackers,* the authors note:

We realize that SATAN is a two-edged sword—like many tools, it can be used for good and for evil purposes. We also realize that intruders (including wannabes) have much more capable (read intrusive) tools than offered with SATAN. We have those tools, too, but giving them away to the world at large is not the goal of the SATAN project.

FOR MORE ASSISTANCE Consult the SATAN Web site at **www.fish.com/satan**.

Authoring/Design Tools

It seems like there is a new high-powered, "Swiss Army Knife," commercial Web authoring tool appearing everyday. There are also several respectable shareware and freeware tools and utilities that are worth referring to. Rather than try to describe each one in detail, we simply provided you with enough information to find out more about them if you are interested.

HTML Authoring Tools

HTML authoring tools are what you use to build Web pages. Here we discuss a few of the better ones.

HOTMETAL (XWINDOWS/WINDOWS FREEWARE) SoftQuad, Inc., is a commercial software company that specializes in SGML authoring tools. They sell a commercial version of the HoTMetaL product, HoTMetaL Pro. You can download and use the non-Pro version for free. It has fewer features, but is still a robust HTML tag editing environment. Features include support for HTML 3.0, WYSIWYG tables editor, and HTML validation. Visit the Web site at **www.sq.com/products/hotmetal/hmp-org.htm**

HOT DOG/HOT DOG PRO WEB EDITORS (WINDOWS SHAREWARE) A strong contender for best HTML editor for Windows. From Sausage Software, **www.sausage.com.**

WEBBER (WINDOWS SHAREWARE) From Cerebral Systems Development Corporation, this Web editor fully supports HTML 2.0 and 3.0, Netscape, and Internet Explorer tags. It also has a built-in SGML parser for HTML validation. Check out the Web site at **www.csdcorp.com/webber.htm.**

Graphics Utilities

You use graphics utilities to manipulate graphics on your Web pages.

MAPTHIS! (WINDOWS FREEWARE) MapTHIS! is a graphics utility for generating server side image maps to be used with clickable Web images. Developed by Todd C. Wilson of Molly Penguin Software. **galadriel.ecaetc.ohio-state.edu/tc/mt**

GIFTOOL (UNIX/MS-DOS FREEWARE) GIFTOOL is a multipurpose graphics utility that can batch convert images for interlacing and creating GIFs with transparent backgrounds. **www.homepages.com/tools/.**

LVIEW PRO (WINDOWS SHAREWARE) A full featured image file viewer, editor, and format converter developed by Leonardo H Loureiro, Lview Pro is also capable of interlacing and transparency. You can download LView Pro from Loureiro's home page at **http://world.std.com/~mmedia/lviewp.html.**

GIF CONSTRUCTION SET (WINDOWS SHAREWARE) GIF Construction Set from Alchemy Mindworks is a collection of tools to work with multiple-block GIF files, commonly known as "GIF animations" or "animated GIFs." **www.mindworkshop.com/alchemy/gifcon.html**

Conversion Utilities

Conversion utilities come in handy when you already have documents in a certain format, for example Microsoft Word, and you want to convert them to HTML documents to publish over the Web.

THE ANT (WINDOWS SHAREWARE) The ANT_HTML.DOT template works with Word 6.0 and above to facilitate the creation of hypertext documents. HTML tags can be inserted into any new or previously-prepared Word document or any ASCII document. **mcia.com/ant/.**

EXCEL TO HTML CONVERTER (WINDOWS FREEWARE) Excel macro that converts Excel files into HTML tables. **rs712b.gsfc.nasa.gov/704/dgd/xl2html.html.**

Microsoft also has an Excel converter, part of the suite of Internet Assistant tools for Microsoft Office (see PowerPoint below). Visit the Web site at **www.microsoft.com/msoffice/internet/**

WP2HTML (MS-DOS SHAREWARE) Wp2Html is a stand-alone program for converting WordPerfect files into HTML. It converts tables, text, styles, and most formatting codes. Visit the Web site at **www.res.bbsrc.ac.uk/wp2html/.**

INTERNET ASSISTANT FOR POWERPOINT 95 (WINDOWS FREEWARE) Microsoft developed a plug-in to PowerPower 95 that allows presentations to be converted to HTML format. Point your browser to the Web site at **www.microsoft.com/mspowerpoint/Internet/ia/default.htm.**

Additional Applications and Tools

In this last section we call your attention to two of the other principal applications included on the CD-ROM that is bundled into the back of this book. These applications are freely available on the Internet, and if combined with other freely available software in this chapter (the Apache Web server, mSQL database, freeWAIS search engine, and log analysis software), would enable you to develop a commercial-quality Web server application on a shoestring budget.

The two applications discussed in this final section are Linux, a freeware implementation of UNIX for Intel-based computers, and the Perl programming language.

Linux (UNIX)

Linux is a freely distributed UNIX clone developed from the ground up primarily by Linus Torvalds at the University of Helsinki in Finland. It runs on Intel-based computers, 486 class or higher, preferably Pentium. The Linux operating system can be selected at boot time, making it possible to switch between DOS/Windows and the Linux/UNIX OS.

Linux is capable of running X Windows, TCP/IP, Emacs, mail, news, and many other standard UNIX applications. Much of the software available for Linux was developed by contributing programmers and teams, including the GNU project at the Free Software Foundation in Cambridge, Massachusetts.

FOR MORE ASSISTANCE A vast amount of information on Linux is available on the Internet. If you are new to Linux, we suggest that you start by perusing the resources in the "For Beginners" subdirectory of Yahoo's Linux directory. See **www.yahoo.com/Computers_and_Internet/Operating_Systems/Unix/Linux/For_Beginners/**

A fairly clear and thorough introductory Linux tutorial is maintained by Matt Welsh at **sunsite.unc.edu/mdw/LDP/gs/gs.html**.

More experienced users may wish to check out the links from the Linux Organization, a not-for-profit group dedicated to supporting the Linux community. See **www.linux.org**.

Perl (UNIX/NT)

Perl, which may or may not stand for "Practical Extraction and Reporting Language," is an easy-to-use, interpreted programming language. Perl, the eclectic creation of Larry Wall, has characteristics of several other programming languages, including features of C, sed, awk, and sh.

Because Perl is particularly adept at manipulating text files and system processes, it has become one of the preferred programming languages for CGI programs, the standard glue that links external data and applications to your Web server.

The current version of Perl, as of this writing, is 5.0.1. Perl 5.0 is included on the CD-ROM that accompanies this book. For installation information, see the Appendix, "Using the CD-ROM and Web site."

FOR MORE ASSISTANCE A wealth of information resources devoted to Perl proliferate on the Internet. Here are a few Web sites to begin your search:

www.perl.com/perl/
www.metronet.com/perlinfo/perl5.html
infoweb.magi.com/~steve/perl.html.

Conclusion

This chapter provides an overview of some of the software applications, tools, and utilities that have been developed as part of the explosion of interest in the Internet. We have attempted to focus on applications that are readily available to anyone. Obviously, if you have a solid budget for your Internet development project, you may not be interested in freeware or shareware software, which tends to require more from the user than the typical commercial product.

Commercial development of Internet software is still just emerging from its infancy. In many cases, the free tools have been around for far longer, and have received far more testing and patching. In addition, if you are still at the prototype stages of your project development, you'll find it more efficient to use freely available tools in the beginning to build your first working model before making recommendations for spending larger sums of money on commercial tools. And you will have the satisfaction of knowing that by using these tools you are participating in the true spirit of Internet application development. Happy developing!

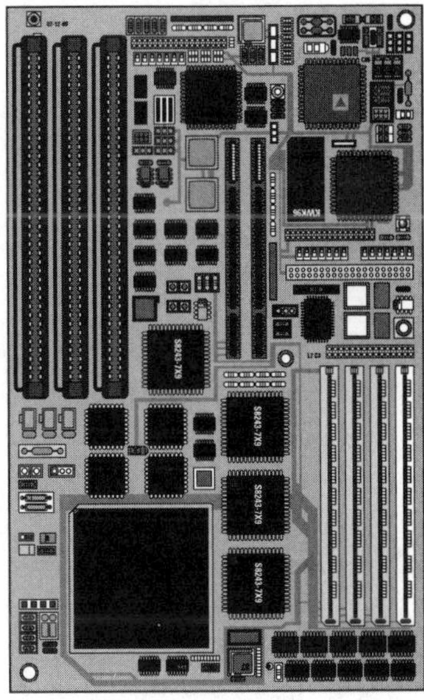

APPENDIX

USING THE COMPANION CD-ROM AND WEB SITE

This Appendix is an attempt to help you install the software you'll find on the CD-ROM in the back of this book. It also contains information on the companion Web site for the book, located at **http://www.idgbooks.com/idgbooksonline/**.

Licensing

Much of the software on the CD-ROM in this book is subject to the GNU General Public License except as noted otherwise below. The terms of the GNU Public License are available on the CD in the file "copying."

The following software is not under GNU GPL and is provided for evaluation purposes only. It is *not* freeware or shareware. If you intend to continue to use this software commercially you must contact the vendor and obtain commercial licenses:

- **MSQL (mini-sql)**
  In the directory \servers\database\msql
- **WebObjects from NeXT Inc.**
  In the directory \midlware\webobj

- **Cold Fusion from Allaire Inc.**
  In the directory \midlware\coldfusn
- **Web.sql from Sybase Inc.**
  In the directory \midlware\websql

Overview of the Material on the CD-ROM

The CD-ROM contains language and development tools useful for building business Web sites. We attempted to provide a small set of tools that will give the beginning Web site builder a start without an exorbitant outlay for hardware and software.

The tools are a combination of freeware, shareware, and trial versions of commercially available tools. We attempted to provide a combination of standard tools and also some tools not commonly found on other such CDs.

The tools on this CD are for the following platforms:

- Windows NT and Windows 95
- Unix (Solaris and Linux)

Using tools from this CD will require you to be very familiar with your platform of choice especially if you need to build software from the sources. If you have never built software from sources before we strongly urge you to get your hands on some books dealing with the subject. For Windows platforms this includes books on Microsoft or Borland C/C++ compilers. For Unix this includes one or more of the excellent books from O'Reilly and Associates on the subject.

Philosophy—Why Solaris and NT?

The platforms supported were chosen to be the predominant platforms on the Internet as of today (circa mid-1996). We also focused the tools on the small- to medium-sized business attempting to bootstrap itself on the Web.

If you're graduating from Windows 3.x to NT and want to be on the Net, NT is a good platform (not quite there yet but tools are fast appearing). Where possible we included versions of tools for NT—Perl, Tcl/Tk, WebObjects, and Cold Fusion. Some tools are just not available on NT yet but this availability is likely to change.

You will find that the Unix tools are for Solaris (Sun Microsystems), which is the platform you would use if you have the financial resources to buy commercial Unix hardware.

Extracting Software from the CD

The software has been compressed using .ZIP, and .Z formats. Utilities to uncompress these have been provided on the CD-ROM in the utils directory.

The following instructions hold for the software in all the directories except the MIDLWARE directories.

1. Create a separate directory on your hard drive to extract the software. Call it, for example, temp.
2. Copy the file from the CD into the directory on the hard drive.
   Unix
   cp/<cdrom-dir>/filename /temp
   Windows
   Either use drag-and-drop in File Manager or Explorer or use the DOS window.
   copy d:/<cdrom-dir>filename c:/temp
   where <cdrom-dir> is the directory containing the file. It is assumed that d: is your CD drive and c: your hard drive. If not, substitute the appropriate drive letters.
3. Change to the target directory.
   Unix
   cd/temp
   Windows (in DOS window)
   cd c:\temp
4. Similarly copy the appropriate executable from the CD-ROM utils directory to the temp dir on your hard drive.
5. Use the following commands to uncompress the files depending on the file extension (.ZIP, .TRZ, or .gz).
   .ZIP
   UNZIP <filename>
   .TRZ (this is a tar file which has been compressed using Unix "compress")
   rename the file:
   - mv <filename>.TRZ <filename>.tar.Z (case sensitive)
   uncompress <filename>.tar.Z
   tar -xvf <filename>.tar
   .gz
   gzip -d <filename>.gz (the gzip utility can be FTP'd from sunsite.unc.edu for Solaris)

For Contents of the MIDLWARE Directory

The contents of this directory are *not* freeware. You must contact the vendor for full commercial licenses if you intend to continue to use the software. This software is for evaluation purposes only.

COLDFUSN (Cold Fusion)

Windows NT Only

This contains Cold Fusion Web-database middleware from Allaire Inc. This is for the Windows NT platform *only.*

Full details are on the Allaire Web site at **www.allaire.com**.

Copy all the files in this dir from the CD into a directory on your hard drive.

In the Windows File Manager (or Windows Explorer) double-click on setup.exe and follow the directions.

If you wish to use this beyond a trial period commercially, you must contact Allaire Inc. and obtain the appropriate licenses.

WEBOBJ (WebObjects)

Windows NT Only

This is NeXT Inc.'s WebObjects for Windows NT only. Other more recent versions of software for this and other platforms may be obtained from Next Inc.'s Web site at **www.next.com**.

Copy the single file with the .EXE extension from this directory to a directory on the hard drive. Then double-click on it in File Manager or Windows Explorer and follow the directions.

WEBSQL

Solaris Only

Copy the file wssol1ga.trz to a directory in which the web.sql files will reside. Then do the following:

1. Rename the file:
mv WSSOL1GA.TRZ wssol1ga.tar.Z
2. Uncompress it.
uncompress wssol1ga.tar.Z
3. Untar it.
tar xvf wssol1ga.tar

The Sybase Web site is located at **www.sybase.com**, and you can download the latest version of web.sql from there.

BROWSERS

The following is a description of files on the CD-ROM for all the other directories with instructions where applicable. This assumes that the CD-ROM is in a Windows machine on the d: drive.

A098LNXA ZIP—Arena WWW browser for Linux a.out format
A098LNXE ZIP—Arena WWW browser for Linux elf format
LYNXDOS8 ZIP—Lynx text mode WWW browser for DOS
LYNXLNUX ZIP—Lynx text mode browser
LYNXLNXN ZIP—Lynx text mode browser for ncurses

DATABASE

MSQL is not freeware and you must contact the author at bambi@bond.edu.au for commercial use.

MSQL—Directory containing the msql .TRZ file
MSQLJAVA.TRZ—Interface between MSQL and Java

MIDLWARE (Middleware)

This directory contains commercial software—it is not freeware or shareware.

See licensing information at the beginning of this Appendix. Also see comments earlier in the Appendix for installation information.

COLDFUSN—Contains the Cold Fusion software.
WEBOBJ—Contains the WebObjects software from NeXT Inc.
WEBSQL—Contains the Web.sql software from Sybase Inc.

TCL-TK

JAVA_TCL ZIP—Interface between Java and Tcl.
MANIFEST—Contents of directory with details on authors.
QUICKREF ZIP—Tcl quick reference.
SOLAR_24 ZIP—Tcl binaries for Solaris 2.4.
TCL7_5 ZIP—Tcl 7.5 sources.
TCLHTML ZIP—Tcl resources.
TCLTKMAN ZIP—Tcl Tk man pages.
TCLX7_3A ZIP—Extensions to Tcl.
TCLX7_5A ZIP—Extensions to Tcl 7.5.
TCL_DP33 ZIP—Distributed Computing extensions for Tcl.
TK40 ZIP—Tk 4.0 sources.
TK41A2 ZIP—Tk4.1 alpha2.
TKNT40R1 ZIP—TclTk binaries for NT.

PERL

P5WINNTB ZIP—Perl5 for NT binaries.
PERL5001 ZIP—Perl 5.001 sources.
PERL5002 ZIP—Perl 5.002 sources.

UTILS

UNIX—UNZIP and GZIP utilities for Unix. This directory also contains SATAN 1.1 which is a Network Security tool for System Administrators.

WIN-NT

SERVERS\WEB

AP101LNX ZIP—Apache Web Server binaries for Linux

APACH100 ZIP—Apache Sources

HTTPS099 ZIP—Emwacs HTTPS for NT

NC14LNXD ZIP—NCSA server 1.4

W3V3CERN TXT—CERN copyright notice

WWWLIB31 ZIP—CERN WWW library which contains a line-mode browser useful for building Web robots.

This Book's Companion Web Site

Visit the book's companion Web site at

http://www.idgbooks.com/idgbooksonline

Borwankar Research and Development

Borwankar Research and Development is one of the top sources of consulting expertise on interfacing relational databases (Sybase, Oracle, and so on) to WWW sites, and connection to payment systems such as First Virtual Holdings and CyberCash. It also consults on strategy for introducing new products into the Internet product space.

Its principals are currently defining Internet standards to interface SQL databases to the Internet via MIME.

Its clients include or have included:

Sybase Inc. Strategic business consulting.

Ascend Communications Inc. WWW-WAIS interface for text database.

Time Warner Inc.'s Pathfinder. web.sql training.

Mayfield Fund (a venture capital company). Evaluating Internet business plans.

First Virtual Holdings Inc. An Internet Payments System company.

Geonet Communications. A high-end Internet Service Provider.

Preview Media. www.vacations.com (Sybase/Web interface).

Intouch Group. www.worldwidemusic.com (Oracle/Web/CyberCash interface).

For more details on what Borwankar Research and Development can do for your high-end business Web site, please send e-mail to info@borwankar.com or fill out the following form and mail it to:

Borwankar Research and Development
5543A Fremont Street
Oakland, CA 94608

Name ____

Address ____

Telephone ____

Fax ____

E-mail ____

Interested in/Need advise on:

Current level of knowledge of the Internet:

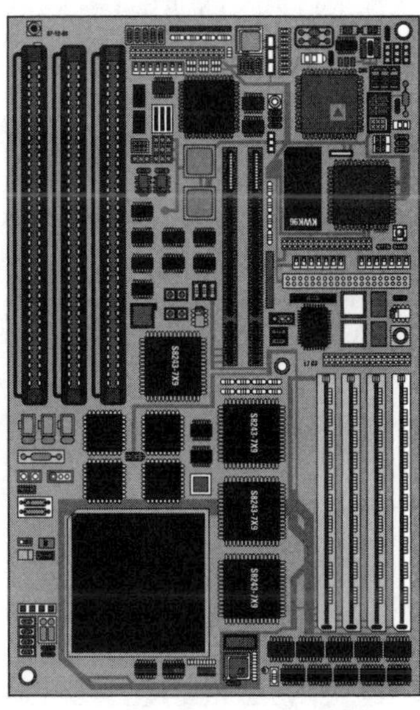

EPILOGUE

BUILDING A CORPORATE INTRANET

Throughout this book we emphasized the fact that Internet development is evolving from building Web sites to building business applications. When we started to draft this book several months ago—roughly an eon in Internet years—we felt that there was enough momentum in this direction to warrant such a book. In fact, the trend to develop business applications has developed faster than this book.

One clear sign of the push to develop business applications is the current fervor surrounding intranets. Six months ago, the word *intranet* barely existed; now it is difficult to avoid. An intranet is a closed version of the Internet, typically residing within a single company and inaccessible to outsiders. In one sense, this inward turn indicates some of the dissatisfaction or discomfort businesses have felt in their initial forays into Internet development. Many companies that rushed to put up Web sites have been left wondering why in fact they did. As an advertising vehicle, or a revenue-generating engine, the Internet has yet to prove itself to the vast majority of small and mid-sized businesses. The basic premise, on the other hand, that an intranet could improve corporate productivity and the flow of information and communication, is highly attractive.

Even though it seems motivated by Internet skepticism, the current interest in intranets illustrates that the business world is beginning to look past the Internet as a place to put up marketing materials and to see its potential as a channel. In this epilogue we examine some of the reasons for building an intranet and the applications you might want to include in an intranet. We also provide a brief case study of Sybase's development of a mixed Internet/intranet environment to facilitate the flow of information both internally and to their customers.

What is an Intranet?

An intranet is a closed network built around the Internet protocols, such as TCP/IP and Internet services, and especially e-mail and the World Wide Web. An intranet can be closed in any of a variety of ways. It can be developed on an internal LAN or a proprietary WAN network that is not physically connected to the Internet at all. Alternately, the intranet may use the Internet physical connection and rely on secure firewalls to protect the flow of information into and out of the intranet.

Why All the Interest in Intranets?

It is worth reflecting for a moment on the cause of all of this enthusiasm for intranets. Given the relatively sudden explosion of interest in the Internet, it may appear that the corporate world has simply been collectively seduced by some rather savvy media hype and marketing. In fact, however, several business trends have been consolidating for a number of years, and have come together to make an intranet appear like a viable solution. Consider briefly some of the major changes in the wind.

Downsizing and Cost-Cutting

In response to increased competitiveness and lower margins, many companies looked for ways to scale back the number of people and the amount of time required to complete a given task or to sustain a given operation. An intranet offers a means of streamlining information flow. It also makes it possible for those who need information to be more self-directing—another time-saver.

Increasing Rate of Change

Companies have also been feeling an increasing sense of urgency around the need to decrease the time-to-market for their new and updated products and services. Here, too, an intranet increases efficiency, allowing businesses to stay competitive. Isn't it interesting, by the way, that the Internet is also routinely blamed for demanding an increased pace?

Changing Employment Patterns

Mobility has become a fact of life for a large segment of the workforce. With mobility, whether for telecommuters, traveling sales teams, or remote satellite offices, comes the need to stay in direct communication. An intranet facilities this over wide area networks.

Increasing Customer Service Needs

In recent years customer support and service have become an increasing part of businesses. This is partly the result of the need to keep a competitive edge, partly because so many products have become more complex, and partly because the value of retaining a customer has become increasingly apparent to businesses. At any rate, the intranet raises the prospect of letting customers get answers directly, allowing support personnel to focus on the thornier problems. This application straddles the border line between intra- and internets by allowing limited customer access to corporate knowledge bases. The result is an erosion between corporation and the world, in effect the flip side of the mobile employee.

What Are the Advantages of an Intranet?

Looking at the business trends that have fueled the interest in intranets already gives us some indication of what the advantages of having one might be. The headlines here are that the intranet increases productivity by decreasing the amount of time required for tasks such as document management, information flow, and project or task management. This decrease in time translates into cost savings. Developing from an open standards-based environment also decreases the cost involved in integrating applications and enabling cross-platform communication. Finally, an intranet typically opens direct access to an increasing range of information—at once relieving the burden of the traditional keepers of the information and empowering the rest to obtain the information directly.

The following is a complete check list, with some repetition, of potential advantages of having an intranet.

- Enables departments to manage and publish data and information documents
- Improves inter-department and enterprise communications
- Simplifies the task of cross-platform application development
- Allows smooth integration of existing legacy applications
- Makes possible global linking of branch offices
- Facilities remote management of global teams
- Provides mobile employees access to corporate data
- Erodes barriers between customers and needed information

What Are the Principal Uses of an Intranet?

All of the advantages of an intranet may sound great, but they are only realized when a corporation gets down to deciding how to use its intranet. Some of the more common applications for intranets include the following:

- News and announcements
- HR employment services, including job listings, benefits information, career planning, and training workshop registration
- Searchable employee directories
- Scheduling/calendar of events
- Conferencing/groupware applications
- Work flow/project management and tracking
- Product inventory and tracking
- Customer service problem resolution tracking
- Customer access to relevant non-confidential data
- Remotely accessible sales and marketing information and demonstrations

What Are Some Potential Problems?

So far we focused on the positive gains your business might realize by investing in an intranet. As you may have already suspected, however, these pluses do not happen magically. They come by recognizing and surmounting the new challenges presented by a change of this extent. Keep in mind that we are not simply talking about a few internal departments putting up some home pages. You can do that, of course, but don't be surprised if the result is as disappointing as many companies have found about their external Web sites.

We are really talking here about redefining the infrastructure and channels of information flow in your company. The bigger your company is and the more ingrained the existing channels and modes of operation are, the bigger the challenge you are likely to face. The key here, no surprise, is adequate planning and a detailed migration path.

The following are some of the issues you are likely to confront along the way.

Centralized versus Departmental Control

In existing companies, it is not uncommon for the interest in intranet applications to begin at the department level. Several Web servers may be in place before the central management of the corporation begins to formulate a strategy for intranet development, which is typically driven from information systems (IS) departments. So the question becomes, how much control should the central organizations retain and how much should they hand off to departments or divisions?

There is no single answer to this question It depends a great deal on the corporate culture of the particular business. It is important to remember, though, that the more decisions are centralized, the more the advantages of efficiency and rapid deployment of information are likely to be diminished. Conversely, the more control placed in the hands of departments, the less consistency there will be and a greater likelihood that the same wheel will be reinvented several times.

One typical solution is to empower IS to enact standards and to assist departments in the construction of applications that suit their particular needs. This keeps the burden of content management and some of the administration off of IS and yet ensures consistency across the company.

Outsourcing versus In-House Development

This is a perennial issue that boils down to a simple dilemma. Hire a contractor and you get an expensive expert who you may have a harder time controlling but who is used to getting things done on impossible deadlines. Use internal resources and you may be slowed down by learning curve requirements as well as by the imposition of other day to day demands on the part of employees.

Most companies end up compromising on this one and build a development team that is made up of an in-house core team supplemented by contractors. In this way the contractors can bring expertise to the core team, and the core team can provide a modicum of stability to the project. Eventually, many larger companies get around to hiring in-house some of those experts.

Staffing and Training Requirements

Someone will need to be responsible for managing the information flow generated by your intranet. Someone, too, will need to be responsible for managing new content. These are roles that have traditionally been confined within IS departments. Depending on how your intranet is ultimately configured, it may be necessary to reorganize the way systems are managed.

Even if job requirements do not change, you will have to provide a good deal of training and support for the new systems you introduce. Intranets are heralded as providing easy-to-use interfaces, which may be true relative to some of the network and enterprise applications currently in use in corporations. But don't forget that only a year ago most people were still complaining that the Internet was an arcane, alien environment that could only be deciphered by certified nerds. Don't assume that employees will intuitively understand this new environment.

Sybase's Support Online Services (SOS—register for it at **http://www-es1.sybase.com/registergw.html**) represents a leading-edge Internet/intranet application. Because it involves both internal staff and external customers, this is a hybrid Internet/intranet application. It is at the boundary of the organization—where it communicates with its customers, vendors, and the external public. It is here where an enterprise can exploit the power of the Internet the most. Sybase's SOS is a superb example of how one company has seamlessly merged it's internal systems with the World Wide Web's framework, and used security technology to enable effective communication between its internal staff and its customers.

PRODUCT DESCRIPTION AND COMPANY BACKGROUND

Sybase, Inc., is a worldwide leader in client/server and Internet software and services and focuses on four major market segments:

- Online transaction processing
- Data warehousing
- Mass deployment
- Online electronic commerce

Sybase's software products—database, middleware, and tools—provide customers with desktop-to-enterprise solutions. The company's mission is to provide customers with an open, adaptable information systems architecture that enables them to develop and deliver complete information solutions to facilitate rapid business change.

Sybase markets products and services under two brands. *Sybase-branded products* are focused on scaleable database and middleware solutions. *Powersoft-branded products* are focused on the development tools marketplace. The combined product lines provide comprehensive solutions to the information systems requirements of small and large companies alike.

BUSINESS MODEL AND MARKETING

In 1995 Sybase merged with Powersoft, making it the world's sixth largest software company with combined 1994 revenues of $826 million and more than 4,500 employees.

Sybase customers are Fortune 500 companies with mission-critical applications that run their businesses. High-quality support is vital to customers. Sybase software runs on Internet sites such as Time Warner's Pathfinder, HotWired, Virtual Vineyards, and C|NET.

In its ongoing efforts to streamline and revolutionize its support infrastructure, Sybase began to look to the Internet as a way to improve its processes. Over a two-year time frame, after many intermediate steps, Sybase's Support Online System (SOS) emerged.

THE USER EXPERIENCE

As currently (Q1 1996) configured, SOS provides Internet-enabled solutions for three key customer support functions.

ECM-ELECTRONIC CASE MANAGEMENT

ECM allows customers to enter cases directly into Sybase's internal case management system and to track them.

ESD-ELECTRONIC SOFTWARE DISTRIBUTION FOR BUG FIXES/PATCHES

ESD allows customers to download bug fixes in the form of patches via FTP.

TIL-TECHNICAL INFORMATION LIBRARY

A large number of technical documents from previously scattered sources are now able o be browsed through in one central repository via one interface: a Web browser.

In each of these three areas the company has achieved significant process improvement by merging World Wide Web, digital certification via Netscape's RSA infrastructure, and FTP (Internet technologies) into its legacy support framework, which consists of phone, fax, Clarify case management software, software distribution using computer tape and overnight courier services, Lotus Notes documents, technical notes, and newsletters.

ECM—ELECTRONIC CASE MANAGEMENT

In this section we describe the before and after scenarios for Sybase in terms of how they handled certain technical support cases.

BEFORE ECM

Before ECM the following process roughly represented the life cycle of a case.

A case was usually initiated by a phone call from a customer who spoke to a technical support representative, who then took notes about the problem, getting as much detail as possible verbally from the customer. After the conversation, the technical support representative then opened a case by entering the details into the internal Clarify case-tracking system. In the process, the technical support person relied primarily on written notes of the conversation. In a situation of this sort, the degree to which technical support can help solve the customer's problem is proportional directly to the amount of detail the customer can provide about the problem and how to reproduce it.

Often with software as large and as complex as a relational database with extensive custom code at customer sites, reproducing the problem is an involved process with detail needing to be provided about specific hardware platforms, operating systems, configurations, and user input, along with resulting error messages. As can be imagined, multiple phone calls, faxes, and e-mail communication is the rule rather than the exception for completely delineating the parameters of a case.

Once the case is logged with all of the requisite information, the case is assigned to an engineer for solution. As the case progresses toward a solution—this may involve multiple partial solutions—the customer communicates with the technical support person who then communicates with the engineer about ongoing problem status. The engineer often updates the case information in Clarify, and when the customer calls, the technical support person reads the status from the Clarify system. The insulation of the engineers from the customer is not a process inefficiency or a system defect. Rather, it is necessary for the engineer to do his or her work effectively without constantly being interrupted by impatient, and sometimes irate, customers.

Often a case must be escalated (increase its priority) if it has been open too long or the customer feels that it is important to do so. In these cases, more people become involved in the problem resolution loop with managers at various levels becoming responsible for resolving the case. Coordination of telephone, fax, and e-mail communication is often a difficult, and sometimes frustrating, process, and often an imperfect process. However, this process is not unique to Sybase or relational databases, but is a characteristic of any large, complex piece of software, such as an operating system or an enterprise application for financials.

A large customer with multiple large sites running Sybase may have several cases at different stages of completion open at one time. Tracking and communicating the status of a particular case adds even more complexity to the task of coordinating communications.

When the case is resolved, or when the customer determines that the problem is no longer an issue, the customer calls technical support again and a support person locates the case and closes out a case on the Clarify system.

USING ECM

In ECM, customers communicate directly with the internal Clarify system using Netscape browsers, a Netscape server with Secure Sockets, and RSA digital certification technology. The secure Web framework enables authentication of the client to the server, validating the customer as a genuine Sybase customer while also validating the Sybase site to the customer to confirm that he is connecting to the real Sybase support system and not some impostor.

Once inside the system, a customer can do any of the following:

- **Open a case directly.** Opening a case involves provideing technical details—including any problem reproduction details or "bug scripts," step-by-step instructions on how to reproduce the problem—and error messages by cutting and pasting them into the window. These steps significantly reduce the number of initial communications needed to grasp the problem. Including error message text directly by cut-and-paste removes ambiguity often introduced by incorrect transcription of the message either by the customer or by the technical support person on the phone.
- **Track the status of a case.** Here a significant process improvement is achieved and the customer is now virtually looking over the shoulder of the engineers as they solve the problem. The engineers often make a note that additional information is necessary and with the new system, the customer can post additional information directly into the system. The speed and the accuracy of communicated information is increased, and there is a persistent historical record of the evolution of the case, which will assist future engineers working with the customer.
- **Close out a case.** Again, another round trip is saved by the customer directly closing out a case. Using the Netscape-enabled authentication, ECM makes sure that customers can only browse their own cases and not other customer's cases.

European VARs (*value added resellers* of Sybase software) are in a different category and are allowed to browse all cases so that they are proactively aware of issues that customers might encounter. Thus ECM also improves a Sybase-to-partner communication process along with the customer improvements.

ESD—ELECTRONIC SOFTWARE DISTRIBUTION

In this section we briefly describe the before and after scenarios for the process of distributing software.

BEFORE ESD

Often, closing a high priority case for a mission-critical customer site may involve shipping a custom "bug fix" to a customer (an EBF or Emergency Bug Fix). Before ESD, an additional night was added to the time it took to put the solution into the hands of the customer. The software was put on a tape and then sent by overnight courier. EBF's then had to be archived and tracked historically.

USING ESD

ESD integrates an FTP site with Netscape-enabled authentication so that a customer can download a bug fix shortly after it becomes available.

TIL—TECHNICAL INFORMATION LIBRARY

In this section we briefly describe the before and after scenarios involving Sybase's cataloging of customer accessible technical information and documentation.

BEFORE TIL

Before TIL, Sybase customers accessed technical information in different forms and different media—technical notes, newsletters, case information, and so on.

USING ESD

TIL is a Lotus Notes repository of all customer technical information that is periodically (daily) outputted as HTML marked-up content via Lotus's InterNotes product. Customers can search the repository, where the search works directly on the native Notes content, but the results are translated (by InterNotes) into URLs that point to the corresponding HTML.

By making all of this information directly available to the customer over a ubiquitous framework (the Web), Sybase enables customers to often solve their own problems—making a journey through ECM and the case process unnecessary.

Intranet Applications

One year ago, we began to see a phenomenon in which software developers of all sorts started to insert the words *Internet* and *Web* into their marketing. Suddenly everything was "Internet software." Currently, the key term is *intranet.* However, just because a software application touts itself as an essential intranet tool does not mean that it offers anything different than a standard Internet tool.

In fact, most of the tools you will want to use to develop your intranet are featured throughout the pages of this book. In this section, we mention a few additional tools that are particularly targeted toward intranet applications.

Lotus Domino Server

Lotus Notes was positioning itself as the pre-eminent corporate application development environment until the Internet—and intranets—came along and took the wind from its sales. First Lotus developed InterNotes Web Publisher to provide conversion functions to make Lotus Notes applications available on the Web.

Its latest product, Domino (**domino.lotus.com**), is the next step in the integration process. Domino turns Lotus Notes into a Internet application server, allowing any Web client access to Notes applications. (Domino was available as a beta product as of the writing of this book.)

OpenText LiveLink Intranet

This is one of the most impressive of the first wave of intranet server products we have encountered, at least in terms of addressing the major needs of intranet networks. LiveLink (**www.livelink.com**) is in fact a collection of applications, including search, work flow, document management, project collaboration, and development builder applications.

RadNet's WebShare

RadNet's WebShare is a groupware rapid application development (RAD) tool and server designed with the needs of intranets in mind. The RadNet package (**www.radnet.com**) includes WebShare Designer, WebShare Server, and WebShare Starter Applications. It is for Windows NT.

Netscape's SuiteSpot

Netscape (**www.netscape.com**) has come out early with a fairly aggressive position relative to intranet solutions. This is partly because it has discovered that a substantial majority of its servers are currently being deployed on intranets. As of the writing of this book, Netscape was marketing its SuiteSpot product line as the key intranet solution. The company plans to release a new version of this product sometime in the next year.

NetManage IntraNet Server

The NetManage (**www.netmanage.com**) IntraNet Server contains standards-based technologies for collaboration, information access, and network management. It features the IntraNet Forum Server, a Network News Transport Protocol (NNTP) based server for hosting secured internal discussion forums for corporate use. Also included are components for DNS, Web, NFS file and print, LPD, Directory, and PC NetTime servers.

Additional Intranet Resources

The following is a list of resources to extend your knowledge of intranets.

NETSCAPE AT WORK A useful collection of demos, white papers, and intranet case studies highlighting Netscape products. **home.netscape.com/comprod/at_work/index.html**.

THE NETSCAPE INTRANET VISION AND PRODUCT ROADMAP A longish document that maps Netscape's vision for developing intranet-related Web clients and enterprise servers. **home.netscape.com/ comprod/at_work/white_paper/intranet/vision.html**

THE INTRANET JOURNAL Includes news items, intranet discussion newsgroups, links to white papers and useful software, and an expert's corner. **www.brill.com/intranet/**

LEE LEVITT, PROCESS SOFTWARE CORPORATION "Intranets: Internet Technologies Deployed Behind the Firewall for Corporate Productivity." An informative white paper on the intranet opportunities, prepared for the Internet Society INET96 annual meeting. It includes research statistics and application diagrams. **www.process.com/intranets/wp2.htp**.

INTRANET RESOURCE CENTRE (AUSTRALIA) Another good collection of information and resources for intranet developers. **www.infoweb.com.au/intralnk.htm**.

INDEX

continued

continued

continued

continued

T

continued

continued

About the Authors

David Elderbrock started doing Internet development work at the University of California at Berkeley way back in the early '90s, when gopher servers were still state of the art and HTML programming was considered an esoteric skill. While working on a Ph.D. in English, he designed and developed an Internet-based information system for the U.C. Berkeley Reading and Composition Programs. As the Humanities Focus Group Coordinator for the Instructional Technology Program, he provided training and conducted workshops for professors seeking ways to incorporate computers into the teaching environment. Since 1993, David has been employed building commercial Internet applications. His programming skills include experience with HTML, SGML, CGI, Perl, and C/C++. He designed and implemented a number of database-driven Web sites on UNIX, Windows, and Macintosh platforms. He currently works as an Internet consultant and technical developer. He also serves as Internet Project Manager for Apple Computer, Inc.'s Apple University, where he is assisting in the development of intranet-based management training courses. David can be reached via e-mail at **dhe@aimnet.com**.

Nitin Borwankar is President of Borwankar Research and Development, a consulting firm specializing in interfacing relational databases to the Web and to other Internet messaging environments, such as e-mail. He worked as an engineer and instructor at Ingres, where he taught database technology classes at such sites as General Electric and AT&T. He also worked for Sybase and continues to consult there. His other clients have included Ascend Communications, Mayfield Fund, Geonet Communications (an ISP), and First Virtual Holdings. He is currently working on technology solutions for interfacing SQL databases to the Internet in a standards-based framework using MIME. He can be reached via e-mail at **bizbook@borwankar.com**.

Colophon

This book was produced electronically in Foster City, California. Microsoft Word Version 6.0 was used for word processing; design and layout were produced with QuarkXpress 3.32 on a Power Macintosh 8500/120. The type face families used are Adobe Garamond and Myriad Multiple Master.

Senior Vice President and Group Publisher Brenda McLaughlin
VP & Publisher David Ushijima
Marketing Manager Melisa Duffy
Managing Editor Terry Somerson
Associate Editor Corbin Collins
Technical Editor Stuti Garg
Copy Editor Katharine Dvorak
Associate Copy Editor Suki Gear
Assistant Editor Mark Morford
Editorial Assistants Anne Alvergue, Alia Fitzgerald, Anna Marie Pises
Additional Writing & Research Leslie Lesnick
CD-ROM Technical Reviewer Anu Garg
Production Director Andrew Walker
Production Associate Christopher Pimentel
Supervisor of Page Layout Craig A. Harrison
Project Coordinator Phyllis Beaty
Production Staff Diann Abbott, Vincent F. Burns, Laura Carpenter, Ritchie Durdin, Kurt Krames, Mary Ellen Moran
Proofreader Christine Langin-Faris
Indexer Elizabeth Cunningham
Book Design Margery Cantor
Cover Design Liew Design

IDG BOOKS WORLDWIDE LICENSE AGREEMENT

Important—read carefully before opening the software packet(s). This is a legal agreement between you (either an individual or an entity) and IDG Books Worldwide, Inc. (IDG). By opening the accompanying sealed packet containing the software disk(s), you acknowledge that you have read and accept the following IDG License Agreement. If you do not agree and do not want to be bound by the terms of this Agreement, promptly return the book and the unopened software packet(s) to the place you obtained them for a full refund.

1. License. This License Agreement (Agreement) permits you to use one copy of the enclosed Software program(s) on a single computer. The Software is in "use" on a computer when it is loaded into temporary memory (i.e., RAM) or installed into permanent memory (e.g., hard disk, CD-ROM, or other storage device) of that computer.

2. Copyright. The entire contents of the disk(s) and the compilation of the Software are copyrighted and protected by both United States copyright laws and international treaty provisions. You may only (a) make one copy of the Software for backup or archival purposes, or (b) transfer the Software to a single hard disk, provided that you keep the original for backup or archival purposes. The individual programs on the disk(s) are copyrighted by the authors of each program respectively. Each program has its own use permissions and limitations. To use each program, you must follow the individual requirements and restrictions detailed for each in the Appendix of this Book. Do not use a program if you do not want to follow its Licensing Agreement. None of the material on the disk(s) or listed in this Book may ever be distributed, in original or modified form, for commercial purposes.

3. Other Restrictions. You may not rent or lease the Software. You may transfer the Software and user documentation on a permanent basis provided you retain no copies and the recipient agrees to the terms of this Agreement. You may not reverse engineer, decompile, or disassemble the Software except to the extent that the foregoing restriction is expressly prohibited by applicable law. If the Software is an update or has been updated, any transfer must include the most recent update and all prior versions.

4. Limited Warranty. IDG warrants that the Software and disk(s) are free from defects in materials and workmanship for a period of sixty (60) days from the date of purchase of this Book. If IDG receives notification within the warranty period of defects in material or workmanship, IDG

will replace the defective disk(s). IDG's entire liability and your exclusive remedy shall be limited to replacement of the Software, which is returned to IDG with a copy of your receipt. This Limited Warranty is void if failure of the Software has resulted from accident, abuse, or misapplication. Any replacement Software will be warranted for the remainder of the original warranty period or thirty (30) days, whichever is longer.

5. No Other Warranties. To the maximum extent permitted by applicable law, IDG and the author disclaim all other warranties, express or implied, including but not limited to implied warranties of merchantability and fitness for a particular purpose, with respect to the Software, the programs, the source code contained therein and/or the techniques described in this Book. This limited warranty gives you specific legal rights. You may have others which vary from state/jurisdiction to state/jurisdiction.

6. No Liability For Consequential Damages. To the extent permitted by applicable law, in no event shall IDG or the author be liable for any damages whatsoever (including without limitation, damages for loss of business profits, business interruption, loss of business information, or any other pecuniary loss) arising out of the use of or inability to use the Book or the Software, even if IDG has been advised of the possibility of such damages. Because some states/jurisdictions do not allow the exclusion or limitation of liability for consequential or incidental damages, the above limitation may not apply to you.

7. U.S. Government Restricted Rights. Use, duplication, or disclosure of the Software by the U.S. Government is subject to restrictions stated in paragraph (c) (1) (ii) of the Rights in Technical Data and Computer Software clause of DFARS 252.227-7013, and in subparagraphs (a) through (d) of the Commercial Computer—Restricted Rights clause at FAR 52.227-19, and in similar clauses in the NASA FAR supplement, when applicable.

Fax Order Form On Back ↓

IDG BOOKS WORLDWIDE REGISTRATION CARD

RETURN THIS REGISTRATION CARD FOR FREE CATALOG

Title of this book: **Building Successful Internet Businesses: The Essential Sourcebook**

My overall rating of this book: ❑ Very good [1] ❑ Good [2] ❑ Satisfactory [3] ❑ Fair [4] ❑ Poor [5]

How I first heard about this book:

❑ Found in bookstore; name: [6]

❑ Book review: [7]

❑ Advertisement: [8]

❑ Catalog: [9]

❑ Word of mouth; heard about book from friend, co-worker, etc.: [10]

❑ Other: [11]

What I liked most about this book:

What I would change, add, delete, etc., in future editions of this book:

Other comments:

Number of computer books I purchase in a year: ❑ 1 [12] ❑ 2-5 [13] ❑ 6-10 [14] ❑ More than 10 [15]

I would characterize my computer skills as: ❑ Beginner [16] ❑ Intermediate [17] ❑ Advanced [18] ❑ Professional [19]

I use ❑ DOS [20] ❑ Windows [21] ❑ OS/2 [22] ❑ Unix [23] ❑ Macintosh [24] ❑ Other: [25] ______ (please specify)

I would be interested in new books on the following subjects:
(please check all that apply, and use the spaces provided to identify specific software)

❑ Word processing: [26]

❑ Spreadsheets: [27]

❑ Data bases: [28]

❑ Desktop publishing: [29]

❑ File Utilities: [30]

❑ Money management: [31]

❑ Networking: [32]

❑ Programming languages: [33]

❑ Other: [34]

I use a PC at (please check all that apply): ❑ home [35] ❑ work [36] ❑ school [37] ❑ other: [38] ______

The disks I prefer to use are ❑ 5.25 [39] ❑ 3.5 [40] ❑ other: [41] ______

I have a CD ROM: ❑ yes [42] ❑ no [43]

I plan to buy or upgrade computer hardware this year: ❑ yes [44] ❑ no [45]

I plan to buy or upgrade computer software this year: ❑ yes [46] ❑ no [47]

Name: Business title: [48] Type of Business: [49]

Address (❑ home [50] ❑ work [51]/Company name:)

Street/Suite#

City [52]/State [53]/Zipcode [54]: Country [55]

❑ **I liked this book!** You may quote me by name in future IDG Books Worldwide promotional materials.

My daytime phone number is ______

IDG BOOKS®
THE WORLD OF COMPUTER KNOWLEDGE

YES!

Please keep me informed about IDG's World of Computer Knowledge. Send me the latest IDG Books catalog.

NO POSTAGE NECESSARY IF MAILED IN THE UNITED STATES

BUSINESS REPLY MAIL

FIRST CLASS MAIL PERMIT NO. 2605 FOSTER CITY, CALIFORNIA

IDG Books Worldwide
919 E Hillsdale Blvd, STE 400
Foster City, CA 94404-9691